SICILY

World Travel Guide

Author: **Patrick de Panthou**
Translation: **Penelope Poulton**
Editor: **Lisa Davidson-Petty**
Photo credits: **Alain Camus,** pp. 133, 158 — **Jean-Claude Lemoine,**
p. 227 — **Patrick de Panthou,** pp. 10, 15, 19, 23, 41, 46, 61, 81,
88, 95, 110-111, 125, 136, 149, 167, 171, 214 — **Sevoz Ramos,**
pp. 129, 176, 204-205 — **Thérèse Tisserand,** pp. 69, 115.

This edition published in Great Britain by **Bartholomew**, 12 Duncan
Street, Edinburgh, EH9 ITA.

Bartholomew is a Division of HarperCollins*Publishers*.

This guide is adapted from *en Sicile,* published by Hachette Guides de
voyage, 1989.

© Hachette Guides de voyage, Paris, 1991. First edition.
English translation © Hachette Guides de voyage, Paris, 1991.
Maps © Hachette Guides de voyage, Paris, 1991.
City maps © Touring Club Italiano, 1991.

British Library Cataloguing in Publication Data
Panthou, Patrick de
Sicily. — (Bartholomew world travel guide).
1. Italy. Sicily — Visitors' guides
I. Title II. En Sicile. *English*
914.5804929

ISBN 0-7028-1252-8

Printed in France by Aubin Imprimeur, Poitiers

· Bartholomew ·

SICILY

World Travel Guide

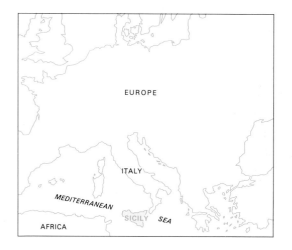

Bartholomew

A Division of HarperCollins*Publishers*

HOW TO USE YOUR GUIDE

● Before you leave home, read the sections 'Planning Your Trip' p. 11, 'Practical Information' p. 16, 'Sicily in the Past' p. 29 and 'Sicily Today' p. 33.

● The rest of the guide is for use once you arrive. It is divided into chapters discussing either cities (Palermo, Catania) or regions (Palermo to Trápani, Catania to Messina). Each chapter includes sections pointing out what to see and provides practical information about the particular area (accommodation, useful addresses and so on).

● Practical advice and information about people, places and events can be located quickly by referring to the 'Index' p. 251. A 'Glossary' p. 248 provides definitions of architectural and geological terms frequently used in this guide. For further information about Sicily, consult the 'Suggested reading' section at the back of the book.

● To easily locate recommended sites, hotels and restaurants on the maps, refer to the map coordinates printed in blue in the text. Example: II, C3.

SYMBOLS USED

Sites, monuments, museums and points of interest

*** Exceptional
** Very interesting
* Interesting

Hotels

See p. 16.

Restaurants

See p. 22.

MAPS

▬ CONTENTS

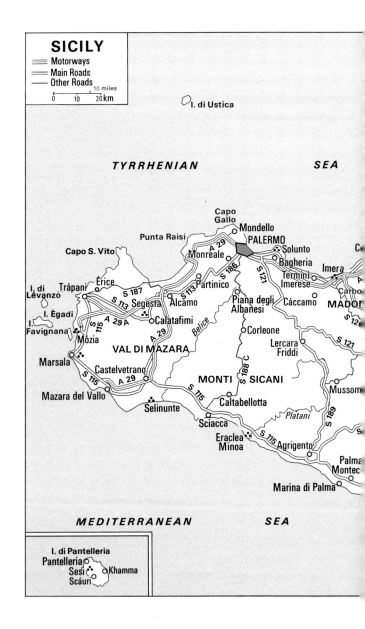

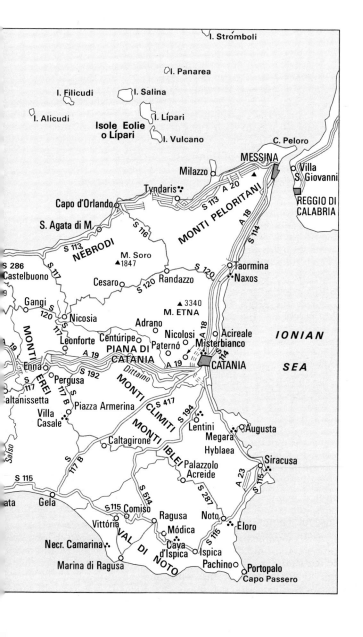

INTRODUCTION TO SICILY

To explore the island of Sicily is to explore the history of the Mediterranean. Few countries in the world have been occupied by a longer succession of foreign rulers: the Phoenicians, Greeks, Romans, Arabs, Normans and Spanish all believed they could make the strategic island their own forever. None managed to dominate it entirely, however, although all left permanent traces of their presence in the wealth of monuments and artifacts that delight both native Sicilians and visitors today.

Sicily is a land of contrasts. Within a few kilometres the landscape can change abruptly from barren hillside to green plain, from snowy mountain slopes to sandy beaches.

Sicily's people are just as varied; the national character takes such diverse forms that it is difficult to define. Sicilians can be audacious and boisterous, 'cutting a fine figure' and then uncomfortably shy. They can appear taciturn and then suddenly break out in a wild display of emotion. Like the mainland Italians, they are great lovers of music, strong defenders of the family, and, even more than their northern neighbours, highly suspicious and disrespectful of authority.

Since the 1950s Sicily has undergone radical social change, due largely to the discovery of oil. The mineral deposits on the island are feverishly mined. At the beginning of this century, 80% of the population was illiterate; today schooling is compulsory and the three universities cannot meet student demand. The island is densely populated, with 90% of the people living in close-packed towns while the countryside is virtually empty. Farmers often travel many miles from their homes in rural slums to work in the fields. Their traditional bright-coloured carts are a thing of the past, sequestered away in museums, replaced by modern tractors. Radio and TV have turned the public attention away from storytellers and puppet shows. In a few years, a feudal agricultural society has become a modern industrial one.

The 1950s also saw an economic resurgence in Europe that tempted many Sicilians to emigrate north. Some of the island's best scholars and artists were among these expatriates, such as Giuseppi Thomasi di Lampedusa, author of *The Leopard.*

Sicily conjures up many images in the foreign mind: long hot summers and long hot tempers; the vice-grip of the Mafia; male chauvinism; Catholic ceremonialism — a culture quite alien, even to other Italians. But while there is some truth in these images, it must also be remembered that Sicily — so long considered the poor man of Italy — is among the richest regions in Europe culturally and historically. Nowhere else have African and European cultures blended more intriguingly.

Not only is Sicily the largest island in the Mediterranean in terms of its geographical area, it is the largest in spirit as well.

Sicily in brief

Location: Sicily lies in the middle of the Mediterranean and is its largest island. The Strait of Messina separates it from mainland Italy by a distance of 1.9 mi/3 km. Between Sicily and Africa (Straits of Sicily) there are 68.4 mi/110 km. Sicily's landscape can be described as a plateau with a mountainous northern edge (up to 6000 ft/1829 m) that plummets to the sea on the north side of the island and slopes gradually to 1000-ft/305-m hills near the southern coast. The most outstanding natural feature of the island is its active volcano, Etna, which rises to an altitude of about 10,902 ft/3323 m. Catania is considered to be the only real plain (166 sq mi/430 sq km) and is located on the east coast between Etna and the Iblei Mountains.

Total area: 9830 sq mi/25,460 km; including the outlying islands: 9926 sq mi/25,709 sq km.

Population: Estimated at six million people.

Administrative division: Palermo is the capital of Sicily, which has regional autonomy.

Religion: Catholicism (90%).

Natural resources: Forty percent of the population make their living from farming, with agriculture representing 20% of the GNP. 25,000 fishermen account for 20% of Italy's fishing industry. Sicily produces 90% of the nation's oil and lemons.

PLANNING YOUR TRIP

WHEN TO GO

Sicily has an exceptionally warm climate with an average of 2200 hours of sunshine a year, or more than six hours a day. The record for Italy as a whole is held by Catania, with an annual average of 2525 sunshine hours.

The best time to visit Sicily is in April and May when the flowers are in bloom and the fragrance of orange blossom pervades the island. June and October are also very pleasant, while July and August are extremely hot, especially inland, where August temperatures can reach 104° F/40° C. November is often rainy but January and February weather is generally fine — so good, in fact, that winter tourism is developing considerably. Although rain is infrequent, when it comes (in winter and spring) it can last for days. The same is true of the hot sirocco wind that blows sand from the Sahara over the entire island.

Average minimum and maximum temperatures

	Palermo		Catania		Taormina	
	°F	°C	°F	°C	°F	°C
Jan	46/57	8/14	43/59	6/15	48/59	9/15
Feb	48/59	9/15	43/61	6/16	48/61	9/16
March	50/63	10/17	45/64	7/18	50/61	10/16
April	54/66	12/19	46/68	8/20	54/68	12/20
May	59/75	15/24	54/75	12/24	59/75	15/24
June	66/82	19/28	61/82	16/28	64/82	18/28
July	72/86	22/30	66/88	19/31	72/88	22/31
Aug	72/88	22/31	66/90	19/32	73/90	23/32
Sept	68/82	20/28	64/86	18/30	70/86	21/30
Oct	61/75	16/24	57/77	14/25	63/77	17/25
Nov	55/66	13/19	50/68	10/20	55/68	13/20
Dec	50/61	10/16	45/63	7/17	50/61	10/16

Average water temperature

	May	June	July	Aug	Sept	Oct
	°F/°C	°F/°C	°F/°C	°F/°C	°F/°C	°F/°C
Palermo	66.7/19.3	72.3/22.4	82.0/27.8	79.7/26.5	75.2/24.0	72.1/22.3
Taormina	64.9/18.3	73.4/23.0	74.3/23.5	75.5/24.2	73.9/23.3	65.1/18.4

From the table above you can see that it is possible to swim as early as May.

A young Sicilian dressed as an angel for the Holy Week procession in Enna.

GETTING THERE

Boat

A visit to Sicily by car can be combined with a boat trip. The main sea links are: Genoa to Palermo (23 hours, four times a week), Naples to Catania or Syracuse (19 hours, once a week), Naples to Palermo (10 hours, nightly), Reggio di Calabria to Catania ($3\frac{1}{2}$ hours, three times a week) and Reggio di Calabria to Syracuse (7 hours, three times a week). During the tourist season it is advisable to book your passage ahead of time. You should check conditions with shipping lines. For example, special rates apply to people traveling in a foreign car who intend to stay for a minimum of six days. Contact the Italian National Tourist Office for information (see 'Useful addresses' p. 15).

The railway company, Ferrovie dello Stato, runs continuous 35-minute crossings for cars and passengers between Villa San Giovanni and Messina. It also runs a twice-daily 55-minute crossing between Reggio di Calabria and Messina. Another company, Siremar, runs a link between Naples and the Aeolian Islands at varying frequencies according to the season. If you are not traveling by car you may want to use the *aliscafo* (hydrofoil) service that runs continuous 15-minute crossings between Reggio di Calabria and Messina.

Car

It is not particularly worthwhile to travel by car unless you intend to spend a long time in Sicily.

Possible itineraries

From England, take one of the ferry crossings between Dover and Calais or Boulogne (Hoverspeed, P & O or Sealink), or Folkestone and Boulogne (Sealink) to reach Paris. From Paris to Rome several routes are possible: The Autoroute du Soleil is the fastest though it is the longest in mileage (1012 mi/1629 km) and the most expensive. The route via the Mont Blanc tunnel is the shortest (870 mi/1400 km) and will be the quickest once the entire A40 highway is open.

You can also drive via Lausanne and from there take the Simplon Pass (894 mi/1438 km) or the Trafaro d. Gran S. Bernardo (884 mi/ 1422 km). Another possibility is via Chambéry and the Fréjus tunnel (890 mi/1432 km).

From Rome, the Autostrada del Sole leads south to Reggio di Calabria (478 mi/770 km) via Villa San Giovanni, where ferries leave for Sicily (frequent 35-minute crossings).

In summer there are daily car-trains between Milan and Villa San Giovanni.

Formalities

When you reach the Italian border you will need to show a valid national driving license with an Italian translation or an International Driving License, car registration papers, an international 'Green Card' for insurance, a red danger triangle in case of breakdown and a national identity sticker for your car. If you are bringing a caravan (trailer) into Italy you should have three copies of an inventory of its contents on plain paper.

Gasoline coupons

Gas in Italy is expensive. You can, however, save 15% by buying a book of gasoline coupons beforehand. These can be bought with foreign currency outside Italy in some Italian banks, at CIT travel agents (see p. 15) and at the ACI (Automobile Club d'Italia) border crossings. You can also check details with your automobile club or with the Italian Tourist Information Office (ENIT). Accompanying the coupons are vouchers for toll reductions on highways (for a value of L20,000). The ACI also offers drivers a card guaranteeing free road service (dial 116) if you break down. These advantages do not apply, however, if you rent a car. It is highly recommended to take out comprehensive insurance for the reasons given in the 'Driving' section on p. 18.

Plane

From London, there are two direct flights to Sicily (Wednesdays and Saturdays) on British Airways. All other flights to Palermo and Catania go through Rome or Milan with a change of plane. Charter flights sometimes offer advantageous fares and dates — check with your local travel agents for details. Alitalia also operates flights from London to Rome and on to Sicily.

From the United States or Australia, you will have to go through Rome or Milan, then change to a domestic flight to Sicily.

Airports

The two main airports for international flights are in Palermo (see p. 48) and Catania (see p. 178).

Train

The train is cheaper than regular flights but not necessarily less expensive than charters, and the 42-hour trip from London will not leave you refreshed and ready to explore Sicily on your arrival. However, if you choose to travel by train, it is best to reserve a seat or, even better, a couchette. Most trains from London to Italy go via Paris. The *Palatino* leaves the Gare de Lyon in the early evening and arrives in Rome the following morning at about 10am. It will take you another 12 hours or so from Rome to Palermo (568 mi/914 km) by either the day train or the night-time *Trinicaria* or *Freccia del Sud*. There is also the *Napoli Express*, which leaves Paris in the evening and arrives in Naples the following afternoon. From here various train connections take you south toward Messina, Taormina, Syracuse or Catania. You can also go via Milan (on the *Stendhal*), Turin, Nice and Ventimiglia. Contact the CIT offices for tickets and information (see p. 15).

Organized tours

This is by far the best and least expensive arrangement for visiting Sicily and it by no means requires traveling with a group. You can leave the organization of your trip to a travel agent who will supply you with a package including airfare, hotel accommodation and car hire. Going through travel agents and tour operators is usually a good idea because they obtain cheaper rates with airlines, hotels and car-rental firms.

ENTRY FORMALITIES

Passports and visas

American, Australian, British, Canadian and New Zealand citizens are required to have a passport to enter Italy. If your stay is likely to exceed three months, you may need a visa. Ask the Italian Embassy for the latest regulations (see 'Useful addresses' pp. 14-15).

Customs

In general, Italian customs follows the same rules as in other EC countries, although you should always check for the latest details. The current regulation regarding lira allows you to enter or leave Italy with up to L500,000 per person. You can also bring back about £147/$232 worth of presents per person, or £38/$60 for those under 15 years of age. It is advisable to travel with receipts for all valuable objects to avoid any problems with customs officials.

Insurance

Health: If you are a member of the EC you will need form E111 from your social security office to benefit from health care in Italy. Otherwise you should take out ordinary travel insurance.

Breakdown, accident: The *Carte Carburante Turistica*, delivered by the

Italian Automobile Club when you buy gasoline coupons, guarantees free breakdown service (see p. 12).

Pets

You will need to show a veterinarian's certificate indicating that your pet is in good health and that its rabies vaccination is up-to-date. If you have a dog, be aware that it will not be allowed in most hotels; and you will have to muzzle it in towns and on public transport.

▬ MONEY

Italy's monetary unit is the lira (plural lire). Coin denominations come in 50-, 100-, 200- and 500-lire pieces while notes are issued for 1000, 2000, 5000, 10,000, 50,000 and 100,000 lire. The Italian Parliament is currently studying monetary reform. Sometimes, rather than coins of small denomination, you will be given telephone tokens (200 lire) as change.

It's safer to use traveler's checks than to carry cash. These can be ordered from banks in lire, dollars or pounds and can easily be cashed.

Exchange rate

The rate at the time of publishing is 2203 lire to the pound sterling, 1120 lire to the US dollar. Inquire about commission rates before changing foreign currency, especially at hotel reception desks (the best rates are usually given by major banks).

Credit cards

These are indispensable for travel and are usually accepted by restaurants and hotels in Sicily (especially Visa, American Express, Eurocard and Diners Club). Note that service stations rarely accept credit cards.

Budget

Sicily is no less expensive than other Mediterranean vacation areas. You may find that eating there can be fairly cheap, especially in little *trattorie*, but accommodation compared to prices in France, for example, can be expensive.

▬ BEFORE YOU LEAVE: SOME USEFUL ADDRESSES

Australia

Embassy
12 Gray St., Daken, Canberra ACT 2000, ☎ (062) 73 3333.
Consulate
6169 Macquarie St., Sydney NSW 2000, ☎ (612) 27 8442.

Canada

Embassy
275 Slater St., 11th floor, Ottawa, Ontario K1P 5H9, ☎ (613) 232 2401.
Consulate
136 Beverly St., Toronto, Ontario M5P 1Y5, ☎ (416) 977 1566.

Great Britain

Embassy
14 Three Kings Yard, London W1, ☎ (01) 629 8200.
Consulate

2 Melville Crescent, Edinburgh EH3 7JA, ☎ (031) 226 3631.

View of Taormina from the Greek theatre.

United States

Embassy
1601 Fuller St. N.W., Washington, DC 20009, ☎ (202) 328 5500.

Consulates
690 Park Ave., New York, New York 10021, ☎ (212) 737 9100; 500 North Michigan Ave., Suite 1850, Chicago, Illinois 60611, ☎ (312) 467 1550; 11661 San Vincente Blvd., Suite 911, Los Angeles, California 90049, ☎ (213) 826 5998; 2590 Webster St., San Francisco, California 94115, ☎ (415) 931 4924.

Italian National Tourist Offices

Canada: Store 56, Plaza 3 Place Ville Marie, Montreal, Quebec, ☎ (514) 866 7667.

Great Britain: 1 Princes St., London W1R 8AY, ☎ (01) 408 1254.

United States: 500 North Michigan Ave., Suite 1046, Chicago, Illinois 60611, ☎ (312) 644 0990; c/o Alitalia, 8350 North Central Expressway, Dallas, Texas 75206, ☎ (214) 692 8761; 630 Fifth Ave., New York, New York 10111, ☎ (212) 245 4961; 360 Post St., Suite 801, San Francisco, California 94108, ☎ (415) 392 6206.

CIT offices

Canada: 2055 Peel St., Suite 102, Montreal, Quebec H3A 1VA, ☎ (514) 845 9101.

Great Britan: 50 Conduit St., London W1, ☎ (01) 434 3844.

United States: 666 Fifth Ave., New York, New York 10103, ☎ (212) 397 2666.

PRACTICAL INFORMATION

ACCESS

Airports

Sicily has two international airports: **Punta Raisi,** which is 19 mi/30 km west of Palermo, and **Fontanarossa,** 5 mi/8 km south of Catania. The Trápani airport, which is 9 mi/15 km south of the town, serves only domestic and national flights.

See p. 48 for Palermo and p. 178 for Catania.

For access by train, boat or car, see pp. 12-13.

ACCOMMODATION

Sicily has a well-developed hotel infrastructure. Establishments are classified by category ranging from Luxury to Class I, II, III and IV. We have not followed these official ratings, which are sometimes debatable, but have adopted our own, rating hotels according to comfort and price.

▲▲▲▲ Luxury hotel
▲▲▲ First-class hotel
▲▲ Moderately priced hotel
▲ Inexpensive hotel

Prices may vary within a given category according to the amenities offered, for example, location, view and terrace. You should request the exact price when reserving, as rates also vary according to the season.

Hotels

As in any tourist area, hotel accommodation varies tremendously. Compared to neighbouring France, for example, prices are generally higher and the service is of a lower standard. On arrival at the hotel, you will be requested to hand in a passport or an identity card; it will be returned to you in a few hours. You should certainly tip a porter for carrying your bags, but do not expect to find one in every establishment. Room prices are always posted on the back of the door. Breakfast is never included in the price of the room.

Camping

Sicily has a lot of well-equipped campgrounds which, like hotels, are officially rated. Tourist information offices will give you a list showing prices and facilities. Most campsites are open from April to the end of September. Unauthorized camping is not advisable.

Youth hostels

Known as *ostelli per la gioventu,* youth hostels are few and far between. Tourist offices have information regarding admission. As a rule an international card is required. There are also inexpensive student hostels *(Casa dello Studente)* for which you will need a student card.

The Virgin dell'Addolorata in Enna.

Parking

Finding a parking space is a serious problem in towns with narrow streets; you will do better to use parking lots, which are generally located near tourist sites. Don't forget to tip the guard, and never leave anything visible in your car.

Road service

The **ACI** (Italian Automobile Club) operates a 24-hour breakdown service. Telephone **116** if you need their help. All foreign vehicles can benefit from free road service on national roads and highways.

Speed limits

In theory, speed limits are as follows: 30 mph/50 kph in built-up areas, 50 mph/80 kph on ordinary roads and 75 mph/120 kph on highways.

▬ ELECTRICITY

The electrical current almost everywhere in Sicily is 220 volts. Bring along an adapter for electrical appliances such as hair dryers and portable irons.

▬ FESTIVALS

Civil or religious holidays are celebrated throughout Sicily. Each town and village organizes feast days for patron saints and commemorates important historical events, such as the victory of Roger the Norman over the Saracens in 1091.

Holy week

Settimana santa is celebrated fervently all over the island. The most dramatic and jubilant processions take place in Caltanissetta, Trápani,

Choose your procession

Enna: Good Friday and Easter Sunday, long processions of penitents.
Trápani: Good Friday and *Misteri*.
Marsala: Maundy Thursday, procession of the Passion.
Messina: Good Friday and *Varette*.
Caltanissetta: Easter Wednesday and *Real Maestranza*.
San Fratello: Maundy Thursday, Good Friday and *Festa dei Giudei* (Feast of the Jews).
Érice: Good Friday and *Misteri*.
Gangi: Palm Sunday, feast of the palms.
Prizzi: Easter Sunday, dance of the devils.
Delia: Good Friday, representation of the Passion.
Piana degli Albanesi: Easter day, Byzantine mass.

Enna, Marsala and Messina, where the Resurrection is celebrated according to the rites and customs of each place.

On Good Friday in San Fratello, a figure of Christ (accompanied by offerings in the form of bank notes) is escorted by trumpet players in a procession through the streets. The celebration is called the *Fiesta dei Guidei*, 'Feast of the Jews,' who are 'restored to favour'. To identify with them, the locals wear shoulder straps and gaiters and are disguised in crimson masks with gold eyes. On the same day in Trápani there is a procession of *misteri*, Baroque sculptures laden with flowers, representing scenes from the Passion. A solemn crowd follows them through the narrow alleys.

In Marsala the members of the procession work themselves into a frenzy of ecstasy to perform a realistic and sometimes cruel interpretation of the Passion. The actress playing Saint Veronica is costumed in gold with all the finery of a princess. In Caltanissetta various guilds reenact or mime the scene at Golgotha to the accompaniment of slow, mournful oriental-like chants.

In Piana degli Albanesi there is a Byzantine Orthodox service with sumptuous costumes where, during the ceremony, blood-red Easter eggs are blessed. Young women try to outdo each other in their dress, flaunting an abundance of jewels, precious stones, lace and patterned brocades.

Christmas

Christmas in Sicily is very much a family affair with closely guarded traditions. Children are encouraged to make models of the Nativity scene, which are less conventional in Sicily than elsewhere. Along with the usual decor, Sicilian children add minutely detailed scenes of the countryside, peopling them with peasants and washerwomen. Remember that Sicily claims to be the land of refuge in the 'Flight to Egypt'. In order to escape Herod, the Virgin Mary fled not to Egypt but to Taormina, to a cave in the rocky hilltop where today you can see the ruins of an ancient castle and the sanctuary of Madonna della Rocca. The people of Taormina carry on an ancient Christmas tradition (still also found in Rome) whereby a child goes to the pulpit and, helped by the priest, delivers the sermon at midnight mass.

Patron saints

Each region commemorates its patron saint. In the past, villagers held plebiscites to elect the saints they wanted to protect them. If a saint did not fulfil their hopes, he or she was disowned and a replacement chosen. In Caltanissetta, for example, a statue of St Michael the archangel was exiled to a ruined church and clad in an old robe for having failed to bring rain to the crops. He was not reinstated in the cathedral until he had satisfied the congregation.

FOOD AND DRINK

See 'Useful vocabulary' p. 243 for food and restaurant terms.

The Sicilians not only love their food — they are gourmets. Added to the typical Italian dishes are the numerous specialities of the island. Bear in mind that over the centuries Sicily was subjected to various foreign influences, which is reflected in the island's richly varied cuisine.

Restaurants

Don't hesitate to leave your hotel and try local restaurants, where you will more often than not make pleasant culinary discoveries. Different types of eating places include: the traditional *ristorante*, the simpler *trattoria* (which generally has less choice), the *pizzeria* and the *osteria*. Theoretically more modest and cheaper than the others, the *osteria* originally served only *antipasti* and cold dishes to accompany wine-tasting. There are also *rosticcerie*, which serve meat dishes as well as pizzas, and *tavole calde*, which have a limited choice of dishes that you eat standing up. Distinguishing between these different types of restaurants is so perplexing that sometimes even the Italians get confused.

Unless the restaurant is in a tourist area it may not display a menu outside. The cover charge *(coperto)* is never included in the price but is added at the end of the meal (between L2,000 and 3,000). Service (also usually charged at the end) is generally quick. *Vino locale* served in a carafe is always good and inexpensive. Mineral water is either *gasata* (carbonated) or *naturale* (non-carbonated). The choice of desserts in restaurants can be limited considering the wonderful pastries and ice creams to be had elsewhere. Expect to pay between L30,000 and 40,000 for a meal including one or two bottles of the local wine.

The ratings given for each restaurant are calculated on the basis of a first course, main dish, dessert, cover charge and wine. Fish dishes are always more expensive. Some restaurants have tourist menus which are generally reasonably priced (between L15,000 and 20,000).

Pasta

Long
Spaghetti: string-like pasta strands
Tagliatelle: long flat strips, known as *fettuccine* in Rome
Bucatini: thick tubular spaghetti with a narrow centre
Tonnarelli: squared spaghetti, white or green (with spinach)
Lasagne: wide, long, flat, layered pasta; white or green
Margherita: literally 'little marguerite', shaped like the flower

Short
Rigatoni: grooved tubular pasta with a wide centre
Penne: tubular pasta, smooth and trapezoidal
Conchiglie: shell-shaped pasta
Gnocchi: shell-shaped and usually made with a potato base
Gnochetti: a smaller version of gnocchi

Filled with meat, ricotta cheese and/or spinach
Cannelloni: large pasta tubes like bolsters
Ravioli: pasta 'cushions'
Tortellini: small pasta rings
Tortelloni: a larger version of tortellini

In soup
Quadrucci: flat and square
Capellini: thin, hair-like pasta
Occhi di pernice: literally 'partridge-eye' in shape
Puntine: small pasta dots
Farfalle: butterfly-shaped pasta
Maltagliati: literally 'badly cut', uneven pasta

LLLL   Deluxe
LLL   Expensive
LL   Moderate
L   Inexpensive

Pasta

Honour where honour is due! When speaking of Sicilian cooking we should begin with pasta, first because it is the basic foodstuff of the island and second because macaroni was invented in Sicily in 1250. This *primo piatto,* without which a meal would not be a meal in Italy, bears no resemblance to the second-rate fare we are used to back home. Here it is an indispensable prelude to any meal.

In Palermo you can try long *maccheroni con le sarde,* seasoned with a sardine sauce, anchovies, raisins, fennel, saffron, onions and olive oil, or *spaghetti alla carrettiera,* with garlic, cheese and chilli. Another specialty is *annelletti alla Palermitana,* pasta rings with meat balls and tomato sauce.

In Catania you will find *pasta alla Norma* in honour of Bellini. This consists of macaroni layered alternately with hard-boiled eggs, aubergines (eggplant) and soft white cheese.

In Messina, ask for *pasta con le cozze,* served with cockles, mussels and a dash of garlic.

Other pasta varieties include wide lasagne strips, generally served with a meat stew, and spaghetti with cuttlefish served in its inky juice.

If you are feeling timid or can't make up your mind, you can always ask for an *assagiata,* an assortment of pastas prepared with different sauces, or fall back on a rice dish, *risotto,* which is usually excellent and often served with seafood.

Antipasti

Antipasti are appetizers served before the main pasta dish but may sometimes replace it. You will often find vast tables spread with an impressive selection of hors d'œuvres. In this category you also have *prosciutto* and *brissaola* — thin slices of smoked meat.

Fish

Sicily, with its coastline of 932 mi/1500 km, is not lacking in fish. The most common is swordfish, and it is also considered the best. You will find the following fish on all menus, especially in coastal towns, though that does not neccesarilly mean that they are all available: tuna, squid, mullet, sardines, crayfish or lobster, and octopus. Restaurants are now required by law to tell clients if the fish they serve has been frozen. Fish is often sold by weight. To avoid surprises on your bill, it's a good idea to agree on the price before you order.

Meat

Well worth trying are the delicious *involtini* (meat slices rolled and stuffed) and *brociolettini alla Palermitana,* small rolled escalopes stuffed with a mixture of fried bread crumbs, cheese, basil and sausage, then cooked in the oven.

Contorni

As in the rest of Italy, fish and meat dishes are served without any accompaniment; these side dishes are ordered separately. The choice is often between spinach *(spinaci),* aubergines *(melanzane),* tomatoes *(pomodori)* and artichokes *(carciofi),* prepared in different ways and sprinkled with olive oil.

Cheese

There is not a wide variety of cheese, but it is used often in cooking, especially *canestrato,* which is very salty, and *piacentino,* which is

An olive merchant in Vucciria, Palermo's most picturesque market.

peppery. Otherwise the most common type is probably *caciocavallo*, which 'owes its name to the fact that the cheeses are fixed in pairs astride *(a cavallo)* rigid sticks and left to mature' (Ada Boni, *Regional Cooking in Italy*). Cheese is often served with olives and tomatoes as hors d'œuvres *(antipasti)*.

Two other cheeses, *pepato fresco* and *pecorino fresco*, are also worth trying.

Desserts

Apart from the famous ice cream (see p. 25) restaurants serve a cake called *cassata*, originally an Easter specialty, made of marzipan, glazed nougat and candied fruit. Fresh fruit in Sicily is excellent. Pastries are rarely featured on restaurant menus; you find them in *pasticceria*. You should also try *cannoli*, rolls of fried flaky pastry filled with ewe's milk cheese, almond paste and pistachios, with a dash of Marsala.

Perhaps you'll have the chance to taste *Tartuffe*, 'virgin's breasts', described by Fulco di Verdura as 'immodest cakes shaped like breasts... moulded life-size, made of stuffed almond paste and fashioned in a very suggestive way with a little flesh-coloured nipple at the top delicately browned in the oven'.

Candied fruits, another island speciality, rival fruit modeled from almond paste for imitative perfection. Both are so convincing you can easily mistake them for the real thing.

Wines

A good meal is not complete without wine; luckily local vineyards produce excellent ones. This was recognized as far back as the days of Julius Caesar, who sang the praises of Mamertino, the island's leading wine.

Italy is the Common Market's second-largest producer and consumer of wine. Production is controlled by certain rules, and the finished product falls into one of two categories according to quality: either DOC *(delimitazione di origine controllata)* or the higher rating of DOCG *(delimitazione di origine controllata e garantia)*.

Each of the nine provinces produces an 'ordinary' wine that satisfies local demand and is also exported (notably to France, where it is used for blending). Among the Palermitan varieties are: Zucco, white; Regaleali, red and white; Corvo, red and white; Zilibbo and Stravecchio, reds.

In Catania province the dry white wine from the slopes of Etna is a straw-colour with a light, earthy taste. Syracuse province produces mainly Pachino, a strong, full-bodied red wine with a proof of never less than 15°. Eloro, another wine from Syracuse, comes in white and red, and Moscato di Siracusa, a light white muscatel, is a delicious dry wine with a proof between 14° and 17°. In Messina province there is Faro, a red wine, and Mamertino, a dessert wine made from white grapes grown on the high ground surrounding the town.

Mention must also be made of Malvasia di Lipari, produced on the islands of Strómboli and Salina from grapes that are left to rot for eight days, giving a strong wine with a 15° or 16° proof. Finally, there is the famous golden Marsala, known throughout the world as a delicious dessert wine.

GETTING AROUND SICILY

Bus

Bus travel, although usually more expensive than train travel, is reliable and generally fast. Several bus companies operate on the island; the two main ones are **SAIS** and **AST** (see p. 48 for addresses in Palermo). You can get almost everywhere using the regional bus system, although schedules may be hard to find. Bus services are usually drastically reduced on Sunday. Check with the local tourist office or the bus station *(autostazione)*. Wherever possible, the station is indicated in the 'Useful addresses' of each section.

Car

See the section 'Driving' p. 18.

Train

Traveling by train is an inexpensive way to get around in Sicily, although you should be prepared for the irritation from often-delayed trains. Lines coming from mainland Italy are much faster, but delays of an hour or more are common. The local trains are often slow and winding; because of the improvements in the bus system, for many destinations you may be better off traveling by bus.

You can get information from the local tourist offices or railway stations. The Italian State Railways also publishes two books. The first, *Principali Treni,* lists the main routes throughout Sicily. If you plan to travel extensively by train, the more comprehensive *Pozzario,* issued twice yearly, details individual train lines and schedules. These books are available at major railway stations.

Inter-rail passes are valid on the Sicilian railway system, although a supplement may be required for the fast trains. Two passes offering reduced fares can be purchased in Italy: a *Biglietto turistico libera circolazione* (unlimited-travel ticket for 8, 15, 21 or 30 days), valid for travel on all Italian State Railway trains; and the *Chilometrico,* valid for 3000 km and for up to five people at the same time. These passes can be purchased before you leave (contact the CIT office, see p. 15) or picked up at the Palermo or Messina railway station.

HEALTH AND MEDICINE

Your hotel reception should be able to direct you to a doctor or dentist if you become ill. There is also an emergency *(pronto soccorso)* department in hospitals, which you can contact by telephone: **113.**

Pharmacies keep the same hours as other shops. In the main towns there is usually one that stays open all night and over the weekend. A notice posted on the door of every closed pharmacy will tell you where to find one that is open.

The religious origins of pastries

Each religious house specialised in one particular form of confectionery or pastry, and since this was one of the principal means of livelihood competition became sufficiently intense to produce a wealth of designs and recipes. The fact that many daughters of noble parents chose the religious life perhaps accounts for the fastidious and elaborate decoration of the cakes. All are typically Sicilian in their extravagant colour and cloying sweetness. The simplest sort is the imitation of fruit or vegetable, smaller than life size, made in almond paste. As though in some fabulous greenhouse, strawberries and cherries, figs and oranges, apples and pears all ripen together in the confectioner's window, as they once did at the church doors. The small orange-coloured *nespole*, which appear in May and taste half-apricot and half-orange, are shown cut in half, revealing the large seeds which resemble chestnuts. Wild strawberries and raspberries are fashioned with such cunning that it is almost impossible, before they are tasted, to distinguish them from the real. Heaped together in a wide bowl, their opulence of colour is as cloying as their tropically sweet taste.

Vincent Cronin
The Golden Honeycomb
Rupert Hart-Davis, 1954

ICE CREAM (GELATO)

The Sicilians have a passion for ice cream that is perfectly justified. After all, the inventor of sorbets was born here, and the famous *cassata gelata*, a cake made with rícotta and candied fruit (or marzipan), originated here. The local *gelateria* is a popular meeting place, especially at the end of the day during the *passeggiata* when people go out for their evening stroll. Apart from ice cream, you should also try *frutali*, different kinds of fresh fruit mixed with crushed ice.

LANGUAGE

See 'Useful vocabulary' p. 243.

In most hotels and restaurants there is someone who can speak English. Young people tend to use it more nowadays and like trying out their skills. In the depths of the country you will of course find fewer people who understand English, but no matter where you are on the island, always try to use your Italian, however faltering. The Sicilians will appreciate your efforts and regard them as a sign of respect.

LAVATORIES

Public conveniences *(gabinetti)* in streets are rare. You will, however, find them in train stations, airports, gas stations, museums, hotels and restaurants. When there is one in a bar it is usually very basic. In Italian *uomini* means 'men' and *donne* means 'ladies'. Sometimes the signs read *signori* for men and *signore* for women.

METRIC SYSTEM

Sicily uses the metric system. Some useful conversions: 15° C=59° F, 25° C=77° F, 40° C=104° F; 100 km=62 mi; 1 l=approximately 1 US quart or 1.8 British pints and 1 kg=approximately 2.2 lb.

NATURE RESERVES

Sicily is becoming seriously interested in the protection of its natural environment. There are regional nature reserves in the Gulf of Castellammare (Zingaro), in the Nebrodi and Madonie mountains, and especially in the Etna region. Information on the Etna regional park can be obtained from **Azienda Foreste Domaniali,** via Liberta 97, Palermo, ☎ (091) 40 4387. For information on excursions to the Lo Zingaro reserve ask in Alcamo at via Ugo Manno 71, ☎ (0924) 20 542. Palermo has a zoological park and there are aquariums at Messina and Syracuse.

ORGANIZING YOUR TIME

If traveling by car you will need a minimum of two weeks to visit the whole island. An ideal vacation would last three weeks, two spent sightseeing and the last spent in a seaside resort or on a trip to the outlying islands. If time is really short, it is possible to tour the main sights in a week.

Sicily in one week

First day: Palermo; second day: Palermo and Monreale; third day: Segesta, Selinunte and Agrigento; fourth day: Agrigento, Enna and Piazza Armerina; fifth day: Syracuse; sixth day: Catania, Taormina and Etna; seventh day: Messina to Palermo with a stop at Tíndari and another at Cefalù.

PASSEGGIATA

In the evening around 6pm the streets suddenly come to life. It's time for the *passeggiata,* a tradition that follows age-old rules. Girls walk slowly together arm in arm while boys look on admiringly. They follow the same route walked by generations before them, occasionally stopping at the *gelateria.* Over recent years the procession has changed with the introduction of a new technique, the 'immobile, motorized' *passeggiata,* which means having one's car admired while sitting inside, watching the world go by.

POST OFFICE

Post office in Italian is *ufficio postale.* Stamps can also be purchased from tobacconists *(tabacchi)* and from some postcard vendors, where you can also buy envelopes *(una busta)* singly. Mailboxes, easily recognizable, are red. If you want letters sent to General Delivery, you must have them addressed Poste Restante, Fermo Posta, Posta Centrale di (followed by the name of the town). Because letters mailed home take a long time, it is advisable to send them *espresso* or, if it is urgent, ask someone returning to take it with them. In the larger hotels the reception desk will usually take care of stamping and sending your mail.

PUBLIC HOLIDAYS

Sicily has far more public holidays than Anglo-Saxon countries do, more even than many other Catholic countries. In August over Assumption and in December over Christmas everything closes down for a week, apart from hotels and other tourist-oriented facilities.

The main public holidays are as follows:
January 1: *il Capodanno*
January 6: *Epifania*
March 19: *San Giuseppe*
Easter Monday: *lunedì di Pasqua*
April 25: *Liberazione de 1945*
May 1: *Festa del Lavoro*
Ascension Day: *giovedì dell'Ascenzione*
Corpus Christi: *Corpus Domini*
June 2: *Festa della Repubblica*
July 15: *Santa Rosalia*
August 15: *Festa dell'Assunta, Ferragosto*
November 1: *Ognissanti*
November 4: *Commemorazione della vittoria de 1918*
December 8: *Festa dell'Immacolata*
December 25 and 26: *Natale* and *San Stéfano.*

SAFETY PRECAUTIONS

Italy as a whole, though more particularly the south and Sicily, has a bad reputation abroad as far as safety is concerned. There are certainly more unsafe towns in the world than Palermo, but it is advisable to take a few elementary precautions. You don't have to worry about the Mafia, which does not take an interest in tourists. It leaves that to the *scippi*, juveniles who practice petty theft using well-tried methods tested over generations on thousands of pedestrians.

You should either leave behind — or be very discreet about — jewelry and valuable objects that are likely to attract attention. Never let your luggage out of your sight. Entrust it whenever possible to the hotel reception, together with your passport and foreign currency. Never leave anything conspicuous in your car and always lock the doors. Car radios in particular are highly prized.

Be discreet about cameras and all photographic accessories. To foil the *scippi*, who operate in groups or on scooters, rather than carry a handbag, use a shoulder-bag worn diagonally across your body. Avoid walking on the edge of the sidewalk in city centres and be particularly careful in crowds. Finally, always put money and credit cards in a pocket that is difficult to get at. These simple measures make it much harder for young thieves to get the better of you. Report any infraction to the police. If you are not happy with service in hotels, restaurants or shops, go to the tourist office or to the police to register your complaint *(denuncia)*.

Emergencies

SOS: Fire, theft, ambulance: ☎ 113
Police *(Carabinieri)*: ☎ 112
Breakdown and ACI road service: ☎ 116

SHOPPING

If you are hoping to find a variety of local crafts, you may be disappointed as the cottage industry in Sicily has practically disappeared. Apart from a little pottery, ceramics and wickerwork, local production is virtually non-existent. What is left is amateur in quality, with the exception of terra-cotta ware, on sale mainly in Taormina. These *terracotte,* scenes with human figures, are very expressive and usually inexpensive. Be careful, though, because some are plastic!

Also for sale are copies of *pupi* (puppets) in full tin-plate armour. Antique shops have been stripped bare by generations of tourists, although it is still possible to come across painted *carretti* panels or real marionettes. Of course, their prices reflect their rarity.

SIROCCO

A wind from the deserts of North Africa, the sirocco sweeps across the island, increasing the temperature considerably and sometimes blowing with such force that it causes widespread damage. When it blows, mainly in spring, Sicilians usually stay indoors.

SPORTS

Where relevant for each town and each hotel, we have mentioned the sports facilities available. For further information ask at the local tourist office.

It is possible to ski on the slopes of Etna and to go hiking in the area. For information contact: **CAI,** via Vecchia Ognina, 169, Catania, ☎ (095) 387 674.

▬ *TELEPHONE (TELEFONO)*

Public telephones have a yellow telephone sign and take cards or tokens, *gettoni,* which are on sale in *tabacchi* and cafés. For inter-city calls dial the area code *(prefisso)* before the number. Because a lot of numbers are changing in Sicily, those in this guide should be checked beforehand by consulting directories on the spot. Emergency numbers are listed at the beginning of the yellow pages. 'Hello' in Italian is *'Pronto'.*

Phoning abroad from Sicily: Dial 00, followed by the country code (44 for England, 61 for Australia, 1 for the US and Canada), the area code and the number, without waiting for the dial tone. Phoning abroad from your hotel is easier (though much more expensive) than phoning from a public booth, where you have to feed in a large quantity of *gettoni.*

Phoning Sicily from abroad: Dial 010 from England, from Australia and from the US and Canada, followed by 39, the area code and the local number.

▬ *TIME*

The time in Sicily is one hour ahead of London time, six hours ahead of New York time and nine hours ahead of Los Angeles time.

▬ *TIPPING*

Tipping, or *mancia,* is always welcome. In Sicily it has the magic power of opening formerly closed doors.

In a café it is customary to pay the cashier first, then present your receipt *(scontrino)* at the counter to receive your order. You are not expected to tip, but leaving an extra coin or two is appreciated. On the other hand, if you are served at a table you should leave something even if the service is included.

In a restaurant, if you are satisfied, certainly leave a tip over and above the service, which is always included in the bill. However, you should not feel obliged to do so.

In a hotel both the porter and the doorman, if he calls a taxi for you, will expect a tip.

If you take a taxi, round off·the fare shown on the meter; this obviously does not apply if you've fixed the price in advance.

It is customary to tip guides, especially if they have acted as commentators on your tour of a monument.

▬ *TOURIST INFORMATION*

Each province has an **APT** office *(Azienda de Promozione Turistica),* which centralizes all the information for the region. This official bureaucratic service is not always open to the public. To simplify the matter, we have mentioned where possible the offices open to the public in the 'Tourist information' section for each town. The towns with a big budget for tourism have an independent office, the **AAST** *(Azienda Autonoma di Soggiorno e Turismo).* Another source of information is the **Pro Loco,** which is dependent on the town council.

You can also telephone **116,** which, in addition to being the road-service number, operates a 24-hour assistance service for foreigners. The personnel speak several languages and give advice as well as information.

SICILY IN THE PAST

Man's presence in Sicily evidently dates from the Upper Palaeolithic period, judging by cave paintings found in the Grotta del Genovese on Lévanzo Island and the Grotta dell' Addáura on Monte Pellegrino. The first people on Sicily were probably the Sicans *(Sicani),* who came from the Italian continent and inhabited the island before 10,000 BC. They were driven out by the Indo-European Sicels *(Siculi),* who gave the island its name.

THE GREEKS (8TH CENTURY BC)

Before the arrival of the Phoenicians of Carthage, Sicily was already part of the Mycenean civilization of Crete. The fertile volcanic soil and prime geographic position of the island attracted navigators from all over the Mediterranean, and the 8th century marked the beginning of Phoenician and Greek colonization. Syracuse was founded in 733 BC, Messina in 724 BC and Gela in 691 BC. By 635 BC, the Greeks had pushed back the Phoenicians to the western part of the island.

Sicily prospered under Greek rule. The fertile areas around the coast were farmed, and by the 5th century BC Syracuse developed into the most important of all Greek cities: 'the Athens of the West'. Its outstanding wealth made it a popular target for raids, however, and for years the city suffered continual attack.

Pericles of Athens (who had just triumphed in the Peloponnesian War against Sparta) tried in vain to destroy Syracusan predominance in 413 BC; the Athenian army was devastated by the Syracusans, under the vengeful leadership of a Spartan general, Gylippos. Seven thousand Athenian Greek soldiers were imprisoned in limestone quarries *(latomiae)* where they were left to die.

As established as their power was on Sicily, the Syracusan Greeks never managed to wrench the western half of the island away from the Carthaginians, whose stronghold on that region lasted until the middle of the 2nd century BC.

THE ROMANS (250 BC)

In 408 BC, the Carthaginians, under Hannibal, tried to capture the entire island. They destroyed Selinunte, Agrigento and Gela but were so weakened by the plague by the time they reached Syracuse that they were easily vanquished. The conflict between Syracuse in the east and the Carthaginian stronghold in the west was an old one; the island was ravaged continually by internal war. The Syracusan tyrant, Agathocles, went so far as to extend the war onto Carthaginian territory in North Africa.

It was Roman intervention that finally resolved the conflict. The Romans had conquered Italy and now turned to Sicily, where they clashed with the Carthaginians in the First Punic War (264-242 BC). During the Second Punic War (218-202 BC), Syracuse united with the Carthaginian forces against Roman attack, but the Roman consul, Marcellus, weakened the Sicilian forces by cutting off their food supplies, and the island fell to Rome.

With its status as a Roman province, Sicily was governed by a praetor, or magistrate. Two quaestors — one at Syracuse and the other at Lilybaeum — controlled the growing of wheat (the island's main source of wealth), ran the treasury and collected taxes.

Roman rule continued until the beginning of the 5th century AD, during which time slaves were brought from the island of Delos and from Asia to work with free peasants on Sicily's rich private domains. Sicilian towns tended toward decline under Roman rule, devastated by epidemics of malaria and increasing emigration. Exceptions were Catania, Taormina and Palermo.

THE ARABS (AD 826-962)

With the fall of the Roman Empire in AD 476, Sicily was invaded by the Vandals of Gaiseric and, shortly afterward, by the Goths. In 535, the Byzantine general Belisarius captured the island. But by 780, the Saracens began to make frequent forays into Sicily. They had become masters of the Mediterranean, and the result of their 50-year conquest of Sicily was that they gradually took complete control of the island (by AD 827). Under Arab rule, irrigation systems were developed, fruit trees were cultivated and mining techniques were improved — all resulting in economic growth. Social improvements coupled with economic prosperity to ensure the well-being of Sicily under the Arabs, and Palermo, particularly, became a respected cultural center of the Arab Empire.

THE NORMANS (AD 1061-1189)

The Muslim presence in Sicily, which might have served as a bridge between Africa and Europe, was not appreciated by the West, however. The pope promised the Normans, who had settled Southern Italy, that he would grant them sovereignty over Sicily if they managed to chase out 'the infidels'. In response, the French count Roger de Hauteville set out with his knights to conquer the island; his siege lasted from 1060-91. During the ensuing reigns of three Norman kings — Roger II (1105-54), William I (1154-66) and William II (1166-80) — Sicily entered its most splendid epoch, not only economically, but also in terms of art and culture. The Normans governed with tolerance, adapting to a life-style that had been influenced by the East while remaining mindful of their Christian origins.

THE SWABIANS AND ANGEVINS (1198-1282)

After the de Hauteville line of rulers, Sicily was governed by the emperors of Swabia (Hohenstaufen). In 1198, the Hohenstaufen Frederick II, son of the Holy Roman Emperor, Henry VI, inherited the crown of Sicily through his mother, Constance. He established Palermo as his capital, centralized the administration of the island, and encouraged a great outpouring of art and science. Known fondly as 'Stupor Mundi', the pope crowned him Holy Roman Emperor in 1220.

His death, in 1250, dealt a terrible blow to Sicily. Pope Urban IV conferred the Sicilian crown on Charles of Anjou, brother of the French king, Louis IX.

In the war that ensued, the son of Frederick II, Manfred, was killed, whereupon Charles took control of the island. He transferred the capital to Naples, levied heavy taxes on the Sicilians and plundered the island. In 1282, the Sicilians revolted against the French feudal lords in the uprising known as the Sicilian Vespers. Thousands of French living on the island were massacred, and Angevin rule in Sicily was put to an end.

THE SPANISH (1282-1860)

Peter of Aragon, who had married one of Manfred's daughters, came to the aid of Sicily during the Sicilian Vespers, then took advantage of the situation to occupy the island himself. The Angevins retained possession of Southern Italy (and Naples) while the Spanish controlled Sicily. Naples and Sicily were thus separately ruled until 1504, when the Spanish managed to repel a French invasion and unite Naples and Sicily under the Spanish crown.

During the 18th century, Sicily was tossed around from one power to another, either as one of the rewards for victory or as a consolation prize in the various struggles for dominion in Europe: In 1713, it was given to Savoy; in 1718, conquered again by Spain; in 1720, ceded to Austria; and conquered by Spain again in 1734. In 1759, the Bourbon king of Spain, Charles III, gave Sicily to his son Ferdinand IV, decreeing that it should never again be united to the Spanish monarchy.

Thereafter the Bourbon kings ruled Sicily (except for a brief period during the Napoleonic wars) until the final battle for the unification of Italy started in 1860.

THE ITALIANS (19TH CENTURY ONWARD)

Having been treated so often as a pawn in the political games of larger powers, Sicily was a particularly fertile ground for revolutionary movements in the second half of the 19th century. On April 4, 1860, a police informant upset a revolutionary plot in Palermo, and a group of conspirators was arrested. Though stifled in the town, however, the revolution continued to foment in the countryside, and by May 15, Giuseppe Garibaldi and his volunteer soldiers (Garibaldi's Thousand) were able to land in Marsala and win a first victory over the Bourbon troops. The Sicilian peasants, who were fighting for their land and livelihood, regarded Garibaldi as a hero; under his guidance they chose (by plebiscite) to unite with the young kingdom of Italy in October 1860. In 1861, the Kingdom of Italy, to be ruled by the House of Savoy, was officially proclaimed, and the island of Sicily was part of it.

Chronology of historical events

850 BC	The Phoenicians establish trading stations on promontories and small islands around the coast.
733	The Corinthians found Syracuse, greatest city of ancient Sicily.
254	Rome captures Palermo in the First Punic War.
43-36	Sextus Pompeius occupies Messina; Sicily comes under Greek control.
AD 276-278	Sicily is invaded by the Barbarians.
533-535	Byzantine general Belisarius destroys the Vandal kingdom, Belisarius occupies Sicily and makes it part of the Justinian Empire.
726	Italians revolt agains the Byzantines; the emperor confiscates all papal estates in Sicily and southern Italy.
831	Saracens take Palermo from the Byzantines; by 965 all of Sicily is under Arab control.
1072	The Bourbon, Roger de Hauteville, conquers Palermo 'for Christendom'. Under his son King Roger, Palermo becomes the most splendid capital of Europe.
1282	Rebellion of the Sicilian Vespers; 2 000 Frenchmen killed by Sicilians. Start of the 20-year War of the Vespers.
1302-1713	Spanish occupation of Sicily.
1487	Inquisition is introduced and all the Jews are driven out of Sicily.
1713-1759	Control of Sicily transferred to Savoy, then to Austria, and finally back to Spain.
1759-1860	Bourbon kings rule Sicily.
1860	Garibaldi lands in Messina with his '1000' and drives out the Bourbons.
1861	United Kingdom of Italy, including Sicily, proclaimed.
1943	Sicily invaded and conquered by Allied troops during World War II.
1946	The Italian parliament grants regional autonomy to Sicily.

SICILY TODAY

About 600,000 years ago, Sicily and its satellite islands were torn from the Italian peninsula by a violent earthquake. The Pezzo headland in Calabria and Peloro in Sicily would fit together perfectly if joined — a fact pointed out 2000 years ago by the geographer Strabo. Sicily and the Aeolian Islands are thus like pieces of a puzzle that gradually drifted apart after the cataclysm, each developing in a unique manner. 'In spite of its classical Greek elements and the Byzantine occupation, Sicily mainly evokes North Africa. Arab influence has had a tangible effect' (French author Brandon-Albini). Although the Strait of Messina is only 1.9 mi/3 km wide, Sicily is a world apart, even from a geographical point of view.

THE LARGEST MEDITERRANEAN ISLAND

With its 9830 sq mi/25,460 sq km, Sicily is the largest Mediterranean island and the largest region in Italy. Numerous small neighbouring islands come under Sicilian administration: the Aeolian Islands (Lípari, Strómboli and Vulcano), Ústica, the Égadi Islands (Favignana, Lévanzo and Maréttimo), the Pelágie Islands (Lampedusa and Linosa) and Pantelleria, which is half-way between Sicily and Tunisia. The total surface area of Sicily, including the satellite islands, is 9926 sq mi/25,709 sq km.

Sicily is triangular, which explains its ancient Greek name, *Trinacria,* or three-cornered land. Its three coastlines correspond to three distinctive regional areas:

The north coast is bordered by mountains that line the Tyrrhenian Sea from Messina to Termini Imerese; the Peloritani Mountains, the easternmost range, are formed of ancient granite rock like those of the Aspromonte Mountains on the other side of the strait on mainland Italy; heading west, the Nébrodi or Caronie mountains are limestone, and the Madoníe range farther on, with heights of 6600 ft/2000 m, completes the chain of Appennines that runs the entire length of continental Italy extending into Corsica and Sardinia. The Madoníe Mountains rise between two rivers, the Himera to the west (15.5 mi/25 km from Cefalù) and the Pollino to the east.

The east coast facing Greece is comprised of the large volcanic formations: the Iblei Mountains and Mount Etna. The limestone Ibleans, located in the south-east, are crossed by

narrow gorges known as *cave,* most common in the area around
Ragusa where fruit farming is widespread. Etna, to the north, is a
volcanic mountain composed of lava and ash that dominates the
entire landscape. At 10,646 ft/3226 m, spreading over an area of
612 sq mi/1570 sq km, it is one of the earth's most formidable
volcanoes and the largest in Europe.

The south coast of Sicily is about 90 mi/145 km from
Tunisia, and the limestone hills and semi-desert plateaus of the
Sicilian interior are indeed reminiscent of Africa. The southern
shores are inhospitable at times, swept by the sirocco winds that
carry sand all the way from the Sahara. Sulphur, asphalt and oil
are produced throughout the region.

AN ANCIENT GRANARY

Up until the 3rd century BC the island, considered Rome's
bread basket, was the most prosperous region in the empire.

Orange and lemon trees were introduced later by the Arabs,
who occupied the island during the 9th and 10th centuries. They
also cultivated cotton and sugar cane (the latter no longer grown)
and cleared much of the forest that covered the island to make
room for the vast wheat fields so essential to the survival of the
rapidly growing population.

Despite this early cultivation there are few plains in Sicily
today. The Catania plain between Etna and the Iblean Mountains
is the largest, formed by alluvial deposits from the Simeto River.
The other plains are located along the coast of the Tyrrhenian
Sea and on the far west of the island, near Trápani, Marsala
and Marzara.

The region's tuff (a porous rock formed of volcanic ash and
dust) is covered by a thin layer of fertile red soil suitable for vine
growing. The island's major problem is the lack of water. The
droughts common throughout the south, coupled with the power
of owners of *latifundia* (large private estates) are serious obstacles
to land reform and development in Sicily.

THE PEOPLE

Six million people live in Sicily alone. With more than
200 inhabitants per square kilometre (0.38 sq mi), the island is
the most densely populated area in Italy. For the most part the
people are farmers, fishermen and shopkeepers, but many are out
of work. Sicily's unemployment problem is rife, which explains
the ever-growing number of Sicilians emigrating to America
or Australia.

If you are accustomed to the boisterous exchanges and
exuberant gestures of the Italians on the mainland and the easy
contact you can have with them, you are likely to be surprised by
the Sicilian character. The contradictory island temperament can
blow hot and cold; beneath the reserve and the apparent shyness
there sometimes lies a fierce and volatile nature.

Ethnically, the Sicilians are a mix of many elements,
including Greek, Roman, Arab, French and Spanish. They

are usually shorter than the northern Europeans, with olive complexions and dark hair and eyes. They share many traits with mainland Italians: strong family loyalty, practical humanitarianism and a dislike for militarism and authority.

As you explore the island you will often have a strange impression of emptiness. There's practically no one in the countryside; 90% of the people live in cities or large market towns. For centuries, in order to try to fight off invaders, the Sicilians banded together in fortified villages, often built in the difficult-to-reach regions. You will come across large expanses of deserted countryside devoid of farms and villages, with only the occasional 'dormitory town' inhabited by farmers who have to travel long distances every morning to their fields. In the past they transported their tools and lunches in brightly painted, carved carts, or *carri*. These were once the pride of their owners but have since been cut into boards (for museums and antique shops) and replaced by noisy three-wheeled scooters.

The villages are empty during the day. Here and there you may see women passing, dressed in black, or elderly men chatting outside a *circolo* (a sort of bar or club), dressed in velvet suits. The streets do not come alive until evening, when almost everyone in town takes a daily stroll, called the *passeggiatta*.

CUSTOMS AND BELIEFS

Marriage is considered the most important event in a lifetime. The trousseau and the ceremony itself are scrupulously prepared down to the last detail. From her wedding day on, a woman will do everything to satisfy her family and to bring up her children according to the values passed on to her by her parents and grandparents. Children have an important place in the home, and every attention is paid to them, even in the poorest families, although parents rule over them with jealous authority. There is a Sicilian proverb: 'Your mother is your soul, he who loses her will never find her. Honour your father and listen to him always, then even the stones will love you'.

As with marriage, it is very much in the Sicilian tradition to celebrate death. The concept of reincarnation, inherited from Eastern religions, is still widespread today, as is the belief in the resurrection of the dead — both of which tend to render the event itself less dramatic. During the celebration of the dead (All Souls' Day), children receive presents, supposedly from the dead. Large wreaths and heartrending obituaries are posted along streets and on doors. These traditions date back thousands of years, to Greek, Arab and Byzantine civilizations.

The practice of magic also plays a part in Sicilian life, serving to heal or guard against illness, to keep death at bay and even to put curses on enemies. Men known as *jettatori* are reputed to use magic to cause a crop to catch fire or a flock to be wiped out by an epidemic or even to kill unsuspecting rivals. For protection from the evil eye, Sicilians wear something red or carry a little coral horn. Although these beliefs have been seriously disputed over the last few years, especially in the towns, they still endure to this day.

THE MAFIA, THE 'HONOURED SOCIETY'

It is impossible to speak about the Sicilians without mentioning the Mafia, but to understand the Mafia we must look at Sicilian history. During the Arab occupation in the 9th and 10th centuries, the large private estates *(latifundia)* dating from the Byzantine era were divided among the peasants. The tyranny of the Roman governors was stamped out, and Sicily regained its former prosperity. The invasion of the Normans, however, put everything into question again. On their return from the Crusades, the Normans arrived in Sicily as liege vassals to the pope and set up a new feudal system on the island. The ensuing conflicts between the lords and the pope, and later between the various interested monarchies and barons (always to the detriment of the people) were to mark the history of the island for several centuries. A movement was created, an association that little by little built up a code of honour, secret rites, and recognized leaders who 'imposed their law and their justice, however basic, against the law and justice of the lords, who were indifferent to the public good' (Brandon-Albini). The word 'mafia' is derived from the Arabic *mu'afah; mu* means 'courage' and *afah* means 'to protect'. Thus the original meaning of 'mafia' was the defense of the weak against the strong. The word expressed the idea of revolt against invaders or protection from feudal abuse. The settling of scores approved by the Mafia was aimed at ensuring the peasants' safety, protecting them from oppressive foreign authorities. At that time, the order was known as the 'honoured society' *(societa onorata)*. Honourable it was, for a few centuries, but gradually it became customary to dispense 'quick justice', to use violence, blackmail and crime, and the Mafia began to degenerate into the dangerous secret society it is today.

The modern Mafia was born when the island was united with the kingdom of Italy on October 21, 1860. The new laws and taxes were not welcomed by the islanders, and when military service was made compulsory most conscripts either refused to join up or deserted. Those who escaped became outlaws but were often given cover by a population that had learned through history to love adventurers.

'See nothing, hear nothing, say nothing'

The Mafia operates according to a well-established hierarchy in which the main rule for *mafiosi* is obedience. They abide by the Sicilian law, 'see nothing, hear nothing, say nothing.' Codes of silence *(omerta)* and honour even forbid giving evidence against a guilty man in court; victims do not dare name their persecutors. Every one of the Mafia's members is a link in the murky chain — from the *gabellotti* (lessors of large estates), to the *soprastanti* (stewards and wardens), on down to the *picciotti* (hired men) who are often recruited from shepherds, ex-prisoners, deserters and the unemployed. Should these different groups *(cosche)* indulge in ruthless fighting, the law is always held at bay when it comes to a settling of scores. Furthermore, the Mafia offers its own police services; for a fee, it will watch over stock and crops and protect property.

The Mafia's activities in Sicily have not diminished since the end of World War II. The Sicilian separatist movement

(1943-45), which resulted in the establishment of regional autonomy, opened new pathways for the Mafia. In Palermo, the Mafia opposed all attempts at industrialization, fearing that workers would organize and become intractable; this meant industrialists avoided Palermo for years. Gangs fought for control of the food market, for suburban land and, more recently, for the drug market.

The Mafia still controls public officials and has judges and police chiefs transferred when they prove too zealous. During elections, the Mafia imposes its own candidates. During auctions, it controls the bidding, and the buyer has to pay a bribe known as *il pizzo*. As the island's economy develops, the Mafia takes over towns; Palermo is its present stronghold. It is still quick to 'dispense justice', often in the form of a pistol shot from a window or from behind a bush. Even if a murder is committed in public the witnesses will have heard and seen nothing; they'll stay at home and keep their mouths shut.

The Mafia is structured roughly as follows: at the bottom of the ladder the *mafia di borgata* hold power over local tradesmen; those just above control funerals, the citrus-fruit market and contraband cigarettes; on the next rung up are those *mafiosi* who supervise public works, drug trafficking and kidnapping *(anonima sequestri)*. They are all under the control of the 'honoured society', whose leaders, thanks to political support, have until recently acted with complete impunity.

The drug trade has become the major interest of the Sicilian Mafia. In 1981 an estimated 20 billion lire changed hands in drug deals. The year 1984 was an eventful one: several high-ranking civil servants and elected representatives were charged with drug trafficking. On February 10, 1986, important legal proceedings opened in Palermo, which lasted two years, as an attempt was made to break down the barrier between the law and the Mafia. Sentences of life imprisonment were pronounced, which helped to restore the Sicilian people's faith in their legal system. Even more important than the trial, however, is the present movement among young Sicilians to break the stronghold the Mafia has on their lives.

Rest assured, the Mafia does not attack tourists; they have more important business to attend to. You could rub shoulders with its most dangerous members without ever realizing it.

Floating coffins

The rise of fascism dealt a blow to the Mafia. Mussolini's government united with major landowners and managed to imprison most of the lesser *mafiosi*. The leaders were exiled, and some were smuggled by ship out of the country in coffins built by port *mafiosi*. Once on board they 'came to life again' and mingled with the unsuspecting passengers. The crossing to America was usually fairly uneventful, apart from the occasional Mafia stowaway being thrown overboard by sailors in the pay of a rival gang. Those who survived reunited in America, and the Mafia became known as 'Cosa Nostra'. The American army used Mafia leaders to weave a network of collusion with their friends in Sicily, which facilitated the American landing there in World War II. The operation was so successful there was even talk about Sicily joining the United States as the latest star in the American flag. In the United States, where it now controls gangsterism and drug trafficking, the Mafia had found fertile ground for its activites.

GOVERNMENT ADMINISTRATION AND ECONOMY

On May 15, 1946, Sicily was granted regional autonomy and has been ruled by its own parliament since the first was elected in 1947. This regional parliament or assembly consists of 90 deputies who function under an executive committee, formed of a president and a group of advisors known as the *giunta*. Power, however, is limited to regional decisions of an administrative nature. The island would not survive without help from Rome, which finances, among other things, a large percentage of the public works projects.

Sicily is divided into nine provinces: Agrigento, Caltan-issetta, Catania, Enna, Messina, Palermo, Ragusa, Syracuse and Trápani.

A difficult economy

Sicily is wealthy along the coasts and poor in the interior — a division accentuated these past few years with the development of industry on the coast. In Augusta, Syracuse, Gela and Milazzo, the metallic structures of large petrochemical complexes stand out against the skyline as they do near the methane deposits and oil fields discovered in the Ragusa and Gela regions. There is also a mechanical engineering industry centred in Palermo, Catánia and Messina.

Although fishing is still very much a cottage industry, it nonetheless plays an important role in the economy. Sicilian ships represent almost 25% of the national fishing fleet.

Forty percent of the island's working population is involved in agriculture, which accounts for 20% of the GNP. Citrus fruit is grown in the well-watered areas, while the centre of the island is mainly devoted to wheat.

The subsoil is particularly rich in minerals. Deposits of sulphur, potassium and rock salt are still worked, though it is mainly gas and oil that are responsible for the island's rapid industrial expansion since the 1950s. Given Sicily's natural beauty, tourism has not played a negligible role either. Finally, financial aid from the Cassa del Mezzogiorno, created in 1950 for the economic development of the south of Italy including Sicily, has helped the island to adapt to modern times.

Nonetheless, Sicily is currently experiencing a serious economic crisis due to unemployement and the corruption that has spread to all the country's economic and administrative sectors. The Mafia's influence and the international drug trade's importance to the island cannot be ignored.

ART AND ARCHITECTURE

A visit to Sicily is a fascinating complement to a trip to Greece. You will see not only splendid landscapes but also some of the Mediterranean's most remarkable monuments.

ARTISTIC HERITAGE

Prehistoric art

Cave paintings dating from the Upper Paleolithic period, the first traces of man in Sicily, were discovered in the Grotta del Genovesi on Lévanzo Island and the Grotta dell'Addaura near Palermo. Evidence of the Neolithic civilization has been found at Megara Hyblaea and on the Aeolian Islands. Remains from the various Bronze Ages can be seen on the Punta Milazzese headland on Panarea Island, at Castelluccio near Noto and in the necropolis at Pantálica.

Greek architecture

Some forms of Greek art found their fullest expression in Sicily. For example, during the 6th and 5th centuries BC temples in Syracuse, Gela, Selinunte and Agrigento were built in the purest Doric style. Hoping to dazzle the world, the tyrants of Antiquity threw themselves into the construction of colossal monuments such as the Temple of Olympian Zeus in Agrigento (see p. 123) and Temple E at Selinunte (see p. 109).

Sicilian temples of the Doric order were built according to strict rules. They consist of a stylobate, the base of the building; columns grooved with 20 flutings that end in a geometric capital; an architrave, or beam which rests on the capitals, above which is a frieze composed of metopes (panels, carved or plain) which alternate with panels decorated with three upright grooves; a

---

The Greek temple in Sicily

Different types of temples can be distinguished by the position of the colonnade:
— in antis: only two columns on the façade
— prostyle: a portico with columns on the front only
— amphiprostyle: columns at both ends
— peripteral: a row of columns on all four sides.
Nearly all Sicilian temples are 'peripteral hexastyles' — they have six (hexa) columns on each side.

A Norman itinerary

The main Norman monuments in Palermo are: Ponte dell'Ammiraglio, the churches of San Giovanni dei Lebbrosi, La Magione, La Martorana, San Cataldo, San Giovanni degli Eremeti, the Cathedral and the Cappella Palatina of the Norman palace.

Traveling counter-clockwise from Palermo other Norman buildings can be visited in Monreale (Cathedral and Cloisters), Castelvetrano (Santíssima Trinitia di Delia), Mazara del Vallo (Cathedral and San Nicolò Regale), Sciacca (San Nicolò la Latina), Caltanissetta (Santo Spirito), Catania (Duomo), Paterno (castle), Adrano (castle), Forza d'Agro (San Pietro e Paolo), Messina (Santa Annunziata dei Catalini, the Duomo and La Badiazza), Frazzano (San Filippo di Fragala) and Cefalù (Cathedral).

---

cornice surmounting the frieze; and the pediment, which is triangular because of the slope of the roof.

In addition to the temples, mention must be made of Sicily's theatres, the most impressive being the theatre of Syracuse, one of the largest in the Greek world (see p. 168). The castle of Euryalus, near Syracuse, is one of Antiquity's most ambitious fortresses and should not be missed, but in general the best-preserved Greek monuments can be seen at Agrigento, which has the richest archaeological site on the island. Akrai (Palazzolo Acréide), Segesta, Selinunte and Syracuse are also well worth a visit.

Roman architecture

Little remains of Roman architecture in Sicily. The major examples are the Syracuse Amphitheatre, the splendid Taormina Theatre and the Piazza Armerina Villa, where the grandeur and beauty of the mosaic tiling are unique.

Christian and Byzantine art

The earliest traces of Christian art can be seen in the catacombs, mainly in Syracuse (2nd-4th centuries), where fragments of paintings have been preserved. Over the centuries some of the ancient temples were converted into churches, as was the case with the Temple of Concord at Agrigento and the temple of Athena in Syracuse. The Byzantines introduced the mosaic — an art form which flourished later under Norman rule. Examples can be seen in the Cappella Palatina in Palermo and in the cathedrals of Monreale and Cefalù.

Arab and Norman art

When they conquered Sicily, the Arabs had been masters of the south of Spain for over a century and had made Cordoba, their Andalusian capital, a luxurious city that rivaled Baghdad. They introduced new techniques for building and decorating that contributed to a flowering of architectural masterpieces: palaces, mosques, fountains and gardens. Unfortunately almost all the monuments from this period have either disappeared or been disfigured.

The Normans were so taken with the excellence of Muslim architecture (which harmonized perfectly with the Sicilian landscape) that they continued building in the Arab tradition while

Detail of a capital in the Monreale cloisters.

adapting it to their Christian requirements. The mingling of Arab, Byzantine and Norman styles gave rise to a new, eclectic art form. When the Norman princes built their churches in keeping with the canons of Rome, they were unable to shake off Arab influences entirely. The Cefalù cathedral, probably the most Roman of Sicilian churches, has numerous Eastern elements, such as Arab arches and mosaic overlays set in a golden background. In building their palaces, the Normans gave way totally to Muslim influences; the monuments from this period mirror the spirit of the court of Palermo, a veritable Tower of Babel where French, Greek, Arabic, Latin and Sicilian were spoken.

13th- to 16th-century art

During the 13th and 14th centuries Sicilian art was influenced by the northern Gothic style that dominated France. Gothic elements can be seen in the castles of Syracuse (Castello Maniace) and Catania (Castello Ursino), as well as in some of the palaces built by feudal families (notably the Chiaramontis), such as the Scláfani and Steri palaces in Palermo. During the 15th century, when Sicily was under Spanish occupation, Catalan-Gothic art was favoured; examples of the style can be seen in the portico of Palermo Cathedral or in the San Stéfano and Corvaia palaces. Toward the end of the century, the architect Matteo Carnelivari designed the plans for Santa Maria della Catena, and the Abbatellis and Aiutamicristo palaces in Palermo, in keeping with the ornamental style of the Catalan-Gothic school. The much-admired fresco *The Triumph of Death,* now in the National Gallery of Sicily, also dates from this period.

Sicily's most famous painter was Antonello da Messina (1430-79). Influenced by the Flemish and Venetian schools, he produced paintings that rank among the major works of the 15th century. Among them are the *Portrait of an Unknown Man,* in Cefalù, and the *Virgin Annunciate* and three portraits of saints displayed in the National Gallery in Palermo.

The Renaissance style was introduced to Sicily by the sculptors Francesco Laurana (1458-1521) and Domenico Gagini (1420-92). The latter was the first in a long line of sculptors whose works are displayed in almost every church on the island. There were at least ten artists in the amazing Gagini family, of whom the most famous, after Domenico, was Antonello, his son (1478-1536).

Sicilian Baroque

Baroque has been defined as anything 'that deviates from the norm'. With its origins in the Counter-Reformation, Baroque was imported by the Spanish to Sicily. It took no time at all for Sicilian artists, inspired by the exuberance of its shapes and the luxuriance of its decor, to develop a real passion for the new style. The most characteristic Baroque buildings in Palermo are the churches of Santa Caterina, San Giuseppe dei Teatini and Casa Professa. The abundance of spiral columns, precious marble inlays, gold decorations, lacey stucco-work and dramatic statuary make these churches look more like palaces than religious sanctuaries.

The Baroque movement came to Sicily during a period when towns such as Catania, Noto and Ragusa, all destroyed by the earthquakes of 1669 and 1693, were being rebuilt. The style reaches its fullest expression in Noto, where the architecture of the whole town is so homogenous that you can easily believe it was the work of a single man. This was in fact the case; Noto was fortunate to benefit from the talent of one of the greatest architects of the time, Rosario Gagliardi (1680-1762). Mention must also be made of other noteworthy architects, such as Giovanni Vermexio (1621-57) from Syracuse; Giovanni Battista Vaccarini (1702-68), who was largely responsible for the reconstruction of Catania; and Andrea Palma (1728-54) of Palermo.

PAINTING, LITERATURE AND MUSIC

Painting

At the beginning of the 17th century the presence on the island of two great foreign painters, Van Dyck and Caravaggio, gave new impetus to painting in Sicily. Van Dyck came to Sicily to paint the viceroy's portrait, and Caravaggio took refuge on the island in 1608, fleeing arrest in Rome and Malta. He produced two major works on the island: a *Nativity* (stolen in 1969) and the *Burial of St Lucia.*

Another mysterious foreign visitor, Filippo Paladino, who was born in Florence in 1544, came to Sicily for the last 15 years of his life and brought the culture of the Florentine Mannerists with him.

Sicilian painting found its most striking expression in the works of Pietro Novelli (1603-47), Mario Rossi and Vito d'Anna (1720-69). Together with Guglielmo Borremans (1670-1744) from Anvers and Filippo Paladino, they covered convents, churches and palaces with frescoes and paintings.

Literature

Throughout its eventful history Sicily has served as a refuge for poets and artists. In particular the island welcomed

---

A prodigious sculptor

One of the most famous Palermitan sculptors of the Baroque period in Sicily was Giacomo Serpotta (1656-1732), a versatile artist who also excelled in playing the lute. At the age of 20 he decorated his first church and gained celebrity so quickly that the viceroy commissioned him for an equestrian statue of Charles II. His reputation was such that he came to be known as the Watteau of sculpture. He fell in love with a young girl from Palermo who died while bearing him a son out of wedlock, leaving him to bring up the child. He devoted his entire life to his art, working in stucco, a beautiful malleable plaster made of white marble dust, chalk and lime, so resistant it can last for centuries. In Palermo the oratories of San Lorenzo, San Domenico and Santa Zita, and the churches of Sant'Agostino, Santa Catarina and San Francesco, all bear his stamp. In his will he asked to be wrapped in a monk's frock and buried in San Matteo. He left everything he owned to religious orders and to his son only the wherewithal to buy mourning clothes and the responsibility of continuing his father's work.

He was a mysterious, secretive man whose work was always very personal even though it was commissioned by the Church. This is borne out by his oratories, which have the energy and verve of ballrooms, and by his portrayal of the Virtues who look like princesses at the viceroy's court.

13th-century French troubadours from Provence who were forced to flee the devastation inflicted by the Albigensian Crusade. The mixture of cultures resulting from occupation by Greeks, Arabs and Normans left its mark on Sicilian literature and gave rise to colourful popular poetry that was passed on by *cantastorie.* These storytellers journeyed from village to village reciting the poems in public, especially at fairs. The poems were similar to the French *chansons de geste* and related the heroic deeds of knight-errants, crusaders, Charlemagne's Paladins and the Moors, as well as tragic local stories and, much later, the exploits of Garibaldi.

More recently, Sicily has provided the world with a number of important writers, including Luigi Capuana (1839-1915), Giovanni Verga (1840-1922), and the most famous, Luigi Pirandello, who was born in Agrigento in 1867 and died in Rome in 1938. A playwright of international repute, Pirandello drew upon his experience of Sicilian life to develop such themes as social taboos, fanaticism, superstition and sexual prejudice.

Leonardo Sciascia is perhaps the best known of contemporary Sicilian writers. His first book was published in 1956 when he was 35. This prolific author continued to write satirical social documentaries, short detective stories, and novels, up to his death in 1989, at the age of 68. Some of his works, *Cadaveri Eccellenti* and *Todo Modo,* for example, have inspired films.

For more information on books and literature, see the section 'Suggested reading' p. 250.

Opera dei Pupi

Puppet theatre is probably the last living example of ancient Sicilian folklore. The most common theme addressed is the struggle between Good (the Christians) and Evil (the Saracens). There are strict rules: battle scenes alternate with love scenes; Christian knights are always on the left of the stage while Saracens are on the right; Roland (Orlando) always wears a helmet with an eagle and carries a shield with a decorative cross while Rinaldo always has a lion for his emblem. The marionettes themselves are at least 39 in/1m tall and are controlled by visible iron rods and wires. The characters are always represented in the same easily recognizable way: Charlemagne, for example, is portrayed as a grumpy old miser while Rinaldo is a Don Juan. It's impossible to understand the subtleties of the text because 'the language used in these "dramas" is a spicy mixture of bombastic rhetorical images taken from famous Italian chivalric poems of the 16th century and the *chansons de geste* of the Middle Ages' (Brandon-Albini). Spectators often get involved in the action and either encourage the performers or shower them with abuse.

Music

To this day, Sicilian shepherds play a strange musical instrument, the *scacciapensieri,* which roughly translates as 'worry-chaser'. It's a kind of metal ring with a thin strip that is played by the mouth. The strip vibrates, producing a rather monotonous sound originally thought to attract love or ward off misfortune. Those sold now are mass-produced and make a different sound than the old-fashioned kind.

Two internationally famous musicians were born in Sicily. The first, Alessandro Scarlatti, was born in Trápani in 1659. He founded the Neapolitan School of Music and is considered to be the originator of Baroque opera. His work includes some 200 masses and 600 cantatas. The second, Vincenzo Bellini (1801-35), was born in Catánia and died in Paris. He is considered to be the founder of romantic opera.

Two major lyric works drew their inspiration from events in Sicily. The *Sicilian Vespers* by Giuseppe Verdi was created at the Paris Opera for the Grande Exposition of 1855, and Pietro Mascagni's *Cavalleria Rusticana,* a Sicilian village drama, was inspired by a novel by Giovanni Verga. Composed in 1890, it is still highly appreciated in lyric performances throughout the world.

PALERMO

Called Panhormos (many harbours) by the Greeks, the capital of Sicily is located on a wide bay bounded to the northwest by Monte Pellegrino and to the east by Capo Zafferano. It stretches along the seaward edge of the Conca d'Oro (Golden Shell), a fertile valley bordered by mountains that form a natural amphitheatre. Surrounded by vineyards, palm trees and orange groves and blessed with a mild climate, Palermo was once a paradise that delighted a succession of sovereigns.

Colonized by the Carthaginians in the 5th century BC in an attempt to control the spread of Greek influence, Palermo later fell under Roman, Arab, French, German and Spanish rule (see p. 29). Remains from the Arab and Norman days have been miraculously well-preserved, as have a number of Baroque buildings. Yet Palermo was very badly damaged during World War II, and much of the city's charm was lost when the older quarters were destroyed.

With a population today of 700,000, the city is suffering from rampant urbanization, and the damage wrought by the war has still not been repaired. A newcomer to the city may be shocked by the peeling façades, the feverish construction of new buildings, garbage left out in the sun, the houses in varying states of collapse and the 'every-man-for-himself' attitude that seems to govern daily life. It may take time to realize that Palermo is also the site of many of the artistic splendours that remain as testament to Sicily's fascinating, if troubled, history.

▬ PRACTICAL INFORMATION

Map coordinates refer to the maps pp. 49, 50-51.
Telephone area code: 091.

Access

Boat
There are regular boat services between Palermo and Naples and between Cagliari and Genoa. The overnight ferry between Palermo and Naples is inexpensive and runs daily. Fast hydrofoils *(aliscafi)* link Palermo to the Aeolian Islands and the Italian continent in half the normal crossing time. The *motonave* boats carry passengers and freight only, and the *traghetti* take passengers with cars. The main boat companies are:

The via Porta di Castro in Palermo.

Grandi Traghetti (to Genoa and Livorno), via Mariano Stabile, II, C4, ☎ 587 832.

Siremar (to Ustica), via Francesco Crispi 120, II, B5, ☎ 582 403.

Tirrenia (to Naples, Genoa and Cagliari), via Roma 385, II, D4, ☎ 585 733.

Bus

If you don't have a car in Sicily, the bus is the most pleasant means of transport. Pullman buses are comfortable, fast, air-conditioned and no more expensive than the trains. There are regular services between the main towns (Palermo-Catania, Palermo-Trápani). Ask for details at a tourist office. The main bus companies are:

AST, piazza Stazione Lolli, II, C2. Buses run to Marsala, Salemi, Castelvetrano and mazara del Vallo.

Autoservizi Segesta, via P. Balsamo 26, II, F5, beside Stazione Centrale. Buses run to Monreale, Alcamo and Partinico. A Segesta Pullman leaves Palermo every hour for Trápani.

Cuffaro, via Lincoln 42, II, F5, near Stazione Centrale. Buses run from here to Agrigento.

SAIS, via P. Balsamo 16, II, F5, beside Stazione Centrale. Buses run to Catania, Trápani, Caltanissetta, Gela and Enna. For Messina, Syracuse and Taormina, change at Catania.

Car

Palermo is 144 mi/231 km west of Messina, 129 mi/208 km west of Catania and 165 mi/266 km north-west of Syracuse. See information on boats above for ferry information. For car rentals, see p. 57.

Plane

All planes arrive at the **Punta Raisi International Airport,** 19 mi/30 km west of the city. An APT tourist office there can provide you with all the information and maps you will need for your stay. If you are flying out of Palermo arrive at the airport in advance, as customs checks can take a long time. There is a regular bus service into town that runs between 6:30am and 10:45pm from the airport to the Politeama Garibaldi Theatre, via I. La Lumia, II, C3, and Stazione Central, II, F5. Expect to pay about L4,000. If you are driving, the road is well indicated. However, there are large road works that can disrupt traffic on the ring road. You can also take a taxi, which will be expensive — between L40,000 and L45,000.

Train

All trains from Milan, Rome and Naples via Messina and the Villa San Giovanni ferry boat, plus the domestic trains from Trápani, Caltanissetta, Enna and Catania, arrive at Stazione Centrale II, F5. Some stop first at Stazione Notarbartolo in the north-west section of the city; make sure you are at the right station before getting off the train.

Be sure you know what kind of train you want: a *Rapido*, or *Espresso*, which, as its name indicates, is the quickest train; a *Diretto*, which stops at most stations; or a *Locale*, which stops everywhere. It's best to reserve a seat if you're going on a long trip, and be aware that you must pay a supplement for many trains (particularly the *Rapido*).

The most frequent connections are to the north coast (Trápani and Messina) and across the island to Enna and Catania, but it is possible to visit any point on the island by train, including the archaeological site at Segesta. Train travel is a convenient, cheap means of transport.

For train information, call Stazione Centrale, ☎ 230 806.

Accommodation

A list of all accommodation and prices is available from the tourist bureau in piazza Castelnuovo 35, II, C3 (see p. 58).

▲▲▲▲ **Villa Igiea,** Salita Belmonte 43, I, C4, ☎ 543 744. 177 rooms.

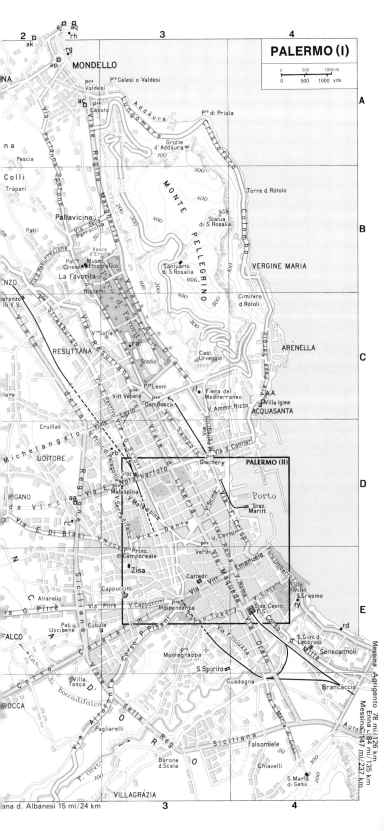

PALERMO (I)

2   **3**   **4**

0   500   1000 m
0   500   1000 yds

aj   aq
ak   rh

rg

ap   **MONDELLO**

P.ta Célesi o Valdesi

P.za
Valdesi

Addáura

Lungomare

P.ta di Priola

ac

P.za
Caboto

Grotte
d'Addáura

Cristóforo

A

na

Pescia

Colli

Trápani

MONTE

300

400

Torre d. Rótolo

PELLEGRINO

B

Pallavicino

Via d. Resurrezione

Via della
Parrocchia

Vasca
d'Ercola

458
Statua
di S. Rosalia

VERGINE MARIA

Via Strasburgo

Pal.
Cinese

Museo
Etnográfico

La Favorita

P.za
Niscemi

Santuario
di S. Rosalia

606.

Cimitero
d. Rótoli

NZO

lorenzo
li F.S.

V.le d. Favorita o Diana

V.le d. Favorita o Diana

400

500

Sérgio

C

RESUTTANA

Via Resuttana

V.la Sofia

Stádio

300

Cast.
Utveggio

ARENELLA

laro

Michelangelo

Cruillas

UDITORE

Viale Lazio

Viale Croce

V. d. Retiro

P.za
Vitt. Veneto

P.za
Leoni

Don Bosco

V. Sampó

Fiera del
Mediterraneo

V. Ammir. Rizzo

A.A.

Villa Igiea

ACQUASANTA

RIGANO

Via F. di Blasi

Via della Vincia

rc

V.le del Fante

V. E. Restivo

P. Princ. di Patagonia

V. Nolli

V. N. Bartolo

Libertà

Via Dante

Giachery

Staz.
Malaspina

V. Malaspina

V. Serradifalco

V. Noce

V. Crispi

V. Cavour

V. Roma

Foro Umberto I

PALERMO (II)

Porto

Staz.
Marítt.

D

N

P.za Princ.
di Camporeale

Zisa

Cappuccini

V. Cappucini

Via Pitrè

Siciliana

P.za
Indipendenza

Cattedr.

Verdi

P.za
Vitt. Emanuele

Via Vitt. Emanuele

Via Maqueda

Via Roma

Villa
Giulia

S. Erasmo

Staz. Centr.
F.S.

G. Pitrè

Altarello

Pal.
Uscibene

Cubula

Corso P. Pisani

Corso Tuköry

Via Lincoln

Corso d. Mille

S. Giov. d.
Lebbrosi

Settecannoli

rd

E

FALCO

ROCCA

Corso di Boccadifalco

Via Calatafimi

Villa
Tasca

P.za
Montegrappa

S. Spirito

Via Filiciuzza

Via Oreto

Guadagna

Brancaccio

Pagliarelli

Via Altofonte o della Regione

Barone
d. Scala

F. Oreto

Via S. Maria di Gesù

Siciliana

Falsomiele

50

Chiavelli

100

200

S. Maria
di Gesù

Autostr.

VILLAGRÁZIA

ana d. Albanesi 15 mi/24 km

3   **4**

Messina 147 mi/237 km
Messina/Enna 84 mi/135 km
Agrigento 78 mi/126 km

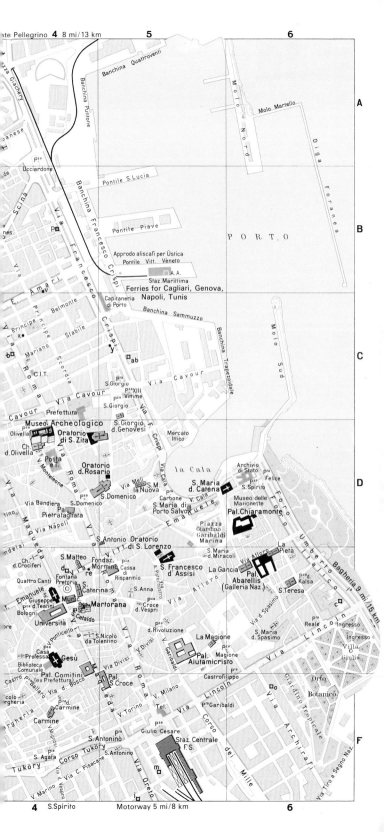

An exceptional establishment, one of the island's most beautiful hotels set in an Art Nouveau villa with a swimming pool, tennis court and magnificent gardens giving a view of Conca d'Oro. A wonderful dining room that in warm weather spills out onto a large terrace overlooking the sea. A large winter room decorated by Ettore de Maria Bergler. There are six sumptuous suites. **La Terrazza** restaurant is renowned (see p. 54).

▲▲▲ **Astoria Palace Hotel,** via Montepellegrino 62, I, D3, ☎ 637 1820 or 362 816. Brand-new hotel with every comfort, bar and restaurant. Outside of centre.

▲▲▲ **Excelsior Palace,** via Ugo Marchese 3, II, B3, ☎ 625 6176. 86 rooms. Opposite viale della Libertà near piazza Mordini. It opened for the National Exhibition at the beginning of the century and has just been refurbished; well located.

▲▲▲ **Grande Albergo delle Palme,** via Roma 396, II, C4 b, ☎ 583 933. 187 air-conditioned rooms. Built in Art Nouveau style, in the centre of town, this charming hotel is the oldest hotel in Palermo. Maupassant came to Palermo on pilgrimage and stayed in the apartment where Wagner composed the end of *Parsifal*. Beautiful reception rooms and magnificent entrance hall. Two restaurants: **La Palmetta** and **La Terrazza Fiorita** (see p. 54).

▲▲▲ **Jolly Hotel del Foro Italico,** Foro Italico 22, II, E6 c, ☎ 616 5090. 277 rooms. Garden and swimming pool on the seafront. Annex with 15 rooms. A good example of the Jolly chain with every comfort.

▲▲▲ **Motel Agip,** viale della Regione Siciliana 2620, I, D2 aa, ☎ 552 033. 105 rooms. Recently renovated; very comfortable.

▲▲▲ **Politeama Palace,** piazza Ruggero Settimo 15, II, C3 g, ☎ 327 777. 102 rooms. Right in the centre of town, with a restaurant, bar and conference room.

▲▲▲ **President,** via Francesco Crispi 230, II, B4 p, ☎ 580 733. 129 rooms. Garden on the terrace. A new hotel with a view of the port and a good restaurant on the roof.

▲▲ **Elite,** via Stabile 136, II, C4 n, ☎ 329 318. 13 rooms. Centrally located.

▲▲ **Europa,** via Agrigento 3, II, B3 q, ☎ 625 6323. 73 rooms. A small new hotel, quiet and near the centre.

▲▲ **Grande Albergo Sole,** corso Vittorio Emanuele 291, II, E4 d, ☎ 581 811. 152 rooms. In the heart of the old town.

▲▲ **Metropol,** via Turisi Colonna 4, II, B2 f, ☎ 588 608. 44 rooms. A few minutes from viale della Libertà.

▲▲ **Ponte,** via Francesco Crispi 99, II, C5 ab, ☎ 583 744. 137 rooms, many of which face the port. Bar and restaurant.

▲▲ **Sausele,** via Vincenzo Errante 12, II, F5 i, ☎ 616 1308. 38 rooms. A very well-run establishment, recommended in its category.

▲▲ **Touring,** via M. Stabile 136, II, C4 n, ☎ 584 444. 13 air-conditioned rooms. Parking lot. Central.

▲▲ **Villa Achirafi,** via Achirafi 10, II, F6 o, ☎ 285 827. 26 rooms. Garden. No restaurant. Beside the Botanical Gardens. Quiet, with lovely surroundings.

▲▲ **Wagner,** via Ammiraglio Gravina 88, II, C3, ☎ 585 311. Simple but well-run and central.

Campgrounds

Internazionale Trinacria, 8 mi/13 km north-west of Palermo, in Sferracavallo, via Barcarello, ☎ 530 590. *Open all year.* Bungalows. Extremely comfortable. Facing the sea.

Private Camping Club dell'Ulivo in Sferracavallo, via Pegasso,

☎ 584 392. *Open May 1-Sept 30.* 711 yds/650 m from the sea. There are also three campsites at Isola delle Fémmine, 10 mi/16 km west of the capital (see p. 91).

La Plaia, Lungomare dei Sacareni, ☎ 677 001. *Open all year.*

La Scogliera, via Palermo 20, ☎ 867 7315. *Open June-Oct.* 55 yds/ 50 m from the sea.

Pepsi Cola, via Marino 69, in Pozzillo 1.2 mi/2 km from Isola delle Fémmine, ☎ 677 654. *Open April-end Sept.* On the beach.

Emergencies

Some useful telephone numbers:

Police (Pronto intervento): 113

Pharmacies on duty: 192

Emergency medical service: 321 860

Road assistance (road police): 116

Gendarmerie (in an emergency): 112

Tourist police: 616 1361

Entertainment

Opera dei Pupi

If you are interested in puppet theatre, an art which unfortunately is dying out, we recommend a visit to the **Museo Internazionale delle Marionette** (see p. 66). Contact the APT office for program information. The few remaining theatres in Palermo are now usually closed, but check at the tourist office for information concerning occasional performances.

Concert halls and theatres

Either ask at a tourist office or look at a copy of *Un Mese a Palermo,* which lists all the shows and cultural events. See also 'Festivals and cultural events.'

Festivals and cultural events

Music

October to June: Opera and symphony season at Politéama Theatre, II, C3. Shows and concerts organized by 'Amici della Musica', performed at Biondo Theatre. Concerts by the Sicilian Symphony Orchestra in the auditorium of San Salvatore.

October: Week of sacred music in Monreale.

Jazz concerts organized by The Brass Group, via Butera 14, ☎ 616 6480 and 561 6513.

Religious festivals

January 6: Epiphany. A family event celebrated around a crib or a Christmas tree.

March 19: St Joseph's fire. In the poorer quarters it was customary to burn the year's accumulation of useless objects in large bonfires. Because this presented a high risk of fires spreading, the authorities opposed the tradition. Nonetheless, occasional fires are still discreetly lit.

July 11-15: Feast of Santa Rosalia, patron saint of Palermo.

August 15: Feast of the Assumption. Children in the poorer quarters set up altars to the Virgin Mary and organize processions in her honour. They ring a little bell to announce their arrival.

September 3: Second part of the feast of Santa Rosalia celebrated with a nocturnal torchlight procession. Pilgrims climb to the sanctuary on Monte Pellegrino along *'la Scala Vecchia'* singing hymns as they go. Prayers are said in front of the statue of the *santuzza*.

November 2: All Soul's Day and also a day for children, who are given presents 'from the dead'. Substitutes for our Santa Claus/Father Christmas.

December 8: Immaculate Conception.
December 13: Santa Lucia, patron saint of Syracuse honoured.

Food and drink

Restaurants
LLLL Charleston, piazza Ungheria 28, II, C3 s, ☎ 321 366. *Closed Sun and June 1-Sept 15.* A wonderful restaurant with Art Nouveau decor and excellent cuisine that deserves its reputation as Sicily's best. The pastries come from its Mazzara annex (p. 56). Excellent service. A wide choice of wines and spirits. In summertime, the restaurant moves to Mondello Lido, in an old palace on viale Regina Elena.

LLLL Gourmand's, viale della Libertà 37/e, II, B3 t, ☎ 323 431. *Closed Sun and Aug 10-25.* Decor is light and ultra-modern like its cooking. The speciality — smoked fillets of fish — now all the rage, originated here. Ask for fish *carpaccio.*

LLLL Renato l'Approdo, via Messina Marina 28, II, C3, ☎ 470 103. *Closed Wed.* Beautiful antique furniture, tasteful decor. Excellent food and service. An unusual menu. For *antipasti* try the delicious raw fish (swordfish, tuna and others) served with a great variety of oils and herbs.

LLLL Terrazza del Grande Hotel Villa Igiea, salita Belmonte 43 I, C4 a, ☎ 543 744. Elegant restaurant in a fine setting. Good food grilled specialities. A varied menu and a wide choice of wines and champagnes.

LLL Friend's Bar, via Brunelleschi 138, I, D2 just off the map, ☎ 201 401. *Closed Mon and throughout Aug.* Away from the centre on a by-road to the airport in a lovely summer garden. The chef favours traditional country fare. When in season, mushrooms are served with local cheese, and asparagus is served with anchovies.

LLL Harry's Bar, via Ruggero Settimo 74, II, C3, ☎ 586 517 *Closed Sun.* Tasteful decor, imaginative menu in the Harry's Bar tradition. Frequented by regular customers.

LLL Ristorante di Pino Ingrao, via Torrearsa 22, II, B3 r, ☎ 582 173. *Closed Sun.* A newly established restaurant in the old Chamade premises (Chamade now has only its Mondello restaurant). Tempting menu. Very reasonable prices given the quality of the food.

LLL Scuderia, via del Fante 9, I, C3 ra, ☎ 520 323. *Closed Sun evening.* The 'stables' *(scuderia)* is an attractive restaurant set in a succession of terraces and fountains at the entrance to Favorita Park. Among its renowned specialities are *involtini di cernia Nettuno* cooked over charcoal, *risotto di mare* stuffed in aubergines *fettuccine azzuro mare* and *spaghetti alla Lampara.*

LLL Terrazza Fiorita del Grande Albergo delle Palme, via Roma 398, II, C4 b. *Closed Sun. In July and August open only in the evening.* Excellent barbecue. Also try smoked swordfish and *risotto alla siciliana.* Terrific variety of pastas. Fine choice of wines.

LLL Trattoria Trittico, largo Montalto 7, I, D3 rb, ☎ 294 809 *Closed Sun.* It may be called a *trattoria* but is in fact a restaurant Ultra-modern decor. Everything comes in threes — hence the name There's a choice of three *antipasti,* three first courses and three main dishes. Recommended for its creative cooking.

LL Al Buco, via Principe di Granatelli 33/c, II, C4, ☎ 323 661 *Closed Mon and throughout Aug.* Good food served in pleasant modern decor. Recommended.

LL A'Cuccagna, via Principe di Granatelli 21/a, II, C4, ☎ 587 267 *Closed Mon.* A classic. Large, pleasant dining-room. Wide choice of *antipasti.* Excellent *prosciutto.* Good value.

LL Al 59, piazza Verdi 59, II, D3, ☎ 583 139. *Closed Wed*

Attractive terrace facing Teatro Massimo. Lively place, good service and very reasonable prices. Remains open late.

LL Aloha d'Oro, via P. Bonanno 42/b, on the road to Monte Pellegrino, ☎ 547 657. *Closed Mon.* Unusual setting. Good food.

LL Bussola 2, via Autonomia Siciliana 117, ☎ 294 692. *Closed Mon.* Good food and efficient service. Wide choice of *antipasti.*

LL Catari, via Giacomo Cusmano 25, II, C2, ☎ 322 992. *Closed Sun and throughout Aug.* Good local cooking. Hot *antipasti* and 30 different kinds of pasta cooked on request. Tasty fried fish.

LL Cotto e Crudo, piazza Marina 45, II, D5. *Closed Tues.* All the cooking is done with home-grown produce. A great variety of dishes. Recommended.

LL Da Gino, via Imperatore Frederico 23, ☎ 547 467. *Closed Mon.* Good couscous.

LL Hong Kong, via Amari 28, II, B4, ☎ 322 172. *Closed Sun.* Chinese restaurant with attractive decor.

LL Lo Scudiero, via F. Turati 7, II, C3, ☎ 581 628. *Closed Sun and throughout August.* Great variety of fish soup, meat and vegetable dishes. Good wines.

LL N'Grasciata, via Tiro a Segno 12, in Sant'Erasmo, ☎ 230 947. *Closed Sun.* Another friendly *trattoria* with a wide choice of fish dishes.

LL Osteria Paradiso, via Serradifalco 23, ☎ 213 919. *Open only for lunch except Sun.* A tiny *trattoria* where fish is the speciality.

LL Papoff, via Isidoro La Lumia 28/b, ☎ 325 355. *Closed Sun.* Art Nouveau decor. A warm atmosphere with unusual cooking.

LL Peppino, piazza Castelnuovo 49, II, C3, ☎ 324 195. *Closed Wed.* A large, popular *trattoria* right in the centre. Good pizzas. Stays open very late.

LL Regine, via Trápani 4/a, II, B3, ☎ 586 566. *Closed Sun.* Quiet, intimate restaurant run by two brothers. International food.

LL Salanitro, piazza Sturzo 15, II, C4, ☎ 324 348. *Closed Sun.* Another good address, just behind Teatro Politeama.

LL Spano, via Messina Marina 22, II, 3C, ☎ 470 025. *Closed Mon.* Fish specialities: pasta with sardines and cockles, seafood risotto, stuffed swordfish, assorted fried fish.

LL Trattoria Stella (Patria hotel), via Alloro 104, II, E5, ☎ 616 136. *Closed Sun.* Don't look for the hotel, it's just an old ruined palace. Stella, the local *trattoria,* is in the courtyard and serves excellent food. It is frequented by Palermitans.

L Antica Focacceria San Francesco, via Paternostro 58, ☎ 320 264. *Closed Mon.* First and foremost it's a bakery cum *rosticceria* where you can buy food to take away. You can also sit at old marble tables to eat *panelle* specialities with sesame seeds and drink *angelica,* a refreshing drink made with a red wine base and fizzy water. This is a popular, inexpensive place.

L Al Duar, via E. Amari 92, II, C4, ☎ 329 560. *Closed Mon.* This restaurant serves Tunisian specialities, including excellent couscous, at very reasonable prices.

L Astoria, viale della Libertà 145, II, B3, ☎ 268 109. A pleasant setting for excellent pizzas and pastries.

L Il Brodo, discesa dei Giudici 24, II, 4E, ☎ 237 520. *Closed Sun.* Brodo means 'broth'. You see large pots of it simmering as you enter. A small friendly restaurant.

L La Capricciosa, via Sampolo 218, ☎ 250 295. *Closed Sun.* A small *trattoria* where fish is the speciality. Truly inexpensive.

L Pizzeria Bellini, piazza Bellini, II, E4, ☎ 283 337. *Closed Tues.* In the former town theatre. Better-known for its position in the heart of the historic quarter than for its food. A large and lovely terrace juts into the square so that you can dine near the illuminated monuments. Quick, efficient service. Open until 2 or 3am.

L Ristorante Tipico I Normanni, via Amari 59, II, C4, ☎ 583 775. Very attractive decor and good food.

L Shanghai, piazza Caracciolo, in Vucciria market, II, D5 (you enter from vicolo dei Mezzani), ☎ 589 573. *Closed Tues.* A modest, lively restaurant with a terrace overlooking the market. Good simple fare. Most of the dishes are oven-cooked in front of you.

L Trattoria Primavera, piazza Bologni 4, II, E4, ☎ 329 408. *Closed Fri.* Small local *trattoria* in a picturesque square. In summer tables are set out beside the statue of Charles V of Spain. Simple food. Inexpensive tourist menu.

L 'U Strascinu, viale della Regione Siciliana 2286, ☎ 401 292. *Closed Mon.* A good address for a wide variety of pizzas.

Cafés

It is difficult to find a place where you can just sit and have a drink. In bars, as in snack-bars, people usually stand at the counter. The only surviving cafés in the centre are the **Roney,** viale della Libertà, II, B3, with a popular terrace where it's considered good to be seen, and the **Nobel,** on the same street.

Right in the centre, the via Principe Belmonte, II, C4, has been partly transformed into a lively street where traffic is forbidden. Numerous small cafés with terraces and gardens.

Café, via Enrico Parisi 7, II, B3. This has a tearoom, restaurant and bar.

Ciro's Bar, via Notarbartolo 25, II, A2. Very pleasant with tables outside.

Ri Bar, piazzale Ungheria 40, II, C3, has a wide variety of beers. Snacks are also served.

Treffpunkt, viale Lazio 49. *Closed Mon.* A place to go for a beer.

Sicilian wines

Al Drink, via Torrearsa 3, II, B3. A small tavern where good snacks accompany local wines.

Di Martino, via Mazzini 54, II, B3. Very popular; frequented mainly by young people.

Genova, via Patania 54, in a courtyard. Very near the Archaeological Museum. *Closed Sat.*

Politeama Vini, via Isidoro La Lumia 3. A big wine shop where you can taste as well as buy.

Saverino, via Dante 76, II, C3. A lively, popular tavern.

Pastry

Alba, piazza Don Bosco 7. *Closed Mon.* A bar that serves good pastries and ice creams. Almond paste is also a speciality.

Amato, vicolo Paterna 9. A classic establishment.

La Martorana, corso Vittoria Emanuele 196, II, E4. Best known for their 'hearts of Jesus', 'Turkish heads', *cannoli* and *cassatine*.

Magri, via Isidoro Carini, II, B3. A small pastry shop with delicious specialities.

Mazzara, via Generale Magliocco 15. *Closed Mon.* A veritable institution, considered by many to be Palermo's best pastry shop.

Monastero delle Vergini, piazzetta delle Vergine 2. Their excellent pastries, such as 'virgin's breasts' and 'glutton's triumph' (this only on request) are made according to traditional recipes.

Pasticceria Svizzera e Siciliana, via Stabile 155, II, C4. A bar that has been making pastries for generations.

Samuele, via Toselli 129. Another classic; highly recommended.

Valenti, piazzetta delle Virgine 10. A good traditional establishment with excellent chocolates.

Ice cream

Al Gelato, viale Strasburgo 348. They have tables outside.

Cofea, viale della Libertà 36.

Cremeria, via La Farina 14.

Gelato, piazza Europa 2.

Ilardo, foro Umberto 12. A well-known classic.

La Ferla, piazza Generale Cascino, where you will find good ice cream served from a large stall.

Stancampiano, on the corner of via Notarbartolo and via Boito, another stall with amazing specialities.

Getting around Palermo

By bus

There are about 50 different bus routes. Tickets are sold in *tabacchi,* but you can also pay on the bus; have some change ready. Stops *(fermata)* are well marked.

By car

If you attempt to drive in Palermo you'll be letting yourself in for a frustrating experience; the town was designed by viceroys for horses and carriages, not cars. Parking lots are nonexistent and the main streets are one-way. Visit the town on foot; that way you'll be sure of seeing something! If you decide to hire a car to explore farther afield, the major car-rental companies are:

Avis, via Principe di Scordia 12, II, C4, ☎ 586 940; airport: ☎ 591 684.

Budget, via Francesco Crispi 120, II, C5, ☎ 585 322; airport: ☎ 591 680.

Conca d'Oro, via Francesco Crispi 86, II, C5, ☎ 329 035.

Europcar, via Guardione 70/c, II, C4, ☎ 321 949; airport: ☎ 591 688.

Hertz, via Messina 7/e, II, B3, ☎ 331 686; airport: ☎ 591 682.

Holiday Car Rental, via Amari 85/a, II, C4, ☎ 325 155; airport: ☎ 591 687.

Inter Rent, via Cavour 61, II, C4, ☎ 328 631; airport: ☎ 591 683.

Maggiore, via Agrigento 27, II, B3, ☎ 297 128; airport : ☎ 591 681.

By carriage (carrozza)

You'll find barouches waiting beside monuments and the larger hotels. This is an original mode of transport for visiting Palermo, but modern pollution and traffic jams spoil the fun somewhat. If you would like a ride in one, the best time to go is in the evening or on a Sunday. Always negotiate the price and the length of the ride beforehand.

By taxi

Taxis are very expensive. Their meters serve only to give you a basic idea of the sum you will negotiate at the end of the ride. Drivers always add extras, which leads to endless arguments. Official rates are listed with the tourist office but they are totally unheeded. You'll find a taxi almost anywhere in the city, especially near hotels and monuments. For a radio-taxi: ☎ 513 311, 513 198, 513 374 or 625 5911.

Markets

The oldest and largest is the **Vucciria*** market, II, D5. Don't miss it. It's described in the third itinerary on p. 70.

Ballaro, II, F4, stretches between the piazzo Ballaro and the piazza del Carmine in the heart of the old Albergheria quarter, one of Palermo's most colourful. The market is set up around the 17th-century Chiesa del Carmine in a lively atmosphere of shouts and smells.

Capo, II, D3, around Sant'Agostino on vie Cappuccinelle, Beati Paoli and Porta Carini. Specializes in fruits and vegetables.

Nightlife

In Palermo the streets are deserted after dark and cafés generally close around 10pm. On the other hand, the monuments are lit up at night, and we recommend a walk around the historic centre (taking all the usual safety precautions). Nightlife is centered mainly in restaurants where the Palermitans dine late. There is also a fair amount of activity along via Principe di Belmonte, II, C4 (pedestrian street).

Eating late

Al Piu, via Campolo 94, ☎ 560 823. *Closes around 1am.*

Bodadilla, via Restivo 94. *Closes around 1am.*

Peppino, via Castelnuovo 49, ☎ 324 195. *Closes around 3am.*

Pizzeria Bellini, piazza Bellini 16, II, E4, ☎ 283 337. *Closes at 2am.*

Pizzeria Madison, piazza Don Bosco 10, ☎ 362 341. *Closes at 2am.*

For nightclubs, piano-bars, and discos you should ask at your hotel reception as there are new ones opening all the time.

Organizing your time

Starting on p. 59 we have listed four historical itineraries, and a fifth on modern Palermo, that take in all the main monuments and the different quarters of town. The maps (pp. 49, 50-51) and index (p. 251) will help you find your way around.

If your stay is short you should at least see the piazza Pretoria**, Quattro Canti**, the Cathedral**, La Martorana**, Cappella Palatina***, San Giovanni degli Eremiti**, Vucciria market*, Oratorio del Rosario*, Oratorio di San Lorenzo*, the Catacombs*, the Museo Archeologico Regionale** and the Galleria Regionale di Sicilia***, plus take a trip out to Monreale***.

Post office and telecommunications

The Central Post Office, via Roma 319, II, D4, is open *Mon-Fri 8:30am-7:30pm, Sat 8:30am-noon.* There are other, smaller post offices in different quarters.

Press

English newspapers can be bought at Stazione Centrale, II, F5, and at the news-stands on the piazza Ruggero Settimo, II, C3, where the street of the same name joins the square.

Shopping

After staying for a while in the capital you'll come to appreciate the variety of shops. Luxury shops are all on viale della Libertà and via Ruggero Settimo, between piazza Politeama and piazza Verdi, II, C3. Clothes are relatively expensive, but the designs are gorgeous. They are, after all, Italian.

Arts and crafts

You will find an interesting assortment of reasonably priced local products at **Artigianato Siciliano,** via Emerico Amari 13, II, C4. **De Simone,** via Stabile 133, II, C3, is one of Sicily's best ceramists. Near the Norman palace, at via del Bastone 44, **Arte e Mestieri** II, F3, specializes in craftsmanship on a small scale, selling ceramics, pottery and souvenirs.

Tourist information

APT (Aziende Provinciali del Turismo) offices:

Piazza Castelnuova 35, II, C3, ☎ 583 847. *Open daily 8am-8pm, Sun and holidays 8am-2pm.*

Punta Raisi Airport, ☎ 591 698. *Open 6am-11pm.*

Stazione Centrale, II, F5, ☎ 230 806. *Open 8am-10pm.*

CIT, viale della Libertà 22, II, C3. ☎ 582 294. *Open Mon-Fri 8:45am-1pm, 3:30-6:30pm; Sat 9am-12:30pm.*

Useful addresses

American Express, Ruggieri agency, via Emerico Amari 40, II, C4. *Open Mon-Fri 9am-1pm, 4-7pm; Sat 9am-1pm.*

Bookshops: Feltrinelli, piazza Verdi, II, D4. Good choice of Italian and English books. Welcoming, helpful staff. **Flaccovio,** via Ruggero Settimo, II, C3.

Left luggage, Stazione Centrale II, F5. *Open 24 hours.*

THE HEART OF THE TOWN

Map coordinates refer to the maps pp. 49, 50-51.

You need a day to see everything in detail. Half a day is enough for a quick look at the main sights. Because of museum opening hours and especially if you are short of time, you may need to follow this itinerary in a different order, beginning, for example, with San Cataldo.

Via Maqueda* II, E4

Start out from Stazione Centrale on piazza Giulio Cesare, II, F5. Via Roma, one of the town's main shopping streets, will be in front of you. Head left, skirting the piazza Giulio Cesare, which extends into piazza Sant'Antonio, and from here enter the via Maqueda.

This street had its beginnings in the 16th century and now crosses a picturesque part of town with busy streets leading off it. On the right at n° 55 is the Assunta Church with a decorated stucco interior.

At n° 85 you will see the magnificent façade of the Palazzo Santa Croce, now abandoned. A little farther to the left another 18th-century building has been restored and houses the Palazzo della Provincia.

The Gesù Church* *(Casa Professa)* II, E4

Open Mon-Sat 9-11am, 5-6:30pm; Sun 7am-12:30pm, 5-6:30pm.

Continuing along the left-hand side of the road you come to via Ponticello, which leads to the Gesù Church, or Casa Professa, built by Jesuits between 1564 and 1636. The front may strike you as ordinary, but the splendid decoration of the interior will amaze you with its rich stucco-work and marble inlays. The church is one of the best examples of Sicilian Baroque. Look closely at the incredible inlays that cover the walls and to the right of the choir at the altar panel with its trompe l'œil decoration, which will give you an idea of the skill of marble masons at that time. Behind the main altar are a number of works; two, set in niches, are Old Testament scenes by the sculptor Gioacchino Vitaliano (1669-1739). The fine funerary monument beside the last pilaster on the left was designed by Ignazio Marabitti in 1755.

Biblioteca Comunale

Open Mon-Fri 9am-3pm, Closed Sat, Sun and public holidays.

The library, to the right of the church, was founded in 1760 in the former Jesuit oratory. There are at least 1000 incunabula (early printed books), 300 16th-century works and 500 manuscripts. Among them is Bellini's original score for *I Puritani*. There is also a collection of Arab and Sikel coins and a portrait gallery.

San Cataldo* II, E4

Retrace your steps and continue along via Maqueda. After a short distance on your right you'll come to a raised bank on which stands the Norman Church of San Cataldo, built in the Arab style in 1160. It is a distinctive building, a rectangle crowned by three small red cupolas. Today it belongs to the Order of the Knights of the Holy Sepulchre. The church has kept its simple shape with pointed arched windows, stone lattice-work crenelations, an external apse and three raised domes. There is a strip of inscriptions around the building where in places you can still see quotations from the Koran. The interior is not open to the public.

La Martorana** II, E4

Open daily 8:30-7:30pm in summer, 5pm in winter; closed Sun afternoon.

Santa Maria dell'Ammiraglio, a contemporary of San Cataldo, is more often referred to as La Martorana in memory of Eloise Martorana, who founded the adjoining Benedictine convent. The church was presented to the convent in 1433.

The church was founded in 1143 by one of King Roger II's admirals, George of Antioch, who, though probably of Syrian origin, was brought up in the Greek religious tradition. This is an important point because this amazing man (who is also credited with bringing the silk industry to Palermo) called upon Greek craftsmen to build the church according to the design of an Arab mosque. Unfortunately, the building was disfigured in the 15th and 16th centuries. You enter it beneath an elegant 12th-century **campanile**, a gem of Norman architecture. It is an unusual design on four different levels with corner columns and twin windows. Unfortunately, the dome was destroyed by an earthquake in 1726.

Once inside you will see the extent to which the original plan has been modified over the centuries. The first part you enter was added in the 17th century and has frescoes by Guglielmo Borremans, Grano and Olivio Sozzi. Two very beautiful **mosaics*** in the aisles at the west end (restored panels in Baroque frames) mark the position of the former façade. The one on the right represents King Roger II in his splendid *basileus* costume being crowned by Christ; the one on the left shows George of Antioch at the feet of the Virgin. As you walk toward the choir, you enter the original church, which is decorated with 12th-century **mosaics****. In the dome is Christ Pantocrator with four archangels; around the drum are eight Prophets; in the corner vaults are the four Evangelists. There are figures of saints on the arches and, on the walls, scenes of the Nativity, the Dormition of the Virgin, the Annunciation and the Presentation at the Temple. Notice also the impressive paving and the lovely marble and mosaics around the choir. The apse was destroyed in 1693 and replaced by a Baroque chapel decorated with frescoes and multi-coloured marble.

Santa Caterina*** II, E4

Closed for restoration.

Facing La Martorana across piazza Bellini, where the former town theatre has been converted into a restaurant, is the Church of Santa Caterina. The church dates from the 16th century but the façade was added in the 17th. The interior, one of the finest examples of Baroque art from that period, is adorned with a profusion of marble, stuccoes and frescoes. In the transept chapel on the right is a statue of St Catherine by Antonello Gagini (1534).

Piazza Pretoria** II, E4

The left side of the church faces the piazza Pretoria, which is largely taken up by a monumental **fountain****. The fountain was begun in 1552, commissioned by a Florentine noble for his villa. It was later acquired by the Senate of Palermo for 30,000 écus, then transported and reassembled on the piazza in 1575.

Surrounded by a protective balustrade, the fountain is composed of a series of circular terraces connected by flights of steps. It is richly decorated with allegorical statues of sea divinities and animals in a style imitative of Michelangelo. These sculptures offended certain citizens, who christened the monument the 'Fountain of Shame' because of the realistic nakedness of the figures. It is said that nuns from a neighbouring convent were so shocked that they hammered off the noses of all the immodest male figures, while not actually daring to emasculate them. To the left of the square is the Palazzo del Municipio, the former

The fountain in Palermo's piazza Pretoria formerly adorned the gardens of a Florentine villa.

Santa Caterina

As soon as one enters, one experiences that absolute satisfaction together with a penumbra of bewilderment which only a perfect work of art can give. Every visible square inch of this vast building (it is almost two hundred feet in length) has been cultivated to add its yield to the total harvest of beauty. A garden in full bloom, a granary heaped to the rafters with corn, an orchard teeming with fruit — none of these gives quite the same effect of abundance, for none has been harmonised and concentrated with deliberate and inspired art. The combination of colours — rose-brown, white and black — and the added dimension given by the relief work are the immediately striking features, conveying a sense of chiaroscuro and pale light which draws one into the nave.

The richness of the meanest chapel here would dignify the high altar of many another church. That of Santa Caterina in the south transept shows the *tour de force* at its highest pitch. Here the detail of decoration is carried to a point beyond which all form would disappear under the weight of ornament and the whole would be lost in the profusion of the parts. It is as though the flowers in a large garden had attained such luxuriance that it is uncertain whether the garden has not reverted to its primeval state; as though a snowstorm had been depicted in the medium of marble; as though a frenzied mind, the mind of a Rimbaud, were throwing out powerful and extravagant images before tumbling over the verge of madness. The first principle is that nothing shall remain simple: the straight line of a column must be twisted, or the flutings painted: the bases must be inlaid with bulging pieces of marble: the recesses must be filled with flowers: at all costs nothing must remain bare, lest it prove that other worlds exist, simpler and quieter than this extravangance of flowers and frozen fountains, abandoned to a perpetual state of tension.

Vincent Cronin
The Golden Honeycomb
Rupert Hart-Davis, 1954

Pretorio. It was built in 1464 but lost its original character when restored in 1875.

Facing the piazza Pretoria across the via Maqueda is the Church of **San Giuseppe dei Teatini***, built in 1612 by Giacomo Besio for the neighbouring Teatini convent. Today the university is housed in the part of the convent to the left of the church. The lovely church dome added in 1725 is covered in glazed tiles that can also be seen in the side-chapels. The interior is highly decorated with pink marble, rich stuccoes and frescoes. St Cajetan, the founder of the Theatine order, is commemorated by a statue. the central dome rests on eight columns and each of the side aisles is surmounted by five small cupolas adorned with cherubs. The church was damaged during the last war and has been remarkably restored.

Quattro Canti** II, E4

Via Maqueda crosses via Vittorio Emanuele at the Quattro Canti intersection, also known as the piazza Vigliena. This is the real centre of the old town, where the four quarters of Baroque Palermo meet. Corso Vittorio Emanuele, then known as Cassaro, was the main street stretching from Porta Nuova down to Porta Felice by the sea. It was intersected by Strada Nuova, which took the name via Maqueda after a Spanish viceroy.

The **four fountains** on the corners of the square represent the Seasons and were built in 1611 by Viceroy Vigliena. They are set against beautiful concave buildings with upper levels that carry statues of the four kings of Italy and the patron saints of the four quarters: the Kalsa, the Amalfitani, the Sincaldi and the Albergheria.

Duomo (Cathedral)** II, E3
Open daily 7am-noon, 4-7pm.

From the Quattro Canti take via Emanuele left, past the sober church front of San Giuseppe dei Teatini. You come to the piazza Bologni, II, E4,

which has an unusual bronze statue of Charles V of Spain (1630). Opposite are the remains of the Belmonte Palace (under restoration). The piazza is surrounded by Baroque palaces, mostly abandoned. After passing the severe façade of the Biblioteca Centrale (n° 431), you reach a garden, out of which rises the grandiose amber cathedral.

In 1185 the English archbishop Gualtiero Offamiglio (Walter of the Mill), chancellor to King William II of Sicily (known as the Good), built the cathedral — considered a masterpiece of Sicilian-Norman architecture. Unfortunately, the harmony of the building has been broken by various alterations — especially the dome that was added in 1801.

The eastern end remains intact, however, with all its 12th-century finesse. The exterior is well worth looking at; you should walk all around before venturing inside. The main façade on the via Bonello has a Gothic portal dating from the 14th and 15th centuries. Spanning the road, two pointed arches link to join a strangely shaped belfry (altered in the 19th century). Continue around the cathedral, passing the remains of the Loggia dell'Incoronata (a 12th-century structure, altered in the 16th century, where the kings of Sicily appeared after their coronations) until you reach the three **apses****, which have retained their 12th-century character.

Having walked the whole way around, come back to the garden and enter the cathedral through the monumental Gothic porch dating from 1465. Beneath the three pointed arches are magnificent carved wooden **doors****, the work of Francesco Miranda (1432). Above is a mosaic of the Virgin, a masterpiece of Catalan-Gothic art (1426). In contrast, the cold and empty interior of the cathedral, altered in the 18th century by the Florentine architect Ferdinando Fuga, will probably disappoint you.

Nevertheless you should see the Roman-Byzantine royal tombs in the chapels at the end of the right-hand aisle. These include the tombs of: Frederick II (died 1250), Henry VI (died 1197), Roger II (died 1154) and his daughter, Constance (died 1198). The two sarcophagi embedded in the wall contain the remains of Duke William, son of Frederick II of Aragon, and the remains of Constance of Aragon, the first wife of Frederick II of Swabia. In the transept to the right of the choir is a chapel with a silver reliquary urn (882 lb/400 kg) containing the remains of Santa Rosalia, patron saint of the town.

The main exhibit of the Treasury to the right of the chapel is the golden crown of Constance of Aragon (died 1222). It was found in her tomb and is a sort of velvet cap adorned with precious stones, enamel and pearls. Opposite is the Sacristy, with a fine 16th-century porch through which you enter a chapel where there is a Madonna by Antonello Gagini (1503). The Sacristan will also show you around the crypt, which has two columned aisles dating from the 12th century and seven small apses containing sarcophagi from the Middle Ages and the Renaissance. Above, in the choir, you can see lovely 15th-century statues. In the left-hand transept are bas-reliefs by the Gagini brothers and a wooden crucifix dating from the 15th century. On the fourth pillar in the nave, facing the side entrance, is a font with a canopy attributed to Domenico Gagini, and, in the last chapel, a beautiful marble baptistry.

The Museo Diocesano in the Palazzo Arcivescovile across the via Bonello, I, E3, is being refurbished and is currently closed (1990).

Palazzo Dei Normanni* II, F3

Continue along via Emanuele, which passes the Bonanno Gardens and ends at Porta Nuova. This triumphal arch was built in 1553 in memory of Charles V, who had visited Palermo 20 years earlier after freeing Tunis from the hands of a pirate. The lower part of the arch, restored in 1668, is curiously topped by a loggia and a handsome pyramidal roof of coloured tiles. You have to go through the arch to see four statues of infidels on the other side. Retrace your steps and take the little stairway, which leads to the vast esplanade of the Norman palace.

Of this immense edifice, built by the Arabs in the 9th century over the ruins of a Roman fort and converted into a palace by Roger II in the 12th century, only the Torre Pisana (or Torre di Santa Ninfa) remains in its original state. Above it is the observatory. The second part of the palace, to the left, was entirely restored in the 17th and 18th centuries and is now the seat of the Sicilian Parliament. The Palatine chapel and royal apartments are hidden behind.

Cappella Palatina*** II, F3

Open Mon-Fri 9am-noon, 3-5pm; Sat 9am-noon; Sun and holidays 9-10am, noon-1pm. Closed Easter Mon, Apr 25, May 1 and Dec 26. When Parliament is in session, use the entrance behind the palace through the garden adjoining the piazza Independenza, II, F2.

You enter the palace through a door on the far left in front of the monument to the first viceroy of Sicily, Philip V of Bourbon. The courtyard, with its three-tiered porticoes, was built at the beginning of the 17th century by Viceroy Maqueda. From here take the staircase to the left, which leads to the entrance of the Cappella Palatina. This is one of the oldest Palermitan churches and a brilliant example of Norman-Saracenic art. The chapel portico's seven columns are decorated with mosaics restored in 1800.

It is impossible to enter the chapel without a sense of awe. Construction was begun in 1132 by Roger II, and in 1140 the chapel was dedicated to St Peter. Although not large (105 ft/32 m long), the interior is lavishly decorated with Byzantine **mosaics***. Its three aisles are supported by antique columns with Corinthian capitals. The nave has a remarkable wooden **coffered ceiling**** in the Arab style, with rose interlacing set in octagonal stars painted in the Persian manner. The paving is porphyry and marble, and the walls are covered with marble facing, studded with multicoloured enamel and mosaics, as is the royal throne between the two doors at the entrance. It takes a moment to adjust to the half-light, but little by little the patterns on the mosaics emerge in an exquisite glistening of precious stones against a golden background.

In the cupola, Christ Pantocrator is surrounded by eight archangels and the figures of eight saints: David in the centre and, from left to right, Luke, Zachariah, Matthew, Solomon, Mark, John the Baptist and St John. On the arches are scenes of the Annunciation and the Presentation in the Temple. In the central apse, Christ and the Virgin Mary are shown surrounded by Mary Magdalene, John the Baptist, Gabriel, Michael, James and Peter. St Paul is represented in the right-hand apse and St Peter in the left. The wall on the right-hand side is covered with scenes from the life of Christ; on the left wall are scenes of Mary and various saints.

The artwork throughout the chapel was created according to pure Byzantine tradition. The scenes in the nave are from the Old Testament; from Genesis to the Flood on the upper part and from the Flood to Jacob on the lower. Medallions of saints can be seen on the arches. The more recent decoration in the aisles illustrates scenes from the lives of St Paul and St Peter, to whom the church is dedicated. These two saints are shown with Christ above the royal throne.

To the right of the choir is a marble **pulpit*** embellished with mosaics. Beside it is the paschal **candlestick***, a beautiful example of 12th-century sculpture.

The chapel's fortunate location in the middle of the former royal palace, where it served only members of the court, explains why it has been so well preserved. What we see today has changed little from the chapel planned by anonymous artists eight centuries ago. Most of the mosaics were made by local Sicilian craftsmen under the tutelage of Byzantine artists.

Royal Apartments*

Open Mon, Fri and Sat 9am-12:30pm.

An impressive staircase leads to the second floor to the former royal apartments and the seat of the Sicilian Parliament. The most interesting room is the **Sala di Re Ruggero***. The vault and the upper part of the walls are covered with splendid mosaics (1170) that illustrate hunting scenes with stylized animals and trees. Stone inlays are set in the foliage to represent fruit.

San Giovanni degli Eremiti*** II, F3

Open daily 9am-7pm; holidays 8:30am-2pm.

After leaving the Norman palace, head toward the monument of Philip V of Bourbon and go down the steps leading to the piazza di Pinta, II, F3, where you turn left onto the via dei Benefettini. N° 18 is the entrance to San Giovanni degli Eremiti (St John of the Hermits), set in a peaceful garden. Constructed by Roger II in 1132 over the foundations of a former church built in 581, it is one of the best examples of Norman churches in Sicily, with a simple campanile and five small red domes that add an Eastern flavour. The interior consists of a single nave, three apses and a small adjoining room, which was part of a former mosque.

Beside the church are the remains of a delightful 13th-century **cloister*** with twin columns and Gothic capitals adorned with figures. A lush garden lends charm to the site.

Retrace your steps to the Norman palace and cross the Bonanno Gardens, where the remains of a Roman house have been discovered. On the corner of the piazza della Vittoria and piazza San Giovanni you will see the **Palazzo Sclafani***, II, E3, which dates from 1330. Legend has it that it took only a single year to build. The main façade, on the piazza San Giovanni, has an interesting portal and Gothic windows. One of the major works displayed in the Galleria Regionale di Sicilia (see p. 67), the *Triumph of Death*, was taken from here. The palace has since been converted for military use. Via Vittorio Emanuele takes you back to the Quattro Canti crossroads.

As an alternative to the above itinerary, after leaving San Giovanni degli Eremiti you could take **via Porta di Castro***, II, F3, a lively, colourful old street that leads to the Casa Professa, II, E4, described at the beginning of the itinerary on p. 59.

FROM QUATTRO CANTI TO THE SEA

You need half a day for this itinerary, not counting the Galleria Regionale di Sicilia which alone takes several hours.

With the Quattro Canti, II, E4, as your departure point, turn right onto the via Vittorio Emanuele, which stretches down to the sea. You pass the Baroque 16th-century church of San Matteo *(open daily 8am-noon, 4-7pm)*. The interior is decorated with marble and there are four statues by Giacomo Serpotta beneath the dome.

San Francesco d'Assisi* II, E5

Open daily 7-10:30am, 4-6pm.

Not far beyond the intersection with via Roma, turn right on via Paternostro to the Church of San Francesco d'Assisi. It has been altered many times over the centuries but the interior was recently restored to its original shape. The façade has a fine 14th-century Gothic portal with zigzag ornamentation, above which are three frescoes and a **rose window****. Inside are three aisles separated by Gothic arches. The ceiling has triangular vaults of painted wood. There is a statue by Giacomo Serpotta in the nave. Gothic and Renaissance chapels in the aisles nearly all contain statues and relief work from the Gagini school. The most beautiful chapel is the fourth in the left-hand aisle, decorated by Francesco Laurana and Pietro de Bonitate in 1468. Also of note are the 16th-century choir stalls and the Immacolata chapel in the right-hand apse, decorated with polychrome marble.

Oratorio di San Lorenzo* II, E5

Usually open Sun morning. Telephone beforehand: 337 719 or 581 698.

To the left of the church at nº 5 via Immacolatella is the oratory of the San Lorenzo brotherhood. This is no bigger than a country house dining room but is adorned with a high ceiling and walls decorated with stucco panels illustrating scenes from the lives of St Lawrence and St Francis. Between 1699 and 1707, Giacomo Serpotta worked on these three-dimensional scenes, alternating them with allegorical statues of the Virtues. The overall effect is a 'cave of white coral' decorated with joyful tumbling cherubs. The carved benches on either side of the nave are inlaid with mother-of-pearl and ivory. The pink-and-green marble altar, topped by a blue tabernacle, once set off a painting of the Nativity, the last work of Caravaggio, completed in 1609 but stolen in 1969.

Around Giardino Garibaldi II, D5

Return to via Vittorio Emanuele and turn right along it until you reach piazza Marina, where there is a beautiful fountain known as the Garraffo (1698) with a statue on top called *Abundance*. The centre of the square is taken up by the Giardino Garibaldi, planted with magnificent banyan trees. Several interesting, though dilapidated, monuments surround the garden, which is worth a detour beginning on the right. On the first corner is the Church of Santa Maria dei Miracoli dating from 1547. It was decorated by Fazio Gagini. At nº 46 the Palazzo San Cataldo has fine Gothic windows; nº 51 is Palazzo Notarbartolo di Villarossa, where on the façade two telamons (male figures used as supporting columns) are holding up portraits in medallions.

Farther along at nº 60 is the **Palazzo Chiaramonte*** dating from the beginning of the 14th century — a rather austere building but a good example of medieval Sicilian architecture. It is now used by the university and cannot be visited. Its walls harbour particularly painful historical memories as it was here that, for two centuries, the Inquisition had its seat under Spanish rule. Executions were carried out in front of the façade, including that of Andrea Chiaramonte, decapitated in 1392 for rebelling against the king of Aragon.

Santa Maria della Catena* II, D5-6

Open only for service, at 8am during the week and noon on Sun.

Continue full circle back to via Vittorio Emanuele where you will see the Church of Santa Maria della Catena on the corner. The name derives from the chain that used to close off the harbour at night. This 15th-century building is a skillful combination of Catalan-Gothic and Renaissance styles. Leading up to it is a staircase and a porch with a bas relief by Vincenzo Gagini.

The interior has lovely Gothic vaults. Columns separate the three aisles. In the second chapel on the right, a little deeper than the others, is a canopied altar of the Gagini school. In the third chapel you can see a relief, dating from 1400, of the Madonna and angels. The choir contains 15th-century sarcophagi.

Santa Maria di Porto Salvo II, D5

Open only on Sun.

This is not far from Santa Maria della Catena on the corner of via Vittorio Emanuele and via Porto Salvo. It retains two portals by Antonello Gagini and an interesting interior.

Museo Internazionale delle Marionette II, D6

Open Mon-Sat 10am-1pm, 5-7pm, Sun 10am-1pm; puppet shows (in summer) on Sat 5:30pm, ☎ 328 060.

The museum is right behind Santa Maria della Catena, on the piazza Santa Spirito at via Butera 1. Its fine collection of puppets from all over the world is growing continually. Much of the museum is devoted to Sicilian *pupi* (dolls or puppets).

Kalsa, Grandeur and Decline II, DE6

Beyond Santa Maria della Catena, continue right along via Vittorio Emanuele to the Porta Felice, II, D6, an important survivor of the historic quarter that was so badly damaged during the war. Turn right onto Foro Italico, a wide avenue along the seafront. After about 437 yds/400 m cross onto the piazza della Kalsa, II, E6. Kalsa is a corruption of the Arabic word *khalisa* meaning 'pure'. This whole area near the sea, once the domain of the sultan and his court, is now one of the poorer parts of Palermo; it consists of a series of insalubrious blocks bounded by narrow alleys. Nevertheless it still harbours monuments that bear witness to its former splendour.

On the other side of the piazza, notice the striking Baroque façade of Santa Teresa, designed by Giacomo Amato (1643-1732), who was also responsible for the Church of La Pietà, among other churches.

Church of La Pietà** II, E6

Via Torremuzza leads to the recently restored La Pietà with its sumptuous façade. It was inspired by the Baroque school in Rome, where Giacomo Amato studied.

Inside there are frescoes by Guglielmo Borremans in the choir and beautiful galleries of gilded wood. Notice also the quality of the finely worked balustrade. In the third chapel on the left is a 16th-century *Pietà* by Vincenzo da Pavia.

Galleria Regionale di Sicilia*** II, E6

Open Mon-Sat 9am-1:30pm; Sun and holidays 9am-12:30pm; Tues and Thurs also open 3-5:30pm.

Via Alloro, II, E6, brings you to the Galleria Regionale housed inside the Palazzo Abbatellis, which was built between 1490 and 1495 by Matteo Carnelivari. The palace façade, an elegant combination of Catalan-Gothic-Renaissance styles, is pierced with fine windows. Two crenelated towers, embellished with gargoyles, rise above the building. An exceptional collection of works, beautifully displayed by the museum, is naturally enhanced by the surroundings of this Sicilian palace.

The ground floor is taken up mainly by the sculptures of Francesco Laurana and the Gagini family, artists whose work was so prolific it can be seen in churches all over Sicily. Among the most remarkable works are the *Bust of Eleonora of Aragon*** by Laurana and the marble *Head of a Young Boy*** by Antonello Gagini, from the church of San Vito. The *Triumph of Death*** is also exhibited on the ground floor in its own room. This magnificent 15th-century fresco by an unknown artist comes from the Palazzo Sclafani.

The first floor is devoted entirely to Italian and Flemish painting from the 12th to the 18th centuries. The collection includes fine examples of triptychs, frescoes and crosses painted on both sides. Among the works are a *Pietà* by the Master of the Pentecost (16th century), the Malvagna triptych of the *Virgin and Child in a Choir of Angels*** painted in 1510 by Jan Gossaert, known as Mabuse (1472-1536). There also are two works by Antonello da Messina (1430-79): the *Annunciation*** , his most famous painting, dating from around 1473 (see box), and his *Three Saints*.

La Gancia, La Magione and Palazzo Gangi

Church of La Gancia** II, E5-6

Open 8-9:30am, holidays 8am-1pm.

Beyond the museum the Church of La Gancia was built on the site of a former hospice and dedicated to Santa Maria degli Angeli. Its sober 15th-century façade with two Gothic portals was designed in the bare style favoured by convent churches.

The recent restoration of the **interior**** enhances the wooden ceiling, the organ case and the rich marble altars. Among other works of note are a Nativity by Vincenzo da Pavia and two reliefs by Antonello Gagini, *Descent into Limbo* and *St Michael*.

The *Annunciation* by Antonello da Messina

The work is a small wooden panel depicting with the utmost simplicity a single figure: indeed this perhaps is the secret of its greatness, for nothing, neither subsidiary figures, nor furnishings nor fine clothes nor background, stands between us and the Mother of God. To see the picture is immediately to be with her, in the same room, at the same intersection of time and eternity: she is there — we are as close to her as the angel Gabriel — looking up from her prayer-book, her dark, oval face at once strong and submissive, her eyes unsurprised and quite passive, her lips firm and untroubled. With her left hand she draws together across her breast the folds of her single blue garment, covering head and shoulders, for even an angel is an intruder. The gesture is simple and without urgency yet it reveals virtues which a whole litany could not list. Her right hand is lifted forwards and raised at a slight angle, fingers spread out towards the invisible angel, a gesture so mysterious that, while we seem to understand its purpose, in fact we know far less than its whole meaning. She is, before all else, simultaneously accepting and — without declining — hesitating· submitting at the spiritual level, hesitating at the human, but such are the gentleness and delicacy of the movement, it is certain beyond doubt that when the will of God has been made clear to her, she will already have accepted.

Vincent Cronin
The Golden Honeycomb
Rupert Hart-Davis, 1954

It was from La Gancia that Francesco Riso organized an unsuccessful rebellion against the Bourbons in 1860. He was executed along with 13 companions.

Church of La Magione II, E5
Open daily 7-11am, 4-6pm; holidays 7:30am-noon. Closed to visitors during services.

After visiting La Gancia, walk left onto via della Vetriera until you reach a garden and the fine Norman apse of La Magione, II, E5. Just before the entrance on via Magione is a Baroque portal and then a drive lined with laurel trees. At the end of it rises the sober façade of the church with its three porches. It was built by Chancellor Matteo d'Ajello for a Cistercian convent and dedicated to the Trinity in 1150 in the middle of the Norman period. During World War II it was badly bombed but has since been admirably restored. Inside are three aisles with raised columns and crown arches. The left-hand apse has a beautiful Renaissance portal. If you would like to see the 12th-century cloister ask the sacristan to show you round.

In front of the church, via Magione leads to via Garibaldi, where at n° 41 the long façade of Palazzo Aiutamicristo begins. It was built by Matteo Carnelivari between 1490 and 1495. Only the portal and several windows of the original building remain, but at n° 23 you should make your way into the second courtyard to see the very fine portico with its loggia and columns. Via Garibaldi continues to the piazza della Rivoluzione, named in memory of the first revolutionary stirrings against the Bourbon regime in 1848. The fountain in the middle is known as 'il genio di Palermo'.

From the piazza take via Aragona, passing in front of the classical Santo Carlo church, and when you reach the intersection turn left onto via Alloro, which leads to the piazza della Croce dei Vespri, II, E5. A commemorative plaque on the right indicates the location of the palace where Jean de Saint-Rémy (the Angevin governor of Palermo) and his garrison were besieged on Easter Monday, March 31, 1282 — the beginning of the Sicilian Vespers rebellion (see p. 74). The French who were massacred

The Triumphal Arch in Palermo, built by Charles V to commemorate his victory over the Infidels in 1533.

during the uprising were buried in the palace grounds. The column in the middle of the square was erected in 1737 to commemorate the 2000 victims.

Palazzo Gangi

The modest appearance of the Palazzo Gangi (overlooking the square) belies the fact that it possesses a magnificent staircase and sumptuous rooms where Visconti filmed the famous ballroom scene in *The Leopard* in 1963. Unfortunately, these cannot be visited.

When you head back toward the Quattro Canti along via Roma you will pass a striking church built in 1736 by Giovanni Amico (1684-1754), the architect from Trápani responsible for many of Sicily's churches. This particular one, Sant'Anna, built in three architectural styles, has a fine curved Baroque façade and is embellished with columns. The upper part of the church crumbled as a result of an earthquake.

▬▬ *PIAZZA SAN DOMENICO AND ORATORIES*

Count on half a day, bearing in mind that the Archaeological Museum requires several hours. A stroll around the market is highly recommended. You should follow this itinerary in the morning because some of the buildings are closed in the afternoon.

Vucciria* II, D5

Start out from the intersection of via Roma and via Vittorio Emanuele, II, E5. The strange church on a platform is Sant'Antonio, which has retained its original square plan and interesting interior, despite numerous transformations. Walk along via Vittorio Emanuele in the direction of the sea until you come to via Pannieri, the first small street on your left. This picturesque, lively street crosses the piazza Caracciolo and ends up at the piazza San Domenico leading you through Vucciria, Palermo's oldest market. The name derives either from the French word *boucherie* (butcher) or from the Italian *vucci* (voices or shouts). The whole area is popular and busy — a chance to see an aspect of everyday Palermitan life. The market sprawls over three main streets, one leading toward the sea and the others converging on the piazza San Domenico.

Piazza San Domenico* II, D4

Rising above the square is the 18th-century Colonna dell'Immacolata crowned by a statue of the Virgin. Behind it is the Church of San Domenico *(open 8:30am-noon, 5-6:30pm)* where many famous Sicilians are buried. The façade, flanked by towers, is late Baroque (1726). At the entrance to the church there are two fonts dating from 1500. The fourth chapel on the right, San Giuseppe, has rich 17th-century marble decoration. Notice the two beautiful 1781 Rococo organ cases of gilded wood in the upper part of the nave.

Outside to the left of the church at via Gagini 1 is a former Dominican convent where you can see a three-sided cloister dating from the 14th century.

Oratorio del Rosario di San Domenico* II, D4-5

To visit, contact the custodian at via Bambinai 16.

You can easily reach the national Archaeological Museum from the piazza San Domenico but a detour to the oratory of the brotherhood of Rosario di San Domenico is worthwhile. Turn right at San Domenico Church and continue to the piazza Giovanni Meli where you turn left into via Bambinai.

In the vestibule you can see a wooden figure of Christ dating from the 16th century. This elegant oratory owes more of its charm to the **stuccoes**** of Giacomo Serpotta than to its conventional and somewhat murky religious wall paintings. The paintings were already there when Serpotta was asked to take on the decoration, so he had to make do with the remaining space. His lively figures look down from beneath the cupola as though they were in a theatre. Here, as in many Palermitan churches, ask for something always precede your request with a *'per favore'* ('please') and never forget to express your thanks with a *'gracie'*, to which the reply will be *'prego'* ('not at all'). When you are introduced, say *'piacere'* ('delighted') and avoid *'ciao'*, which is very familiar. In a restaurant, address the waiter with *'senta'*, which translates as a polite 'listen'.

CURRENCY EXCHANGE

You will get the best exchange rates at the major banks and exchange offices licensed by the Bank of Italy. The main banks in Sicily are the **Banco di Sicilia**, the **Banca Nazionale di Lavoro** and the **Cassa di Risparmio**. *They are open Monday to Friday, 8:30am-1pm. Some also have afternoon hours, 2:45-3:45pm.* Large hotels and some of the main railway stations also provide currency exchange services, but the rates will be lower than in the banks.

DRIVING

We cannot advise you strongly enough to take the greatest care when driving. Sicilians have their own idea of how this should be done, coupled with a total disregard for the highway code. Road signs, including traffic lights, are there just for show, or so it seems. It is against the law to use your horn, but that fact does not stop drivers in Sicily from honking away from the moment they get behind the wheel until they reach their destination.

It is often impossible to get out of cacophonous traffic jams in town, especially during rush hours, when total anarchy reigns. Sometimes hundreds of cars are temporarily immobilized by a single vehicle blocking the road simply because the driver has stopped to chat with a friend. Keep calm, count to ten, then try to wind your way out of the mess Sicilian-style, by disregarding the *semafori* (traffic lights). Always be ready to apply the brakes and keep your eye on cars in front, behind and beside you; the reactions of other drivers can be unpredictable.

Sicilian roads

The Sicilian road network is excellent, with the exception of a few secondary roads. Highways have been deliberately omitted from the itineraries because traveling on them is not compatible with peaceful tourism. If you are in a hurry, however, highways link the major towns in no time at all and pass through beautiful countryside. The following highways are currently open:

A18: Between Messina and Catania.

A19: Between Catania and Palermo via Enna, with a short leg to Caltanissetta.

A20: Between Messina and Palermo along the Tyrrhenian coast. It joins the A19 south of Cefalù. The stretch between Sant'Agata di Militello and Cefalù is not yet open.

A29: Between Palermo and Trapani, with a leg out to the Punta Raisi Airport and another one to the airport at Birgi. The A29 also branches down to Mazara del Vallo via Castelvetrano.

While 'SS' *(strade statali)* roads are always good, the 'SP' *(strade provinciali)* are sometimes narrow and winding.

Gas

Gas is expensive in Sicily but less so if you use gasoline coupons (see p. 12). There are lots of service stations available but they rarely accept credit cards.

Hitchhiking

Hitchhiking is widespread during the tourist season. It is forbidden on highways.

▬ *BUSINESS HOURS*

Chiuso, always posted on closed doors, is a word you'll get used to quickly. The reasons for its ubiquitous presence in churches, museums and national monuments are varied and seemingly unavoidable. In certain cases, however, a tip works wonders. Among the most common reasons are strikes (*scioperi*, widespread in Italy), a lack of personnel, the temporary indisposition of the guard, a celebration in the church attendant's family or simply the siesta of the key keeper. Nonetheless, here are the official opening times :

Banks

These are open Monday to Friday, 8:30am-1pm. There are also a few that open for an hour in the afternoon from 2:45-3:45pm.

Churches

Most open only for services, which generally take place in the morning or in the evening between 5 and 7pm. For 'church-museums' we give official opening times in the text. You are most likely to find churches open on Saturday mornings, a popular time for weddings.

Museums

These almost always close at 1 or 2pm. Some reopen in the afternoon on certain days of the week. As a general rule, the weekly closing day is Monday. Public buildings have variable opening hours according to the season. Museums close earlier in winter, on Sundays and on public holidays. Archaeological sites close according to when the sun goes down. The times given in the text are summer times, valid from April to October.

Post offices

Open Monday to Friday, 8:15am-1:40pm. On Saturdays and the last days of the month they are open 8:10-11:15am. They are always closed on Sundays.

Restaurants

Sicilians have their meals relatively late. Restaurants usually serve at 12:30-2:30pm and again at 7:30-10:30pm. A lot depends, of course, on the size of the town. In the Palermo section we have included restaurants that are open late at night. Don't forget that cafés close earlier than restaurants, almost at the same time as shops.

Shops

Most shops are open 9am-1pm and again in the late afternoon 5-7:30pm. They are closed on one weekday and on Sunday. Grocery stores are closed on Wednesday afternoons. Towns shut down entirely on Sundays, apart from the odd bar that opens only in the morning.

▬ *COFFEE (CAFFE)*

Some of the best coffee in the world is drunk in Italy, and the choice is marvelous: *espresso* (single), *doppio* (double), *americano* (a longer drink served in a large cup), *caffé freddo* (cold), *frappé* (espresso coffee mixed in a shaker with ice), *cappuccino* (with foamy milk, sprinkled with chocolate) and *macchiato* (with a little milk). If you don't like coffee try a *cioccolata*, a thick, creamy chocolate-and-milk drink.

▬ *COURTESY*

It is customary to address a person as *Dottore* or *Dottoressa* if you want to show more respect than with a simple *Signore* or *Signora*. You may also use *Professore* for a person with social position. Sicilians are always very polite, love using titles and are very particular about them. You should at least learn to say *'Buon giorno'* ('Good day' or 'Hello'), which becomes *'Buona sera'* ('Good evening') after siesta time. Whenever you we find his statues symbolizing the Virtues. The artist's hallmark, a lizard, can be seen climbing up the gilded column of the second statue on the right. The *Coronation of the Virgin* by Pietro Novelli, a Sicilian Renaissance painter and pupil of Van Dyck, adorns the ceiling. Van Dyck himself painted the famous altarpiece representing the Virgin of the Rosary surrounded by St Dominic and the patron saints of Palermo.

Oratorio del Rosario di Santa Zita* II, D4

Open daily 8am-noon, 4-6pm. Either ring for the sacristan or inquire at the Conservatory across the street.

Continue along via Bambinai, then via Squarcialupo, to the 1369 church of Santa Zita, II, D5. It was built in 1369 and restored after World War II. Inside, in the apse behind the altar, is a marble representation of the Nativity and scenes from the life of Santa Zita, all by Antonello Gagini (1515). To the right of the choir the lavishly decorated chapel of the Rosary is adorned with polychrome marble and sculptures by Gioacchino Vitaliano.

The entrance to the oratory is at via Valverde 3, to the left of the church. It is on the first floor and is magnificently decorated inside with stuccoes by Giacomo Serpotta. This is the artist's masterpiece, created between 1688 and 1718. On the entrance wall the relief of the *Battle of Lépanto* reminds us we are in a religious building — a fact easily forgotten in the distracting presence of cherubs playing in clouds and clinging onto garlands of flowers. Notice the masterful work of the two boys below the *Battle of Lépanto*. On the main altar is Carlo Maratta's *Virgin of the Rosary with St Catherine and St Dominic*. On either side of the nave are ebony seats inlaid with mother-of-pearl.

Continuing along via Valverde you reach via Roma. From here via Bara leads on to the piazza Olivella. On the way you pass the Central Post Office, II, D4, built in 1933 in the heavy style of the day. The Church of Sant'Ignazio, more commonly known as all'Olivella, was built in 1598 and houses some interesting works. In the third chapel on the left is an altar beneath a crucifix set theatrically in a rich decor of rare marble inlays and precious stones with jasper columns supporting the arches. Outside to the right of the church is the Oratorio di San Filippo Neri by Venanzio Marvuglia (1769).

Museo Archeologico Regionale** II, D4

Open Mon-Sat 9am-2pm, 3-6pm, Sun and holidays 9am-12:30pm.

Adjoining the Church of Sant'Ignazio all'Olivella is a former 17th-century monastery, now a museum. The collections are being reorganized, which may mean you will not be able to see all of them. You first enter a small 17th-century cloister with a fountain statue of Triton. From here you pass into a larger cloister where Roman works are displayed.

Misadventures of an ephebus 25 centuries old

In 1882 a Selinunte peasant found the fragments of a bronze statue in a field. He took them to the Town Hall in Castelvetrano and sold them for 50 lire. In 1926 a specialist puzzled over the pieces and discovered the shape of an adolescent figure, probably designed by a local artist in about 480 BC. The work was considered one of the finest examples of ancient Sicilian sculpture and was returned to Castelvetrano. But in October 1962 the statue was stolen and not heard of again until 1969, when it was recovered. Once more the ephebus was handed over to specialists, Roman ones this time, who restored its original splendour and eternal youth.

To protect the sculpture from the covetousness of admirers it was placed in the national Archaeological Museum in Palermo. There it has remained an enigmatic young man who, for the last 25 centuries, has looked at the world with amazement through eyes of glass.

Most of these were excavated in Sicily. Of particular interest are the **Selinunte temple metopes****. Those from Temple C (6th century BC) represent the quadriga of Helios, Athene protecting Perseus as he slays the Gorgon (from which sprang Pegasus the winged horse) and Herakles punishing the Cercopes dwarves. The metopes from Temple E (460-450 BC) depict Herakles fighting an Amazon, the wedding of Zeus and Hera, Actaeon being attacked by hounds while Artemis looks on, and Athene fighting a giant. You should also see the Etruscan collection from Chiusi (from 7th to 1st century BC) and the Egyptian room with the *Stone of Palermo*, a long chronology and genealogy of the first five Egyptian dynasties (3200-2500 BC). Don't miss the *Ephebus of Selinunte***, one of the major pieces in the museum (in the Selinunte room), or the *Ram of Syracuse***, an admirable Hellenistic bronze work from the 3rd century BC.

Other noteworthy works include the lion head **water-spouts*** from the temple at Himera (5th century BC), *Herackles Overpowering the Stag** (the Roman copy from Pompeii of a Greek original from the 4th century BC), the *Satyr Filling a Drinking Cup** (another Roman copy of a Greek original) and finally, a fragment of the Parthenon frieze.

Teatro Massimo II, D3-4

As you leave the museum, take via Bara to the piazza Verdi, where you will find one of Europe's biggest theatres, Teatro Massimo (83,205 sq ft/7730 sq m). The theatre is neo-Classical in style and was built between 1875 and 1897 by the architect Basile and his son. Unfortunately, it has been closed for work over the last ten years, serving merely as a decorative centrepiece in the middle of the lively square.

Church of Sant'Agostino II, D4

Open 7am-noon, 4-6pm; holidays 7am-12:30pm. Closed to visitors during service.

To get to Sant'Agostino from the Teatro Massimo, walk around the left side of the theatre and take via Favara, the third street on the left. The church dates from the 13th century, but of its original structure only the portal remains, with a lovely 14th-century rose window. The interior is decorated in stucco by Serpotta (1711). In addition to the statues of the Virtues, as in most of Palermo's oratories, Serpotta's saints also decorate the nave in Sant'Agostino. He gave free rein to his imagination and interpreted the characters with a great degree of realism. At the end of the nave to the left a door opens onto a small cloister. Outside, turn the corner onto via Sant'Agostino where you will have the best view of the side doorway by Domenico Gagini.

You are now in the Capo quarter and should wander through its lively market down via Sant'Agostino. This street brings you to via Maqueda and its elegant shops. If you follow via Maqueda for long enough you'll reach the piazza Cesare, II, F5, and Stazione Centrale, the departure point for the first itinerary. On the right of the piazza, approaching from via Maqueda, is the Church of Sant'Antonino where you can see the last work of Fra Úmile da Petralía (1639); it was left unfinished by him but later completed by Fra Innocenzo da Palermo.

▬▬ THE MODERN CITY

During the preceding walks you will have had a brief glimpse of the modern part of town to the left of the ancient city; it deserves a longer look.

From the piazza Verdi, II, D4, set out along via Ruggero Settimo, one of Palermo's main shopping streets. You will pass the piazza Ungheria, II, C3, on the left with its large modern buildings and the famous Charleston restaurant (see p. 54). A little farther along to the right is via Principe Belmonte, II, C4, now partly closed to traffic, where you have a pleasant choice of open-air cafés. Via Ruggero Settimo ends at its own piazza dominated to the right by the vast neo-Classical theatre, Politeama Garibaldi, built in 1874. Major shows and operas are presented here.

On the left side of the theatre at via Turati 1 is the **Galleria d'Arte Moderna** *(open Tues-Sun 9am-1pm, also Tues and Thurs 4:30-7pm)*. This houses mainly the works of Sicilian sculptors and painters, although there are sometimes exhibits by artists from the continent and international retrospectives.

Piazza Ruggero Settimo is flanked to its left by yet another large square, the piazza Castelnuovo, with its garden of palm trees and a small neo-Classical building in the middle. At n° 34 you will find the APT Tourist Office (see p. 58).

Leading off from the large double square is **viale della Libertà***, II, C3, the most elegant street in Palermo. The wide avenue is lined with shady side lanes, impressive buildings and luxury shops.

Viale della Libertà stretches all the way to the piazza Vittorio Veneto but before this it narrows at piazza Crispi and leads to some fine gardens (see below) and to Villa Zito, on the corner of via Notarbartolo, II, A2, home of the **Museo Archeologico, Mormino**. The museum displays the rich collections of the Mormino Foundation *(open Mon-Fri 9am-1pm, 3-4:45pm; closed Sat afternoon, Sun and holidays)*. The collections include ceramics from prehistoric and Greek times, terra-cotta pieces, diverse objects from excavations financed by the foundation, and a good collection of Sicilian coins.

Palermo's gardens

Palermo has many public gardens to escape to when it gets too hot. Unless otherwise indicated, these parks are open during daylight hours.

Orto Botanico*, via Lincoln, II, E6, *(open Mon-Fri 8am-12:30pm, Sat 8-11am)*. This botanical park, covering an area of 24.7 ac/10 hec, was created in 1879 by King Ferdinand IV. It contains a wide variety of European and tropical plants and flowers, used in various industries — chemical, textile, medical and food. The strange-looking Egyptian-style building in the centre is the work of a French architect, Léon Dufourny. Of special interest are the palm trees, the giant magnolia, the Yucca plants and all the exotic shrubs in the winter garden greenhouses.

Giardino Garibaldi, piazza Marina, II, D5, is justly famous for its banyan trees (see p. 66).

Villa Giulia, via Lincoln, II, E6. The garden was laid out in the 17th century and named after the wife of Viceroy Marcantonio Colonna. There are several fountains one of which, the *'Genius of Palermo'* by Marabitti (18th century), is unfortunately quite dilapidated.

Villa Bonanno, piazza della Vittoria, II, E3, is a cool oasis in the historic centre. You cross it on your way to the Palazzo dei Normanni (see p. 63).

Parco d'Orleans, II, F3, behind the Palazzo dei Normanni, belongs to the residence of the president (but can be visited) and is therefore well maintained!

Giardino Inglese, viale della Libertà, II, A3, is a vast garden on both sides of the avenue with a variety of plants. There is an equestrian statue of Garibaldi in a square on the left.

Parco della Favorita, on the way to Monte Pellegrino, I, BC2-3. The garden is described on p. 82 in the 'Environs of Palermo' section.

Villa Tasca, corso Calatafimi 446, I, F2 *(open only by previous appointment)*. This is a private park known for its rare species of trees surrounding a lovely house built in 1777 for the prince of Trabia. From the terrace you have a splendid view of the Conca d'Oro. Richard Wagner came here during his visit to Sicily in 1881.

Villa Malfitano, via Dante, II, C1. An immense garden in an area of town seldom visited by tourists.

IN SEARCH OF THE NORMANS

This itinerary includes three Norman churches in the south of Palermo that are far apart. You might like to visit them on your way to Bagheria and Solunto.

San Giovanni dei Lebbrosi I, E4

Open Mon-Sat 4:30-5:30pm, Sun 8-11:30am. Ring for the custodian next to the church. Buses 11, 26 and 31.

On leaving Palermo, take the corso dei Mille south and cross the Oreto River near the Ponte dell'Ammiraglio, a bridge built by George of Antioch in 1113 (no longer in use because the river has been diverted). Not long after the piazza Scaffa take the first street to the left, via Salvatore Capello, which leads to San Giovanni dei Lebbrosi (St John of the Lepers). This is one of the earliest Norman churches in Sicily. Founded by Roger I in 1070 and completed under Roger II, its style is Arab-Norman. The church was once part of an Arab castle, of which almost nothing remains. At one time it was also used as a leper hospital. The interior consists of three aisles separated by pillars, a cupola resting on pendentives and three apses.

Santo Spirito** I, E3

Open 9-11am. Buses 2 and 42.

Take via Oreto to the right of the Stazione Centrale and turn right onto via Palermo, which runs to the hospital. Then follow via del Vespro to the piazza Orsola, in front of the cemetery (there's a parking lot). The church is in the cemetery to the left of the main lane. It is a fine Norman edifice built in 1178 by Gualtiero Offamiglio. Pointed arches and inlaid bands of lava and tuff embellish the sides and transept. The restored interior is beautiful, in spite of its austerity. Columns separate it into three aisles, and on the coffered ceiling there are traces of paint from the original decoration. The choir is raised and has a 15th-century wooden crucifix.

It was in Santo Spirito that, after vespers on Easter Monday in 1282, the Palermitans rose against their Angevin rulers. It was customary at the time for peasants to come into the neighbouring fields to celebrate religious holidays, whereupon Angevin soldiers searched them for any weapons hidden in their clothes. On this particular day the soldiers intended to search some of the women. The Sicilians reacted immediately, and an uprising followed that led to the massacre of 2000 Frenchmen. Those who could took refuge in the mountains or left the island. The insurrection marked the beginning of a long series of conflicts that spread to the mainland and only came to an end in 1302, when the treaty of Caltabellotta was signed.

Santa Maria di Gesù I, F4

Continuing south of Palermo, via Santa Maria di Gesù, I, F4, climbs Monte Grifona and leads to the church. Built in 1429, the church stands in a cemetery at the top of a flight of steps. On its façade is a splendid marble Renaissance portal and surrounding the inscribed credo are the figures of saints. The 16th-century side portal on the left is remarkable; inside is an unusual Catalan-Gothic chapel (15th century). The Gru-Talamanca, with traces of frescoes, is said to represent the life of St Bernard of Sienna. Beside the church is a convent with a small cloister. One of the monks will accompany you to the belvedere where the **view*** of the Conca d'Oro is breathtaking.

OUTSKIRTS OF PALERMO

This excursion will show you different aspects of Norman architecture, enriching what you've already seen in Palermo. Count on half a day to visit the sites.

La Cuba* II, F1

Open Wed and Sun 9am-noon; for entrance, inquire at the guardroom.

Take bus n° 819 or n° 9 to corso Calatafimi 100, about 0.6 mi/1 km beyond the Porta Nuova.

During Norman times this whole area was one large park with country pavilions, lush gardens and artificial lakes. The few vestiges that remain of this past splendour are now hemmed in by a chaotic arrangement of new buildings.

A good example, behind the entrance to the Tukory barracks, is La Cuba, built by Arab artists in 1180, during the reign of William II. It was named after its high dome (Arabic for 'dome' is *kubbeh*), which has since crumbled. The palace is solid and severe, with turrets in the middle of each of the sides. Arcades embellish the building, and high up the wall there is an inscription in Arabic mentioning the name of the king and the date the palace was built. Other Norman remains from this era are **La Cubula** and **La Zisa** (see p. 76). To visit La Cubula, I, E2-3, corso Calatafimi 575, ask the custodian at the Villa Napoli. This little kiosk, commissioned by William I, has four heavy arches and is topped by a red dome. If you happen to pass corso Calatafimi 446, I, F2, between 9 and 10am, ask to see the magnificent garden of the Villa Tasca (see p. 73).

The Catacombs* II, EF1

Open 9am-noon, 3:30-5pm; Sun and holidays 9am-noon.

Continue along corso Calatafimi to the first intersection with traffic lights and turn right onto via Pindemonte. Follow this to the end where you will find the **Convento dei Cappuccini**, renowned for its catacombs. You can also take bus n° 27 from the centre of town.

From the 17th to the 19th century, whenever there was a death in a noble family or among the clergy, the deceased was taken to an embalmer, who removed the insides and left the body to dry for several months. The body was then dressed in the deceased's best clothes and taken to the Capuchin monks, who placed it in one of the long underground corridors you can see today. There are about 8000 bodies of Palermitans in the catacombs, more or less preserved by the extreme dryness of the air. Some of them still have a ticket pinned to their chests

---

The catacombs

The bodies were taken underground to the Capuchins 24 hours after death, without an injection or any kind of preparation whatsoever, and were laid on a grill made of terra cotta tubes inside a small cellar, which was then carefully walled up. After a year the dried bodies were removed from their 'draining boards', now rid of all their secretions. They were then put in a bath of vinegar and aromatic herbs and left in the sun to mummify. Finally, reduced now to skin and bones, they were dressed, adorned and placed in the galleries.

There's a particularly well-preserved body in the men's corridor — that of Antonio Prestigiacomo, standing in his greatcoat, his eyes and hair extraordinarily life-like. His body was plunged into an arsenic bath whereupon the poison fossilized him. Another method was to immerse the body in quicklime. Such was the case with Giuseppe Siciliano, a young boy of 14 who died in 1851.

Not all the bodies reacted in the same way to the drying process. Some of them came out twisted, with dislocations or detached arms and legs. Afterward, in the gallery, they fell prey in time to decay and mice. Sometimes a head would roll off or an arm would fall to the ground. Then the relations who had dressed and made up the bodies when they left the 'draining board' would fix the appendages back on again with wire.

D. Fernandez,
The Gorgon's Raft
Le Radeau de la Gorgone, Grasset, 1988

with their name, address and date of death, which helped their families identify them once their clothes had been eaten by moths. The bodies are arranged in categories according to social rank and profession. You can, for example, see members of the clergy grouped in a gallery, their skeletons wearing cardinal's hats, which lends a black humour to the scene. This is not a visit for sensitive souls.

La Zisa* II, D1

La Zisa palace has just been restored and was still closed to the public at the time of this writing. If it is open during your visit, take via Cipressi from the convent to the right and follow it to the piazza Ingestone, where the second street to the left, via Zisa, leads to the piazza San Stefano and the palace. You can also take bus n° 24 from the city centre. La Zisa (from the Arabic *el aziz*, meaning 'magnificent') is modeled on an Arab design and was begun in 1154 by William I, whose son completed it. It is a fine rectangular building decorated with 16th-century arches and crenella-tions and has two small towers on the shorter sides. The interior recalls the decorative splendour of oriental palaces. The hall is preceded by an entrance arch and is embellished with stalactite vaults and a mosaic frieze of hunters and peacocks.

These itineraries guide you to the essential sights of the city, but there are many more worth seeing if time permits. Palermo has no less than 90 churches and 50 palaces. Not all have the same interest, of course, and we have omitted some because of their poor state of repair. But to really get to know the town, you need to spend time wandering through its maze of alleyways and venture into what is left of the old city. Although the bombing during World War II destroyed many of its most picturesque areas, it is still well worth seeing.

ENVIRONS OF PALERMO

There are many wonderful places to visit outside Palermo, the most interesting of which are mentioned in the following excursions. Monreale and Mondello are high priorities. If you are going all the way around the island, Bagheria and Solunto can wait until you return. Piana degli Albanesi and Ustica are of special interest if you have no time to venture into the interior or to visit the Aeolian Islands.

MONREALE***: THE BIBLE IN IMAGES

Monreale is the main tourist centre on the outskirts of Palermo and is well known for its magnificent cloister and cathedral. It's a trip not to miss, as the Sicilian proverb says: 'He who goes to Palermo without seeing Monreale leaves a donkey and comes back an animal.'

Monreale was supposedly built after a dream by one of Sicily's rulers. William II (1153-89), also known as William the Good — third of the Norman kings in Sicily — was resting under a carob tree after hunting on Mount Caputo when the Virgin appeared to him in a dream. She told him where his father, William the Bad, had hidden his treasure. The king followed her instructions and dug up a pile of gold, which he used to build a church — the masterpiece which was to earn the young sovereign everlasting renown. In 1183 Pope Lucius III declared that 'no similar work has ever been created by any king since time began'.

The treasure must have been quite fantastic because it financed the building of both a church and a monastery. To do this William II summoned the greatest artists and architects of his kingdom and numerous craftsmen from Greece, Provence, Arabia, Pisa, Venice and Naples. In 1176, during a grand ceremony, the king dedicated the church to Maria Assunta and put it in the charge of Teobaldo, the first abbot of Monreale, who had already gathered together 100 Benedictine monks. Monreale rivaled the lavish religious buildings of Rome and Byzantium, the two great imperial cities of the Christian world at the time. We will never know what other wondrous buildings the discerning young king might have financed had he not met with an early death at age 37. His death put an end not only to the works of Norman kings but to their dynasty as well. William II was buried in his cathedral in a white marble sarcophagus.

The road to Monreale twists above beautiful panoramas of the Conca d'Oro and skirts two Marabitti fountains. They were originally put there so that pilgrims on the climb to the cathedral could quench their thirst. You arrive at the piazza Vittorio Emanuele with the left flank of the Duomo in front of you.

Duomo (Cathedral)***
Open Tues-Sun 8am-noon, 3:30-6:30pm.
Before going inside, take a look at the façade and central portal, the side portal and exterior apses.

Façade and portals**

The apogee of Arab-Norman art was reached in 1176 with the building of this glorious cathedral — one of the wonders of the medieval world. The façade is framed by two solid towers, one unfinished. Between them is an elegant portico added by the architect Marabitti in 1770, with semi-circular arches and Doric columns.

The magnificent pointed **portal**** has five sets of sculpted bands of garlands, human figures and animals. These alternate with strips of mutlicoloured mosaics, making a sumptuous frame for the **bronze door**** (1186) by Bonanno da Pisa. The door's 42 panels illustrate the main events of the Old Testament and New Testament.

Walk around to the left of the church where there's another portico, by the Gagini brothers, built between 1547 and 1569. The bronze door, by Barisano da Trani (1179), is smaller than the first and decorated with 28 bas-relief illustrations, three of which depict the life of Christ. The artists responsible were probably inspired by Byzantine ivory-work. Resist going in for the moment and walk around to the apses by skirting the palace; this will give you a full idea of the cathedral's architectural structure.

Apses**

The decoration on the apses consists of three levels of interlacing, superimposed arches. The first seems sober, but the artists who worked on the other two levels treated the inlay's of limestone, black and grey lava and coloured brick as if they were rare woods.

Interior ***

The interior (335 × 131 ft/102 × 40 m) was designed along the same lines as the Capella Palatina (see p. 00) but was more ambitious. The three aisles are supported by 18 granite columns from Roman monuments; only the first one on the right is marble. They are crowned by classical or Corinthian capitals with sculpted heads of Ceres and Proserpine. These in turn are topped by blocks decorated with Byzantine mosaics, from which spring the pointed arches.

The paving is the work of an unknown Palermitan artist (1569) and consists of a mosaic of white marble, porphyry and granite. The ceiling in the nave was restored after a fire in 1811. It has exposed beams and is decorated with paintings. The ceiling of the choir is Arabic stalactite, recalling the muqarnas (or honeycomb patterns) in the Cappella Palatina.

Mosaics ***

The mosaics on the upper part of the walls cover an area of 68,244 sq ft/6340 sq m, the second largest area covered by mosaics in the world after St Sophia in Istanbul. Unknown artist worked on them from the 12th to the 13th century. They differ from the ones in the Cappella Palatina and are thought to be the work of Sicilian or Venetian artists rather than Sicilian craftsmen under the direction of Byzantine artists. Many of the scenes are more realistic, with more life-like vitality in the figures than is typical of Byzantine art. The illustrations of the Miracles bear this out — the ten lepers are covered in black pustular spots; the man suffering from dropsy has a huge swollen stomach; the body of Lazarus has reached such a state of putrefaction that those present cannot help holding their noses; the two blind men are stretching out their hands imploringly to be healed; and finally, the possessed man is wearing a straitjacket and his feet are in chains.

To see the mosaics at their best, glistening with gold, turn on the lights (there are special coin meters to operate them). It's useful to have a pair of binoculars because some of the scenes have fascinating details you will otherwise miss.

Right apse **

The red porphyry sepulchre of William I (1166) and the white marble sarcophagus of his son William II, the Good, are in the right apse.

A finely worked door leads into the **Cappella di San Benedetto*** containing six marble bas-reliefs by the sculptor Giovanni Marino. The barrel-vaulted ceiling is adorned with stucco work. On the altar is a large marble culture representing the Glory of St Benedict, carved by Marabitti in 1776. The stuccoes and white marble tableaux contrast beautifully with the multicoloured marble on the walls.

Left apse and Treasury***

The three marble tombs lined against the wall were restored in the 19th century. They contain the remains of Marguerite of Navarre, the wife of William I, and their two sons, Roger and Henry. The heart of St Louis, the French king who died of the plague in Tunis in 1270, is buried in the altar.

On the left are very fine **brass railings** around the **Cappella del Crocifisso***, a polygonal chapel and part of the **Treasury*** (admission charge). It was built between 1687 and 1692 by a Capuchin friar from Monreale under the Jesuit, Angelo Italia (1627-1700). Sumptuously decorated in marble, with bas-reliefs and statues, it is one of the most beautiful examples of Baroque art in Sicily. Everything in it was created in relation to the wooden 15th-century crucifix above the altar. There are four large statues of prophets under polychrome marble hangings with little angels holding the folds. They are impressively framed by four cabled columns made of red stone from Piana degli Albanesi. Notice also the detail on the altar panel, a fine example of marble inlay.

Terrace

For an interesting **view** of the cloisters, Conca d'Oro and Palermo, climb the 180 steps to the top of the tower.

Cloisters***

Open Mon-Sat 9am-7pm, Sun and holidays 9am-1pm.

The entrance to the cloisters is beside the Duomo on the piazza Guglielmo. Built by William II as part of the Benedictine monastery (of which only a dormitory on the southern side remains), the cloisters form a square of four galleries 154 ft/47 m long. The Arab arcades are decorated with geometric patterns of lava inlays and are supported by

---

A gigantic illustrated Bible

The most interesting mosaics are in the nave covering either side in two bands, one above the other, illustrating events from the Old Testament. Above them is a frieze of saints and angels in medallions.

In the upper strip the series begins on the right-hand side with the creation of the earth and sky, followed by the moon, the sea and the firmament, right up to the Garden of Eden. On the left-hand side, moving toward the choir, the scenes portray the temptation of Eve, the banishment from the Garden of Eden and the murder of Abel by Cain.

The lower band, again beginning on the right, illustrates the building of Noah's Ark, the Tower of Babel, the destruction of Sodom, Abraham's sacrifice, Jacob's dream and his fight with the angel.

In each of the aisles, a selection of Christ's miracles are portrayed in ten paintings. In the transept, where the royal tombs are located, there are scenes from the life of Christ: in the middle his birth and early years; to the right his miracles and Passions; to the left his death and Resurrection.

The side apses contain illustrations of St Peter (left) and St Paul (right). The most impressive, however, is the central apse with the figure of Christ Pantocrator taking up the whole upper curve representing the point of convergence for the theological poem. Beneath is the Virgin enthroned, surrounded by angles and Apostles.

In the central apse to the right, just above the episcopal throne, you can see William II offering his church to the Virgin and, to the left, above the royal throne, the same king being crowned by Christ.

228 twin columns which are grouped in fours on the corners. All the columns are white marble and every second pair has a mosaic decoration spiraling up its shafts. The shape and decoration of the capitals are extremely varied; the artists gave free reign to their imaginations to create a wonderful sequence of images the whole length of the galleries, alternating sacred subjects with profane. Among the scenes are the banishment of Adam and Eve, the murder of Abel, the story of Samson, the Annunciation, the Allegory of the months, hunting and harvesting scenes and William II offering his cathedral to the Virgin.

In one of the corners is a fountain in a charming enclosure with three arches on each side. The fountain itself is a single shaft crowned by 12 small lion heads, standing in the middle of a basin. It has often been said that this cloister is far more like the Alhambra in Grenada than a Benedictine monastery. This is probably because William II used the cloister to express his fondness for Islamic art, with its geometric designs and Arab arches.

When you leave the cloisters, walk past the Baroque front of the convent, which houses the Institute of Mosaic Art *(open daily 8:30am-noon)*, and go through the doorway on the left, which leads to a belvedere in a little garden. From the terraces you have a wonderful view of the Oreto valley and Palermo.

Environs of Monreale

San Martino delle Scale

This is a resort 3.7 mi/6 km north-west of Monreale, set in the middle of a pine forest on the slopes of Serra dell'Occhio, at an altitude of 1798 ft/548 m. The little village (350 inhabitants) is based around a Benedictine Abbey founded in the 6th century by Gregory the Great. The abbey was rebuilt in the 14th century and enlarged by Venanzio Marvuglia from 1770 to 1786. There are several noteworthy paintings in the church *(open daily 8am-1pm, 4-7pm)* and in the right-hand transept is a 1396 font near a lovely portal dating from the same era. The sacristy contains a collection of vestments. Outside, to the right-of the church, is a very elegant Oreto fountain by Ignazio Marabitti (1784).

San Cipirello

The archaeological site at San Cipirelli is 14,6 mi/23,5 km south-west of Monreale. Excavations have brought to light the remains of ancient Jetae, a city dating from the 4th century BC. Diverse objects, including colossal statues, are exhibited in the town in a little **Museo Civico** *(open Tues-Sat 9am-noon, 4-6pm; Sun and holidays 9am-noon; closed Mon)*.

Telephone area code: 091.

Access

Bus: Take bus n° 8/9 or 9 from the piazza dell'Indipendenza, II, F2.

Car: Monreale is 5 mi/8 km south-west of Palermo. Take via Vittorio Emanuele from the city centre; this street becomes the corso Calatafimi, which goes to Monreale. If you are coming from La Zisa, head back to the corso Calatafimi and turn right onto it (away from the sea).

Parking is very difficult in Monreale. Try to find a spot before arriving in the centre. The streets are very narrow, many are one-way, and there are no parking lots.

Accommodation

▲▲ **Carrubella Hotel**, via Umberto 1, ☎ 640 2187. 30 rooms. Overlooking a garden, with a beautiful view.

Food

LL **Restaurant La Botte**, contrada Lenzitti 416, 1.8 mi/3 km from

The beautifully preserved cloisters of Monreale, constructed by William II in 1176.

Monreale along the Trápani road beyond the cemetery. *Closed Mon, Aug and Sept.* An old *osteria* with country decor and veranda for open-air dining in warm weather. Relatively limited choice but good food.

LL Villa Tre Fontane, on the circonvallazione, 3 mi/5 km from Palerme heading toward Monreale on the Partinico road, ☎ 411 274. *Closed Tues.* Large terrace.

There are several *trattorie* and *pizzerie* in Monreale itself; try the **Guglielmo,** just opposite the Duomo.

Useful address

Tourist information, piazza Vittorio Emanuele, beside the Duomo, ☎ 640 4448. *Open 9am-1pm, 4-8pm; Sat 9am-1pm. Closed Sun.*

▬▬ FROM PARCO DELLA FAVORITA TO MONTE PELLEGRINO

Buses nº 14 and nº 15 leave from the station or from via Roma in the town centre.

If you have a car, leave Palermo on via Giardino, II, A3, which runs along Giardino Inglese (see p. 73). At the end of the street, turn right and then immediately left onto via Sampolo. This leads to the piazza Leoni and on to via del Fante, which runs beside Parco della Favorita.

You really need a whole day to enjoy this itinerary fully.

Parco Della Favorita* I, BC2-3

This former hunting ground, now an enormous park in a sad state of neglect, stretches for almost 1.5 mi/2.5 km at the foot of Monte Pellegrino. A large area of the park is comprised of sports grounds. There are a number of entrances off via del Fante, but the most convenient is the last gate on the piazza Niscemi, I, B3, near Palazzina Cinese, 1.5 mi/2.5 km from the piazza Leoni.

Palazzina Cinese: Royal Delirium I, B2

This strange construction (now deteriorated and closed to the public) was built in 1799 for Ferdinand III and Queen Maria Carolina. The king himself drew up most of the plans, leaving the architect Venanzio Marvuglia to adapt his wild imaginings. The resulting style is mainly Chinese, although there are also Gothic, Arab and Egyptian influences. Ferdinand and his queen took refuge here while Naples was occupied by Napoleon's army. It was also in these extraordinary surroundings that Admiral Nelson and Lady Hamilton conducted their love affair.

Museo Etnografico Siciliano Pitre I, B2

Open Tues and Thurs 9am-1pm, 3:30-5:30pm.

The palace's former outbuildings to the right now house the ethnographic museum, founded in 1909 by Professore Giuseppe Pitre.

This wonderful museum of Sicily's popular arts and traditions exhibits objects that belong to the country's past folklore, such as carts, costumes and utensils. The collections are classified by theme and well documented in the large library. The most unusual displays are on the themes of superstition, witchcraft and religion. There are fine collections of votive tablets, ceramics and cribs. Don't miss the 18th-century one on Trápani, which is of special interest.

Mondello, I, A2

6.8 mi/11 km north of Palermo. Buses nº 14 and nº 15 leave from the station or via Roma in the centre of town.

On leaving the ethnographic museum, take viale Duca degli Abruzzi to the right, then right again onto via della Parrochia and left onto viale Regina Margherita. This wide avenue runs along the foot of Monte Pellegrino to the piazza Valdesi, the centre of Mondello (1.8 mi/3 km).

A former fishing village, Mondello today is one of Sicily's most important seaside resorts, mainly because of its exceptional position on the magnificent bay between Monte Pellegrino and Capo Gallo. Unfortunately the beach has been overrun by bathing huts and is packed in summer, and the water is polluted. This, however, has not dissuaded numerous Palermitans from making it their main place of residence.

Telephone area code: **091**.

Accommodation

▲▲▲ **Mondello Palace,** viale Principe di Scalea 2, I, A2 ap, ☎ 450 001. 83 rooms. A lovely garden, swimming pool, private beach and tennis courts.

▲▲ **Conchiglia d'Oro,** viale Cloe 9, ☎ 450 032. 50 rooms. Private beach, garden.

▲▲ **Splendid Hotel La Torre,** via Piano del Gallo 11, I, A2 aq, ☎ 450 222. 179 rooms. Beach, tennis courts, swimming pool, garden.

▲ **Esplanade,** via Piano del Gallo 22, I, A2 aj, ☎ 450 003. 32 rooms. On the beach.

Food

LLLL Charleston le Terrazze, via Regina Elena, I, A2 rg, ☎ 450 171. *Open only mid-June to mid-Sept.* Remarkable food is served either in a dining-room with an atmosphere similar to the Palermo Charleston or on their elegant terrace. Very good choice of wines.

LLL Chamade Mare, via Regina Elena 43, I, A2, ☎ 450 512. *Open June to Oct.* Another restaurant of quality, splendidly located in a villa in the middle of a large garden. Fish and seafood specialities. Ravioli with salmon or caviar.

LLL Gambero Rosso, via Piano del Gallo 30, I, A2 aq, ☎ 454 685. *Closed Mon and the second half of Nov.* Their large terrace overlooking the sea is an ideal setting for enjoying very good food, mainly fish dishes.

LL Sympathy, via Piano del Gallo 18, I, A2 rh, ☎ 444 570. *Closed Thurs.* Another good spot to enjoy fish.

Monte Pellegrino

You can return to Palermo from Mondello along the coast road, lungomare Cristofo Colombo. This skirts the mountain passing near the **Addaura caves,** the deepest in Sicily, where you can see prehistoric inscriptions and Paleolithic drawings. For admission go to the Soprintendenza Archeologica in Palermo, via Bara 24, ☎ 580 642. You can also return from Mondello by the more pleasant mountain road. To do this, leave Mondello on viale Regina Margherita going toward Palermo. After about 0.6 mi/1 km turn left onto via Ercta, which winds up into Monte Pellegrino (4.3 mi/7 km) — you will have striking views of the bay, Parco della Favorita and Palermo. A road off it to the left leads to a belvedere (500 yds/458 m) and a statue of Santa Rosalia. To reach the cave chapel of the saint, Santuario di Santa Rosalia, return to via Ercta.

Santuario di Santa Rosalia

The complex was built in 1625 and comprises a cave and a convent that runs an orphanage. The cave where St Rosalia retired to pray is about 82 ft/25 m long and has been converted into a chapel *(open 7am-noon, 3-8pm).* A complex channel network collects the water, considered miraculous, which seeps out of the rock. To the left a statue of the saint lies in an elaborate glass structure, surrounded by gifts from her devotees. Her clothes are made of gilded silver, and her head and hands

---

Rosalia, patron saint of Palermo

Daughter of a Palermitan nobleman, Duke Sinibald, Lord of Quisquina and the Roses, Rosalia decided to retire to a cave and lead a life of prayer and penance. There she died in 1166. Five centuries later an epidemic of the plague broke out in Palermo. The inhabitants called upon their traditional patron saints — St Nymph, St Olive, St Christine and St Agatha — to no avail; the plague continued to decimate the population. Then somebody had the idea of carrying the relics of Rosalia in a procession around the town, whereupon the plague ceased. The population decided to make this understanding saint their patron. The Senate in Palermo, which had commissioned Van Dyck for a picture of the four guardian saints of the town, had to hastily ask the famous painter to add a fifth. Santa Rosalia became the main saint of Palermo and is venerated throughout the island. There's an important pilgrimage to her shrine on September 4, and a festival is held in her honour every year from July 11 to 15.

---

are white marble — a rather strange representation of a troglodyte (a cave hermit) who vowed to live in poverty, although it should be noted that the statue was a royal gift.

To return to Palermo (8.6 mi/14 km) continue along the panoramic road. It leads down toward the Conca d'Oro and crosses Strada Antica (known as Scala Vecchia), the footpath still taken by pilgrims to the sanctuary. You pass near Utveggio, a derelict castle on a ridge that commands superb views of the city. At the bottom, take via Pietro Bonanno, which runs to the piazza Generale Cascino near the Fiera del Mediterraneo buildings. Continue straight along via Imperatore Federico until you arrive at viale della Libertà.

▬ *BAGHERIA, SOLUNTO* AND CAPO ZAFFERANO*

You need half a day for the 27 mi/43-km trip there and back.

Take either Autostrada A19 toward Messina or the very congested N113 coast road, which you reach from Foro Italico, II, E6.

Nightmarish decor

There are 62 monsters in the Villa Palagonia, each more grotesque than the last: deformed beggars, hunchbacks playing weird musical instruments and dwarves on mounts with human faces. If the chroniclers of the time are to be believed, there were once more than 600 in the garden, among them 'a mythical beast with the head of a lion, the neck of a goose, the body of a lizard, the legs of a goat and the tail of a fox' (A. t'Serstevens). It appears that the sculptors tried hard to satisfy the whimsical folly of their prince, who wanted to live surrounded by monsters. This eccentric character had a very pretty young wife whom he kept shut up inside the palace. A large part of the unusual interior decoration has disappeared, which is a pity because most of the rooms were covered in mirror fragments, pieces of rock crystal, bits of polychrome marble, crystals and coloured glass. This decoration went right up to the ceiling; to complete it the prince, an ardent collector, piled up obelisks of porcelain, chandeliers, saucers, teapots and even chamber pots. The tables were shaped like tombs, and there was a clock inside one statue that made the statue's eyes move as it ticked. The prince's bedroom went beyond the realms of the imagination for sheer outlandishness: there were reptiles, toads, scorpions and multicoloured marble spiders everywhere. In the chapel was a bust of a woman being devoured by centipedes and a St Francis with luminous hands and feet hanging from his neck. Most of these bizarre objects, which would have delighted the surrealists, have unfortunately disappeared. All that remains are the detailed, sometimes enthusiastic descriptions of them by travelers of the time. Not everyone appreciated the prince's strange taste — Goethe, for one, was appalled by the eccentric decoration.

Bagheria: A Sicilian Versailles

After 9 mi/14 km along the N 113 you come to an intersection: left to Aspra and Capo Zafferano, right to Bagheria (0.6 mi/1 km, 42,000 inhabitants). You will see the first of Bagheria's villas on the left, the 17th-century Villa Cattolica, which now houses a modern art gallery *(open Apr 1-Sept 30, Tues-Sat 9am-7pm, Sun 9am-2pm; closed Mon).* Follow the corso Butera to the centre of town.

Bagheria was founded in 1657 by Prince Branciforte, who decided to build his country house there. Other splendid residences began to spring up among the orange groves as Palermitan nobles followed suit. Today the modern town has completely taken over the former aristocratic centre, and the gardens have mostly disappeared.

At the beginning of the corso to the left is Villa Cuto, with its central arches holding up a wide belvedere. Villa Inguaggiato is a little farther along at n° 92. The corso ends in front of Villa Butera, which dates from 1658 and is now a nursery school. Enter through a porch to the left of the façade (restored in the 18th century) into a vast courtyard where you can see the remains of the former building. Back on the corso Butera, take corso Umberto to the right, passing through the piazza Vittorio Emanuele opposite Chiesa Matrice to Villa Trabia, not far from the piazza Garibaldi. The façade was restored in 1890, and the basin in front has a statue of Abundance by Ignazio Marabitti. The corso ends at the piazza Garibaldi; to the left is the entrance to Villa Palagonia, guarded by statues of monsters.

Villa Palagonia

Open Mon-Fri 9am-1pm, 4-7pm; Sat and Sun 11am-12:30, 4-8pm.

By far the most interesting and unusual of the villas, this was built in 1715 for the prince of Palagonia, a Spanish grandee related to the royal family. The villa is an elliptically shaped building comprised of the elegant dwelling and its surrounding semi-circle of outbuildings. The prince of Palagonia's nephew did not find this arrangement to his liking when he inherited it in 1747, and he set about embellishing it in his own way (see box). The extraordinary invasion of monsters all over the walls is the product of his eccentric imagination.

To the right across the piazza Garibaldi is the entrance to Villa Valguarnera. A staircase leads up to the magnificent façade adorned with statues by Marabitti.

Solunto* and Capo Zafferano

Return to the crossroads on the N 113. Don't take the road opposite to Aspra but continue to the right toward Messina for 1.8 mi/3 km (where you are 10.5 mi/17 km east of Palermo). Turn left here along the road to Porticello. A little farther on (there's a signpost) is a road to the left that winds up 0.9 mi/1.5 km to the Solunto ruins *(open 9am to one hour before sunset).*

The ancient town of Soloeis (or Solus) stands at 712 ft/217 m on Monte Catalfano, in a magnificent setting overlooking the sea. The town was one of the earliest Phoenician trading posts in Sicily, taken by the Romans in 254 BC and then destroyed by the Saracens in the Middle Ages. The visit begins at the archeological museum that displays finds from various local excavations.

The most spectacular ruin is a house, named the *gymnasium,* which retains six of the original Doric columns, three of which still support the entablature. On the side of the hill above, you can see the tiered rows of a small theatre and an odeon. The breathtaking **view*** from the top of the hill stretches all the way from Capo Zafferano to Cefalù.

Return to the Porticello road and turn left for a tour of the peninsula along a lovely panoramic road that goes through the fishing village of Porticello, then on to **Capo Zafferano** and Capo Mongerbino before it reaches Aspra. Then return to the N 113, which takes you back to Palermo.

Telephone area code: 091.

Accommodation

▲▲▲ **Zagarella Sea Palace,** in Solunto, via Nazionale 55, 2.4 mi/4 km along the Messina road, ☎ 937 077. 414 rooms. A very attractive vacation centre with two swimming pools, an immense garden overlooking the sea and a private beach.

▲▲ **Kafara,** in S. Elia, 1.8 mi/3 km along the road to Capo Zafferano, ☎ 957 377. 63 rooms. Tennis courts, swimming pool, private beach, garden.

▲▲ **Lido Sporting,** in Torre Colonna, ☎ 959 052. 59 rooms. Swimming pool, beach.

▲▲ **Torre Normanna,** in Piano Torre, 4.3 mi/7 km along the Messina road, ☎ 951 322. 299 rooms. Garden, swimming pool and elevator to the beach.

Food

LL **Francu u Piscaturi** (also called **Trattoria dell'Arco**), in Porticello, largo Pescheria 26, ☎ 957 758. *Closed Mon outside the tourist season.* Overlooking the sea. Serves good fish.

▬▬ *OTHER SITES*

Piana degli Albanesi, the Albanian Plain

15 mi/24 km south of Palermo.

Leave Palermo from the piazza dell'Indipendenza on the corso Pisani, II, F1. This leads into via Altofonte, which winds up to the picturesque village of Altofonte (7.4 mi/12 km). You follow a panoramic road around Monte Moarda to Piana degli Albanesi, a town of 7000 inhabitants on the shores of a large artificial lake. Piana was founded in 1488 by an Albanian colony that has persevered its customs, dialect, religious rites and costumes to this day. Weddings, important holidays and feast days, such as Easter, Epiphany, San Giorgio (April 23) and Madonna Odigitria (Tuesday after Pentecost and September 2), are all performed accor-ding to tradition. On Sunday you can attend a service celebrated in accordance with Italo-Greek tradition in the church of San Demetrio, which is decorated with Byzantine paintings and frescoes by Pietro Novelli.

All the other churches in Piana are Baroque.

Ústica, Lost Sister of the Aeolians

Ústica rises out of the Tyrrhenian Sea 35 mi/57 km from Palermo. It looks like a lava shell with occasional patches of greenery and a steep wild coastline. The highest point is Monte Guardia dei Turchi, with an altitude of 800 ft/244 m. The area of the island is only 3.3 sq mi/8.6 sq km for a population of 1300. There are practically no roads, and vehicles are not allowed on the island during the tourist season.

The only place of real interest on the island is the town of Ústica. For the last few years a biennial event for painting the walls of the houses has been staged, resulting in the picturesque appearance of Ústica's alleys.

There is a small **Museo di Archeologia Sottomarina** (Museum of Marine Archaeology) in Torre di Santa Maria with objects from the buried city of Osteodes (the Greek name for the island, meaning 'ossuary'); 6000 Carthaginian rebel soldiers perished here after having been abandoned. The remains of a Roman necropolis can be seen on the rock above the town, and an archaeological park is being planned at Faraglioni, a Bronze Age village.

The excursions on and around the island are varied: donkeys can be rented from farmers; you can take a boat to see the caves and creeks around the island; and scuba diving, underwater fishing and snorkeling enthusiasts have a whole world of exceptional flora and fauna to explore. **Telephone area code: 091.**

Access

There is regular boat service between Palermo and the island (crossing takes $2\frac{1}{2}$ hours) as well as a daily hydrofoil service, sometimes three times a day in summer (crossing takes 75 minutes). Departures from molo V. Veneto in Palermo. For boat information, see p. 47.

Accommodation

▲▲▲ **Grotta Azzura,** ☎ 844 9048. 66 rooms. Swimming pool. Quiet with a beautiful view. *Open only in summer.*

▲▲ **Diana,** in San Paolo, ☎ 844 9109. 34 rooms. Private beach.

▲▲ **Punta Spalmatore,** in Spalmatore, ☎ 844 9323. 100 rooms. Swimming pool.

Festival

Island holiday: August 24, feast day of San Bartolomeo.

Food

LL Restaurant Clelia, via Magazzino 7, ☎ 844 9039. Part of a small hotel; intriguing location on a rock, with a grotto and swimming pool. Good food, mainly fish.

Useful address

Tourist information, piazza Vito Longo *(open daily 9am-1pm, 6-8pm).*

PALERMO TO TRÁPANI:
WESTERN SICILY

There are three routes from Palermo to Trápani: the first through Segesta on the N186 and N113, 62 mi/100 km; the second through Castellammare del Golfo on the N113 and N187, 65.8 mi/106 km; and the third on highway A29, which is quick and direct. You can also take the train, which stops at Segesta, getting you to Trápani in about two hours.

THE SEGESTA ROUTE

Monreale (5 mi/8 km south-west of Palermo)

The Palermo-Monreale itinerary is described on p. 80.

Borgetto (16 mi/26 km south-west of Palermo)

A small road (2.7 mi/4.5 km) climbs from here to the sanctuary of Madonna del Romitello (2355 ft/718 m), where you have a panoramic view of Segesta and the gulf of Castellammare. May 10 is feast day at the sanctuary.

Álcamo (30 mi/49 km south-west of Palermo)

This is an industrial town and agricultural centre of 45,000 inhabitants located at the foot of Monte Bonifato (2710 ft/826 m; an hour's climb). Alcamo's origins are Arab (from a fortress named Alkamuk). The 13th-century poet Ciullo d'Alcamo, who was also one of the first singers of Italian lyric music, was born here.

There are several fine churches in the town. At the beginning of corso VI Aprile (which crosses the entire town) is the Church of San Francesco with two statues by Antonello Gagini and a marble altarpiece by Giovanni Gagini. A little farther along on the left, in via Caruso, you come to the Church of Badia Nova with its 18th-century façade. There is a painting inside of San Benedetto by Pietro Novelli and five statues by Serpotta. At the corner of via Tomaso you will see the church of San Tomaso. To the right, in via Rossotti, the church of Badia Grande contains allegorical statues and a marble tabernacle by Antonello Gagini; it also has two of Novelli's paintings: *Santa Teresa* and *The Assumption*.

The cathedral, Chiesa Madre, is on piazza IV Novembre. Although rebuilt in 1669, it has retained part of its original structure, including its attractive 14th-century campanile and 15th-century marble portal. Inside, on the cupola in the apse, you can see frescoes by Guglielmo Borremans (1737). There are also sculptures by Antonello Gagini and his pupils and a painted crucifix dating from the 15th century in the last chapel on the right. Facing the cathedral is the small former church of San Nicoló. The 17th-century Church of Sant'Oliva on piazza Ciullo has a fine statue of the saint by Antonello Gagini in the fourth chapel on the right. At the end of the square a road leads to the town's 14th-century castle with its distinctive round and square towers.

The Segesta Temple is one of the best examples of Doric architecture in Sicily.

North of the town is the sanctuary of Madonna dei Miracoli, the town's patron saint, whose feast day is around June 20.

To reach **Castellammare del Golfo** (see p. 92), turn right 36 mi/58 km outside Palermo; you can thus also follow the second itinerary to Trápani on the road that leads past the thermal baths of Segestane (sulphurous waters).

SEGESTA***

To reach the Segesta ruins, turn right 39.7 mi/64 km from Palermo onto a small road and follow it for 1.8 mi/3 km. An alternative is to take the train from Palermo that stops at Segesta Tempio station, less than 1 mi/1.5 km from the site. The road ends in a parking lot (with a refreshment stand) at the foot of the hill where the temple is located. In the summer, a minibus leaves every 10-15 minutes up the short road (0.6 mi/1 km) that leads to the ancient theatre on Monte Bárbaro. Cars are not allowed.

Greek Egesta, capital of the Elymians, was once located on the plateau facing the hill where the temple still stands. The city played an important role in the history of both Greek Sicily and Greece, but today it retains only the temple and theatre. Legend has it that Acestes, king of Érice, founded Egesta to create a home for refugees from Troy. Egesta's history was marked by perpetual conflict with its southern neighbour, Selinunte. The city allied with Athens in 453 BC but was forever victim of struggles between Carthaginians and Greeks. In 307 BC the town was massacred by Agathocles, tyrant of Syracuse. Some had their limbs dislocated on the wheel, others were hurled afar by catapults. One of Agathocles' tortures was similar to that known as the Bull of Phalaris (another Sicilian tyrant), whereby a bronze bed was made in the shape of a human body with a grill in it to which victims were strapped. The whole was set alight and the victims were burned alive. Those who were not massacred were deported as slaves.

Although the town lost everything — even its name — it was rebuilt gradually, and was later called Dikaeopolis. But during the first Punic War in 260 BC the Carthaginians attacked it again. Liberated by the Romans, it enjoyed a short period of peace, only to be plundered later by Verres and finally destroyed by Vandals and Saracens.

Temple***

The fact that the temple remains intact is nothing short of miraculous. Standing on a hill covered in flowers and aloes it is the strangely peaceful survivor of an ancient city that suffered countless sackings, conflicts and crimes. Of all Sicily's antique edifices, this solitary temple in its grandiose desert setting is probably the one that most inspires an impression of divinity. It is most beautiful in the morning light.

The estimated date of its construction is 425 BC. The temple is peripteral, Doric in style, with 36 columns — 6 on the façades and 14 on the sides. Its peculiarity lies in the fact that it was never completed — only the entablature, pediments and colonnades were built; there is no trace of paving or interior work. In addition, the columns have been left unfluted; at their bases you can still see the bosses used to facilitate transport. Some archaeologists believe it was never intended as a closed structure but as an 'empty shrine' around a sacrificial altar. Whatever the case may be, the Segesta temple is one of the most perfect examples of the Doric order, 'a testimony to reason, order and intelligence in the middle of the chaos, indifference and anarchy of nature' (B. Berenson, *Travels in Italy*). Notice the slight bulging in the columns to correct optical illusion — an example of architectural refinement that can also be seen in the Parthenon in Athens.

Theatre*

In the 3rd century BC, when Segesta had been delivered from the Carthaginians and was enjoying a new period of prosperity, the theatre was built into the rock on the summit of Monte Bárbaro near the ancient city. Its outstanding position commands a view of the mountains and plain down to Golfo di Castellammare. The 20 rows of seats (207 ft/63 m diameter) are divided by steps into seven sections.

At the foot of Monte Bárbaro, near a little village called Mango, a rectangular sanctuary has been discovered along with the ruins of two Doric temples dating from the 6th and 5th centuries BC.

Calatafimi

Continuing along the N113 you pass Calatafimi (41 mi/66 km south-west of Palermo), an agricultural town with Arab origins (Kalat-al-Fimi) where Garibaldi gained one of his first victories over the Bourbon troops (May 15, 1860).

Telephone area code: 0924.

Accommodation

▲ **Mille Pine**, piazza Vivona 2, ☎ 51 260. *Closed Tues and through Nov and Dec.* 10 rooms. Modest but extremely pleasant establishment in the middle of a pine wood. Restaurant with good local cooking.

Trápani (62 mi/100 km south-west of Palermo)
You will cross through mountains onto the Trápani plain. To the right is a view of mount Érice (see p. 92 for a description of the town). Trápani is described on p. 94.

THE CASTELLAMMARE DEL GOLFO ROUTE: THE CAPE ROAD

Leave Palermo on the A29 highway, then follow the smaller coast road.

Sferracavallo
The road runs along the coast past this little fishing village/seaside resort, with its pretty houses and gardens.

Isola delle Fémmine
This is another fishing village, opposite an islet of the same name surmounted by an ancient fort. The beach is about 3.7 mi/6 km long.

Carini
Off to the left a small road leads inland for 1.8 mi/3 km to a hillside where Carini, a town of 16,000 inhabitants, commands a good view of the coastal plain and gulf. The medieval castle contains a statue of the Madonna by Mancino (1500) in the ground-floor chapel. There are a number of fine Baroque churches in the town, all with noteworthy paintings and stuccoes. You can also visit limestone caves in the vicinity, in some of which (the Maccagnone cave for example) Palaeolithic artifacts have been discovered.

Punta Raisi
The road passes near the airport.

Terrasini
This is a little resort 9.3 mi/15 km south-west of Carini with a number of museums: Museo Civico, via Calarossa 4, *(open Tues-Sat 9am-1pm, 4-7pm);* a museum of painted Sicilian carts, Museo del Carretto Siciliano, via Roma 38, *(open Mon-Sat 9am-12:30pm, Sun 10am-noon; July and Aug also open 7-11pm);* Antiquarium, piazza Kennedy *(open Sun 10am-noon and in July and Aug 7-11pm);* and a botanical exhibition of wonderful plants *(to see them ask at the local library,* ☎ *868 2467).* There is also a zoo in contrada Piano.

To also follow the first Palermo-Trápani itinerary, after driving 26.7 mi/43 km south-west of Palermo, take the branch of the N113 that leads to Partinico (3.7 mi/6 km) and the road from Palermo to Trápani through Segesta.

Álcamo Marina (36.6 mi/59 km): see p. 89.

Castellammare del Golfo (40 mi/65 km)

This small town (population 14,000) is named after the bay and is a port on the former site of the Segesta harbour. There are no noteworthy monuments in the town apart from an Aragonese castle overlooking the sea that dates from the 14th and 15th centuries. You have a magnificent **view*** as you leave the town on the road to San Vito lo Capo. A festival of Sicilian songs is held in August.

The Segestane thermal baths (4.9 mi/8 km to the south) are open from May to November. Another 4.9 mi/8 km further on are Segesta's ancient **temple** and **theatre** (see p. 90).

> **Accommodation**
>
> ▲▲ **Al Madarig**, in village, ☎ 33 533. 22 rooms. Modern, well decorated hotel facing the port. Bar and restaurant.

Scopello* (5.5 mi/9 km on the road to San Vito lo Capo)

This is a little fishing village located below a *tonnara* (tuna fishery). Its *faraglioni* (rocky islets) rise picturesquely out of clear water, making it one of the most pleasant places in the environs of Palermo. Several ambitious building projects have been planned, and the region has already set aside one nature reserve, the nearby Riserva Naturale dello Zingaro.

Swimming is good below the village, in Tonnara di Scopello, where the seascape is impressively dominated by two circular towers in the middle of the rocks.

▬ ÉRICE**: SENTINEL OF THE WEST

On leaving Valderice 18.6 mi/30 km west of Castellammare, a short detour to the small town of Érice would be well worth your while before visiting Trápani. Leave the N187 and take the steep road into the town (4.5 mi/7.4 km).

The origins of the ancient town of Eryx (named after Eros) are steeped in myth. Perched on an enormous rock that seems to rise from the sea and dominating the western part of the island, Eryx was best known for its temple to Aphrodite, or Venus Erycina, Goddess of Fertility. Built by the Elymnian cult, who claimed to be descended from both Greeks and Trojans, the temple was mentioned as a landmark in Homer's *Aeneid*. Later, Virgil wrote that Aeneas, the Trojan leader, who was thought to be Aphrodite's son, erected the temple. Daedelus is said to have presented Aphrodite with the gift of a golden honeycomb when he visited Eryx; in another legend, Eryx — also son of Aphrodite — was Hercules's host when he visited Sicily.

Érice's fate was linked with that of Carthage until the 5th century BC, when it came under Greek rule. During the first Punic War, the Carthaginians removed many of its inhabitants to Drepanon (present-day Trápani). Although nothing remains from ancient times, there are ruins from the Middle Ages, when the city was taken by Count Roger. The Norman renamed it Monte San Giuliano, inspired by a dream in which he saw St Julian chasing out the Saracens with a pack of greyhounds. In 1934 Mussolini renamed it Érice.

Érice is one of the last vestiges of medieval Sicily — now an isolated mountain citadel of 27,000 inhabitants. Surrounded by a pine forest and protected from the world by ramparts, the town is often swathed in mist because of its altitude and is usually cool, with a temperature several degrees lower than that of Trápani. Érice may well be Sicily's most picturesque city, lost as it often is in banks of clouds, as if it belonged to another world. A strange silence reigns over its maze of sleepy alleys. The streets are narrow and pebbled, the houses old with austere façades that hide the abundant private flower gardens within.

Chiesa Matrica*

The road to Érice ends on piazza Grammatico near the Porta Trápani —
the best place to leave your car. Immediately on the left via Vito Carvnin
brings you to Chiesa Matrica (Mother of God Church). Its solid detached
campanile with twin windows was probably intended as a lookout tower
during the reign of Ferdinand of Aragon. Stones from ancient temples
were used to build the church façade (1314), where the porch
with pointed arches shelters a magnificent Gothic portal. The interior
was rebuilt in 1865 in imitation Gothic style with heavily worked
ornamentation on the vaults. In the choir you can see a marble
altarpiece by Giuliano Mancino (1533).

Museo di Érice and San Giovanni

Back at Porta Trápani, via Vittoria Emanuele leads to piazza Umberto
and the Museo di Érice *(open Mon-Fri 9am-2pm, 3-5pm; Sat, Sun
and holidays open only in the morning)*. Among the displays is *The
Annunciation**, a group of marble figures by Antonello Gagini (1525)
and a head of Aphrodite dating from the 4th century BC.

From here follow via Guarrasi to via San Cataldo, which leads to the
Church of San Giovanni Battista with its 12th-century portal. There are
several statues inside, including St John the Evangelist and St John the
Baptist by Antonello Gagini.

Villa Balio and Castello di Vénere

Turn right outside the church and continue until you reach the gardens
of Villa Balio on the site of the ancient acropolis. Castello Pepoli, dating
from the Middle Ages, has square towers and a massive keep that was
entirely rebuilt in the 19th century. Castello di Vénere, with its twin
windows, was built in the 12th and 13th centuries partly with ancient
stones from the temple of Venus Erycina. The remains of the temple
are inside. Venus Erycina was believed to give protection to sailors who
showered her with gifts of jewels, coins and jars of wine on their return
to land; a great number of broken amphorae have been found during
excavations here.

From the castle terrace you have a stupendous **view*** of Trápani, the
western coast and the Égadi Islands. On a clear day you can even see
Cape Bon in Tunisia.

Beside the Balio gardens is the 18th-century church of San Giuliano with
its pink onion-shaped tower rising above the rooftops. Walking along via
Nunzio Nasi, viale del Cappuccini and viale delle Pinete, you will have a
splendid **view**** and see the rest of the ancient fortifications. The lower
part of these consists of 5th-century BC megalithic blocks that the
Romans are said to have taken from ancient sites. The upper parts of the
three gateways (Spada, Carmine and Trápani) were added by the Normans.
Telephone area code: 0923.

Accommodation

▲▲ **Elimo,** via Vittorio Emanuele 75, ☎ 869 377. 21 rooms. Agreeable decor and restaurant. Centrally located.

▲▲ **Ermione,** via Pineta Comunale 43, ☎ 869 138. 48 rooms.
Located outside the town, with a garden, swimming pool and
beautiful view. The restaurant is unexceptional.

▲▲ **Moderno,** via Vittorio Emanuele 63, ☎ 869 300. 39 rooms. In
the old town with a terrace and good restaurant.

▲ **Edelweiss,** cortile Padre Vincenzo, ☎ 869 158. 15 rooms.
Modest but pleasant and quiet.

Youth hostel, viale delle Pinete, ☎ 869 144.

Festivals

The procession of Misteri on **Good Friday.** Numerous artistic and cultural
events throughout the summer, particularly in July and August.

Food

LL Ciclope, viale Nunzio Nasi. *Closed Tues except during the holiday season.* At the very end of the town facing the sea. Lovely view. Fish and seafood.

LL Erice, via Vittorio Emanuele, near piazzo Umberto. Very central and frequented by tourists.

LL Taverna di Re Aceste, viale Conte Pepoli. *Closed Wed and throughout Nov.* Marine setting. Good local dishes. Trápani wines.

L Ulisse, via Chiaramonte. Pizzeria where you can eat outside in a pleasant garden.

Pastry

Grammatico, via Vittorio Emanuele (second store on via Guarnotti). Renowned throughout the region; crowds jostle at the door to try their unforgettable almond paste and cakes. Their recipes are age-old, handed down through generations.

Useful address

Tourist information, viale Conte Pepoli II, ☎ 869 388. *Open daily in summer 8:30am-2pm, 4:30-7pm; closed Sun in winter.*

▬ TRÁPANI*: GATEWAY TO THE WEST

From Érice to Trápani: 9.3 mi/15 km on the scenic route or 11 mi/18 km on the Valdérice road.

Trápani, formerly Drepanon, the ancient port for Eryx (Érice), derives its name from its sickle-shaped promontory. It started to flourish as a city in 260 BC when the Carthaginians sent part of their population here from Eryx. But the Romans took it in 241 BC, and under Roman rule its importance was eclipsed by ancient Lilybaeum (present day Marsala). In turn, Vandals, Byzantines and Saracens sacked the port and not until the 13th-century did the town flourish again, as a port between Europe and Tunis. In 1282 Peter of Aragon stopped here on his return from North Africa to accept the crown after the Sicilian Vespers (see p. 74). Charles V later enlarged the ramparts for protection against pirates and

---

Trápani's procession of Misteri

When the Spanish occupied Sicily they brought with them the tradition of enacting scenes from the Passion of Christ, whereby actors identified with different people from the story to create living tableaux. At the beginning of the 16th century the actors were replaced by carvings. The first groups of sculptures were carved in 1603 by the Brotherhood of the Blood of Christ, which then joined with the Brotherhood of St Michael and later with various guilds of town craftsmen to be able to meet the expense and ensure the maintenance of the figures. The sculptures are astonishingly expressive, with realistic bodies and tortured faces hiding neither the cruelty of the executioners nor the sadism of some of the soldiers.

The scenes showing the arrest, scourging and trial of Christ are extremely sensual and violent. The dying Christ is portrayed with eyes rolled upwards while around him are faces distorted with hate. Fists are raised above his swollen, bleeding flesh while spears, swords and whips are poised, itching to be let loose again.

The procession of Misteri through the old town begins in the late afternoon on Good Friday and lasts all night accompanied by penitents and communicants. The various groups of sculptures are placed on flowery bases and carried by different teams employed for the occasion by local guilds.

These craftsmen still organize the event according to an ancient tradition in which art, folklore and faith are inextricably linked. The *scippi* come out in force to mingle with the crowd and are far more interested in tourist handbags and wallets than in the weeping Virgin.

Church of the Annunziata in Trápani.

used Trápani as his headquarters in the Tunisian campaign. Today the town has 72,000 inhabitants and functions as a busy port, a trading partner with nearby North Africa and a commercial centre that owes its prosperity largely to salt marshes, vineyards and tuna fisheries.
Count on about three hours to visit the main sights.

Church of the Annunziata*

Open daily 7am-noon, 5-7pm.

The road from Palermo as you enter Trápani becomes via Pepoli while the Érice road, which runs parallel, becomes via Fardella. Via Pepoli is bordered by a garden in the middle of which is the town's main monument, Church of the Annunziata, next door to Museo Nazionale Pepoli.

The first church on the site of the Annunziata was built between 1315 and 1332 but was entirely transformed in 1760. All that remains of the original building are the Gothic portal and a beautiful rose window (restored) on the façade, together with the portal on the left-hand side. The Baroque campanile with its pyramidal roof was added in 1650.

As you enter the Church on the left-hand side you come into a votive chapel. From here you have access to a richly decorated chapel dedicated to the Virgin, with a marble Renaissance arch carved by Antonello Gagini. A bronze gate (1591) leads to the choir, which houses the well-known *Madonna di Trápani*. A wooden door under the organ leads into the basilica with its wide nave, which was restored in the 18th century. Don't miss the 14th-century Cappella dei Pescatori on the right, a square chapel with a Gothic arch, octagonal cupola and 16th-century frescoes of scenes from Genesis. To the left of the choir is the 16th-century Cappella dei Marinai with a cupola, a semi-dome vaulting in the apse and an arched niche with shell-shaped motifs.

Museo Nazionale Pepoli★★
Open Tues-Sat 9am-1:30pm, Sun 9am-12:30pm, Tues Thurs and Sat also open 4-6:30pm. Closed Mon.

In a garden to the right of the church, a former Carmelite convent now houses one of Sicily's most interesting museums.

The portal and balcony together with the Renaissance cloisters give an idea of the wealth of the convent. It was designed by Giovanni Amico. Judging by the splendid **staircase★★** of 17th-century polychrome marble the Carmelite community could hardly have vowed to lead a life of poverty; the splendour of the interior is more like Versailles than a monastic retreat, although the rules governing Sicilian convents were much less strict than they were elsewhere in Italy.

The works were mainly collected by Count Pepoli and blend well with the decor. This is a rare, well-presented and tastefully arranged museum. In addition to the many collections of sculpture, painting, ceramics and silver ware, are the 17th- and 18th-century coral objects by Trápani craftsmen as well as the display of crib figures.

Other important pieces are the *Pietà★* by Roberto di Oderisio, *St Francis of the Stigmata★* by Titian and the *Madonna* by the Master of Trápani. The finest sculpture is the *San Giacomo* by Antonello Gagini.

The old town
Trápani is a clean white town with a distinctly oriental flavour located gently along the sea front. A pleasant walk through the old town is one of the best ways to take in its charm. The *Pescheria* (fish market) is very lively in the morning, and in the afternoon the locals stroll along viale Regina Elena on the waterfront opposite the Égadi Islands and the salt-pans.

To reach the old town continue along via Pepoli, which ends at piazza Martiri d'Ungheria; then take via Fardella straight ahead to piazza Vittorio Emanuele, the town centre. Keep going straight and you pass Villa Comunale, then further along the police headquarters and post office on the left and the impressive Municipio on the right. Via Garibaldi leads to a crossroads where via Torrearsa to the left takes you past a palace with a Baroque façade (the former town hall dating from 1693) to the harbour. You should be able to find a place here to leave your car.

To the right of piazza Garibaldi and the jetty is via Giglio, where a little farther along on the left you will see the Church of Purgatorio, where the Misteri are displayed *(open Mon, Wed and Fri 9am-noon)*. It was built by Giovanni Amico, a local architect, and has an intricately decorated façade.

Via Giglio leads to corso Vittorio Emanuele and the recently restored **Cathedral of San Lorenzo★**. Built on the site of a former construction (1300) it has a portico and a Baroque façade dating from 1635. Inside, there are stucco decorations and a painted ceiling.

Corso Vittorio Emanuele continues past the **Church of Collegio★** (currently under restoration). It has a sumptuous Baroque façade dating from 1636 decorated with reliefs of masks, shells and sea nymphs. During the 18th century the interior was decorated with painted medallions framed by blue-and-white stucco-work.

On reaching via Torrearsa turn right, and a little farther on, to the left, you will come to piazza Saturno (with a tourist office) and its fountain, which dates from the end of the 16th century. The 14th-century church of Sant'Agostino on the square was very badly damaged in World War II and no longer serves as a church. However, it still retains the original façade, its fine Gothic portal and beautiful rose window. Continue behind the church past a modern building onto via San Pietro where shortly you come to the early 16th-century Church of Santa Maria del Gesù. The portal on the Gothic-Renaissance façade is Gothic, the one on the right-hand side Renaissance. Inside, the nave has retained its elegant wooden vault. In the transept on the right is a canopy by Antonello Gagini and a lovely polychrome **terracotta***, Madonna of the Angels *(Madonna degli Angeli)*, by Andrea della Robbia (1435-1528).

Access

Plane: Birgi airport, 9 mi/15 km south of Trápani, has flights to and from Palermo and Pantelleria.

Train: The Messina-Palermo and Agrigento-Marsala lines end here.

Bus: Segesta pullman buses leave Palermo for Trápani every hour.

Car: Trápani is 62 mi/100 km west of Palermo (65 mi/105 km on highway A29), 19.8 mi/32 km north of Marsala and 115 mi/185 km northwest of Agrigento.

Telephone area code: 0923.

Accommodation

▲▲▲ **Astoria Park,** lungomare Dante Alighieri at San Cusumano, ☎ 62 400. 93 rooms. Very comfortable hotel overlooking the sea with private beach, garden, swimming pool and tennis courts.

▲▲ **Cavallino Bianco,** lungomare Dante Alighieri, ☎ 21 549. 64 rooms. By the sea.

▲▲ **Vittoria,** via Crispi 4, ☎ 27 244. 33 rooms, some with a sea view. Right in the middle of town.

Festivals

Musicale Trápanese in July; **Mattanza** (tuna massacre) organized as a show in the Ègadi Islands in May; and the **Misteri procession,** famous throughout Sicily, on Good Friday.

Food

LL **Dell'Arco da Enzo,** via Nina Bixio 110, near Campo Sportivo, ☎ 27 796. *Closed Fri.* Sea view. A good address for fish specialities.

LL **P e G,** via Spalti 1, near the Stazione. *Closed Sun and in Aug.* Good local specialities, a wide variety of fish dishes.

L **Trattoria del Porto,** via Staiti 45, in the harbour opposite the hydrofoil wharf. *Closed Wed.* Less chic than the above but very good.

Useful addresses

Bus station, piazza Malta, ☎ 21 641.

Post office, piazza Vittorio Veneto. *Open Mon-Sat 8:30am-1:30pm.*

Shipping lines: Siremar and **Tirrenia,** Molo Sanita 63, ☎ 40 515. For crossings to the islands, ☎ 22 467.

Tourist information, piazza Saturno, ☎ 29 000; via Sorba, ☎ 27 273 and 27 077. *Open Mon-Sat 8:30am-8:30pm; Sun 9am-noon, 4-7pm.* Provides information regarding sea links to the islands.

▬ *ENVIRONS OF TRÁPANI*

The most beautiful beaches in the whole of Sicily are at San Vito Lo Capo. To get there from Trápani, leave the town on via degli Archi and take the road that leads to the sea (2.4 mi/4 km) at San Giuliano lido. You pass Pizzolungo at the foot of Trápani hill and continue to Bonagia, where the road leaves the coast and goes inland through Custonaci. Turn left at Sperone (12.4 mi/20 km). The landscape is rugged and rocky with the

Palatimone mountains (1952 ft/595 m) on the left and the Speziale (2995 ft/913 m) on the right. At Castelluzo (18.6 mi/30 km) the road returns to the coast and brings you to San Vito Lo Capo.

San Vito Lo Capo (24 mi/39 km north-east of Trápani)
This is a fishing village and seaside resort of 3900 inhabitants dominated by Mount Monaco (1745 ft/532 m). Recommended sights are the 16th-century fortress and its interesting church, Chiesa Madre.

Around San Vito Lo Capo
Local excursions include a tour of Piana di Sopra, a trip to prehistoric caves and a climb up Monte Monaco, where you have a wonderful view of the two gulfs. You can also take the road to Torre dell'Impiso (6.2 mi/10 km), but it stops before Scopello so you cannot do a complete tour of the cape.
Telephone area code: 0923.

Tourist information, Pro Loco in the main street, opposite the church.

ÉGADI ISLANDS

The geological origins of the islands are similar to those of Sicily. The group includes three main islands: Favignana, Lévanzo and Maréttimo, and two much smaller ones, Fornica and Maraone. The 5000 or so inhabitants live mainly from fishing. The sea around the Égadis, thanks to the currents, abounds with fish, especially tuna. Neolithic paintings in Lévanzo's Grotta del Genovese include images of tuna, which indicate its importance as a food staple of this region. April to July is the period of the *Mattanza,* or tuna slaughter, once a sacred ritual, vestiges of which remain even today.

Favignana
Ancient Aegusa, 10.5 mi/17 km from Trápani, is the largest of the islands, with an area of 7.3 sq mi/19 sq km. The main town and capital of the islands is Favignana (4600 inhabitants), located on a bay on the northern coast, dominated by Monte Santa Caterina (990 ft/302 m). The house of the town's founder, Palermitan tuna entrepreneur Ignazio Florio, is an impressive building on the dock of the bay.

Favignana is experiencing enough of a tourist boom to warrant a road crossing the island, now almost complete. You can also tour the island by boat (enquire at the harbour or the tourist information office).
Telephone area code: 0923.

There are several boats a day to the islands; numerous hydrofoils from Trápani take 15 to 20 minutes for Favignana and Lévanzo and 30 minutes for Maréttimo. There are also other links between the islands themselves.

Ask for timetables at Molo Dogana in the harbour or, better still, at the tourist information office on piazza Saturno.

Accommodation

▲▲ **Albergo Égadi**, via Colombo 17, ☎ 921 232. 12 rooms.

▲▲ **Club Hotel L'Approdo di Ulisse**, 3 mi/5 km from the centre of town, ☎ 921 287. 72 rooms. Closed Nov-May.

Campgrounds
There are three: **Quattro Rose**, in Mulino a Vento, just under 1 mi/1 km from the port, ☎ 921 223; **Egad**, in Arena, ☎ 921 555 and **Miramar**, in Costecella, ☎ 921 330.

Food

The town has a wide choice of small restaurants. The best is:
LL Albergo Egadi, via Colombo 17. Tuna fish holds the place of honour.

Useful address

Tourist information, Pro Loco, piazza Matrice 7, ☎ 927 647. *Open only in summer.*

Lévanzo

With only one hotel, no fresh water, and a population of 2000, Lévanzo is the smallest and perhaps most peaceful of the Égadi islands (3.8 sq mi/10 sq km), Only 2.4 mi/4 km from Favignana and 9 mi/15 km from Trápani, the island has a forbiddingly rocky coastline. The main town and port, also called Lévanzo, is on the south coast (200 inhabitants).

The main attraction of the island is its wild appearance and more importantly, the prehistoric caves. Of these the best known is **Grotta del Genovese***, which has Palaeolithic and Neolithic incised drawings and cave paintings dating from 10,000 to 5000 BC. The earlier series consists of about 80 black figure drawings. To visit the cave, ask the custodian near the hydrofoil dock to guide you (☎ 924 104). Weather permitting, a boat trip will be possible, otherwise the 2.4 mi/4 km mule ride takes half an hour.

Telephone area code: 0923.

Accommodation

▲▲ **Pensione Paradiso**, via Calvario 133, ☎ 921 580. 8 modest rooms. Excellent food, mainly fish. Reasonably priced.

Food

LL Restaurant Nautilus, via Pietre Varate 2, ☎ 924 008. Local specialities, again mainly fish.

Maréttimo

Iera (meaning 'sacred'), as it was known to the ancient Greeks, is the most isolated, most mountainous and richest of the islands, 23.6 mi/38 km from Trápani and 20.5 mi/33 km from Marsala. It has about 800 inhabitants all in the village of Maréttimo, who live mainly from fishing and who seem to take little interest in the prospects of developing the tourist trade on their dramatically beautiful island. Reserved and independent, the local people appear as inaccessible as their dry mountainous wilderness. The area of the island is 4.6 sq mi/12 sq km, and the highest point, Monte Falcone, reaches 2250 ft/686 m. There are no cars, of course, but you can go on a number of pleasant walks. One leads north to Punta Troia, a castle on a headland. Take the footpath out of Maréttimo port, passing a small Arab-Byzantine church, now converted into a stable, before reaching a zone of mastic trees and wild plants. The path leads on until you eventually reach the 17th-century military fort near a beautiful beach. As with the other islands, if you are interested mainly in the rugged coastline and secluded inlets, a boat trip around the island cannot be beaten.

▬ *ISLAND OF PANTELLERIA*

Pantelleria, the largest island off Sicily (32 sq mi/83 sq km) is nearer Tunisia (43 mi/70 km) than Sicily (68 mi/110 km). Rocky and mountainous, the highest point, is Montagna Grande (2742 ft/836 m), a volcanic crater which last erupted at the end of the 19th century, giving a warning earthquake beforehand.

Pantelleria has been inhabited since the prehistoric era and has had an eventful history. It was colonized by the Phoenicians and became an important stopover point between Africa and Sicily for the Carthaginians. The Romans first took it in 255 BC and then again in 217 BC. When the Arabs arrived on the island in AD 700 they massacred the entire Christian population. Roger the Norman conquered it in 1123, and since then Pantelleria has been ruled by Sicily. It was devastated by pirates in 1551 and by the Turks two years later.

Fishing and farming provide the main livelihood for Pantelleria's 8000 inhabitants. **Pantelleria**, the main town, is located on the northwest coast and is dominated by the austere Castello Barabacane. From here you have a choice of excursions.

The nearest is to **Mursia**, 1.8 mi/3 km, on the road to Scauri, where you can see the ruins of a fortified neolithic village, and then continue to nearby **Sesi,** with its prehistoric tombs reminiscent of the *nuraghi* on Sardinia.

Slightly farther afield, this time on the other side of the island on the Kamma road, take the small road to the right after 3.1 m/5 km. This leads to Bagno dell'Acqua Calda, a crater lake with a diameter of about 1640 ft/500 m. It is fed by underground springs that rise at a temperature between 86º and 140º F/30º and 60º C and that have such a high soda content laundry can be done without soap.

Return to the coast road and continue for another 1.2 mi/2 km, where you will see Cala dei Cinque Denti, the fantastic rock formations eroded into 'teeth' by the sea. If you continue, the rough though picturesque road leads all the way around the island (21 mi/34 km).

Telephone area code: 0923.

Access

Plane: There are daily flights, 30 minutes from Trápani and 1 hour 20 minutes from Palermo.

Boat: There is a daily crossing in summer from Trápani (5 hours 30 minutes) and once a week from Marsala (4 hours).

Hydrofoil: There are crossings three times a week, only in summer; 3 hours from Trápani and 2 hours 20 minutes from Marsala.

Accommodation

▲▲▲ **Cossyra**, in Mursia 1.8 mi/3 km from Pantelleria, ☎ 91 154. 80 rooms. Garden, swimming pool, tennis courts and beach.

▲▲ **Punta Tre Pietre**, in Scauri, 6.8 mi/11 km from Pantelleria, ☎ 916 072. 60 rooms. Swimming pool.

▲ **Turistico Residenziale**, in Blue Marino, ☎ 911 054. 28 rooms. Garden. No restaurant.

Food

LL **Bartolo Miramare**, via Catania 4, ☎ 911 428. *Closed in winter.*

LL **La Lanterna**, in Campobella, 3 mi/5 km from Pantelleria, ☎ 911 634. Best to reserve. *Open only in the evening. Closed Mon.*

Useful addresses

Airport, 2.4 mi/4 km south-east of the town of Pantelleria, ☎ 911 172.

Alitalia, La Cossyra, via Borgo Italia, ☎ 911 078.

Tourist information, Pro Loco, via Sant Nicola, ☎ 911 838. *Open Mon-Sat 9am-12:30pm; in July and Aug also 5-8pm.*

TRÁPANI TO AGRIGENTO: AFRICAN SICILY

MOTYA: PHOENICIAN CITY IN THE VINES

Heading south toward Agrigento from Trápani on via Marsala you can take either the coast road on the right or the faster N115 (118 mi/190 km), which passes Paceco (after 3 mi/5 km) and Birgi airport.

The second road on the right after the airport joins the coast road at contrada Catenazzi where another track leads off for 0.6 mi/1 km into salt-pans, the departure point for the boat to San Pantaleo island and the Motya ruins. The boat leaves from the end of the jetty (ten-minute crossings daily, 9am-1pm and 3-6pm, unless the sea is too rough). It's advisable to reserve ahead of time (☎ 959598), and if you are a group of more than ten persons, special permission is required.

The ruins of ancient Motya (also known as Mozia) spread over the small vine-covered island of San Pantaleo (99 acres/40 hectare). The town was founded by the Phoenicians in the 8th century BC and became the centre of Carthaginian resistance in Sicily. It was destroyed in 397 BC by Dionysius I of Syracuse who wanted to avenge the destruction of Selinunte by Carthaginians several years earlier. Those who managed to survive the massacre founded Lilybaeum, present-day Marsala.

The Ephebus of Motya

The young man's head is turned slightly to the left. His face has been damaged by its long burial but shows classic traits of the first half of the 5th century: above his forehead there are three rows of curls, two more run down the back of his head and neck, leaving his ears exposed. On the top of his rough-hewn head the fragments of five bronze studs (only two remain, holes mark the position of the other three) testify that he once wore a crown or headdress denoting his rank in the city.

You are first struck and then attracted by his unusual, magnificent tunic that covers the entire length of his body. Its thick overlapping folds seem to rise and fall as if the young man were breathing. Its sinuous lines tightly mould each part of the body: chest, hips, legs, and (audaciously) his genitals, which, according to Christian artistic tradition, would normally have been covered. Seen from the back, the cloth's liquid vivacity expresses even more frankly the firmness and roundness of his buttocks. As though rising from a bath streaming with transparent droplets, the Ephebus of Motya is almost more naked than if he were portrayed with no clothes. His wide belt is held by two straps which cross at the back and were once knotted at the front with the aid of a metal buckle, long since lost, the ancient presence of which is indicated by two large holes.

D. Fernandez
The Gorgon's Raft
Le Radeau de la Gorgone, Grasset, 1988

Motya, the first and most important of Sicily's colonies, with ramparts 8202 ft/2500 m long, was then completely forgotten until a series of recent excavations supplied precious historical information. The main discovery, in 1979, a statue known as *The Youth in a Tight-Fitting Tunic*★★, is exhibited in the small museum.

You can walk all the way around the island by following the coastal track, to the left of the landing stage, which leads to the ruins of an ancient Greek house. This consists of a courtyard decorated with mosaics and surrounded by a portico of Doric columns. A little farther along you come to a small inland port connected to the sea by a canal. Motya once had two harbours and was linked to the mainland by a causeway, traces of which can still be seen.

___ **MARSALA**★ (20 mi/32 km south of Trápani)

Map coordinates refer to the map opposite.

You can reach Marsala by the coast road or by the N115.

Marsala was built on a promontory at Cape Boeo, one of three headlands that gave the island the name Trinacria. The town of 80,000 inhabitants, mainly known for its wine industry, is also a busy commercial and agricultural centre.

Marsala, ancient Lilybaeum, was founded by the Phoenicians in 397 BC when the inhabitants of nearby Motya were forced by Dionysus of Syracuse to flee from their island. Lilybaeum resisted successive attacks from Dionysius the Elder, in 368 BC, Pyrrhus in 267 BC and the Romans in the First Punic War. During this nine-year seige (250-241 BC), the town was blockaded by a fleet of 220 vessels; the inhabitants were secretly provided with fresh supplies by pirates, and it wasn't until after the Roman victory over Érice that Lilybaeum also fell to Rome. The Saracens rebuilt the city as their principal port in Sicily, naming it Marsa Ali (the port of God). Garibaldi landed here on May 11, 1860, with his Thousand volunteers (see p.32)

Arriving from Trápani you enter the town by the Corso Gramsci, A3. Leave your car somewhere nearby as soon as you can because the streets are very narrow and often one way; it is easier to get around on foot, beginning with the piazza della Repubblica, B2. Here you can see the 18th-century Palazzo Communale with its loggia and portico and the Baroque façade of the Duomo, the Cathedral of Marsala. This impressive Norman building has been transformed several times and is dedicated to St Thomas of Canterbury (Thomas à Becket). Inside, the three aisles all have massive columns, and the sculptures are by the Gagini family.

The wine war

The Portuguese held a world monopoly in the sweet wine trade in the 18th century, mainly because of the excellent reputation of their port. But then, in 1773, an Englishman named John Woodhouse visited Sicily and decided to export some of the local wine, calling it simply Marsala, after the nearest port. He sent several barrels to London, where they were enthusiastically received. In light of this success, he resolved to set up the first winery. Others followed suit, including the Whitaker, Martinez, Florio and Pellegrino families who, like Woodhouse, were to make their fortunes with dessert wine and by doing so give the town an international reputation. So great was the success of this 'liquid gold' that it became fashionable the world over. Since then annual production has reached almost three million hectolitres — about a third of the island's entire wine production. Today there are almost 300 wineries in the Marsala region. Some of them, with their arches and wooden frames, initiated an attractive new style of architecture. These *bagli* can sometimes be visited, such as Florio, at via Florio 1, ☎ 999 222, where you can see oak casks and precious vintages religiously stocked in the *enoteca* (wine cellar).

Leave the square on via X1 Maggio. This street is dominated by the tower and majolica spire of San Pietro, a former convent, now a library. You pass a 16th-century church with a well-preserved rose window and rich interior. At nº 15 there is the **Foundation of Modern Art** *(open Mon-Sat 10am-1pm, 5-7pm)* with a permanent exhibit of contemporary art.

Via XI Maggio leads through Porta Nuova into piazza della Vittoria. On the right are the Cavallotti gardens and belvedere. To the left of the gate, viale Sauro leads across a field to San Giovanni, B 1, a small church (still closed) with a grotto where the Sibyl of Cumae is said to have spoken her oracles.

Museo Archeologico di Marsala* (Baglio Anselmi) B 1

Open Mon-Sat 9am-2pm, Sun and holidays 9am-1pm.

The museum is superbly located in the former warehouse of a famous wine company. Here, among other interesting exhibits, is the only Punic ship (Liburnian) found to date.

Discovered during excavations off Isola Lunga in the Stagnone Islands, it is reckoned to have weighed no less than 120 tons and to have sunk during the First Punic War in 241 BC. The vessel has been meticulously restored and is preserved at a constant temperature in an enormous tent. A second room with magnificent arches displays archaeological finds from the area.

Roman Villa A1

Ask the custodian of the Museo Archeologico for the key.

Insula Romana, an archaeological zone, stretches from Porta Nuova to the sea. Excavations, begun in 1936, have brought to light a Roman villa from the 3rd century AD with fine mosaics depicting hunting scenes. The most interesting are of four wild animals chasing a stag. Another mosaic represents the four seasons displayed around the Trinacria, symbol of Sicily, while another shows a chained guard dog.

Museo degli Arazzi*** B2

Open daily 9am-1pm, 4-6pm.

Retrace your steps along via X1 Maggio and just before the cathedral take the street that runs beside it to San Cecilia Church, now used as a concert hall. Turn left onto via Garaffa to the small museum, an entirely restored palace, where a magnificent collection of 16th-century Flemish **tapestries*** is displayed. The eight panels of different sizes were a gift from Philip II of Spain and tell the story of the capture of Jerusalem. They are considered among the most beautiful in the world thanks both to the artistry of the work itself and to the fact that they have been exceptionally well preserved. For centuries they have been exhibited only during grand ceremonies in the cathedral, and today great care is taken to keep them intact; the lights are switched on only when visitors are in the room.

Telephone area code: 0923.

Accommodation

▲▲▲ **President,** via Nino Bixio 1, C3 (off the map), ☎ 999333. 72 rooms. A new hotel 1.2 mi/2 km from the centre of town. *Open all year.* Quiet. Swimming pool.

▲▲ **Cap 3000,** via Trápani 147, A3 (off the map), ☎ 989055. 50 rooms. On the Trápani road. Swimming pool.

▲▲ **Stella d'Italia,** via Ripasardi 7. Right in the centre of town, B2 a, near piazza della Repubblica. 50 rooms. Friendly management.

Festival

The traditional **Misteri procession** on Maundy Thursday, with origins dating back to the Middle Ages, is a popular event not to be missed. From 2pm onward the old town is transformed into an immense stage. People are chosen from among the local inhabitants to act the parts of St Veronica, Mary, Judas, Pontius Pilate and the robbers, and they identify dramatically with their characters for six hours. The crowd is not in the least passive either — people hurl insults, groan with suffering or prostrate themselves — reliving the Passion of Christ with great intensity. Scenes from the Way of the Cross are not acted in chronological order but take place all over town in separate groups like detached tableaux of a vast polyptych, accompanied all the while by dirges played by brass bands.

Food

LL **Trattoria Capo Lilibeo,** via Boeo 40, A1. *Closed Thurs.* A new restaurant facing the sea at the end of viale Vittorio Veneto.

LL **Zio Ciccio,** lungomare Mediterraneo 211, C3 (off the map), ☎ 981962. *Closed Mon except in season.* Good sea view. Fish specialities. Recommended.

L **Kalos,** piazza della Vittoria, B1-2 s, ☎ 958465. *Closed Fri.* A large dining room behind a bar-café-caterer's with a pizza oven at the back. Very fine choice of antipasti. A good address for a simple meal. In summer, terrace dining on the lively square.

L Trattoria Garibaldi, piazza Addolarata, B2 r, ☎ 953 066. *Closed Mon.*

Useful addresses

Birgi airport, 9.3 mi/15 km north of Marsala. Flights to and from Palermo and Pantelleria.

Boats for the islands, ☎ 959 060.

Hydrofoils *(aliscafo),* daily to and from Trápani and Pantelleria, ☎ 22467.

Post office, via Garibaldi, opposite the Duomo, B2.

Tourist information, Pro Loco, in the Municipio, via Garibaldi 45, B2, ☎ 714 097. *Open Mon-Sat 8am-8pm, Sun 9am-noon.*

MAZARA DEL VALLO*: LAST OF THE NORMAN CONQUESTS

Map coordinates refer to the map p. 106.

Originally Phoenician, Mazara del Vallo (33.5 mi/54 km south of Trápani) is a pleasant town of 46,000 inhabitants on the mouth of the Mazaro river. Its busy harbour is one of the most important centres for Italy's fishing industry.

Mazara, an ancient colony of Selinunte, was destroyed by the Carthaginians in 409 BC. The Romans then took over, but it was under the Saracens, who captured it in 827, that the town really prospered, even meriting its own emir. El Idrissi, the Arab geographer who visited Mazara in 1154, described it as 'a splendid, superb town'. It was the last town to be conquered by Count Roger, who settled here in 1073 and held the first Norman parliament in Sicily here in 1097.

You enter the town on via Marsala which runs into via Roma, A2. At the end of this street, turn left into via Vittorio Veneto and then right onto corso Umberto, which leads to piazza Mokarta, where you can see the ruins of Count Roger's castle.

From here a street leads off to the right, past a public garden, to the Cathedral, C2. This was first founded in the 11th century but was entirely rebuilt in 1654. Flanking the façade is a massive Baroque campanile. The interior houses a number of interesting works of art: a large marble portal by Bartolommeo Berrettaro (1525) in the aisle on the right, three sarcophagi with relief decorations in the right transept, a **Transfiguration***, a group of six statues by Antonello Gagini (1537) behind the choir, stucco-work by Ferraro, a coloured marble figure of Christ by Ignazio Marabitti and finally, a painted wooden cross in the left transept.

To the left of the cathedral you come to piazza della Repubblica with a statue of the town's patron saint, San Vito, by Marabitti (1771). On the left is an elegant **façade*** with portico and loggia, part of a former seminary built in 1710. Opposite are two palaces: Municipio and Vescovile.

Go through the porch behind the cathedral to see its original three apses. The church on the left with a Baroque façade is that of Santa Catarina. It dates originally from 1318 and has 17th-century alterations. There's a statue of the saint by Antonello Gagini (1524) inside.

Back on piazza della Repubblica take via XX Settembre to the left, which leads to piazza Plebiscito, C1, facing two former 16th-century churches with Arab-style cupolas. On the left are the ruins of the Church of Sant'Ignazio with a Baroque façade, and, a little farther on, a richly decorated portal with caryatids dating from 1675 opens into a former Jesuit college with a fine interior courtyard surrounded by a portico with loggia. This is now the **Museo Civico.** The collection includes artifacts from the region, mainly Roman amphorae, pottery and coins.

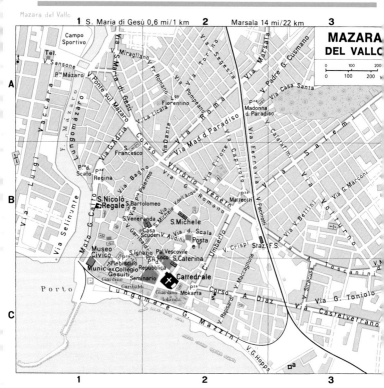

Walk around the palace to lungomare Mazzini, which is joined on the right by molo Caito, B1. This leads to the 12th-century Norman church of San Nicoló Regale, of which only the four walls are original.

If you have time to spare you could finish your visit with a stroll through the centre of town, where every street has an old, probably abandoned, church. Mazara was once home to a great number of convents, as it was from here that pilgrims set sail for the Holy Land.

On piazza San Veneranda, B2, you can see the church of the same name which dates from 1714 and has an elegant wrought-iron balcony, above which rise twin towers. Not far away is another church, San Michele, dating from 1637. Inside are 20 statues of the Serpota school, a 1540 statue of St Michael and the remains of majolica tiling. It has a convent which has attractive windows with balconies and a 1771 campanile.
Telephone area code: 0923.

Accommodation

▲▲ **Hopps**, via Hopps 29, on the lungomare, C3 a, ☎ 946 133. 240 rooms. Garden, swimming pool and private beach.
▲▲ **Mediterraneo**, via Valeria 46, C2, ☎ 932 688. 17 rooms. Located near the railway station; bar and restaurant.

Festival

San Vito fair on the last Sunday in August with a procession of historical costumes.

Food

LLL La Bettola, corso Diaz 20, C2 s. *Closed Mon except in summer.* A pleasant inn with good food.

LL Trattoria da Nicola, via E. Sansone 21, A1 t, ☎ 94270. *Closed Mon.*
LL Trattoria del Pescatore, via Castelvetrano 191, C3 (off map), ☎ 947580. *Closed Mon.* Good food.
L Trattoria Pizzeria Lo Scoiattolo, in Garibaldi gardens, C1. Good simple fare in pleasant surroundings.

Useful addresses

Post office, via Audino, B2 e.

Tourist information, Pro Loco, piazza della Repubblica, C2 d, ☎ 941727. *Open Mon-Sat 8am-8pm, Sun 9am-noon.*

Mazara del Vallo to Castelvetrano

Leave Mazara on via Castelvetrano, C3. After 41 mi/66 km (from Trápani) turn right and follow the road for 0.8 mi/1.3 km to Campobello di Mazara. As you enter the town a rough road on the right leads to the **Rocche di Cusa** quarries (1.8 mi/3 km), from which stones were taken to build the temples at Selinunte. It is possible to reach Selinunte directly from Campobello on a 9.3 mi/15 km road although it is more pleasant to return to the N115, which goes through Castelvetrano.

CASTELVETRANO

A convenient stopover for visiting Selinunte, Castelvetrano (50 mi/74 km south-east of Trápani) is an industrial, commercial centre of 31,600 inhabitants.

Via Campobello followed by via Garibaldi lead to piazza Garibaldi and the **Chiesa Madre** (16th century) with a richly decorated front porch. Inside there are stuccoes by Ferraro and Serpotta, and a statue of the Madonna from the Gagini school in the left-hand apse. Outside the church on the left is an elegant fountain (1615) in front of the campanile. The Municipio stands on the same square (entrance piazza Umberto 4) with a small museum *(open only Thurs 9am-1pm)* displaying sculptures by, among others, Laurana and Pietro de Bonitate.

To the right of Chiesa Madre via Bonsignore leads to the Church of San Domenico (1470), which has been altered several times. The interior, still not open at the time of writing, is richly decorated with stuccoes. On the building's right, in piazza Regina Margherita, is the Church of **San Giovanni,** rebuilt in the Baroque period and containing several 17th-century pantings and a statue of *St John the Baptist** by Antonello Gagini (1522).

Of greater interest still is the Church of **Santissima Trinità di Delia*,** 2 mi/3.5 km west of the centre of town *(closed noon-3pm).* Like the Martorana in Palermo, its style is Arab-Byzantine, with a Greek cross plan and three apses. Its square base is crowned by an Arab cupola supported by four columns. Not far from the caretaker's house you have a good view of Lake Trinità.

Accommodation

▲▲ **Selinus,** via Bonsignore 22, ☎ 41104. 48 rooms.
▲▲ **Zeus,** via Vittorio Veneto 6, ☎ 81200. 31 rooms.

Festival

In the morning on **Easter Sunday,** the 'Aurora' service is held to celebrate the meeting of Christ risen from the dead and the Virgin.

Food

L San Giuseppe, via Marconi 42. *Closed Sat.* Simple restaurant.

Useful address

Tourist information, corso Emanuele 102, ☎ 41015. *Open Mon-Sat 8am-8pm.*

Environs of Castelvetrano

Gibellina Nuova (12.4 mi/20 km north-east of Castelvetrano on the N118 or highway A29). During the night of January 15, 1968, the whole of the Belice river valley was damaged by an earthquake, the most violent recorded since that in 1908, which destroyed Messina. In a matter of minutes the *terremoto* claimed 1000 victims and left nearly 10,000 people homeless. Among the towns most affected was Santa Margherita di Bélice, where the Chiesa Matrice and Palazzo Filangieri (made famous in *The Leopard*) were reduced to ruins. In Gibellina, a large neighbouring market town that was also entirely destroyed, the mayor, Ludovico Corrao, decided to fight against slow administration, fatalism and the Mafia to get something done about his town. It was rebuilt in a resolutely modern style, 12.4 mi/20 km west of the old site. The mayor's 20-year struggle resulted in rebuilding Gibellina Nuova as a city of contemporary art — no small achievement, given that Sicily in general seems closed to all expression of modern art. The best architects produced all manner of modern constructions, among them a spiral maze, a spherical church, a winged spire, a clock tower, and a metallic star which acts as a sort of monumental gateway to the town. There are no shops, no cafés and no hospital, but there is a house shaped like a snail and two museums, one of contemporary art, the other of anthropology and ethnography.

Old Gibellina, now called Ruderi di Gibellina, is also fascinating. The N188 leads you there through 12.4 mi/20 km of beautiful countryside. The famous Italian decorator, Alberto Burri, conceived of converting the ruins into an immense funerary monument. He covered acres of ruins with a large white strip of concrete (about a metre thick) respecting the former layout of the streets so that each block of houses now looks like a tomb. Corrao organizes a festival every year in this extraordinary environment.

Salemi, 4.3 mi/7 km west of Gibellina Nuova on the N118, is an agricultural centre with a castle that was built for Frederick II and now houses a **Museum of the Risorgimento** *(generally open in the morning)*. It was here, on May 14, 1860, that Garibaldi proclaimed himself dictator of Sicily in the name of King Victor-Emmanuel II.

▬▬ *SELINUNTE* ★★★

Leave the town of Castelvetrano on via Selinunte that leads to the N115. After 5.2 mi/8.4 km, the N115 leads left toward Agrigento and the N115d takes you south 3 mi/5 km to Marinella and the archaeological zone of Selinunte.

Marinella di Selinunte is a small seaside resort that has grown around a modest fishing village. Its good sandy beach, and proximity to the famous ruins have contributed to its recent tourist development.

Selinunte derives its name from a plant known in Greek as *selinon,* a sort of wild parsley or celery, which was chosen as the city's emblem and stamped on ancient coins. The city was founded in 628 BC by inhabitants of Megara Hyblaea (Syracuse) who were looking for a peaceful site to set up a colony. Selinunte prospered rapidly, and its citizens hoped to overcome the Elymians, mainly in Segesta, in order to gain new territorial possessions stretching as far as the Tyrrhenian Sea. These pretensions led to intervention by both the Carthaginians and the Athenians. In 409 BC Hannibal laid seige to the town. It resisted heroically for the first nine days but was then sacked and taken with exceptional cruelty; 16,000 people died and an estimated 5000 were taken prisoner. The temples were pillaged and knocked down and the city left in a state of ruin. Hermocrates, an exile from Syracuse, rebuilt some of the walls in a vain attempt to revive the town. But in 250 BC during the First Punic War, the Carthaginians took Selinunte once again and destroyed it after moving the inhabitants to Lilybaeum (Marsala). Reduced to a miserable village, the once flourishing city was overcome by marshes and decimated by malaria. An earthquake knocked down the remaining temples and the site fell into oblivion.

Selinunte consists of three distinct archaeological zones: the Marinella plateau, the Acropolis and the Sanctuary of Demeter Malophorus, west of the site of the ancient city of Selinus. Certainly one of the most moving sights in Sicily, Selinunte recalls Greece by the enormity of its ruins, the grandeur of the site and the beauty of the landcape. You need at least half a day to visit all three archaeological sites, but if you have less time it is possible to see the Marinella plateau and the Acropolis in two hours.

Marinella plateau***

On arrival in Marinella di Selinunte, a road to the right leads off to the zone known as the Eastern group of temples. Inside the enclosure you will find a vast parking lot and a tourist bureau. This 'sacred suburb' consists of three temples parallel to the entrance of the archaeological zone and separated by the road. Selinunte's temples are referred to by letters of the alphabet; Temples E and F are on the left-hand side of the road, Temple G is on the right.

Temple E* can immediately be distinguished by its raised columns. It was built in pure Doric style in the 5th century BC and was probably dedicated to Hera (Juno). It measures 223 × 82 ft/68 × 25 m, and its 38 columns (6 on the façades and 15 on the sides) still support part of the entablature. Four metopes from the temple are now in the Palermo museum. Heading back toward the road you will see the remains of Temple F on the left.

Temple F, the smallest and most damaged of the three, built in the Archaic style, probably dates from 560-540 BC. It was a peripteral temple of 203 × 78 ft/62 × 24 m, surrounded by 36 columns (6 on the ends and 14 on the sides) measuring more than 29.5 ft/9 m.

Temple G on the other side of the road is a gigantic mass of stones in the middle of which rises a restored column. Among the largest in Antiquity it was very likely dedicated to Apollo. Building began around 250 BC and continued until AD 480 but was never completed.

The whole building, including the base, covered an area of more than 64,584 sq ft/6000 sq m. It rose 98 ft/30 m above the ground, thus dominating the other temples, with a length of 370 ft/113 m, a width of 177 ft/54 m and 46 surrounding columns (8 on the ends and 17 on the sides). The columns reached a height of 53.3 ft/16.27 m, and the average diameter on their bases was 11 ft/3.41 m. They supported capitals with a surface area of 172 sq ft/16 sq m. Each drum (blocks placed one on top of the other to form a column) weighs about 100 tons. Some of them are incomplete, left unfluted, indicating that building was most likely interrupted by the destruction of Selinunte. These great stone blocks came from Rocche di Cusa (p. 107), and remains of their coloured stucco covering have been found. The temple cella was preceded by a vast peristyle which was supported on the façade by four columns and on the sides by only two. You get an idea of the immensity of the place by climbing over the huge stone blocks into the middle of the ruins where each section of the building surprises by its sheer size.

The **'dei Templi' road**** winds around Temple E down toward the sea before climbing up again to the Acropolis on the western hill.

Acropolis**

Open daily 9am to one hour before sunset.

The Acropolis spreads over a steep plateau overlooking the sea. It lies between two rivers, the Selinus to the west and the Gorgo di Cottone to the east, the mouths of which once formed the town's two ports, now silted up. The Acropolis (1476 × 1148 ft/450 × 350 m) was surrounded by a walled enclosure 9.8 ft/3 m thick in places, made of

Temple E in Selinunte, built in the 5th century BC. ▶

square blocks and much smaller stones. Part of it can still be seen to the right of the entrance.

Follow the main alley through the excavations toward the only remaining colonnade and on the right you will see **Temple O**, of which only the base and some fluted drums have survived. In structure it is identical to that of **Temple A** situated just beyond. These two buildings, contempories of **Temple E**, are the most recent on the Acropolis and were built in the Classical style between 490 and 480 BC, when the Doric order was at its height. They measure 131 × 52 ft/40 × 16 m and their 36 columns (6 on the ends and 14 on the sides) are 20 ft/6.23 m tall.

After the intersection on the right, on the highest point of the Acropolis, you come to **Temple C**, the oldest and largest of this group of temples. It was built in the middle of the 6th century BC and dedicated to Demeter. It measured 210 × 79 ft/64 × 24 m and included a cella, a pronaos without columns and a sanctuary at the back. There were 17 columns on the sides and 6 on the ends with a base diameter of 6.3 ft/1.94 m. Twelve columns complete with capitals and two others, both incomplete, were raised in 1925. Three metopes from the temple are exhibited in the Palermo museum. The entire cornice was covered with polychrome terra cotta, traces of which can still be seen. The terrace on the right ended with a Doric portico which surmounted stepped ramparts. Between the portico and the temple there was once a large altar, 67 × 25.7 ft/20.40 × 7.85 m, of which parts of the base remain. Standing 32.8 ft/10 m to the right, in front of Temple C, is **Temple B**, a Hellenistic construction attributed to Empedocles. It measured 27.7 × 15 ft/8.45 × 4.60 m and was reached by nine steps.

Temple D, the northernmost of the Acropolis, was built between 570 and 554 BC comprising a pronaos, cella and sanctuary. There were 6 columns on the ends and 13 on the sides measuring 24.6 ft/7.51 m. The stylobate measured 183.7 × 78.7 ft/56 × 24 m. Around Temples C and D are the ruins of a 5th-century Byzantine village that made use of the ancient stones to build its houses.

Sanctuary of Demeter Malophorus

Most visitors to Selinunte forget all about the third archaeological zone 875 yds/800 m from the Acropolis; the sanctuary stands in the middle of wild sand dunes. To reach it take the road down toward the large beach opposite the one at Marinella and cross the bridge over the Modione, the former Selinus river, near the old western port. About 165 ft/50 m farther on turn right into the sacred enclosure, entering through 5th-century BC propylaea which once gave access to the sacred path lined with cypress trees. You pass a small Archaic altar and a large sacrificial one before reaching the temple of Malophorus, the Greek Demeter. Without columns or base, the sanctuary once contained a cult statue and served as a stop for funeral processions on their way to the necropolis of Manicalunga, where more than 12,000 6th- and 5th-century BC terra-cotta figurines (generally of the goddess) have been found. Return to the bridge and follow the Modione river to reach a beautiful sandy beach.

Telephone area code: 0924.

Accommodation

▲▲▲ **Garzia**, via Pigafetta, on the sea in Marinella, ☎ 46 024. Pleasant hotel with a patio and private beach. Lovely well-kept rooms. *Open all year.* Recommended.

▲▲▲ **Paradise Beach Hotel**, contrada Belice di Mare, beside the sea, 4 mi/6 km from Marinella. 250 very large, comfortable rooms. One of the best hotel-clubs in Sicily with fine architecture, organized activities, swimming pool and tennis courts. Telephone beforehand for reservation information: 46 166 or 46 333. (Eldorador Jet Tours can also give information.)

▲▲ **Alceste**, in Marinella, via Alceste 23, ☎ 46 184. 30 rooms. Terrace-solarium.

▲ **Giani**, in Marinella, via Pigafetta, ☎ 46 212.

Campgrounds

Lido Hawai and **Elios**, in Triscina. *Open only in summer.*

Il Maggiolino in Garraffo, ☎ 46 044. *Open all year.*

Food

A succession of restaurants on the seafront along via Marco Polo all serve a wide variety of fish.

LL Ristorante Pierrot, one of the oldest and by far the best. Good grilled fish and excellent *antipasti di mare.*

Useful address

Tourist information, in the archaeological zone of the Eastern group of temples.

SCIACCA

From Selinunte a road leads up 3.2 mi/5.2 km to join the N115 which crosses a fertile, undulating region past Menfi, 62 mi/100 km from Trápani and on to Sciacca.

Sciacca (74.5 mi/120 km south-east of Trápani), the world's oldest spa, is a lively town of 38,000 inhabitants, spread over terraced hills on a plateau sloping toward the sea. It was already famous in Roman times when it was called Ex Acqua and is now Sicily's most important thermal centre.

The N115 leads to piazza Belvedere (where there is a parking lot). Beyond Porta Palermo, via Gerardi leads to **Palazzo Steripinto***, an unusual Catalan-style construction dating from the 15th century. Its front, studded with pointed diamond-shaped stones, is adorned with crenels, three twin windows and an elegant Renaissance portal. A little farther along on the right is the 16th-century Porta San Salvatore. Just opposite, at the entrance to via Incisa, are two churches, **Santa Margherita** on the right and **Chiesa del Carmine** on the left.

Santa Margherita was built for Eleonora of Aragon in the 14th century, then altered in the 16th. The lovely Gothic portal on the façade dates from the original building, while the left **façade*** of the church by Francesco Laurana is in a later Gothic-Renaissance style. The interior is decorated with stuccoes by Ferraro (1623).

Chiesa del Carmine has a majolica dome and a Gothic rose window. A little farther along via Incisa, at n° 48, is the attractive Casa Arone with three Gothic windows and an inside staircase that dates from the 15th century.

From here, corso Vittorio Emanuele leads to piazza Scanaliato, the town centre. On the left, buildings from a former Jesuit college (1615) now house the town hall with its beautiful arcaded interior courtyard. A terrace on the right overlooks the lower town and harbour. Continuing straight ahead you come to the 12th-century Duomo, which was altered in the 18th century but has retained its three original exterior apses. The statues on the façade are by the Gagini.

You might like to complete your visit of the town with the following itinerary: continue along via Vittorio Emanuele to piazza Friscia, where there are pleasant public gardens with a sea view. From here take via Licata immediately to the left to piazza Lazzarini, then follow via Santa Caterina to the right, climbing up to the small Norman church of San Nicoló, now wedged between houses. Behind the church via Castello leads to the ruins of the Luna castle (1380). Beyond via Castello via Ciaccio leads to piazza Noceto, on which stand Badia Grande and the church of San Michele with the ruins of a detached campanile. Not far along to the right you come to the gate of San Calogera, behind which you can see parts of the 16th-century walls.

Telephone area code: 0925.

▲▲ **Garden Hotel**, via Valverde 2, ☎ 21 203. 58 rooms. Recommended.

▲▲ **Grand Hotel delle Terme**, via Nuove Terme 1, ☎ 23 133. 72 rooms. Swimming pool and garden. *Closed Dec-Feb.* Thermal installations.

Around Sciacca

▲▲ **Monte Kronio**, in San Calogero (4.6 mi/7.5 km), near the sanctuary, ☎ 21 840. 27 rooms. Good view.

▲▲ **Torre Macauda**, 5.5 mi/9 km along the Agrigento road, ☎ 26 800. 249 rooms. A holiday village in a beautiful setting with private beach and swimming pool. Meals must be taken at the hotel; check the conditions beforehand.

Campground

Residenza di Baia Macauda, contrada Tranchina, ☎ 92 092. Bungalows for 200. Extremely well located near the hotel. Private beach, organized activities. Reservations: (091) 625 2564.

Sagra del Mare carnival, June 27-29, celebrating the feast of San Pietro. Various shows and cultural events throughout July and August.

▲▲ **Corsaro**, in Stazzone, via Esperando 51, ☎ 24 120. Fish specialities in simple surroundings. Pizzas also served.

Tourist information, corso Vittorio Emanuele 94, upstairs, ☎ 21 182. *Open Mon-Sat 8am-1:30pm, 3-7:30pm.*

Environs of Sciacca

There are three interesting excursions from Sciacca:

Il Giardino d'Incante

This is about 1.2 mi/2 km from Sciacca on the road to Agrigento, which is marked with an arrow indicating 'Fondo Bentivegna'. The garden is full of naïve-style sculptures carved at the beginning of the century by a retired man who literally worked on everything in sight — trees and stones alike. Hundreds of sculpted heads lie scattered on the ground or peep out of trees.

San Calógero (4.9 mi/8 km from the town)

Leave Sciacca on the Palermo road and turn right. A rough road leads to the summit of Mount Kronio (1302 ft/397 m), where you will find the sanctuary of San Calógero. Inside is a statue of the saint by Antonello Gagini (1538). The road to the right ends on an esplanade with a tremendous **view***. The road to the left leads to a thermal centre built over natural caves known as the steamrooms of San Calógero, where the temperature is maintained at 100° F/38° C by hot springs.

Prehistoric remains found in these caves prove that they have been used for therapeutic purposes since earliest times.

Caltabellotta (12.4mi/20 km north-east of Sciacca)

Leave the town on via dei Cappuccini and take the N188 b toward Palermo for 1.2mi/2 km, then turn right onto a minor road that climbs up to Caltabellotta, passing below Rocca Ficuzza (2956 ft/901 m).

Caltabellotta is a market town of 5500 inhabitants clinging to a rock (of the same name) at an altitude of 2785 ft/849 m. According to legend, Daedalus, who was expelled from Crete by King Minos, is supposed to have founded the mythical town of Camicos here for Cocalus, the first Sican king. The town's present name derives from the Arabic *Kal' at al*

Perched high up on a rock, Caltabellotta offers a splendid view over the surrounding countryside.

ballut meaning 'fortress among the oaks'. Because of its geographical position it has been used as a place of refuge from prehistoric times — judging by the many tombs found in the rocky hillsides. Count Roger settled here in 1090 and built the castle where, in 1194, the Norman Queen Sibylla and her son William came for protection from Emperor Henry VI of Hohenstaufen.

Caltabellotta has an exceptional **view*** of a large part of Sicily — especially Piano della Matrice, dominated by Rupe Cocala. To reach the best vantage point, pass the Church of San Salvatore with its Gothic portal and go round to the back of Chiesa Matrice, built by Count Roger after his victory over the Saracens; of its original structure only its portal with pointed arches remains. From behind the church you have a superb panorama of the Verdura river valley.

In another church, Sant'Agostino, there is a very fine Deposition, a group of polychrome terra-cotta figures by Antonino Ferraro (1552).

A picturesque road leads from Caltabellotta to the N115, 12.4 mi/20 km east of Sciacca, on which you can continue toward Agrigento.

ERACLEA MINOA

Leave Sciacca toward Agrigento on via Figuli and, 95.6 mi/ 154 km south-east of Trápani, turn right onto a road that leads to the ruins of Eraclea Minoa (Heracleia Minoa) on a deserted promontory to the east of the Platini River, near Capo Bianco.

As you near the archaeological zone you have a magnificent view of Capo Bianco and the large Bovo Marina beach, one of the most beautiful on this part of the coast. The panoramic **view**** alone justifies the climb to Eraclea.

Pirandello

Before Luigi Pirandello's time (late 19th century) it was thought that a man could be defined by his words and actions. Pirandello hoped to convince us that nothing we can do or say gives a true picture of what we really are — this is the main theme of his revolutionary plays. In *Six Characters in Search of an Author* a father unexpectedly meets his daughter-in-law in a house used by lovers for discreet meetings; he is there as a client and she, without his knowing, has become a boarder there. 'Well', he never ceases to protest, 'you have no right to reproach me for eternity, for what is no more than a minute of my life. You have no right to reduce what I am to a single moment which does not express the whole of my personality'. The father also laments the misleading power of words which artificially dissect or blow out of proportion a small fragment of reality always more complex than what words can say about it. Our reality — and in the final analysis we don't really have one — is always elsewhere than in our gestures, always greater or lesser than the words we use. Can we even be sure of our name, age and family history?

The devastating earthquake that shook Messina in 1908 inspired Pirandello to write another famous play, *Naked Truth,* in which the inhabitants of the town try in vain to force a woman to reveal her identity after everyone's civil status paper have been buried in the rubble. Each of us, like the title of his book, is *One, None and a Hundred-Thousand.* The face we show to others, what they see of us, what we say to them, has only relative importance in comparison with the impenetrable mystery of the real 'me'.

D. Fernandez
The Gorgon's Raft
Le Radeau de la Gorgone, Grasset, 1988.

Eraclea Minoas was founded by inhabitants from Selinunte toward the end of the 6th century BC. Rule of the city was shared by Selinunte and Akragas (Agrigento) until the Carthaginian Wars, when the city was depopulated. Repopulated with Greeks and Carthaginians by Timoleon, the town was abandoned permanently after the 1st-century slave wars.

The visit to the **archaeological site** *(open daily to one hour before sunset)* begins with a small museum housing the finds from excavations on the site. Some of the 4th-century BC walls remain, and inside them are ruins of Roman houses; on a hill to the right is a 3rd-century BC theatre, with its nine sections of white stone rows (the places of honour in the first rows have been particularly well preserved). There is also a necropolis to visit on another hilltop.

To reach Agrigento (118 mi/190 km south-east of Trápani.), return to the N115, which passes through Siculiana, a typical coastal village with a castle.

AGRIGENTO:
'MOST BEAUTIFUL OF
MORTAL CITIES'

Pindar praised ancient Akragas with the above words, speaking of it as the 'lover of splendour' with its 'colossal riches' and 'valley of the Temples'. Not only is the town adorned with magnificent monuments, but also its setting high above the sea between two deep valleys is breathtaking.

Akragas, as it was called in ancient times, was founded in 581 BC by colonists from Rhodes and Gela (Caltanissetta) — a fact borne out by the ceramics discovered in the necropolis of Montelusa. The first small dwellings were probably constructed on the rock of Athena, the site of the present town, but it wasn't until the tyrant Phalaris came to power (570-549 BC) that the first temples and the city walls were built. Pindar, who lived in the town after the rule of Phalaris, claimed that the tyrant had cooked his enemies alive in a gigantic brass bull — an image that recurs in the mythology of Rhodes.

Akragas reached the height of its political power during the reign of a later tyrant, Theron (488-472 BC) who extended the borders all the way to Himera on the north coast. To this daring advance the Carthaginians responded with a military attack, but Theron allied with Gelon of Gela and was victorious over the Carthaginians, using captured prisoners-of-war to work slavishly building temples and other monuments in the ever-growing city of Akragas. The wealth of the city grew to marvelous heights, commemorated much later in the writings of Shakespeare, and also by Empedocles, the pre-Socratic philosopher, who was born here. Empedocles postulated that the world was made of earth, air, fire and water and existence resulted from the ebb and tide created by the opposing forces of 'Love' and 'Strife'. Convinced that hot air would raise him to the Gods, he is said to have thrown himself into the volcanic crater of Mount Etna.

Syracuse was the archenemy of Akragas and, after the victory they won over Athens, they joined with the Carthaginians in a vengeful eight-month seige of Akragas. Citizens of the city are said to have sought refuge in the Temple of Athena, where they ultimately set fire to themselves and to their sacred shrine.

The city was rebuilt in 340 BC by a Corinthian, Timoleon, who also reconstructed the city walls. For a time, Akragas regained some of its former importance, becoming the centre of the coin market under the Romans. But by the 3rd century BC, a gradual decline had set in. In 262 BC the Romans expelled the

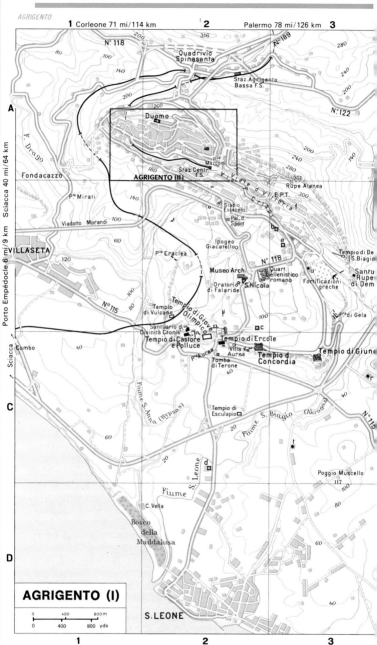

Carthaginians, who remained in the city and sold 25,000 of the town's inhabitants into slavery. The city remained under their rule until the fall of the Roman Empire. In AD 828, the town fell to the Saracens, who destroyed and abandoned it. From this point on the history of Akragas is linked to the history of Sicily at large.

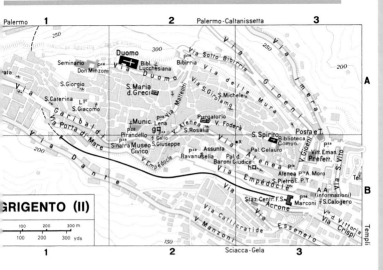

The Greek name Akragas became Agrigentium under the Romans, Kerkent under the Arabs, Girgenti under the Normans and finally Agrigento when Mussolini renamed the city in 1927. The best known of this century's Italian playwrights, Luigi Pirandello, was born here in 1867; he died in 1936.

PRACTICAL INFORMATION

Map coordinates refer to the maps pp. 118, 119.
Telephone area code: 0922.

Access

Car: Agrigente is 35.4 mi/57 km south-west of Caltanissetta, 130.4 mi / 210 km west of Syracuse and 118 mi/190 km south-east of Trápani. Coming directly from Palermo there are two possible routes: the first and fastest (82.6 mi/133 km) is through Lercara Friddi on the N 121 and N 189; the second much slower and rougher route (105.6 mi/170 km) is through Corleone.

Train: There are rail links with Caltanissetta, Enna, Catania, Palermo (very pleasant four-hour journey), Sciacca and Castelvetrano.

Accommodation

▲▲▲▲ **Villa Athena,** via Passegiate Archeologiche 33, I, B2 c, ☎ 596 288. 40 rooms. The only hotel in the archaeological zone, in a converted 18th-century mansion facing the temples, with lovely gardens and a swimming pool. An exceptional setting but the service does not do it justice; the new rooms are small and the food ordinary. No credit cards.

▲▲▲ **Colleverde,** via dei Templi, I, B3 e, ☎ 29 555. 31 rooms. Garden, pool and panoramic view of the temples.

▲▲ **Pirandello,** via Giovanni XXIII 35, I, B3 f, ☎ 595 666. 28 rooms. Located on the edge of town, near the tourist office.

▲ **Bella Napoli,** piazza Lena 6, II, A2 g, ☎ 20 435. 40 rooms. Centrally located.

▲ **Belvedere,** via San Vito 20, II, B3, ☎ 20051. Indoor garden, not far from Stazione Centrale.

▲ **Concordia,** piazza San Francesco 11, II, B3 h, ☎ 596266. 18 rooms. Conveniently located near Stazione Centrale, with restaurant and bar.

On the N 115 heading toward Licata (4.3 mi/7 km east of town)

▲▲▲▲ **Jolly dei Templi,** Parco Mose, ☎ 606144. 146 rooms. Swimming pool and good restaurant, the **Pirandello.**

▲▲▲ **Akrabello,** Parco Angeli, ☎ 606277. 130 rooms. Swimming pool, tennis courts and sauna in a lovely location.

▲▲ **Tre Torri,** Villa Mosè, ☎ 606733. 118 rooms. Modern hotel with a swimming pool, garden, restaurant and bar.

Porto Empédocle (4.3 mi/7 km south-west of town)

▲▲▲ **Dei Pini,** SS115 (the Agrigento road), ☎ 634844. 138 rooms. Swimming pool.

▲▲ **Tiziana Residenza,** SS115, 1.8 mi/3 km west of town toward Sciacca, ☎ 637202. 71 rooms. Swimming pool, restaurant and bar in a garden setting.

San Leone (2.4 mi/4 km south of town).

▲▲▲ **Pirandello Mare,** via de Chirico 17, I, D2, ☎ 412333. 45 rooms. A modern hotel, with restaurant and bar.

▲▲ **Akragas,** via Emporium 16, I, C2 d, ☎ 414082. 15 rooms. Comfortable hotel with restaurant and bar.

Campgrounds

Nettuno, ☎ 606663. *Open June 15-Aug 31.*

San Leone, ☎ 606625. *Open June 15-Aug 31.* On the beach and crowded in summer. Restaurant and small grocery store.

Festivals

Almond Festival, Feb 7-14, with a folklore festival and historical procession near the Temple of Concord.

Feast of San Gerlando, June 16.

Feast of San Calógaro, with a colourful open-air market, viale delle Vittoria, on the first and second Sun in July.

Pirandello Week, in Caos, July-Aug.

Food

▲▲▲ **Le Caprice,** strada Panoramica, I, B3 u, ☎ 26469. *Closed Fri and Feb 1-15.* Excellent Sicilian dishes, good fish, and local wine. Splendid view of the sea. Recommended.

▲▲ **El Vigneto,** Cavaleri Magazzeni 11, I, C3 t, outside the town. Take the Gela road and then turn to the right, following the signs, ☎ 414319. *Closed Tues and Nov.* Overlooking vineyards and temples. Good food.

▲▲ **Taverna Mosè,** contrada San Bagio, I, C3 r, ☎ 26778. *Closed Mon and throughout Aug.* Garden.

▲ **Ambasciata da Sicilia,** via Giambertoni 2, II, B2. Pleasant decor and terrace (in summer).

Useful addresses

Buses, leave from the train station, via Favara Vecchia and piazza Le Rosselli.

Post office, piazza Vittorio Emanuele, II, AB3.

Stazione Centrale, piazza Marconi, II, B3.

Tourist information, viale della Vittoria 255, I, B3, ☎ 20454. *Open 8:30am-2pm, 5-7pm. Closed Mon and Tues.*

GETTING TO KNOW AGRIGENTO

Map coordinates refer to the maps pp. 118, 119.

Excluding a visit to the museum, you need at least a day and a half to see everything, although you could see the main monuments in a day. The **temple zone***** is lit up at night, a sight not to be missed.

Agrigento is split into two distinct areas some distance apart — the modern town (52,000 inhabitants) and the archaeological zone.

The modern town

The modern town spreads over a hillside where part of the ancient city is believed to have stood. It is made up of a mixture of medieval, Baroque and modern buildings with the latter somewhat spoiling the cityscape. The entanglement of alleys, stairways and small irregular squares makes it almost impossible to drive through the town. You would do better to leave your car at the beginning of via Crispi, in front of the station, or in viale della Vittoria, the long tree-lined esplanade that overlooks the valley of the temples. This a lovely place to stroll and there is a terrace with a panoramic **view***.

Abbey of San Spirito* II, B3

Setting out from piazza Aldo Moro, II, B3, near the tourist office, take via Atenea, the colourful narrow main street that winds its way to the Municipio. Turn onto via Porcello (third street on the right) and right again onto salita San Spirito with its staircase up to the abbey of San Spirito. Founded in 1290 this is one of Sicily's most beautiful abbeys. The church has retained its Gothic portal and rose window, and with an encouraging tip you can persuade the guardian (who lives opposite) to open the church, where you will see the more recent Baroque interior decorated with stuccoes by Serpotta. The large panel above the entrance is particularly noteworthy. The coffered ceiling dates from 1758.

To the right of the church the first doorway leads into the convent. Of the former abbey buildings you can see the cloisters, the chapterhouse with its crown-shaped doorway framed by twin bay windows and the old refectory. The convent's Cistercian nuns bake well-reputed pastries, especially those made of almond paste. These are for sale — simply ask the sister in charge (knock at door n° 8).

From the abbey continue straight ahead along via Fodera, which joins via Atenea at piazzetta del Purgatorio, II, A2. Here you will see a small chapel and the **Church of Purgatorio,** also known as San Lorenzo, with eight statues of the Virtues by Giacomo Serpotta. To the left of the church, under a sculpted stone tympanum (with the figure of a lion), is the entrance to an underground gallery of 5th-century water channels, now closed to the public. Diagonally across to the left is via Atenea, which continues to piazza Gallo (church of San Giuseppe on the right) and ends on piazza del Municipio (also known as piazza Luigi Pirandello). On the right are the town hall and the Baroque Church of San Domenico. On the left is the **Museo Civico** (currently closed) with collections of paintings from the 12th century to the present.

Santa Maria dei Greci II, A2

From piazza del Municipio (Pirandello) you have an interesting walk through colourful streets and up torturous flights of stairs (215 steps in all) to the Church of Santa Maria dei Greci. Start on the left of the Church of San Domenico on via Orfane, go up the stairs and turn right onto via Barone. Take the steps to the left in salita Sant'Antonio and then turn right into via Garafo, where you'll find the church; if it is closed, ask for the guardian at n° 8, via Alfonso. The beautiful 13th-century Gothic portal opens into a small Norman church with three aisles. On the right wall are fragments of 14th-century Byzantine frescos. On first sight there seems nothing unusual about the church, but if you venture underneath it, through the entrance in the small front courtyard, you discover that it was built over a Doric temple (5th century BC). You enter a narrow gallery, with the remains of six ancient columns.

Duomo (Cathedral)** II, A2

Take via Alfonso left of the church and follow it to the Church of Alfonso on via Duomo. Turn left for the cathedral along via Duomo. This is lined with 18th-century houses, badly damaged like the rest of the quarter by an earthquake on July 19, 1966.

The Duomo, built on the site of a Greek temple, was also partly destroyed by the earthquake but has been remarkably well restored. Founded in the 12th century, enlarged in the 14th and then altered often during the 17th and 18th, its 15th-century campanile remains massive and incomplete. It is decorated with two rows of false Catalan-Gothic style windows below an arcaded balcony. The condition of the first row of windows shows how brittle the local stone is.

The interior consists of three aisles, Gothic in the lower part of the church, Classical in the upper. The central nave has a beautiful ceiling with painted beams. The different sections correspond to successive restorations, the most interesting of which, near the main portal, dates from 1518. The choir is richly decorated with Baroque **stucco work**** — a profusion of animal heads, graceful sirens ot adolescents, and laughing putti surrounded by flowers, acanthus leaves, shells and bunches of fruit. All the stuccoes are gilded as is the large organ case behind the main altar. A Gothic chapel on the right-hand side with a fine portal houses the silver reliquary of San Gerlando (1639), the first bishop of Agrigento. In another chapel, to the right of the choir, you can see the Virgin and Child by Gagini. Lastly, a grand Roman arch opens onto the baptistry from the nave on the left.

There's a curious acoustic phenomenon in the Duomo: a person who speaks in a low voice at the entrance of the church can be heard in the apse 279 ft/85 m away; the same is not true, however, the other way round.

Beyond the Duomo, on piazza Don Minzoni, is an episcopal seminary in a group of 17th- and 18th-century buildings. To return to piazza Aldo Moro, walk back past the Duomo to piazza Bibirria (good view), then turn right onto via Matteotti, then on to via Atenea, at the end of which is the square. On the left in via Atenea, the Palazzo Celauro, II, B3, permanently houses an instructive exhibition of Sicilian palaeontological and paleoanthropological artifacts.

Archaeological zone of the valley of the temples*** I, C2-3

The eastern zone is unenclosed; it is best to visit the site in the early morning or late evening when there are less people.

This long itinerary includes all the monuments in the archaeological zone, which can, of course, be visited separately. You need a car to get to the valley, or you can take the bus from either piazza Maroni, II, B3, or Porto Empedocle that stops near the temples.

Take via Crispi, II, B3, from the town centre, leaving the Hellenistic quarter on your left and the Museo Nazionale Archeologico on your right — these can be visited on your way back. Continue to the parking lot, I, BC2, at the entrance to the ruins.

Tempio di Ercole* I, C2

Dominating the crossroads is the oldest temple in the valley, the Temple of Hercules, dating from about 520/511 BC. It was once no doubt one of the most remarkable in Sicily but was probably destroyed by earthquakes at the end of the Classical period. A bronze statue of Hercules, much admired by Cicero when he came to Sicily to support charges against the Roman magistrate Gains Verres, was once venerated here.

The temple originally had 38 columns (33 ft/10 m high and 7 ft/2 m in diameter). The eight on the south side were re-erected in 1924, thanks to an Englishman who financed the work.

Villa Aurea I, C2

Continue east along the footpath to Villa Aurea and its garden. Here you can see the Fragapane Grotto, Christian catacombs that are difficult to date (between the 1st and the 5th centuries) and, on the eastern flank of the hill, the remains of a Christian-Byzantine necropolis, with open graves.

Tempio della Concordia★★★ I, C2-3

This simple, majestic temple, one of the wonders of Sicily, recalls the Theserum, or Temple, of Hephaistos in Athens by its symmetry and colour. Although it was built with friable stone it has survived practically intact, due largely to the fact that it was converted into a Christian church at the end of the 6th century. Arches were opened in the temple walls, allowing access to the peristyle, and giving the temple the shape of a basilica with three aisles. In 1748 the building was restored to its original form.

An inscription found in the Valley of the Temples and events that occurred during the building of the temple (450 BC), suggest that it could have been erected in honour of the goddess of Peace and Fertility.

The temple is a marvelous example of Doric architecture with its 4-stepped stylobate and 34 peripteral columns. Like all the Akragas monuments it was covered with a fine layer of resistant stucco and then painted. At sundown, when the stone takes on a golden honey colour, the temple reappears in all its glory.

Tempio di Giunone★★ I, C3

The panoramic route continues east to the Temple of Juno Lacinia standing on a rocky ridge that once formed the town ramparts. This elegant temple (125 × 56 ft/38 × 17 m) was built in about 470 BC in the Doric style; 25 of its original columns (21 ft/6.5 m) are still standing while 9 have been severely damaged. The architrave on the northern side is still intact.

To continue your visit, go back to the parking lot and from there head into the western zone.

Tempio di Giove Olimpico★ I, BC2

Immediately on entering the western zone you will see on your right traces of the vast base of a sacrificial altar. A little farther on are the remains of one of Antiquity's largest monuments — the Temple of Jupiter, which stretches over an area of approximately 64,584 sq ft/6000 sq m.

Built to last for thousands of years, according to a revolutionary plan in Greek architecture, the edifice measured 373 × 185 ft/113 × 56 m, but, unlike more traditional constructions, it was not surrounded by a colonnade; half of the columns were integrated into the wall. Giant statues of men were placed between these columns to carry the weight of the entablature.

These *Giganti,* or male caryatids (sometimes bearded), were placed on consoles to break up the uniformity of the peristyle and add originality to the building. They illustrate the mythological war waged on Zeus (Jupiter) by the giants who were defeated and thereafter condemned to carry huge loads. There is a reproduction of one giant in the centre of the temple that measures 25 ft/7.8 m. Only one of the originals could be reconstructed from fragments, a work carried out in the 19th century by Politi, now in the National Archaeological Museum.

The temple was built by the prisoners of war taken after the victory at Himera and left uncompleted in 406. Everything about it was gigantic, as is shown by the width of the column flutings, which were large enough to hold a human figure.

Tempio dei Dioscuri★ I, BC2

A little farther on, the path leads through a group of ruins to the Temple of the Dioscuri, better known as Castor and Pollux. A Doric temple built in the 5th century BC, it was a mass of rubble when discovered. In 1896 an archaeologist tried to put together some of the fragments which today you can see as the four columns supporting part of the architrave.

Tempio di Esculapio I, C2

Visiting the Temple of Aesculapius completes the itinerary; you now have a collective view of all the temples and can take a different road back to the archaeological zone and the museum. You need your car for this; turn right when you leave the parking lot.

You pass the site of the former Porta Aurea, the gate through which the Romans took the ancient city in 210 BC. The monument on the left is known as the **Tomb of Theron,** I, C2.

You should now take the N 115 to the left, toward Syracuse, for a few hundred metres. On the left you pass the 5th-century BC ruins of the small Temple of Aesculapius. Built near a spring believed to have curative powers, the temple was dedicated to the god of healing and housed a famous statue of Apollo by Myron. From here you have a good view of the ancient city with its precious **crown of temples*** protected by ancient walls. The Greek city, founded in 600 BC, stands out against the sky, bathed in yellow light that changes hue according to the time of day, turning a shade of purple toward sunset.

Hellenistic and Roman quarter* I, B2-3

Open daily 9am to an hour before sunset.

On leaving the Temple of Aesculapius, take the road toward Caltanissetta, and when you reach the crossroads take the Strada Panoramica to the left toward Agrigento. You turn left again onto the N118 to reach the Hellenistic and Roman quarter. This covers an area of 107,640 sq ft / 10,000 sq m and gives you an idea of how the urban centre of Akragas (4th century BC) was organized. Wide straight streets, aqueducts, terra-cotta and stone water channels, cisterns and painted houses with mosaic pavings all testify to the opulence of the town and the perfection with which it was planned.

Empedocles states that the Athenians ate as if they would die the next day and built as if they would live forever. Some of their artwork can be seen in the museum, one of the best in Sicily.

Museo Nazionale Archeologico*** I, B2

Open 9am-1:30pm, 3-7:30pm; holidays 9am-12:30pm. Closed Mon and Sat afternoon.

The National Archeological Museum contains unique, remarkably well-presented, collections of kraters (Greek jars), statuettes and sculptures. There are two sections, the first devoted to Agrigento and the second to the town's provinces and the Caltanissetto region. The visit begins with the rooms on the left. The **krater collections**** (most from the 5th century BC) are exceptional. One of the finest represents the **Battle of the Amazons***. Among the museum's major pieces is the marble statue of the **Ephebus of Agrigento****, which dates from about 470 BC. The centre piece in room 6 is the only *gigante* that was reconstructed from the ruins of the temple of Jupiter (25 ft/7.8 m tall).

San Nicola* I, B2

The Roman-Gothic Church of San Nicola was built by the Cistercians at the beginning of the 13th century with stones from neighbouring temples. It was altered in the 14th and 15th centuries and very well restored in 1966. Its **portal*** (1531) is noteworthy in that it is Roman on the outside and Gothic inside. The single nave has pointed vaulting with heavy ribbing that enhances the church's powerful design. The apse is decorated with 16th-century frescoes.

One of the most beautiful pieces from the former Museo Diocesano, the **Phaedra Sarcophagus***, is in the second chapel on the right. In another chapel you can see a statue of the Virgin by Gagini and a 12th-century fresco of St Ursula. To the right of the choir a corridor leads off to the convent's former chapel, with its Byzantine-style fresco of the Deposition dating from 1575.

The Temple of the Dioscuri, or Castor and Pollux Temple, in Agrigento.

Next to the church is the **Oratory of Philaris,** a monumental Roman tomb dating from the 1st century BC that was converted into a chapel in the Middle Ages. Nearby is the comitium, a type of ancient theatre built for public assemblies.

San Biagio and the Temple of Demeter I, B3

The cemetery road brings you to the ruins of the Greek town walls and ramparts (parking lot nearby) from which a rocky path leads to the Church of San Biagio, on a platform excavated out of the rock. This small 12th-century Norman church was built on the ruins of a 5th-century BC temple in honour of Demeter and Persephone; only the base of the temple remains. Note the two circular altars between the church and the rock.

On your way back from the church take the narrow staircase carved into the rock face on the left. This leads to the ruins of the 7th-century BC Temple of Demeter, the oldest temple in Agrigento. It consists of a complex group of basins, behind which are two caves with corridor extensions of 82 ft/25 m stretching back into the hillside. Water from the caves flowed out into the basins. The caves themselves contained offerings to the gods, among them strange votive vases now exhibited in the archaeological museum. They resemble long tubes with handles that were connected by lengths of hair and sunk into the ground to ensure 'good contact with the Underworld'. The sanctuary is thought to have been used by a water cult, in honour of Demeter, or the mysteries of Eleusis.

Before returning to Agrigento, a visit to the **municipal cemetery** makes an interesting detour. Here you will see elements typical of Italian funerary art including marble statues of weeping cherubs.

ENVIRONS OF AGRIGENTO

House of Pirandello

Take the N115 toward Trápani and follow the sign left to Caos, where you will find the modest house of Luigi Pirandello (1867-1936), now converted into a museum *(open daily 9am-1pm, 3-7pm; winter to 5pm).* The playwright is buried on the edge of the cliff nearby, beneath a solitary pine where he is said to have contemplated the vicissitudes of life.

San Leone Bagni *(2.4 mi/4 km south of Agrigento)*

This is a small seaside resort to the left of the mouth of the San Leone River. To the right is the Bosco della Maddalusa (forest). The environs of San Leone Bagni have a variety of campgrounds, tourist resorts, and hotels (see p. 120).

Porto Empédocle *(4.3 mi/7 km south-west of Agrigento)*

Porto Empédocle, the largest of Sicily's south-western ports, has a population of 17,000, and was founded in the second half of the 17th century. Apart from the fact that it is the departure point for the Pelágie Islands, this industrial centre has little of interest for the tourist. The **Isole Pelágie** is an archipelago comprising **Lampedusa, Linosa** and **Lampione** (uninhabited). Porto Empédocle has hotel accommodation (see Agrigento p. 120) and a choice of restaurants.

PELÁGIE ISLANDS

Lampedusa

The largest of the Pelágie Islands (7.7 sq mi/20 sq km) is also the farthest from Sicily (127 mi/205 km) and quite close to Tunisia (70 mi/113 km). Lampedusa is a flat, windy and barren island — virtually treeless, as a result of deforestation and poor farming techniques that have destroyed the topsoil. It is difficult for today's visitor to believe that the island was once fertile, its forests filled with deer and wild boar.

Nonetheless today's disasterous ecological realities do not deter visitors from coming to the island in search of the pleasant stretches of beach and the vestiges of Phoenician, Greek, Roman and Arab civilizations.

Humans were present on Lampedusa as far back as the Bronze Age, and there is evidence that the island was used as a base for the Romans during the Punic Wars. But generally the island has gone unmentioned in the tale of history. The Arabs colonized it around AD 813, but there is not much of note until 1553, when the pirate Dragut, from Tunis, captured the 1000 inhabitants and sold them all as slaves, effectively depopulating the entire island. King Carlos of Spain gave the island to Giulio Tomasi di Lampedusa in 1630; his inheritors allowed the Gatt family from Malta to colonize it around 1800; then around 1810, the Gatts divided the island with an Englishman called Alexander Fernandez and his 300 colonists.

When the Tomasi family tried to sell the island to the English in 1839, King Ferdinand II stepped in and snatched it up himself for 12,000 ducats, sending the first Bourbon colonists to the island in 1848. In the 1870s, the Italian government set up penal colonies on Lampedusa and Linosa, much to the dismay of the residents. The island was made into a fortress during the North African campaign of World War II, when all native islanders were evacuated.

Today, 70% of the islanders make their living from fishing, another 15% from tourism.

Albero Sole is the highest point (altitude 436 ft/133 m).

Telephone area code: 0922. ·

Access

Boat: Lampedusa is a nine-hour crossing from Porto Empédocle. Daily departures at 11pm (except Sun in winter). For information: **Siremar, ☎ 66 683** and **66 685**.

Plane: There is a daily one-hour flight from Trápani. For information: **Lampedusa Airport, ☎ 970 066; Alitalia, ☎ 970 299.**

Accommodation

▲▲ **Baia Turchese,** in Guitgia, ☎ 970 455. 47 rooms. Garden, restaurant and private beach.

▲ **Lido Azzuro,** in Guitgia, ☎ 970 225. 30 rooms. Comfortable hotel at a reasonable price.

▲ **Vega,** via Roma 19, ☎ 970 099. *Closed Dec 20-Jan-20.* 13 rooms. Simple, small hotel, with a bar.

Food

LL Gemelli, via Cala Pisana 2, ☎ 970 0699. *Closed Oct-May.* Fish specialities.

LL Tommasino, via Lido Azzura 13, ☎ 970 316. *Closed Mon and throughout Nov.* Mainly fish dishes.

Useful address

Tourist information, Le Pelagie agency, via Roma 155, ☎ 970 170.

Linosa

This delightful, out-of-the way island, known as Algusa or Aethusa in ancient times, is 100 mi/161 km from Sicily, 26 mi/42 km from Lampedusa. It is a volcanic island with three extinct craters, including Monte Vulcano, the highest point at an altitude of 640 ft/195 m. The island was inhabited during the Roman era, then in the 9th century by the Arabs and probably by pirates in the 16th century. The Bourbons colonized it in 1845, cultivating the rich volcanic soil and building villages.

If you are looking for peace and quiet that is definitely off the beaten track, Linosa may be just the place. In spring, there is a marvelous blossoming of wild flowers on the craters, and in all seasons the island offers its charming lava beaches, although be warned that in summer it is one of the hottest places in Italy. The people on Linosa enjoy a very simple and natural life, scaled down to the basics. If you need discotheques, video games or roller rinks to amuse you, avoid this stop.

Access

By boat: There is an approximately seven-hour crossing from Porto Empédocle on the same boat to Lampedusa.

AGRIGENTO TO CALTANISSETTA

There are two possible routes: the N122 or the more direct 640.

Favara

Leave Agrigento from piazza Vittorio Emanuelle on via Imera, II, A3, and then take the N122. Favara (8 mi/13 km east of Agrigento) is a small town that grew up around the **Chiaramonte family castle** (1275, partly rebuilt in the 15th century).

Naro

On the N122, 13.6 mi/22 km east of Agrigento, the roads forks to the right for Naro (8 mi/13 km). This is a picturesque town of 11,000 inhabitants perched on an isolated hill covered in almond trees. There are several Baroque churches, among them San Salvatore de San Francesco (1635) and Sant'Agostino (18th century). You can also see a 14th-century Gothic church dedicated to Santa Caterina, the ruins of 13th-century walls and a Chiaramonte castle dating from the 13th and 14th centuries. The 17th-century Chiesa Matrice contains sculptures by Gagini and baptismal fonts dating from 1424.

CALTANISSETTA, 'CASTLE OF WOMEN'

Caltanissetta is believed to have been built on the site of ancient Nissa, which was given the prefix Kalat (meaning 'castle') by the Saracens — hence its modern name. Located in the heart of the island with a population of 61,000, it is an essentially modern, triangular-shaped town at the foot of Monte San Giuliano. Thanks to its sulphur, potassium and magnesium mines, it played an important role in the country's economy during the last century.

As the monuments are very close to each other, you can visit the town in two or three hours.

You arrive from Agrigento on via Rosso di Secondo. Viale Testasecca to the right leads to piazza Garibaldi, the centre of town, where the two main streets, corso Umberto I and corso Vittorio Emanuele, meet. In the centre of the square is a large fountain of Neptune with a group of bronze sculptures by Tioisciano.

Duomo (Cathedral)

The following buildings are on the square: the town hall, the Church of San Sebastiano (not particularity noteworthy) and opposite, the Duomo and its two campaniles, built between 1550 and 1648. The interior with its three aisles and high dome has some fine decoration. The main nave is adorned with stuccoes and **frescoes** by the Flemish painter Borremans (1721). The three major compositions in the vault, framed by Old Testament scenes, represent the *Immaculate Conception,* the *Crowning of the Virgin* and the *Triumph of St Michael,* all of which are still quite remarkable in spite of having needed restoration. In the choir you can see a large painting also by Borremans, near the main altar and a richly decorated 1601 organ case of gilded wood with painted panels.

Walk around the left side of the cathedral to via San Domenico to visit the church of the same name. Inside, above the main altar, is a painting by Paladino, the *Madonna del Rosario.*

Church of Sant'Agata**

On Corso Umberto I, the first street on the right after the *Municipio,*

The brightly painted Sicilian carts, now rare, were used by farmers to carry tools and food.

stands the Baroque Palazzo Moncada, built in 1625. Farther on is the church of Sant'Agata (almost always closed). It is Jesuit in style, and because it is dedicated to St Ignatius it is more suitably known as Il Collegio. It was built in 1605 by a Jesuit architect who gave the façade an extremely austere design. This contrasts greatly with the rich interior where all the altars are decorated with polychrome **marble inlays★★**. The one at the end of the right-hand aisle is dedicated to the Madonna del Carmine, the left-hand one to St Ignatius. The artist Marabitti portrayed St Ignatius allegorically, illustrating the four parts of the known world. Adjoining the church is the Jesuit college, which houses one of Sicily's largest municipal libraries.

Via Angeli leads to two other monuments, the former Church of Santa Maria degli Angeli and the Castello Pietrarossa. Disappointingly, the church stands trapped in a factory courtyard and in poor condition. All that remains is a beautiful Gothic portal made of sandstone. The second monument, a few remaining stones balanced on a rock, cannot evoke Caltanissetta's former citadel.

Museums

The **Museo Civico,** via Napoleone Colajanni, near the Stazione *(open daily 9am-1:30pm; closed holidays),* contains collections of objects dating from the 7th to the 3rd century BC. The finds come from various archaeological sites in the Greco-Sikel village of Gibil Gabib, on the hill of San Giuliano, in Sabucino and also in Capodarso.

Misteri sculptures of the Passion are displayed in the Church of **San Pio X** and can be seen throughout the school year. You can arrange a visit by telephoning 31 280.

Telephone area code: 0934.

Access

Car: Caltanissetta is 63 mi/102 km west of Catania, 77 mi/124 km

south-east of Palermo, 42.8 mi/69 km north-east of Agrigento (direct on
the 640), 51 mi/82 km north-west of Gela and 23.6 mi/38 km south-
east of Enna.

Train: There is rail access with Catania, Agrigento and Palermo.

Accommodation

▲ **Diprima,** via Kennedy 16, ☎ 26088. 106 rooms. The only hotel in
town ; you have no choice but to stay here or arrange accommodation outside Caltanissetta.

Festivals

Folklore Festival in September. At **Christmas** there's a *tableau vivant*, live
manger scene, on the square. At **Easter,** the Holy Week ceremonies of
the Passion last three days, beginning on the morning of Easter
Wednesday with a procession of the Holy Sacrament known as *Reale
Maestranza*. In the evening there's another procession, *Varicedde*. On
Maundy (Holy) Thursday the *vare*, groups of *Misteri* sculptures normally
kept in the museum, are carried through the town by members of
different guilds. It is a day of folklore and religious fervour which draws to
a close around 8pm with another solemn procession. The last procession takes place on Good Friday when a black figure of Christ is
venerated as lord of the town.

Food

LL Cortese, corso Sicilia 166, ☎ 31686. *Closed on Mon and for
two weeks in Aug*. Good Sicilian food. Recommended.

Useful address

Tourist information, via Conte Testasecca, on the corner of via Kennedy,
☎ 21089. *Open Mon-Sat 8:30-noon ; Mon, Tues and Thurs 4-6:30pm.*

▬ *ENVIRONS OF CALTANISSETTA*

A short trip (just over 1.8 mi/3 km) east to the Church of **Santa Spirito** is
worth your while. Take the N122 toward Enna and after 1.5 mi/2.5 km
turn left following the sign to Badia di Santo Spirito, which is about
0.62 mi/1 km farther on. The building was constructed under Roger I
and was consecrated on June 15, 1153, in commemoration of a victory
over the Arabs. It is a small basilica with a single nave and three
Roman apses.

From **Monte San Giuliano,** 1.2 mi/2 km outside Caltanisseta, you have a
panoramic view of central Sicily. On the mountaintop, at an altitude of
2385 ft/727 m, there is the large monument Christ the Redeemer by
Ernesto Basile (1900).

Monte Sabucina (2316 ft/706 m), on the road to Enna (3.7 mi/6 km
from Caltanissetta), was excavated about 20 years ago ; what remains is
in an archaeological park (ask the guardian).

Monte Gibil Cabib, 3 mi/5 km on the N191, was a Sicano-Greek centre.
Prehistoric and Greek tombs have been excavated, many of them carved
into the rock.

Apart from the lovely views from sites, they are mainly of interest to
specialists.

▬ *ENNA**, 'SICILY'S NAVEL'*

Map coordinates refer to the map p. 132.

Enna has a population of 29,000 and is the highest provincial capital
(3054 ft/931 m) in Italy. It is known as 'the belvedere of Sicily' because
of its elevated position in the heart of the island.

Numerous mountain caves discovered in the area prove human presence
in Enna in prehistoric times. Ancient Henna was settled by the Sikans
(see p. 29) then gradually came under Greek influence (8th to 7th
century BC) when it became the centre of the cult of Demeter. From the
6th to the 3rd century BC it was a commercial and agricultural centre,

minting its own coins and becoming so rich that it caught the eye of the tyrant Agathocles, who took it in 307 BC and made it a Syracusian colony. After that Henna fell under the control of the same succession of foreign rulers as the rest of the island, including Romans and Saracens. When Palermo fell to the Muslims in 851 the Byzantine government decided to move to Enna, which held out against the Muslim seige until 859.

When the Normans conquered Sicily, they had difficulty taking the town of Enna, which didn't fall until 1083. It became one of the favourite residences of Frederick II of Swabia, who restored the Castello di Lombardia. Frederick III of Aragon was crowned King of Trinacria here in 1314.

Without visiting the Museo Alessi or the archaeological museum you need a good half day to visit the town.

Coming from Caltanissetta, via Pergusa leads to the centre, piazza Vittorio Emanuele and the 14th-century church of **San Francesco,** A2 (entirely restored), which is dominated by a 15th century campanile. To visit the church enter through the crypt, now converted into a modern chapel, and walk up to the first floor. In the centre of the nave there is a painted wooden cross from the 16th century. Once outside, walk to the end of the square to piazza Francesco Crispi with its fountain, a bronze reproduction of the Rape of Persephone by Bernini. The **view**** from the terrace of the Madonie Mountains, Etna and Calascibetta, is splendid.

From here the main street, via Roma, leads to piazza Coppola and the former Church of **San Benedetto,** A2, now dedicated to San Giuseppe, with its Baroque façade. Inside, in the right-hand aisle there is a reliquary bust of Christ made of painted wood. Above the door to the sacristy is the *Descent from the Cross* by A. Mercurio.

Turn right from piazza Coppola into via Candrilli where you will see the fine **campanile*** of the former church of **San Giovanni Battista** (15th-century) with its three levels of Gothic arches crowned by a small Arab-style cupola. Continuing along via Roma you reach piazza Colaianni where, at n° 467, you will see the Catalan-Gothic ruins of the 15th-century **Palazzo Pollicarini**. Although it has been damaged it retains a fine portal and windows.

Facing the palace is the former church of the Santa Chiara Convent 1725, now a memorial and burial place. The Duomo is a little further along via Roma.

Spanish heritage

Holy Week processions, a tradition inherited under Spanish rule during the 17th century, begin in Enna on Palm Sunday with processions by the brotherhoods of Rettori, del Rosario, della Passione and del San Salvatore. On each day of the week four brotherhoods parade through the town, the penitent's faces hidden by hoods. There are 14 brotherhoods, the oldest of which was founded in 1261, the most recent in 1973. Members once played an important social role: those of the Passion helped the poor, those of Santa Maria La Donna Nuova helped former victims of the plague, and members of the Souls of Purgatory had the sad task of comforting those condemned to death.

On Good Friday the brotherhoods join the processions that start from each church and make their way toward the cathedral, accompanying a statue of the Virgin dell'Addolorata and another one of Christ lying in a glass coffin. The two statues are carried in great pomp, by torchlight, and are impressively life-like. The Virgin is portrayed laden with jewels, shedding realistic tears, a lace handkerchief in her hand. She appears under a canopy while the corpse of Christ lies on a bed of flowers, his head encircled by a crown of thorns and his body bleeding. The crowds sympathize far more with the suffering of the Madonna — who symbolizes both mother and wife — than they do with the tragic death of her beloved son. The meeting of the two on Easter Sunday, after the Resurrection, takes place on the square in front of the Duomo.

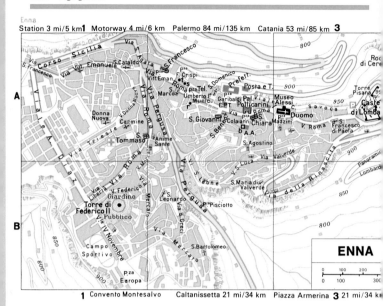

1 Convento Montesalvo   Caltanissetta 21 mi/34 km   Piazza Armerina 3 21 mi/34 km

Duomo (Cathedral)** A3

The cathedral was begun in 1307 under the auspices of Queen Eleonora of Aragon and underwent various alterations during the centuries that followed, mainly in the 16th century. Of its original construction only the transept and apses remain because it was partly destroyed by a terrible fire in 1446. The main façade dating from the 15th century is preceded by a narthex and surmounted by a 17th-century bell tower. The right side of the cathedral bears a portal attributed to Gagini adorned with a bas-relief of St Martin.

The interior is Latin-cross-shaped with three aisles separated by two rows of black basalt columns. These are decorated at the base and crowned by Corinthian capitals. The second columns on the left and right were carved by Gian Domenico Gagini and date from 1460. Note the two marble fonts from 1500 at the entrance. The 17th-century coffered ceiling of the recently restored nave and that of the transept are made of chestnut. On the right-hand side of the nave the white marble pulpit dating from the first half of the 17th-century has a Roman pedestal, which may have been taken from the ancient pagan temple of Ceres. Magnificent organ cases and 16th-century tribunes adorn the nave at the top.

The choir, dedicated to the Virgin of the Assumption, has Gothic arches and lancet windows, stucco decoration and paintings by Filippo Paladino (1613). The chestnut choir stalls (16th century) with their carved backs illustrating scenes from the Old Testament and New Testament are the work of Scipione di Guido. There's a fine 14th-century crucifix painted on gilded wood, known as the *Christ with Three Faces* because the expression changes depending on the angle from which you look at it. In the transept on the left is the *Madonna del Pilar* by Borremans, dated 1722. The left aisle has another Madonna by Salermo and Borremans' *St Peter and St Paul appearing to Constantine*.

The **baptistry** stands on an alabaster vase taken from pagan temples. Its wrought-iron gate once enclosed the Arab harem in the Castello di Lombardia. The cathedral treasures are now housed in the Museo Alessi.

The local guilds play a major role in Enna's Holy Week procession, one of Sicily's most important.

As you leave the cathedral through the side portal you pass the Holy Gate, closed by the Pope after a jubilee in 1447. This was held to enable the restoration of the church a year after it had been destroyed by fire.

Museo Archeologico* A3
Open daily 9am-1pm, 3:30-6:30pm.
This is a new museum in a beautiful house off piazza Mazzini, containing interesting finds from various archaeological sites in central Sicily.

Museo Alessi*** A3
Open Mon-Sat 9am-1pm.
The museum, a remarkably well-arranged building behind the Duomo, houses collections that once belonged to Canon Alessi (1774-1837), a native of Enna who was an historian, an archaeologist and a coin collector. The cathedral's ancient treasury, justly considered one of Italy's most important for both the quantity and the quality of its works, is also on display here.

There are paintings on the ground floor, among them a **polyptych*** by Antonello Crescenzio, a Madonna of the Flemish school and several Byzantine **icons*** of Cretan and Venetian origin. The basement has an exceptional collection of **vestments****; on the first floor are silver and gold works from the cathedral treasury. The most beautiful article is the large silver **reliquary**** made by Paolo Gili in 1536, which is 6.2 ft/1.9 m tall. Note also the gold **monstrance*** by S. Mercurio (1735), the amazing gold **crown**** of the *Virgin of the Visitation* with enamel work and diamonds, and finally the **pelican**** made of precious stones, spreading its wings to feed its young. On the second floor you can see a fine krater collection and 4000 coins of Siculian-Greek and Roman origin.

Castello di Lombardia* A3
Via Roma ends at Castello di Lombardia, an irregularly shaped fortress and one of the largest medieval castles in Sicily (279, 864 sq ft/26,000 sq m) with Byzantine, Norman and Swabian features. Six of its original

20 towers still stand. Of its three courtyards the first, known as **San Nicola,** is used for an open-air theatre and in the third, the most interesting, is the **Torre Pisano,** the tallest and best preserved tower, which gives a spendid view of the island.

A road with panoramic views leads to an isolated rock, the **Rocca di Cerere** (Ceres or Demeter) where there was once a temple which, according to Cicero, housed a giant statue of the goddess whose figure was stamped on the town coins.

Torre di Frederico II (Castello Vecchio) B1

To complete your visit to the town, return to piazza Vittorio Emanuele and then head for the public gardens, where you will see the Torre di Frederico II, more commonly known as Castello Vecchio. Frederick II built this octagonal tower over an older edifice (which cannot be visited). A circular opening on the ground floor may have been the entrance to an underground passage linking it to Castello di Lombardia. It is also believed that for administrative purposes under Arab occupation the platform served as the island's focal point for its three regions: the Noto, Demone and Mazara valleys, which formed the three main axes of Trinacria.

Heading back toward piazza Garibaldi, the centre of town, there are two interesting churches to visit. The first, **San Tommaso,** on the left via Roma, AB1, has a 15th-century tower and inside on the main altar, a fine marble icon by Giuliàno Mancino. Not far behind this church you come to another 15th-century tower, which pre-dates the church of the **Carmine,** built in the 17th century.

Environs of Enna

Calascibetta (43 mi/7 km north of Enna)

This is a market-town of 5000 inhabitants positioned like an amphiteatre on a hill, at an altitude of 2880 ft/878 m. Outwardly it has managed to retain traces of its Arab origins, with clusters of alleys, stairways and little squares offering lovely views of Enna and the surrounding countryside. **Chiesa Matrice** (San Pietro) at the top of the town was founded in 1340 and completely altered later. Inside, its Gothic arches are upheld by columns whose bases are intriguingly decorated with sculptures of monsters. The sacristy contains a rich collection of treasures. In the 16th-century **Cappucini** church near the cemetery you can see an altarpiece by Filippo Paladino (1613), and in the **Carmine** church, an Annunciation by Gagini.

At about 0.6 mi/1 km from Calascibetta on the Petralia road a path leads to the archaeological site of **Calcarella** and to the Realmese **necropolis** where there are approximately 3000 round oven-like tombs dug into the rock Cozzo San Guiseppe, dating from the 7th to the 5th century BC. The whole region is riddled with ancient caves.

Telephone area code: 0935

Access

Car: Calascibetta is 19.8 mi/32 km (highway) or 23.6 mi/38 km (N122 and 177) north-east of Caltanissetta, 54.6 mi/88 km west of Catania, 46.6 mi/75 km north of Gela, 19.2 mi/31 km north-west of Piazza Armerina, 83.2 mi/134 km north-west of Ragusa and 60.8 mi/98 km (N122) or 55.3 mi/89 km (640 direct) north-east of Agrigento.

Train: Enna is on the line between Palermo and Catania. The station is 3 mi/5 km from the town centre.

Accommodation

▲▲ **Belvedere,** piazza Crispi, A2, ☎ 21 020 and 21 026. 52 rooms. Recently opened.

▲▲ **Grand Albergo Sicilia,** piazza Colaianni 5, A2, ☎ 21 644. 70 rooms. Pleasant location, with bar but no restaurant.

Around Lago di Pergusa (6.2 mi/10 km south-east of Enna)

▲▲▲ **Park Hotel La Giara,** via Nazionale 125, ☎ 42 287. 20 rooms. Garden, swimming pool, restaurant and bar.

▲▲ **Riviera,** Autodromo di Pergusa, ☎ 36 267. 26 rooms. Garden, swimming pool and restaurant.

▲ **Serena,** via Nazionale 4, ☎ 36 113. 28 rooms. Bar, restaurant and parking facilities.

Festivals

There are plays in the open-air theatre in Castello di Lombardia during the summer, motor racing around Lago di Pergusa and Holy Week processions. **Harvest Festival** in honour of the Virgin is held at the beginning of July, continuing an age-old tradition from the time when harvests were dedicated to Ceres.

Food

LL Ariston, via Roma 365, A2 s, ☎ 26 038. *Closed Sun.* Large, rather austere dining room. Varied menu. Try the excellent *bressaola* as a first course.

LL Centrale, via VI Dicembre 9, A2 r, ☎ 21 205. *Closed Sat in off-season and throughout Oct.* Large choice of local specialities and good inland wines.

L La Fontana, via Volturno 6, A2 t, ☎ 25 465. *Closed Sun.* Simpler than the two above. Very reasonable tourist menu.

Useful addresses

Bus station and taxi rank, viale Diaz, in the new town.

Tourist information, AAST piazza Colaianna, beside Sicilia hotel, A2, ☎ 26 119 *(open Mon-Sat 8am-2pm, 4:30-6:30pm)*; **EPT,** piazza Garibaldi, in the Chamber of Commerce building, A2, ☎ 21 184 *(open Mon-Sat 9am-1pm)*.

AGRIGENTO TO CATANIA
VIA GELA

Piazza Armerina,
Roman villa at Casale, and Caltagirone

This itinerary features castles, Baroque churches and the ruins of Antiquity. It has suggestions for pleasant strolls among various archaeological curiosities and may even turn out to be a pilgrimage during which you could come across the lost tomb of Aeschylus, who died in Gela in 456 BC.

AGRIGENTO TO GELA

50 mi/80 km on the N115.

Palma di Montechiaro (16.7 mi/27 km south-east of Agrigento)
There are several Baroque churches, the most interesting of which is the cathedral, designed by a Jesuit architect. You can also see the ruins of a 14th-century castle on a hill near the village that was built by Carlo Tomasi di Lampedusa, an ancestor of Tomasi di Lampedusa, who wrote *The Leopard* (the author gave the town the name of Donnafugata in his novel).
A small road leads to a beach in Marina di Palma (3.7 mi/6 km).

Licata (30 mi/48 km south-east of Agrigento)
This is an industrial centre of 42,000 inhabitants, located near the mouth of the Salso river with a port and a beach. In ancient times it was known as Phintias, after a tyrant who destroyed Gela and moved the survivors here. **Palazzo del Municipio** *(open Mon-Fri 9am-2pm)* houses a number of interesting works of art. **The Madre Church** contains a 17th-century chapel with a wooden crucifix dating from the 16th century. There are 16th- and 17th-century tombs in the former **Carmine convent**. The **Museo Civico** *(open Mon-Sat 9am-2pm; closed holidays)* in piazza Linares houses local archaeological finds. West of the town is the 16th-century castle of **Sant'Angelo,** which offers good views.
Telephone area code: 0922.

Accommodation
▲▲ **Al Faro,** via Dogana 6, in the port, ☎ 862 256. 30 rooms. Reasonably priced hotel with restaurant, bar and parking.

Food
LL Logico, via Lido 5, ☎ 862 222. *Closed Mon.*

The famous Villa Casale contains remarkable mosaics from the 3rd century AD.

GELA

Possibly on the advice of the Delphic Oracle, antique Gela was founded in 688 BC by people from Crete and Rhodes who colonized formerly Sikel territory. The name of the town is derived from the name the Sikels gave to a river in the region and is related to the Italian *gelo* (from Latin *gelidus*) meaning 'cold'. By the 7th century BC Gela was a powerful settlement that prospered until the Carthaginians sacked it in 405 BC, razing the walls. The inhabitants made their way back into the city, which remained open and defenseless until 339 BC, when Timoleon, who ruled from Syracuse, decided to repopulate it with people from the Aegean coast. The town spread westward, and new walls were built with towers, gates and even secret entrances (ruins can be seen in the Capo Soprano zone). In spite of this remarkable defense system Agathocles accused the inhabitants of treason in 311 BC, invaded the city and tortured 4000 people to death; they were buried in communal graves, some of which have been unearthed. On the death of Agathocles in 264 BC, mercenaries came from Messina and attacked the town. Then Phintias, a tyrant from Agrigento, destroyed everything (except for the temples) and decided to rebuild the city at the foot of Mount Ecnomos, naming it after himself (modern Licana). Gela, now deserted, sank into oblivion. In 1230 Frederick II of Swabia founded a new city on the site. This was Terranova, a name that remained until 1927 when Mussolini restored it to Gela in memory of its glorious past, of which very little remains. Archaeologists have searched in vain for the tomb of Aeschylus, who died during his second visit to Sicily, supposedly when an eagle dropped a tortoise on his head. What has been found may be more valuable than the tomb of Aeschylus: oil. Both oil and methane were discovered off the coast in 1957 and have greatly boosted the economy of the town, which has 77,000 inhabitants.

If you are interested in archaeology stop in Gela for an hour or two; in addition to the excavations the museum is well worth a visit.

Capo Soprano fortifications*

Open daily 9am to an hour before sunset.

The Capo Soprano zone, which comprises the long high wall that formed the western ramparts of the ancient city, is of considerable archaeological interest.

The Greek wall, the finest in Sicily, has been exceptionally well preserved because it was covered by a dune very early in Antiquity. Excavations begun in 1948 revealed a wall about 984 ft/300 m long, which runs parallel to the sea and then turns north, reaching a height of 26 ft/8 m in some places. Because of the scarcity of stone in the region the upper part of the wall was made of dried clay bricks.

After leaving the archaeological zone head for the area behind the hospital, where you can see ruins of **thermal baths** dating from the Hellenistic era. These public baths are unique in Sicily.

The main street, corso Vittorio Emanuele, runs the entire length of the town, passing piazza Umberto I and the 18th-century Chiesa Madre.

Museo Archeologico***

Open daily 9am-1:30pm, 3:30-6:30pm.

This is located at the very end of corso Vittorio Emanuele in the Molino a Vento quarter.

Although Gela's monuments have left few traces of its prestigious history, archaeologists have unearthed extraordinary treasures which are exhibited in the museum. For centuries Gela was plundered by secret collectors, who sent their finds all over the world; furthermore the official excavations, begun in 1901, served only to enrich the museum in Syracuse. However, the importance of the discoveries, especially the Greek wall in 1948, led to the creation of a national museum in Gela in 1958.

The well-presented collections cover the period from the 7th to the 3rd century BC. They include Greek vases, statues, ceramics, terra-cotta figures and bronze artifacts. One of the finest exhibits is the superb terra-cotta **head of a horse*** found in Molino a Vento. It was probably part of the pediment decoration on a temple. Don't miss the **Navarra Collection**** on the 1st floor, which includes beautiful Greek pottery.

Molino a Vento

The Molino a Vento quarter, right beside the museum, was once the acropolis of Gela. Ancient houses have been brought to light, as have the ruins of two temples from the 6th and 5th centuries BC. A Doric column and part of a stylobate can be seen in the **Parco di Rimembranza** where the ancient town once stood. The interest of these ruins to nonspecialists lies more in the remarkable treasures they have produced than in the buildings themselves. From here you have a view of the beach and the sea, evoking the town's more recent history when on a morning in July 1943 the American fleet arrived. Gela was once more partly demolished but has risen again thanks to the new wealth brought by the oil business.

Environs of Gela

Lago di Disueri (10.5 mi/17 km from Gela)
Discoveries have been made of ancient tombs carved into the rocky shores of this irrigation dam. It is one of the largest prehistoric Siculian necropolises.

Butera (13 mi/21 km north of Gela) is a picturesque village of 6000 inhabitants overlooking the Gela plain and the sea. There is an 11th-century fortified castle and a **Palazzo Communale** with a beautiful 15th-century portal.

Falconara (13 mi/21 km west of Gela) is a seaside resort. Its 14th-century castle drops steeply to the shore, overlooking Roccazzelle and Mangria, two fine beaches.

Telephone area code: 0933.

Access

Car: Gela is 49.7 mi/80 km east of Agrigento, 51 mi/82 km south-east of Caltanissetta, 60 mi/97 km south-west of Catania, 128.6 mi/207 km south-east of Palermo, 36 mi/58 km west of Ragusa and 89 mi/144 km west of Syracuse.

Train: Gela is on the rail link from Syracuse to Canicatti and Caltanissetta.

Accommodation

▲▲ **Motel Agip,** on the N117 where it crosses the N115, ☎ 911 144. 91 rooms. Modern hotel with restaurant, bar and TVs in the room.

Food

L **Centrale Toto,** via Cascini 63, ☎ 913 104. *Closed Sat.* Good, simple food — try the daily suggestions. Recommended.

Useful address

Tourist information, AAST, via Navarra Bresmes, ☎ 913 788. *Open Mon-Sat 9am-1pm, 4-7pm.*

▬ *PIAZZA ARMERINA***

Piazza Armerina reached its height under the Normans during the reign of Count Roger. In 1296 Frederick III of Aragon summoned the parliament here before deciding to wage war against his brother Jacques and Charles II of Anjou, who were preparing to take the island. In 1299 the House of Anjou made a vain attempt to beseige the town.

Piazza Armerina has retained a number of interesting monuments from Norman and Aragonese times but mainly owes its fame to the **Roman villa***** at Casale, discovered in 1950 after a century-long search.

Today Piazza Armerina has a population of 22,000 and is spread over three hills at an altitude of 2365 ft/721 m.

Many people visit only the Roman villa and not the Piazza Armerina itself, which is unfortunate because it is a charming town with some remarkable monuments.

Entering the town on via Manzoni, viale della Libertà leads to piazza Cascino, the modern centre. From here via La Malfa and via Mazzini, which intersect with Marconi, lead to piazza Garibaldi, the historic centre of the old town, which has a square lined with monuments. The first building on the right is the former Church of **San Rocco** (1613), also known as Fundrò, which has a beautiful **portal***. The monastery buildings now serve as a municipal administrative centre.

On the other side of via Cavour is **Palazzo di Città** (1773), with a Baroque façade and a large balcony. It houses a cultural centre.

Duomo (Cathedral)**

Continuing along via Cavour you come to the Duomo after passing Palazzo Demani (17th century) on piazza Santa Rosalia and the Franciscan monastery, which was converted into a hospital a century ago. You can take a shortcut to the Duomo, through alleys and up flights of stairs, starting at the bottom of via Cavour on the left.

Piazza del Duomo, on the hilltop at an altitude of 2365 ft/721 m, has a splendid view from its belvedere. The long, noble façade of Palazzo Trigona (18th century) closes off one side of the square.

The Duomo itself is a grandiose Baroque edifice which was begun in 1604 (on the site of a much older church) and was completed in 1719. Of the original church, the tall Catalan-Gothic **campanile** (144 ft/44 m) remains on the right, with two levels of **arcaded windows****.

The cathedral façade has been altered several times. It has fine cabled columns around the porch above the stairs. Note the theatrical use of the front stairs and those on the right-hand side leading into the church.

The cathedral, shaped like a Latin cross, is 230 ft/70 m long and crowned by a cupola 46 ft/14 m across, giving a total height of 257 ft/77 m. An impressive building, it has recently been restored to its former splendour, including being given a new coat of white paint with blue motifs similar to the decoration on certain kinds of English porcelain. There is a fine Baroque tabernacle on the main altar, a Byzantine Virgin in a rich silver frame, and admirable carving on the wooden choir stalls.

In the chapel to the left of the choir (you can switch on the lights) is a large 15th-century wooden **crucifix**** painted by an unknown artist referred to as the Master of Piazza Armerina. The nave has two exceptionally fine **organ cases*** of gilded wood, and in the right aisle over the baptismal fonts is a theatrical **arch*** carved by the Gagini studio (1594). There are also some noteworthy paintings. The church is so richly decorated it is more like a ballroom than a religious building.

Old quarters*

From the cathedral walk down via Monte, a street that crosses a working-class quarter full of alleys at right angles that form the fishbone pattern characteristic of 13th-century town planning. After passing Palazzo Sant'Elia, beside Palazzo Trigona, take via Crocifisso on the right to the 17th-century church of the same name.

You will also find San Martino, which was the town's most important church in the 15th century.

Return to piazza Duomo and take via Floresta to your right past Palazzo Sant'Elia and the Trínita to Castello Aragonese and the church of the Madonna delle Neve. Via Vittorio Emanuele leads back to piazza Garibaldi past the church of the former Jesuit college and the former Sant'Anna convent with its convex Baroque façade. Cross piazza Garibaldi into via Umberto I to see Chiesa del Purgatorio, Palazzo Mandrascati, Chiesa dei Teatini and the church of San Stefano. Returning along via San Stefano ınd piazza Martiri, you have the chance to see the church of the former convent of Santa Chiara, that of the Dominicans and finally San Vincenzo n largo Seminario.

Returning to piazza Cascino in the modern part of town, just beyond Garibaldi gardens at the entrance to viale Ciancio, you might like to see the Church of San Pietro, which dates from the beginning of the 7th century. Inside, it has a fine coffered ceiling, sculptures by the Gaïni studio and a decorative inlaid altarpiece. All these monuments, many of which are no longer in use, testify to the town's former wealth.

Environs of Piazza Armerina

Sant'Andrea Priory* is located on the road to Park Paradiso just before ou reach the hotel, on the left. This large church, the oldest in Sicily, is one of the best examples of medieval art on the island. It was founded in the 11th century, although the present structures dates from the 12th century.

The church and convent of **Santa Maria di Gesù** are a little farther on, beyond the hotel. The convent has recently been restored, its present structure probably dating from the 16th century. On the façade there is an interesting portico composed of monolithic columns above which is a oggia with five arches.

*Villa Romana del Casale**** (3.7 mi/6 km south-west of the town)
Open daily 9am to an hour before sunset.

Starting out from piazza Cascino, first follow via Sturzo and then turn right at via Principato. At the end of the street turn right at the road to Barrafranca. After 2.4 mi/4 km you will see a signpost to the left; the entrance to the villa is 0.6 mi/1 km farther on (it has a large parking lot).

A mysterious owner

The **Villa Romana del Casale** is one of the major archaeological discoveries in recent years. It is unique among Roman finds by virtue of its sheer size, the number of rooms, the extent of the mosaics and their artistic originality. No other archaeological centre from the same epoque offers as much. Its 40 polychrome mosaic pavements cover an area of more than 37,674 sq ft/ 3500 sq m.

The location of the villa was established in 1812 by the first archaeological dig, but it wasn't until 1929 that the first mosaic, the *Labours of Hercules,* was discovered by Paolo Orsi. Part of the dwelling was excavated between 1935 and 1939, but it took until 1954 to uncover the country mansion as a whole and to restore its mosaics.

Archaeologists and historians have long argued over the identity of the owner, but it is now generally agreed that the magnificent hunting lodge belonged to Maximian (Maximianus Herculeus), who was born in central Europe in about AD 250. As soldier in Diocletian's army he fought in Gaul and in 287 was promoted to Augustus (a title given to Roman emperors) when he became responsible for Roman interests in the West. Diocletian had been appointed emperor by his soldiers and set up a tetrarchy to be ruled by two Augustuses (Maximian and himself) aided by two seconds-in-command, or Caesars Galerius and Constancius. During their reign Christians were violently persecuted. Diocletian abdicated in 305 and forced Maximian to do the same. He revolted and finally took his own life in Marseilles in 310.

Whoever the owner, his taste and fortune, evident in the villa's layout and decoration, testify to the luxury in which certain people lived at that time. It is possible to date the villa from the 3rd century AD. It was built over a far more modest 2nd-century construction, and some of the mosaics bear traces of restoration carried out in the 6th century.

There is also a regular bus service in summer, check at the tourist office. Because the villa is one of the most popular sights in Sicily you should choose a time to go when you can avoid the bus loads of tourists. A gigantic and unattractive transparent shelter has been built to preserve the mosaics, and walkways have been installed so you don't step on any of the precious ornamental tiling.

You follow a complex series of arrow signs which occasionally lead you out of the shelter or make you walk all the way around the outside of a room before you can enter it (see the floor plan). If you visit the villa in summer the covered ways can become unbearably hot; bring along a bottle of mineral water and a paper fan (on sale at the entrance).

1. Frigidarium. An octagonal room with mosaic of sea creatures surrounded by six small apses, some serving as vestibules and others as swimming pools which were supplied with water by the aqueduct.

2. Small massage room (seen from the outside). People came here for relaxation after their bath — one can easily distinguish the mosaic of a massage scene. The massage room leads to the tepidarium, now ruined which was heated by underground channels connected to an exterior fireplace.

3. Small vestibule. This is a circular room decorated with geometric patterns.

4. Vestibule. After crossing the polygonal court you reach the vestibule which leads to the main part of the villa. Here you can see a mosaic of servants welcoming guests with laurels and candelabra. Walk around this room to the left to enter the large peristyle.

5. Peristyle. This is a large rectangular court (125 × 59 ft/38 × 18 m) surrounded by columns with Corinthian capitals and medallion-shaped mosaics of animal heads. You go down a few steps outside to see the small uncovered latrine.

6. Small latrine. This ladies latrine has rectangular bidets.

7. Palaestra (circus hall). Illustrating races at the Circus Maximus in Rome, the race track is shown in the centre, the spectators and imperial box are on the left and temples to various divinities are on the right. The four teams participating in the chariot races are wearing different colours.

8. Small vestibule. This is a trapezoidal chamber of mosaics depicting a group of people with attendant servants on their way to the baths. From here you walk up a footbridge to look down on the room called the 'Norman oven'.

9. 'Norman oven' room. Used for baking ceramics, this room was mostly destroyed during the Arab period.

10. Room with geometrical decoration of squares, hexagons and stars with six points.

11. Dance room. In the partly damaged scene of six dancing couples note the beautiful figure of the dancing girl encircled in her scarf. It has been suggested that this scene illustrates the Rape of the Sabine Women.

12. Room with geometric decoration and stars with eight points.

13. Room where the mosaics have disappeared.

14. Room of the seasons. Depicted here are fish, birds and four human figures representing the seasons.

15. Room of the small hunt*. The mosaics here are exceptional: the scenes are varied, of superb quality and very well preserved. They illustrate servants with dogs, hunters making sacrifices to Diana and in the middle a group taking refreshment under a red awning.

16. Room of fishing amorini. Depicted here are cupids aboard four boats in the middle of a ballet of dolphins, with a sumptuous villa in the background.

17. Room with square mosaics.

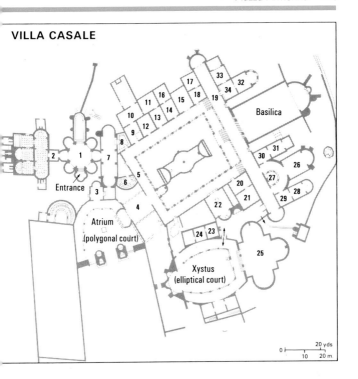

VILLA CASALE

18. **Room** with octagonal mosaics.

19. **Corridor** (ambulacrum) **of the great hunt*****. This is a magnificent mosaic covering an area of 3767 sq ft/350 sq m. It is 197 ft/60 m long and is composed of three parts: the pursuit and capture of wild animals, the loading of the animals onto a galley ship and their disembarkation. In the centre is a group of officials, with a man in charge directing the loading operations. The two places depicted in the apses at the ends of the galery are Africa and Arabia — no doubt the countries that supplied the animals.

20. **Sitting rooms.** The first, with a geometric decoration, leads into the famous room with girls in 'bikinis'.

21. **Room of young girls in 'bikinis'.** The most famous mosaic in the villa is probably the most recent; it lies over an earlier mosaic dating from the first (more modest) villa of the 2nd century AD. On the upper level the girls are shown taking part in races and doing gymnastics, on the lower they play ball and the winners are crowned.

22. **Room of the Orphic myth.** The legend of the poet Orpheus is depicted here.

The visit continues from here into the elliptical courtyard, which was once adorned with two central fountains and statues of divinities in the niches on the sides.

23. **Room of children picking grapes** (in poor condition).

24. **Room of children pressing grapes** as they are transported in carts to a farm (in very poor condition).

25. **Triclinium** (dining room). This is a large, beautifully decorated room with three apses. In the centre you can see the Labours of Hercules, who is symbolized as a powerful hero combating monstrous creatures. The mosaic in the left-hand apse depicts the glorification of Hercules,

crowned with laurels. The middle strip shows firstly the metamorphosis of Daphne, who, being pursued by Apollo, prayed to the gods to be changed into a laurel tree, and second that of Cyparissos who, on killing his favourite stag, turned into a cypress tree. The apse at the back contains five giants struck by the fatal arrows of Hercules.

On leaving the dining room retrace your steps and walk to the room of the mistress of the house.

26. Room of the mistress of the house. In this room you can see a mosaic of Arion amid Naiads and other mythical characters, abandoning ship to continue his journey in a small boat.

27. Atrium (boudoir) with a mosaic of cupids fishing.

28. Mosaic illustrating musicians and actors getting ready to perform a tragedy. This was a children's room as were the following three.

29. Room of the children's circus. The different teams bear the same colours as those in room 7.

30. Fight between Pan and Eros.

31. Hunting scenes. Next, leave the building and walk around the reception room, which is shaped like a basilica — a style later used for Christian churches.

32. Bed chamber belonging to the master of the house. It has an apse and is decorated with fruit and flowers.

33. Antechamber to the master bedroom with an erotic scene in the centre.

34. Private apartments. There is a mosaic of **Ulysses and Polyphemus** in which the cyclops is portrayed with three eyes.

Aidone and the Morgantina excavations (10 mi/16 km)

Site open daily 9am to an hour before sunset.

Continue along the N117 toward Enna and after 2.1 mi/3.4 km turn right onto the N288, which leads to Aidone. This village of 7500 inhabitants has a gorgeous panoramic view. The church of Sant'Anna contains a fine crucifix by Fra Umile da Petralía. Turn left 3.1 mi/5 km out of Aidone following the sign to Scavi di Morgantina; you can take your car right up to the entrance of the ruins. Excavations have unearthed a pre-Hellenistic city, known as Morgantina, which was destroyed by the Romans.

The entry gate leads to the *agora* (market place). To the right, lining the sides of the enclosure, are the remains of the gymnasium and baths as well as a *bouleuterion* (city council chamber). Walk alongside the large portico on the left to reach a fine trapezoidal stairway. This extraordinarily shaped edifice is the only one of its kind in Hellenistic architecture and is remarkably well preserved. It was probably used for public assemblies. Just beside it on the hill on the right is a 4th-century BC theatre with an orchestra area and rows of seats divided into five sections. To the east, on the hill opposite the theatre, is the residential quarter with its houses and alleys. From here you have a wonderful view of the ruins and especially of the theatre embedded in the hillside.

Telephone area code: 0935.

Access

Car: Piazza Armerina is 28 mi/45 km north of Gela, 30 mi/48 km east of Caltanissetta, 49.7 mi/80 km west of Catania, 21.7 mi/35 km south of Enna, 110 mi/177 km south-west of Messina, 61.5 mi/99 km north-west of Ragusa and 86 mi/139 km west of Syracuse. From Gela, take the N117B.

Train: Trains from Catania, Palermo and Agrigento stop at Dittaino, where a bus takes passengers on to Piazza Armerina.

Bus: Buses from Piazza Armerina to Catania, Aidone (Morgantina), Caltagirone, Caltanissetta, Enna and Gela depart from piazza Cascino.

Accommodation

▲▲ **Park Hotel Paradiso,** contrada Ramoldo, 1.2 mi/2 km from the town centre, ☎ 680 841. 26 rooms. Simple establishment with an average restaurant and pizzeria.
▲ **Selene,** via Generale Gaeta 30, on the way to Enna, ☎ 682 254. 42 rooms.

Festivals

May 3 memorializes the day when Count Roger and his soldiers were beseiged on top of the hill. Miraculously, they found a spring and built the Duomo there as a gesture of gratitude.
Palio dei Normanni (Norman Joust) takes place on August 13 and 14. This is a competition by riders in medieval costume, one of the few still held in Sicily today. On the first day of the *palio* the entrance of Count Roger into Piazza Armerina is commemorated and on the second there are various riding tournaments throughout the town.

Food

LL Da Battiato, just over 2 mi/3.5 km from the centre, near the Villa Casale, ☎ 82 453. Good food, with local specialities.
LL Da Toto Centrale, via Mazzini 29, ☎ 680 153. *Closed Fri.* Good regional dishes. Simple but recommended.
LL Europa da Pipo, piazza Gen. Cascino, ☎ 680 575. *Closed Sun.*
LL Papillon, via Manzoni, ☎ 82 524. *Closed Mon.*
LL Pepito, via Roma 140, ☎ 82 737. *Closed Tues and throughout Dec.* Country trattoria with a few tables outside serving local dishes. Recommended.
LL Primavera di Randazzo, on the 117B, contrada Cameni, 6.2 mi/10 km from Piazza Armerina, ☎ 970 387. *Closed Wed.* Excellent food — everything is made by the restaurant, including the bread.
L Al Ritrovo, on the road to Enna, ☎ 681 890. *Closed Mon.* The only restaurant worth recommending near the site.

Useful address

Tourist information, AAST, via Cavour 15, ☎ 680 201. *Open Mon-Sat 8am-2pm and also Tues, Wed, Thurs and Fri 4:30-7:30pm.*

GELA TO CATANIA

65.2 mi/105 km on the N417.

Caltagirone: ceramic capital (24.2 mi/39 km north-west of Gela)
This is a town of 37,000 inhabitants picturesquely located on three hills, at an altitude of 1998 ft/609 m. It is the centre of the ceramic industry and is popularly referred to as the 'queen of the mountains' although its name is of Arab origin and means 'fortress'. The town was destroyed by the earthquake of 1693 and as a result has tortuous little streets and irregular squares and stairways.

You arrive in Caltagirone from Gela on via Duca degli Abruzzi at the end of which is the Norman church of **San Giacomo,** rebuilt after the earthquake in 1693. The three aisles have monolithic columns and marble arches carved by the Gagini studio. There is also a 16th-century silver reliquary by Giacomo Gagini and a statue of San Giacomo by Archifel (1518).

Continue along via Vittorio Emanuele to piazza del Municipio where you will see **Corte Capitaniale** to your right, a fine 16th- and 17th-century building with decoration by the Gagini on the portals and windows. Just opposite is the new Galleria Luigi Sturzo (named after the founder of the Christian Democrat Party), a popular meeting place.

From piazza del Municipio the second street on the right leads to piazzo Mercato and the church of **Santa Maria di Gesù** (16th century) with its twelve 17th-century statues. There are richly decorated marble altars inside and carved, gilded wooden stalls. Via Luigi Sturzo leads off to the left of the Municipio to a little square where you will find the Rosario and Salvatore (18th century) churches. The latter houses a *Madonna and Child* by Antonello Gagini (1532). At the end of via Sturzo you come to San Giorgio Church, of which only the tower remains from the original architecture. Inside, near the second altar on the left, there is a painting of the Trinity by Rogier van der Weyden, of the Flemish school.

La Scala is a monumental **stairway** that was built between the upper and the lower towns in 1608. It begins at the foot of via Sturzo and has 142 steps adorned with majolica tiles. These were fashioned by artists in 1954 using patterns that were in use in the 10th century. During the Feast of San Giacomo (July 24-25) the steps are illuminated by paper lanterns.

For those brave enough to climb the steps, Santa Maria del Monte is at the top. The church has an elegant campanile by Marvuglia and inside above the main altar, a highly venerated 13th-century *Virgin and Child* and a 15th-century statue of the Virgin. You have a panoramic view of the town from the terrace.

Return to piazza Municipio, which extends into piazza Umberto I where you will find the **Duomo** (San Giuliano). It was altered entirely in the 19th century and has a rich treasury. On the right inside there is a 15th century crucifix and on the left a figure of Christ by Giacomo Vaccaro (1848) made of painted wood. Continue along via Roma where you will see **Palazzo del Monte di Pietà** (18th century) on the right. This was a prison in Bourbon times and is now a Museo Civico *(open Tues-Sat 9:30am-2pm, Sun 10am-noon; closed Mon).*

Via Roma crosses a 17th-century viaduct and then runs alongside public gardens decorated with both terra-cotta and ceramic vases. In the gardens is the **Museo Regionale della Ceramica*** *(open Tues-Sat 9:30am-2pm, Sun and holidays 9am-1pm; closed Mon).* The collections trace the development of ceramics from prehistory to the present day. There is a reconstruction of a potter's oven on the patio.

Telephone area code: 0933.

Accommodation

▲▲ **Grand Hotel Villa San Mauro,** via Porto Salvo 18, ☎ 26 500 92 rooms. Outside the town centre. Swimming pool and restaurant in a lovely setting.

Festivals

Biennial exhibition of Sicilian ceramics; **Feast of San Giacomo** at the end of July and **Feast of the Madonna** in August.

Food

LL Ristorante Scivoli, via Madonna della Via 161. *Closed Tues.*

Useful address

Tourist information, Pro Loco, in Corte Capitaniale palace, ☎ 22 539 Exhibition and sale of ceramics *(open Mon-Sat 9am-1pm, 4-8:30pm).*

Caltagirone to Catania: 41 mi/66 km on the N417.

Caltagirone to Syracuse: On the N124 via Vizzini and Palazzolo Acreide (part of this itinerary is described on p. 157).

GELA TO SYRACUSE: BAROQUE SICILY

Roman ruins, Baroque art, towns perched on rocky spurs, sea vistas, ancient necropolises with cave paintings, troglodyte dwellings, vestiges of ancient Greece, Byzantium, and Arabia reign all merge together to create a tableau of harmonious contrasts in this region of Sicily.

The most convenient road to take for this itinerary is the N115 (90 mi/145 km); it includes Ragusa, Modica and Noto.

GELA TO RAGUSA

Vittória (19.8 mi/32 km east of Gela)

This is a large wine and oil-producing centre with a population of 53,000, located on the slopes of the Iblei Mountains. It was founded in 1607 by Vittoria Colonna, the daughter of a viceroy, and built according to an ordered, regular plan. Of particular interest are the fine, neo-classical theatre, the Church of the Madonna delle Gracia and the Chiesa Madre. There is a wonderful panoramic view of the surrounding countryside from the public gardens. A **Museum of Sicilian Carts** was set up in 1989 with the private collection of a local craftsman; inquire at the Municipio for the latest information *(open Mon-Sat 9am-noon, 4-8pm)*. A road from Vittória leads south (8 mi/13 km) to Scoglitti, a seaside resort in a little fishing village.

Cómiso (24.8 mi/40 km east of Gela)

This is a small town (30,000 inhabitants) that dates in part from the 18th century. The town has often made the news because of demonstrations held here protesting the American nuclear missile base nearby.

Noteworthy monuments in the town include a beautiful fountain of Diana (1937) on piazza Municipio and, behind the town hall, the ruins of thermal baths (of which the mosaic pavement has been transferred to the municipal library). The 15th-century Chiesa Matrice was rebuilt after the earthquake of 1693. The Church of **San Francesco** dates from the 13th century and contains fine altars and the tomb of Naselli by Antonello Gagini. In the 16th-century Church of the **Annunziata** you can see baptismal fonts by Mario Rutelli and the *Assumption of the Virgin* by Bidonio. You should also see the **Castello Feudale** of the Naselli family of Aragona, parts of which date from the 14th century. It was altered in the 16th century but has kept its original low octagonal tower and a Gothic portal. There is a Byzantine baptistry inside.

Camarina ruins: A road leads from Cómiso to the necropolis of Camarina (13 mi/21 km south), an ancient Syracusan town, founded in 598 BC, that was destroyed by the Romans in 258 BC. Here you can see ruins of the original walls and a temple to Athena. Excavations in 1896 unearthed a number of works now exhibited in the museums of Ragusa and Syracuse. Some of the finds are displayed in a small museum on the site *(open Mon-Sat 9am-1pm, Sun 9am-2pm; ruins open daily 9am-6pm*

Cómiso to Ragusa: The N115 twists up into the Iblei Mountain affording spectacular views of the Ippari plain. After 7.4 mi/12 km, a roa on the left leads to **Chiaramonte Gulfi** (9.3 mi/15 km), which has a 14t century castle founded by Manfredi Chiaramonte, count of Módica. (note also are the public gardens and the Sanctuary of Madonna di Gul a place of pilgrimage.

RAGUSA: TWIN CITY

29.8 mi/48 km east of Gela.

Geographically speaking, the ancient Greek city of Hybla Heraea is on of the strangest towns in Sicily, located on a ridge between two rock valleys, the San Leonardo and Santa Domenica gorges. It is divided int two very different parts which were distinct communities until 1926 There is modern Ragusa (at 1634 ft/498 m) on the one hand, whic was rebuilt in a grid plan after the 1693 earthquake; and Ragusa Ibla (a 1263 ft/385 m) on the other, which is far more picturesque and has wealth of Baroque buildings.

The present town (66,000 inhabitants) is thriving, as a result of th petrochemical industry set up near local oil wells and asphalt deposits.

Ragusa

You enter the town on corso Italia. Turn right at via Roma, which lead to Ponte Nuovo. Just before the bridge a flight of steps leads down t the museum.

Museo Archeologico
Open Mon-Sat 9am-1pm, Sun and holidays 9am-2pm.

Among the displays are some beautiful Greek vases discovered in 1972 statuettes found at Scornavacche and two large mosaics from Camarina

Duomo (Cathedral)
Cross the Ponte Nuovo, which spans the Cava di Santa Domenica, an then go on to piazza della Libertà, the administrative centre of town. little farther on you come to piazza del Popolo and via Leonardo da Vinc which leads back to the Ponte dei Cappuccini. This was built at the be ginning of the 19th century and affords an impressive view of the ravin and Ponte Nuovo.

After the bridge you soon reach piazza San Giovanni Battista, a squar built on two levels, where you will see the heavy Baroque Duom (1706-60). The interior consists of three vast aisles separated b monolithic columns with capitals. The decoration includes fine stuccoe and 19th-century paintings. Just behind the cathedral is Casa Canonic with its beautiful balconies.

By taking corso Italia from the square and then via 24 Maggio (whic twists on down the hillside) you come to a bend in the road with the sma church of Santa Maria delle Scale on the right. This was built in th 15th and 16th centuries and then altered entirely at the end of the 18th century. Parking is available.

Ragusa Ibla

You can reach Ragusa Ibla on foot from Santa Maria delle Scale by takin the steps *(le scale)* that lead to the Church of Santa Maria dell'Idria an two 18th-century palaces, Bertini and Cosentini. If you go by car tak corso Mazzini, which ends at piazza della Repubblica; there is a sma parking lot.

From piazza della Repubblica turn left at via del Mercato and via de XI Febbraio and continue to largo Camarina; cross to the right to piazz

The two cities of Ragusa, one ancient and one modern, have bee
united since 192(

del Duomo. Here you will find a finely crafted balustrade closing off a flight of steps, at the top of which rises the beautiful, harmonious façade of **San Giorgio,** built by the architect Rosario Gagliardi between 1738 and 1775. The impressive neo-classical dome was added in 1820 and is 148 ft/45 m high. It rests on a drum supported by 16 columns; unfortunately the spaces between these have been filled in with blue stained glass. The convex façade is extremely elegant with its three tiers and bell tower. The latter has been skillfully integrated into the façade with clever positioning of the columns.

Inside there is a collection of Baroque art. The sacristy houses a marble altarpiece from the Gagini school and a treasury.

There are other places of interest in the town. Below the piazza take via XXV Aprile, which passes Palazzo Donnafugata (on the left) and leads to piazza Pola. Here you see the fine Baroque façade of the Church of San Giuseppe (1590) attributed to Rosario Gagliardi.

On the left, in via Orfanotrofrio, is the church of Sant'Antonio with a Gothic portal on the right flank. Corso XXV Aprile leads off from the end of piazza Pola and continues to a public garden (Giardino Ibleo) with a good view and three more churches. On the right, near the entrance to the garden, is the former church of San Giorgio Vecchio. Of its original 15th-century construction, only the magnificent Catalan-Gothic portal remains, with a worn relief of St George and the Dragon on the tympanum.

Head back toward piazza del Duomo and you will see the noble façade of the Circolo di Conversazione on the right. This is for members only but try all the same to catch a glimpse of the interior with its large sitting area, its red velvet sofas, mirrors, tall windows and *trompe l'œil* ceiling. It's as if time has stood still here for decades; this is the Sicily of Lampedusa's book *The Leopard,* recreated in the film by Luchino Visconti.

Environs of Ragusa

South of Ragusa (1.2 mi/2 km) there are open asphalt mines with a small **archaeological park** nearby *(open daily 9am-1pm).* You can see quarries known as *latomiae* and the tombs of a Christian *hypogeum* (4th to 5th century).

Telephone area code: 0937.

Accommodation

▲▲ **Montreal,** corso Italia 70, ☎ 21 133. 63 rooms. Good service.

Festivals

The religious and folklore **Festival of San Giorgio** is celebrated at Ibla on April 25. That of **San Giovanni Battista** is held August 27 to 29.

Food

LL **Jonio,** via Risorgimento 49, ☎ 24 322. *Closed Fri.* Regional specialities.

LL **U Saracinu,** opposite the Duomo, ☎ 46 976. Excellent, traditional cuisine in lovely vaulted basement.

LL **Villa Fortugno,** on the road to Marina Ragusa, 3.1 mi/5 km from town, ☎ 28 656. *Closed Mon.* Fine decor in a country house.

Campground
Baia del Sole, on the Lungomare, ☎ 39 844. *Open all year.*

Useful address

Tourist information, piazza Duomo in Ragusa Ibla, ☎ 67 330. *Open daily 8:30am-2:30pm, 3-8pm.* Also: via Callodi, on the corner of via Corbino, ☎ 651 510. *Open Mon-Sat 8:30am-2pm.*

MÓDICA

(47.2 mi/76 km east of Gela)

Módica was an ancient Siculian city and later a rural Roman centre mentioned in the writings of Cicero. Today it has a population of 49,000 and is divided into two parts: **Módica Alta** stands on a rocky spur, and **Módica Bassa** was built on the banks of two streams that converge at the foot of the rock. Some fine Baroque churches testify to the town's past splendour.

On corso Umberto, in the lower town, you will find the Church of the **Carmine** with its 15th-century Gothic portal and a rose window on its façade. Inside there is a marble sculpture by Antonello Gagini representing the Annunciation and a painting dating from the first half of the 15th century. Piazza Principe di Piemonte, the town centre, is located at the confluence of the two streams, now covered over. Turn right on via Marchese Tedeschi to the Church of **Santa Maria di Betlem,** which probably originated in the 13th century but was rebuilt after 1693. Its chapel is a good example of the late Gothic architecture that borrowed from Arab-Norman and Catalan styles.

Near the end of corso Umberto, at the top of a flight of stairs adorned with statues of the Apostles, you will see the sumptuous 18th-century façade of the Church of **San Pietro,** patron saint of the town. To reach the upper town, keep to the left side of the church and then take corso Garibaldi.

San Giorgi***

The splendid façade of San Giorgio by Rosario Gagliardi is one of the most beautiful examples of Baroque architecture on the island. It is preceded by a theatrical staircase made of four oval sections with a total of 250 steps. The church itself stands out against the sky like a great stone tabernacle, especially in the afternoon light.

Not only did Gagliardi have an innate sense of spectacle, shown by his church in Ragusa, but also he took the minutest detail into account. Note the quality of the sculptures that adorn the porches, creating a lovely harmony of circles, shells and volutes. At sunset the stone takes on a beautiful honey colour that makes the effect even more striking.

The interior consists of a nave and four aisles and is painted white, blue and gold. In a chapel on the right there is a repository containing the relics of San Giorgio. A meridian figure has been drawn on the pavement in front of the choir. Over the main altar you can see nine panels dating from 1513, illustrating the life of St George and various scenes from the Gospels.

Museo Civico

Open Mon-Sat 8am-2pm; closed holidays.

Before leaving Módica, we recommend a short visit to the small museum in corso Umberto opposite the Church of San Pietro. It houses artifacts found in the area, among them a very strange statue from a temple to honour the Sun, as well as paintings from the 18th and 19th centuries. The **Museo Ibleo delle Arti e delle Tradizioni Popolari** is in the annex, where you can see reconstructed artisan shops and a reconstructed farm.

Environs of Módica

Scicli (6.8 mi/11 km south of Módica)

This town of 25,000 inhabitants is off the conventional tourist trail, in a valley between two hills on a pretty road leading to Donnalucata. Some of its interesting 18th-century palaces have been preserved, such as **Palazzo Beneventano** with its monstrous decorative figures on the balconies and, above the windows, grotesque masks. There are also a number of Baroque churches, including Matrice, San Bartolomeo and

Santa Maria la Nova, that provide a satisfying conclusion to a Baroque art lover's visit to Ragusa and Módica.

La Cava d'Ispica * (8 mi/13 km east of Módica)
Open daily 9am-1pm, Tues and Thurs 3-6 pm.
You have a choice of roads to get here but the best is the one to Ispica (N115). At the Béttola del Capitano crossroads you turn left and take a small country road for 3.4 mi/5.5 km.

This is a valley in one of the limestone plateaus in the Iblei Mountains. Over a distance of more than 6.2 mi/10 km you can see traces of primitive dwellings, the oldest dating from the Bronze Age (Castellucio). There are Siculian necropolises, troglodyte dwellings, Palaeo-Christian catacombs from the 4th and 5th centuries, and caves converted into chapels containing Byzantine paintings. The custodian from Molino Cavallo d'Ispica can accompany you along the track through the valley and show you the most interesting caves.

Módica to Noto

Continue along the N115. It passes just south of **Ispica** where, in the Church of Santa Maria Maggiore, you can see paintings by Stozzi and Vito d'Anna. As you leave town there's a road south-east to **Pachino** (12.4 mi/20 km), a wine-producing centre located in a geological zone with interesting caves in Calafarina and Capo Passero on the tip of the Golfo di Noto.

The N115 continues on to Noto from Ispica, after passing the market town of **Rosolini,** with its ancient catacombs and the Castello del Principe (1668).

Telephone area code: 0932.

Accommodation

▲▲ **Motel di Módica,** corso Umberto 1, Módica, ☎ 941 022. 12 rooms. Inexpensive hotel, with restaurant and garage.

Food

LL Trattoria La Rusticana, viale Medaglia d'Oro 34, Módica. *Closed Mon.* Typical local dishes.

▬▬ *NOTO**, APOTHEOSIS OF BAROQUE*

Map coordinates refer to the map p. 153.
72 mi/116 km east of Gela.
Noto, the largest centre (22,000 inhabitants), in the province of

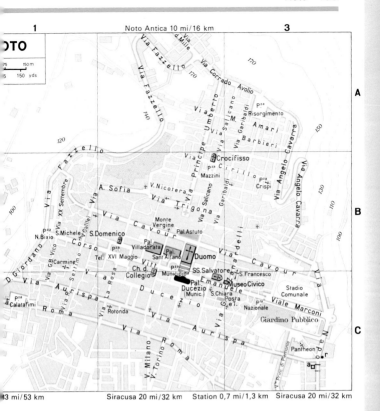

Noto Antica 10 mi/16 km

43 mi/53 km   Siracusa 20 mi/32 km   Station 0,7 mi/1,3 km   Siracusa 20 mi/32 km

Syracuse, is a relatively recent town. It was destroyed by an earthquake in 1693 when ancient Neai or Netum was reduced to a heap of ruins. The inhabitants decided to rebuild their city on a hillside facing the sea. Not only was their choice of site a good one but Giovanni Battista Landolina, a patrician and great patron of the arts, called upon the architect Rosario Gagliardi to design the town. A Noto man himself (already mentioned as the architect of San Giorgio cathedral in Módica) Gagliardi devoted all his talent to the rebuilding of his native town, with the result that it is one of the most beautiful Baroque towns in the world.

Landolina designed the town plan around three main parallel axes which ran horizontally across the hillside. Three squares were introduced to break the monotony of the urban layout and on each of them a church was placed as backdrop. To reinforce the architectural unity of the town, only one type of material was used: a beautifully soft yellow limestone.

The result is striking — so perfectly harmonious that you almost take Noto for a model rather than a real town, a kind of immense stage where you half expect an actor in period costume to appear and deliver a line. Unfortunately, most of the monuments are currently being restored and are hidden behind scaffolding. The work will take several years.

Count on two or three hours to see the town, preferably in the afternoon when the light is at its best.

If you're coming from Módica, continue straight ahead on via Giordano to piazza Bixio, where you turn right into corso Vittorio Emanuele, the town's main street, lined with churches and mansions. Follow this right across the town to viale Marconi, C3, where you can park alongside the public gardens. This is the most convenient starting point for your visit.

Porta Nazionale, C3, a powerful triumphal arch with capitals, stands on corso Vittorio Emanuele. It was built in 1838 for the first visit of King Ferdinand II, who so loved Noto that he returned to the town twice. Immediately on the right, in piazza Immacolata, you will see the façade of the church of San Francesco, C3, built by Vincenzo Sinatra, a local architect. It rises above a theatrical staircase divided into three sections. Across from the church, on the other side of via Zanardelli, is the monastery of San Salvatore — an impressively austere building flanked by a massive keep and adorned with windows protected by finely worked wrought-iron bars.

Museo Civico C2

Open Mon-Sat 9am-1pm.

The museum is located on the ground floor of San Salvatore and contains prehistoric, Greek and medieval works. The latter come mainly from the Norman abbey of Santa Lucia del Mendolo and from ancient Noto. Several works of modern art are displayed in the reception room, once part of the former Santa Chiara Monastery. The Church of Santa Chiara itself, on the other side of the corso, is a small, well-proportioned oval edifice designed by Gagliardi in 1718.

A little farther on you come to piazza del Municipio, B2, where Palazzo Ducezio stands facing the stairs leading up to the Duomo.

Palazzo Ducezio* C2

Another of Sinatra's works, this is a beautiful building inaugurated in 1746. The original design was comprised of only a ground floor with 11 arches upheld by pilasters and half columns. The three central arches curve out from the rest of the building and are reached by a semicircular flight of steps. The palace was converted into a town hall, and a first floor was added in 1951, somewhat spoiling the balance of the whole. We recommend you walk around the building to get an idea of the original design.

Duomo (Cathedral)* B2

Dominating the piazza is the Duomo's impressive façade. The cathedral was completed in 1776 and is dedicated to San Nicola di Mira and San Corrado. The genius of the architects is reflected in the theatrical appearance of the building and the immense tripartite outside staircase.

The long façade is a masterpiece of proportion. Above you can see four statues of the Evangelists crowning the vertical sweep begun by the four columns which frame the side portals. The dome was built in 1872 to replace the original, which was damaged in a minor earthquake. The central door, illustrating the life of San Corrado (patron saint of the town), is contemporary (1982).

Other sites

Closing the perspective on the right side of the Duomo are **Palazzo Vescovile** (the episcopal palace) and the Church of San Salvatore. The sober, elegant, neo-classical façade of the latter's monastery was commissioned in 1791 to replace the original, which was considered too plain for the square.

Continue along the corso to the **Collegio Church,** on the left, or San Carlo, B2, with its convex façade in three different styles. It was designed by Rosario Gagliardi (between 1736 and 1746). Nearby the former Jesuit college now houses a high school. Note the strange sculpted figures supporting the original balconies.

The corso continues to piazza XVI Maggio, B2, planted with fine trees, beneath which is a statue of Hercules from the ruins of Noto Antica. Hercules is triumphantly holding up the town's coat of arms. In the background the walls of a Dominican convent frame the sumptuous façade*** of **San Domenico,** designed by Gagliardi between 1703 and 1727. The influences of Roman architecture and Spanish Baroque are integrated in San Domenico with those of the Sicilian school. It's more a rococo palace than a church. Note the pointed volutes in the side niches; their proportion and balance almost outdo any natural shell.

The furniture inside is 17th century and there is a Madonna del Rosario by Vito d'Anna. Outside, to the left of the church, is the former Dominican convent, which now houses an institute and the communal library.

Continuing along the corso you reach via Settimo which leads to the **Church of the Carmine,** B1. Its concave façade with three styles of pilasters was designed by Sinatra. The oval interior is decorated with white stucco.

Walk back up the street into via Galilei then take vie Sofia, Trigona and finally Principe Umberto to see the **Church of the Crocifisso,** B2. This church was never completed but is crowned by a remarkable dome and has lions standing guard on either side of the doorway. These were salvaged from the ruins of Noto Antica, as was the statue inside of the *Madonna del Nave and Child* by Francesco Laurana (1471).

Return to via Cavour, B2. This runs parallel to corso Vittorio Emanuele and boasts a number of palaces. Near Palazzo di Lorenzo stands the church of **Monte Vergine** (1762) noted for the perfection of its shape and its unusually bare concave façade set between twin campaniles. For reasons of perspective it was intended to be seen from the end of via Nicolaci (mentioned below). To the left is Palazzo Astuto and to the right Palazzo Trigona, with its eight balconies adorned with wrought ironwork. Via Nicolaci connects via Cavour to corso Vittorio Emanuele and runs between Palazzo Sant'Alfano, B2, on the left, and on the right, **Palazzo Villadorata,** designed by Gagliardi in about 1731. The rectangular façade is noteworthy firstly for its wide doorway, which opens onto a sloped courtyard designed for carriages, and secondly for its two rows of impressive windows. Those on top are adorned with 'pot-bellied' balconies of wrought iron shaped like 'the breast of a goose' that bulge out over an unusual assortment of supporting sculptures. They include monsters, griffons, sphinxes, centaurs, cherubs and old men; all masks of 'a theatre of derision' illustrating the apogee of Sicilian Baroque. Look back now to the church of Monte Vergine to see how well it fits into the decor, gracefully closing off the perspective of the narrow street between the two rows of palaces.

Telephone area code: 0931.

Accommodation

▲ **Stella,** via Nuova Aurispa, C3 a, ☎ 835 695. 21 rooms. If you stay the night in Noto, this is the place — it's the only hotel in town.

In Marina di Noto (3 mi/5 km east)

▲▲▲ **Hotel Club Eloro,** ☎ 812 242. 206 rooms. Best to check beforehand on booking availability. This large hotel offers many facilities, including private beach, swimming pool, tennis courts and a restaurant.

You could also try Pachino and environs: Mazarmemi (2.4 mi/4 km) and Portopalo (4.3 mi/7 km), where there are several small hotels and tourist resorts.

Food

L Trieste, via Napoli 17, C3 r. Very simple fare.

Useful address

Tourist information, Pro Loco, Piassa XVI Maggio, B2, ☎ 836 744. *Open April-Oct daily 9am-8pm; Nov-March daily 8am-2pm, 4-6pm.*

▭ ENVIRONS OF NOTO

Noto Marina (5 mi/8 km east of Noto)

Leave town on the road to Syracuse and then follow the signs to the right to reach this small seaside resort. There is a beautiful sand beach. The resort is the most southerly in Sicily, and you can swim here most of the year.

Outside Noto Marina are the ruins of the ancient Greek city of Helorus, and nearby, on a small headland, is a column 34 ft/10.5 m tall, known as Pizzuta. In **Caddedi**, on the Pachino road, archaeologists have excavated a 4th-century Roman villa with magnificent floor mosaics.

Noto Antica (11 mi/18 km north-west of Noto)

Leave Noto on via dei Mille, which leads onto the road to Palazzolo Acréide. You pass the **Hermitage of San Corrado,** located at the end of a gravel drive. Inside, above the main altar, there is a 1759 painting of the saint. After about 6.2 mi/10 km take the small road to the left, which leads to Noto Antica. This was a former Sicilian city and later became capital of one of the three valleys into which the island was divided by the Arabs for administrative reasons. It once spread over a distance of more than a kilometre but was abandoned after being completely destroyed by the 1693 earthquake. All that remains today are a few structures, including the Porta Reale, two toppled bastions and the ruins of a castle.

Palazzolo Acréide* (18.6 mi/30 km north-west of Noto on the 287)

Although it's off the usual tourist track, it's an excursion not to be missed. There are beautiful views on the road from Noto and the ancient city of Akrai is charming.

Palazzolo Acréide is an agricultural centre 1302 ft/397 m high in the Iblei mountains with a population of 10,000. It was founded in 664 BC by the Syracusans; though destroyed later by the Arabs, there are some interesting ruins on the hill at Acremonte. Don't miss the lovely public gardens at the entrance to the town, where there is a good view of the Anapos Valley, a fertile, hilly landscape. Among the buildings of note is the striking **San Paolo Church,** north of piazza Roma. It was designed by Sinatra in about 1750 and has a fine columned portico, a balustrade, blind arches, volutes and statues.

In the centre of town, rising above a staircase on piazza del Popolo, is the **San Sebastiano Church,** dating from 1609. Built in the late Renaissance style it has three different architectural orders on the façade. Nearby you can see the arches on the front of the town hall.

If you take corso Vittorio Emanuele III left from here you reach Palazzo Ludica (nº 10) where there's a collection of finds from excavations of the ancient city. Palazzo Pizzo Gugliemo at nº 38 has a fine doorway. At the end of the corso is the Church of the Immacolato with an interestingly convex façade. To see the statue inside of the *Madonna with Child** by Francesco Laurana, enquire at the college behind the church. The unfinished 18th-century Church of the Annunciata has a striking Baroque portal with cabled columns.

Finally, a group of objects pertaining to Sicilian folklore, that belong to a local collector, Antonio Uccelo, are displayed in the ethnographical museum, which is unfortunately closed at the moment.

Archaeological Zone (Noto Antica)

Open Tues-Sun 9am-an hour before sunset; closed Mon.

You can either continue straight ahead to reach the archaeological zone or drive along a new panoramic road.

A small path leads from the entrance of the zone to the late **Greek theatre** (3rd century BC; altered during the Roman era), an elegant, remarkably well-preserved construction. The 12 rows of the cavea could hold 600 spectators. The orchestra has retained part of its original tiling, and you can still see the altar to Aphrodite on the left, where the actors used to sacrifice a lamb before each performance. Beside the theatre is the **Bouleuterion** (city council chamber) with several rows of seats arranged in a semicircle.

Don't miss the **Intagliata** and **Intagliatella latomiae** (quarries) that were used during the Greek era by members of the cult of Hero, as hypogea and catacombs by early Christians, and finally as rock dwellings in the Byzantine era. In the deepest quarry, Intagliatella, you can still see wall niches where tablets *(pinakes)* were placed for the Hero cult. There is also a relief dating from the 2nd or 1st century BC. As you leave, follow the outer wall which surrounds the ruins to the left and you will come to a magnificent **Roman road** more than 13 ft/4 m wide, paved with lava.

You can ask for a guide at the entrance to the Archaeological Zone to take you into the valley to see the **Santoni*** — rough sculptures carved directly out of the rock in the 3rd century BC. They mainly represent a group of 12 figures of Cybele, seated or standing, accompanied either by her lions or by the Dioscuri (Castor and Pollux) on horseback. Now badly damaged and protected by wooden shelters, the statues nevertheless testify to the importance of the oriental cult in Hellenistic Sicily. Cybele was worshipped as goddess of Fertility in Greece in the 5th century BC and again in Rome in 200 BC.

Palazzolo Acréide to Syracuse (28.5 mi/46 km to the east)

If you want to go directly to Syracuse, the N124 via Floridia is the best route. After about 8 mi/13 km from Palazzolo Acréide a side road to the left takes you 13.6 mi/22 km to the necropolis of **Pantálica***. This is a Siculian necropolis, the largest in Sicily, with about 5000 tombs dug into the cliffs of a limestone plateau. You can also see vestiges of Anaktoron, a palace that dates from the 12th and 11th centuries BC.

Palazzolo Acréide to Caltagirone (37 mi/60 km to the north-west)

For those who wish to explore a little inland this short itinerary into the Noto valley and the Iblei Mountains is recommended.

Buscemi, 3 mi/5 km from Akrai on the N124, is a large village on a hill and **Buccheri**, 4.3 mi/7 km away, is huddled in a valley. Buccheri is famed for its pure air and water and also a fine church dedicated to San Antonio set at the top of a theatrical flight of steps. The façade has a bell tower and twin columns.

Vizzini is a large village (9000 inhabitants) standing on a rocky plateau 9.3 mi/15 km farther on. It became known because Giovanni Verga set the action of his novel *Cavalleria Rusticana* here (the book gained fame thanks to the opera by Mascagni, created in Rome in 1890). The Chiesa Madre houses a badly damaged 1614 picture of the *Martyrdom of San Lorenzo* by the mannerist Florentine painter Filippo Paladino.

Grammichele, about 10 mi/16 km farther on, was built under the Spanish who gave it an unusual, extremely regular layout. All the streets lead to the star-shaped piazza Centrale, which is dominated by Palazzo Municipale and beside it the Chiesa Madre (1724-27). You will find *circoli* (bars) all around the square and the town's elderly citizens dozing on straw chairs set out in front.

Caltagirone (37.2mi/60 km): see p. 145.

Noto to Syracuse (20mi/32km)

The N115 runs alongside the gulf of Noto crossing the town of Cassibile, where the armistice was signed between Italy and the Allies on September 3, 1943. A small coast road leads off to the right to Syracuse through the beach towns of Fontane Bianche and Arenella. For hotel and restaurant suggestions see Syracuse p. 161.

SYRACUSE

Syracuse*** *(Siracusa)* is a provincial capital of 118,000 inhabitants partly situated on an island separated from the mainland by a narrow channel, the Darsena. On a par with Athens and Carthage Syracuse was, in Antiquity, the most important city in Sicily. The ancient town was comprised of four districts: Achradina, Tyche, Epipolae and Ortygia, the island where the *città vecchia* (old city) developed. This is the most interesting part of the present town.

Syracuse is the prettiest and probably the pleasantest of Sicily's towns. You need at least a day to see the town but count on two if you would like to visit the museums.

A MAJOR ROLE IN SICILY'S ANCIENT HISTORY

Ancient Syracuse was founded in 733 BC by colonists from Corinth who chased out the native Sikels. In terms of its location, it was perfect: the offshore island of Ortygia was easy to defend, the plains were fertile and the natural harbour was ideal for maritime ventures. It didn't take long for the new leaders of Syracuse to extend the city's sphere of influence on the island to the borders of the powerful Gela.

The Syracusans overcame resistance from many a Siculian village on the island but were beaten by Hippocrates, a tyrant from Gela, in 491 BC. His successor, Gelon, took advantage of internal political struggle in Syracuse and gained control of the divided town in 485 BC. Realizing the potential of the harbour, he built Syracuse into a sea power and actually moved much of the population of Gela to Syracuse. Having sealed an alliance with the tyrant of Agrigento, Gelon defeated the Carthaginians at Himera in 480 BC.

He was succeeded by his brother, Hieron I. Although Hieron was a cruel tyrant, he was a lover of poetry, and he invited the great scholars of the day to his court — men such as Simonides, Pindar and Aeschylus. On the military front, Hieron helped the Greek navy defeat the Etruscans at Cumae in 474 BC, which ended another threat to Greek holdings.

The steps of the Duomo in Syracuse are a favourite meeting place for tourists and locals alike.

After Hieron died in 466, Syracuse turned to democracy, which in no way lessened its power. Athens was growing jealous: Syracuse had extended its domain over most of Sicily and, worse — had allied itself with Sparta in the Peloponnesian War. In 415 BC, 134 Athenian triremes set sail and nearly succeeded in taking Syracuse, but the city was saved by the Spartans, who sent reinforcements, led by Gylippos. They managed to blockade the Athenian fleet in the harbour, sank half the ships and caught the Greek soldiers who tried to flee south. This sterling victory gave Syracuse such prestige that it overtook Athens as the greatest city in the West. As for the captured Athenians... they were imprisoned in quarries *(latomiae)* in vile conditions, and legend has it that only those soliders who could recite Aeschylus or Euripedes (the most popular poets in Syracuse) ever saw Athens again.

Another in the line of Syracusan tyrants was Dionysius, who is said to have envisioned himself as a poet and who submitted an original tragedy to the theatre festival held in his name, year after year in Athens, until the Athenians begrudgingly awarded him a prize, in 368. The Athenians were avenged for their humiliating loss at Syracuse when Dionysius celebrated his poetic victory so indulgently that he killed himself.

Dionysus, whose poetry has (perhaps thankfully) not survived, was best known for his military genius. He built the fortress of Epipolae Ridge and gathered engineers from all over Italy and Greece to design weapons to help him rid the island of the Carthaginians. The most impressive of these inventions was the catapult. Although Dionysius built Syracuse into a powerful empire, he never vanquished the Carthaginians entirely.

His son, Dionysius II, was a weak successor, and his uncle tried to overthrow him, but was assassinated himself for his efforts. In 343 BC Syracuse was suffering once more from internal unrest and, fearful of another attack from the Carthaginians, the people appealed to Corinth for aid. Corinth sent to Syracuse the humanist Timoleon, who cleared the government of all its petty tyrants and established democracy and peace with Carthage.

When Timoleon died in 336, the feuding started up again, however. In 317, the adventurer Agathocles took power; during his rule Syracuse was constantly at war, conquering most of Greek Sicily. But when Agathocles died in 289 BC with no heir, his empire crumbled, and the Carthaginians once again attacked the harbour, deterred this time by Pyrrhus of Epirus. After the battle, the Syracusans elected one of Pyrrhus's officers, Hieron II, as their leader. He was a godsend for the city of Syracuse; he signed a treaty with the Romans, improved the laws and life of the citizens, built the altar to Zeus, reworked the Neopolis quarter, and invited the great scholars and scientists of the day to his court. His rule (275-16 BC) was a long and favourable one for Syracuse.

Hieron II was succeeded by his grandson, Hieronymus, who incurred the wrath of Rome by pledging allegiance to the Carthaginian Hannibal, in 215 BC. The Roman Consul Marcellus attacked Syracuse, and the Syracusan army defended its territories under the leadership of Archimedes, General of

Ordinance. Archimedes had spent a number of years developing increasingly effective forms of defense, and when the Romans attacked they had 600-lb/272-kg lead weights dropped on their scaling engines. Archimedes lowered his grapnels to attach them to the Roman ships in the harbour and, tipping them up by their hulls, he spilled the Roman sailors into the sea. Legend has it that Archimedes even reflected the sun's rays with mirrors in an attempt to set fire to the more distant Roman ships. However, in spite of his inventiveness, the Syracusan was defeated and slain in a surprise attack during a festival.

Rome now took power over Syracuse, and the city's importance as a Western power waned. In the early 1st century, St Paul stopped in the city en route from Malta to Rome, and thereafter Christianity began to take hold.

Syracuse followed suit with the rest of Sicily from this point on, falling under the rule of the Byzantines, Arabs, Normans and Spanish.

▬ PRACTICAL INFORMATION

Map coordinates refer to the map pp. 164-165.
Telephone area code: 0931.

Access

Boat: Boats from Naples to Malta and Tripoli stop at Syracuse.

Car: Syracuse is 36.6 mi/59 km south of Catania, 19.8 mi/32 km north-east of Noto, 53.4 mi/86 km north-east of Ragusa and 64.6 mi/104 km east of Caltagirone.

Train: There are northern connections from Catania, Taormina and Messina, and western and southern ones from Caltanisetta, Ragusa, Módica and Noto.

Accommodation

The tourist office can supply you with a complete list of accommodation in Syracuse.

▲▲▲▲ **Jolly,** corso Gelone 45, C2 b, ☎ 64 744. 100 rooms. A large comfortable hotel in the centre of the modern town.

▲▲▲ **Fontane Bianche,** via Mazzarò 1, in Fontane Bianchi 9.3 mi/15 km south on the coast road to Avola, ☎ 790 356. 170 rooms. Tennis courts, swimming pool and private beach.

▲▲▲ **Grand Hotel Villa Politi,** via Politi Laudien 2, A4 a, ☎ 32 100. 93 rooms. Located in a former private residence with old-world charm and modest rooms, beside the Latomia dei Capuccini. There is a garden, swimming pool and beautiful dining room. Usually filled with tourists.

▲▲▲ **Motel Agip,** via Teracati 30, A2 c, ☎ 66 944. 87 rooms. Part of the Agip chain — recently renovated, very comfortable.

▲▲▲ **Park Hotel,** via Filisto 80, outside the centre, A4, off the map, ☎ 32 644. 102 rooms. Swimming pool.

▲▲▲ **Relax,** via Monterosa 11, ☎ 740 122. 42 rooms. Garden-like setting and swimming pool.

▲▲ **Aretusa,** via Francesco Crispi 75, C2, ☎ 24 211. 46 rooms. Inexpensive for the service.

▲▲ **Bellavista,** via Diodoro Siculo 4, A4, off the map, ☎ 36 912. 50 rooms. Agreeable location with a garden, restaurant and bar.

▲▲ **Panorama,** via Necropoli Groticelle 33, A1, off the map, ☎ 32 122. 51 rooms. Simple hotel, with bar but no restaurant.

▲ **Grand Hotel,** viale Mazzini 12, D3 a, ☎ 65 101. 47 rooms. An old hotel in Ortygia beside the sea. Very twenties atmosphere.

Campgrounds

Agritourist, 2.4 mi/4 km out of town in Rinaura on the SS115 heading towards Ragusa, ☎ 721 224. *Open all year.*

Fontane Bianche, in Fontane, 9.3 mi/15 km south of Syracuse, ☎ 790 333. *Open April 1-Oct 31.*

Villagio Turistico Il Minaretto in Faro Castellucio, ☎ 721 210. *Open Mar 15-Oct 31.*

Festivals

Festival of classical theatre (in summer) in the Greek Theatre and around the Altar of Hieron; **festival of music and singing** (July-September); **feast day of Santa Lucia** and procession (Sept 13); **feast day of San Sebastiano** (Jan 20).

Food

LLL Arlecchino, lungomare di Levante, D4, ☎ 66 386. *Closed Mon and throughout Aug.* Excellent food in an attractive modern setting.

LLL Darsena da Januzzo, riva Garibaldi 4/6, D3 r, ☎ 66 104 and 105. *Closed Wed.* Lovely covered terrace giving onto the Darsena. Seafood, fish specialities.

LLL Jonico-A Rutta e'Ciauli, riviera Dioniso il Grande 194, A4 s, ☎ 66 639. *Closed Tues.* Good view of the sea. Good food in a pleasant setting but check the bill!

LL Fratelli Bandiera, via G. Perno 6, D4 u, ☎ 65 021. *Closed Mon and throughout Oct.* Simpler establishment than the two above. Large dining room. Not far from the market. Very reasonable prices.

LL Minosse, via Mirabella 6, D4 x, ☎ 66 366. *Closed Mon and the first two weeks in July.* Good traditional fare.

LL La Spiagetta, 9.3 mi/15 km from Syracuse in Fontane Bianche on the seafront. *Closed Tues and throughout Nov.*

LL Vasta, via Capodieci 49, F4, ☎ 66 538. *Closed Mon.* This is a local favourite and one of the best restaurants in Ortygia.

There are also several *trattorie,* such as **Minerva,** in Ortygia opposite the Duomo, and **Al Papiro,** beside the museum, A3, convenient places for lunch when visiting the monuments.

Cafés

You have a good choice of little cafés and bars, especially in Ortygia. The best are near the Duomo and the Fountain of Arethusa, particularly the ones with a terrace on lungomare Alfeo, F4, which has become very lively at night since Ortygia was illuminated.

Useful addresses

Boat trips: Harbour tours leave on quai piazza Marina, E4, every hour from 9am. See p. 173 for excursions to the fountain of Ciane.

Bus station, via Elorina, D1, ☎ 69 555 and via Trieste, D4, ☎ 66 710.

Papyrus Institute, viale Teocrito 66, ☎ 22 100.

Post office, piazza della Posta, D3-4. *Open Mon-Fri 8am-1pm 4-8pm, Sat 8am-2pm.*

Stazione Centrale, via Francesco Crispi, C2, ☎ 67 964.

Telephones: via Brenta 33, behind the station, C2 *(8am-8pm),* and in the Trápani bar, piazza Marconi 19 *(8pm-8am).*

Tourist information, via Maestranza 33, E4, ☎ 66 932. *Open Mon-Fri 9am-2pm, 3:30-7pm; Sat 9am-1pm.* There is also an office in the archaeological zone, ☎ 60 510. *Open Mon-Sat 8am-6pm.*

▬ ORTYGIA***

The road from Ragusa and Noto leads into Syracuse on via Elorina, D1. Just before reaching the Island of Ortygia on the left at n° 56, opposite a barracks, you can visit the ruins of what is called a **Roman gymnasium,** C2. It is not in fact a gymnasium, as once believed, but a small theatre built at the end of the 1st century, surrounded by a portico of arches. Unfortunately the whole site has been badly damaged and only one of the bases of the portico remains. Of the theatre itself the lower rows of seats and the orchestra are under a sheet of water. Marble parts of a peripteral temple can be made out behind the *scena*. Several statues from the original site are now in the archaeological museum.

Further on, via Elorina leads into piazza Marconi, D2, which adjoins the ancient Forum, now entirely destroyed. A small garden stands where the Agora once was. As if the ravages of time were not enough, the municipality has added an unattractive pantheon memorializing the soldiers who died in the war. In fact this whole district has very little of interest so your best bet is to cross it quickly on via Malta to the bridge over the Darsena river between Syracuse's two harbours (Porto Grande to the right, Porto Piccolo to the left). You cross onto Ortygia Island, (Ortygia means 'quail' in Greek) and reach the old town, the *città vecchia*, which juts into the water 'like a ship about to put to sea' (V. Cronin). If you don't have a car, bus n° 1 conveniently links Ortygia to the archaeological zone, stopping at the station en route.

Piazza Pancali D3

Just over the bridge on the island is Piazza Pancali, where you will find the ruins of the Temple of Apollo, the oldest peripteral Doric temple in Sicily. Cleomenes had it built around 565 BC and it was discovered in 1862. Cicero mentions that the temple was dedicated to Artemis (Apollo's twin sister). It is quite possible that the temple honoured both brother and sister because the Artemis cult was greatly respected in ancient Syracuse. All that's left today is the base and fragments of walls and columns. The columns are massive and set close together — characteristic of 6th-century BC architecture. The temple originally had 17 columns on the sides and 6 on the façades, and what we see today gives only a bare idea of its past splendour. It has been converted a number of times, into first a Byzantine church, then an Arab mosque, a Norman church and finally a Spanish barracks (demolished in 1938).

In the mornings there's a colourful market near the temple, with stalls all around via Trento, D4, stretching down toward the sea.

Piazza Archimede E4

Corso Matteotti leads off from the right of the temple to piazza Archimede, which was once lined with palaces. The most interesting is at n° 27, the 15th-century **Palazzo Lanza** with its twin windows. In the centre of the square is a fountain by the sculptor Moschetti of the legendary nymph, Arethusa, who was turned into a spring. To the right of the Banco di Sicilia palace, via Montalto leads to Palazzo Montalto, a Gothic construction dating from 1397.

At the end of Archimede square, take via Roma and then turn into via Minerva to reach **piazza del Duomo,** E4, which was considered sacred ground in Antiquity and where you will now find the Duomo and several Baroque palaces.

To the right of the square is the **Municipio***, the former palace of the Syracusan Senate, a beautiful building (1628) designed by one of the originators of the Baroque style, the architect Giovanni Vermexio. Opposite stands the **Beneventano del Bosco palace*** built by a local architect, Luciano Ali, in about 1780. It was the former headquarters of the Order of the Knights of Malta. The inner courtyard has a magnificent staircase leading to the *piano nobile*, or master's floor.

Duomo (Cathedral)** E4

The Baroque façade of the Duomo was designed by Andrea Palma (from 1728-54) to replace the Norman façade that crumbled in the 1693 earthquake. It is adorned with statues by Marabitti, but the interior is even more striking. After a few moments, when you have adjusted to the half-light, you will be able to discern the bare Roman-style nave with its beautiful ceiling (1518).

In the right-hand aisle, the alignment of the nine Doric columns creates an impressive optical effect. The baptismal font in the first chapel incorporates a Greek vase from the crypt of San Marziano, near the catacombs, mounted on a capital adorned with seven bronze lion cubs (13th-century Norman). The second chapel, dedicated to Santa Lucia, was decorated at the beginning of the 18th century and it contains a chiseled silver casket. The third chapel, of the Holy Sacrament, was designed by Giovanni Vermexio and decorated with frescoes.

At the top of the nave there are two Doric columns and facing them the richly decorated Baroque choir with its 15th-century tribunes. In the left-hand aisle you will see the 11 Doric columns from the original temple (which have had their drums displaced a little by various earthquakes). At the end is the only remaining Byzantine apse, with a statue by Antonello Gagini, the *Madonna della Neve*★ (1512).

The cathedral of Ortygia

The Duomo, the earliest church in western Christendom, was built inside a Greek temple to Athena that was constructed by Gelon I after the battle of Himera in the 5th century BC. During the Byzantine era it became a basilica. Its colourful history explains the hybrid style of its architecture. During its conversion the external columns were incorporated into a surrounding wall, and the walls of the *cella* were embellished with eight arches on each side in order to create a church with a nave and two aisles. Radical modifications were made during the Arab invasion and again after the Norman conquest. The *cella* walls were heightened and given five side windows. When the 1693 earthquake caused the façade to crumble, the new reconstruction was carried out in the style of the day, which meant that the building's original austerity, hitherto preserved, disappeared under an exuberance of stuccowork and ornamental decoration. Furthermore, 16 Doric columns were removed. Despite these unfortunate renovations, the Duomo deserves more than just a fleeting visit.

Beyond the cathedral to the right is Palazzo Arcivescovile, built in 1618 by Andrea Vermexio, a Spanish architect who drew his inspiration from the Renaissance. The second floor was added in 1751 by a French architect, L.A. du Montier. Almost opposite the building at n° 15 there is a Baroque palace.

Palazzo Bellomo** E4
Open Tues-Sun 9am-2pm, in summer 3-8pm.

The Church of Santa Lucia alla Badia stands at the back of piazza del Duomo. Its graceful Baroque façade was designed by Luciano Caracciolo (1700). The doorway is framed by cabled columns and surmounted by an elegant wrought-iron balcony that runs the length of the façade. Take via Lucia, turn right into via Conciliazione then left at via Capodeici to see, at n° 16, the austere Palazzo Bellamo.

Originally a Swabian palace, the Palazzo Bellamo now houses the **Galleria Regionale**** with its collections of medieval art, sculptures from the Byzantine era to the Renaissance and numerous paintings. The most famous is *The Annunciation*** by Antonello da Messina. In this painting the artist has combined Gothic with Italian Renaissance influences; the work is considered one of the most important Italian paintings from the second half of the 15th century. Unfortunately it has undergone certain tribulations, including disastrous restorations that have permanently damaged it. Originally painted on wood, it was transferred to canvas in an attempt to save it.

The museum has been temporarily entrusted with the *Burial of Santa Lucia****, one of Caravaggio's last works. It is an exceptional painting that has recently been successfully restored. These two major works should not, however, entirely overshadow the rest of the exhibition, which is admirably set off by the beautiful palace interior. Don't miss the **drawings*** by Filippo Paladino (1544-1614). There are also collections of old cribs, terra-cotta figurines, vestments, ceramics and majolica ware.

Opposite the palace via San Martino leads to **San Martino Church**, F4, on the left. It was built in the 14th century over the remains of an earlier 5th century church. The interior has been restored and contains relics of St Vincent and a 15th-century polyptych painted on wood.

Fountain of Arethusa F4

Walk back to via Capodeici and follow it left until you come to a sunken terrace where you will see the famous fountain of Arethusa. Don't expect

---

The Burial of Santa Lucia

The *Burial of Santa Lucia*, by Caravaggio, had spent more than ten years' reprieve in restoration workshops before I saw it for the first time. It is one of the last of the painter's works (1608, two years before his death) and probably his best. Standing out from an immense section of dark brown wall that takes up half the picture (only Goya would have dared) a group of relations and friends are standing around the saint's reclining body. An old woman has fallen to her knees, her head in her hands. Another has clasped her hands, resting her chin on them. The foreground is taken up by two muscular, threateningly powerful gravediggers, built like convicts. The one on the left is bearded but it is the one on the right, with his shaved head and pug face, who seems the more menacing. Dull, pallid shades dominate in the picture: browns, blacks, greys, homespun beige for those in attendance, the shroud colour for the breeches of the gravedigger and lead grey for the hand of the bishop held out in blessing. The only bright colour is on the red overcoat of the young man who, with lowered head, is contemplating the corpse.

D. Fernandez,
'The Gorgon's Raft'
Le Radeau de la Gorgone (Grasset, 1988).

Detail of a sculpture in the courtyard of the Palazzo Bellomo, which houses the Galleria Regionale.

conventional fountain — it is more like a small pond with tufts of papyrus. All the same, it is a geological phenomenon — just a few metres from the sea, fresh spring water flows up to fill the pond, and it has been doing so for centuries.

Other sites

You can follow along the *foro* from here right to Porta Marina (15th century), one of the ancient gateways to Ortygia island. Nearby is the little Church of Santa Maria dei Miracoli, with a marble Renaissance portal very much in the Gagini style (1501). Inside, the apse retains its original Gothic-Catalan structure. Via Savoia, D3, leads back to piazzo Pancali and the bridge across the Darsena River, but if you wish to continue exploring Ortygia, the alleys around the Duomo abound in architectural interest. We recommend a sunset stroll along **Foro Italico**, E3. This esplanade was famous in Cicero's day, when he reproached the magistrate proconsul Verres for having turned it into 'a den of iniquity'. Times have certainly changed but the view is still just as enticing.

A love story

Cicero and Strabo have told us the story and Virgil has sung it in his eclogues. The legend begins like a fairy tale: Once upon a time there was an Arcadian nymph who used to bathe in the waters of the river Alpheus. She was so beautiful that the river god fell in love with her and began to pursue her. She was on the verge of succumbing to his advances when she implored Artemis, protectress of virgins, to save her. Artemis then ordered the earth to open at the feet of the nymph who disappeared, crossed the sea, and reappeared in the guise of a fresh-water spring on the island of Ortygia. We are told that Alpheus dug an underground passage beneath the Ionian Sea and pursued her all the way to Sicily, where their two waters intermingled... An unusual phenomenon did in fact occur in Greece — the Alpheus river suddenly disappeared underground.

After visiting the main sites, spend a few hours in Ortygia and wander around the alleyways where you will discover hosts of cherubs, lions and sirens on the façades of former merchant-class residences. These houses, now occupied by craftsmen and fishermen, have finely crafted balconies and heavy, permanently closed shutters. You will see the elderly dozing in terrace chairs, perfectly oblivious to the hubbub of life around them.

A suggestion for a stroll: start out from piazza Archimede and take via Maestranza, E4, a street lined with mostly rundown villas. You will see the Baroque San Francesco Church, also known as dell'Immacolata, built in 1769. The street ends at Belvedere San Giacomo, E4, after crossing (left) via Vittorio Veneto, formerly an important street in the once Spanish town. Return to via Vittorio Veneto, with its many Baroque buildings embellished with balconies, and see San Filippo Neri by Giovanni Vermexio (1652), now part of an Ursuline convent. You pass Palazzo Interlandi (15th century) and then turn left at via Mirabella, D4, where you will see Palazzo Bongiovanni, the Carmine church and, on a little square to the right, the 5th-century San Pietro, which has been altered several times but retains a 15th-century doorway. No longer a church, it serves as a concert hall today. A little farther along you come to Palazzo Abela and the small Church of San Tomaso (12th century).

Another interesting walk is from the Duomo, E4, along via Castello, F4, to **Castello Maniace**, named after a Byzantine general. It was built in 1239 by Frederick II of Swabia on a spur at the tip of the island. Because the fortress is in a military zone it cannot be visited. All that remains of the original building are a fine Gothic **portal*** and the walls with mullioned windows looking out to sea. Walk back along the seafront on lungomare Alfeo and Foro Italico.

ANCIENT SYRACUSE

Neapolis and Achradina** AB1-2

The most interesting monuments from the Graeco-Roman period, the Palaeo-Christian era and the Middle Ages are grouped in these two northern districts of ancient Syracuse where the modern town has developed. The **Archaeological Park** *(open Tues-Sun 9am-dusk, closed Mon and holidays; admission charge)* can be reached from Foro Siracusano (on the mainland) by driving up corso Gelone (the Catania road), a long double-lane street lined with modern buildings. Turn left at viale Augusto after about 0.6 mi/1 km.

On a small square to the right you will see the Church of San Nicolò de Cordari, B1, an 11th-century Norman building which now houses the EPT tourist bureau.

Logically, you should first be able to visit the Roman amphitheatre (opposite San Nicolò) but because you have to get your entry ticket near the Greek theatre, at the end of a lane crowded with souvenir sellers, take a look at this while you're there and see the Roman amphitheatre and the altar of Hieron II at the end of your visit.

Greek Theatre** AB1

This exceptionally beautiful theatre was entirely hewn out of the rock. It probably dates from the 5th century BC and was designed by the architect Democopos. It is one of the largest Greek edifices, 453 ft/138 m in diameter; the Athens theatre is only 328 ft/100 m and the theatre at Delphi 164 ft/50 m.

The theatre played an important role in the life of ancient Syracuse. Aeschylus staged a number of his plays there (among them *The Persians* in 472 BC). It was also the site of the people's assembly.

The *cavea* (ampitheatre), with its 66 rows of seats, could hold 15,000 spectators. It is divided horizontally into two parts by a diazoma, or ambulatory, and vertically into nine sections. These bear the names of divinities and members of the ruling family.

The grotto, or *nymphaeum*, behind the theatre (water still flows there today) echoed back the actors' voices. The wall of rock overlooking the theatre bears traces of niches for votive tablets in which statues of muses were later discovered. The **Street of Tombs** begins at the left-hand end of the wall. This is a large trench cut into the rock where there were tombs and niches for ex-votoes (tablets expressing gratitude to a saint). A little farther on the remains of a small **theatre**, which may have been Syracuse's earliest, have been excavated.

Latomiae del Paradiso** A1

The *latomiae* were quarries from which the ancients extracted the stone needed for building their monuments. Syracuse has five such quarries, of which the best known are the Latomia del Paradiso (which includes the 'Ear of Dionysius' and the Grotta dei Cordari) and the Latomia dei Cappuccini. Unlike conventional open quarries, the *latomiae* are a series of caverns. When parts of them collapsed in the 1693 earthquake they developed into luxuriantly overgrown gardens.

The **Ear of Dionysius*** is an artificial cave that narrows toward the top into a shape resembling the upper part of the outer ear. It is 213 ft/65 m long, 75 ft/23 m high and between 16 to 36 ft/5 to 11 m wide. The name Caravaggio gave the cave in 1588 alludes to a legend that, by placing his ear next to a hole in the roof, the tyrant Dionysius could eavesdrop on the conversations of his prisoners, without his movements being heard by them. The cavern's strange acoustic properties still exist today, and the simple crumpling of a paper at the entrance develops into an amplified echo at the back.

Now closed for safety reasons, the **Grotta dei Cordari** is a vast cavern held up by natural pillars that look like gigantic stalactites. The dampness enabled the ropemakers who once worked here to twist their hemp at a constant temperature.

Altar of Hieron II, B1

On the left you will see the ruins of the altar of the tyrant Hieron II, built in the 3rd century BC for public sacrifices. Its immense size (653 ft/199 m long by 75 ft/23 m wide) testifies to the importance the city placed on the sacrifices, during which priests would offer up animals as thanks to the gods for a military victory. When democracy was proclaimed, the Syracusans slaughtered 450 oxen, cutting their throats so that the blood spurted up onto the altar.

The foundations are all that remain today, hewn out of the rock in the midst of a vast square.

You reach the amphitheatre from the altar of Hieron II by passing through a garden criss-crossed with paths lined with sarcophagi.

Roman amphitheatre* B1

Like the Greek theatre and the altar of Hieron II, the sheer size of the amphitheatre (459 x 390 ft/140 by 119 m) is impressive, and despite its state of ruin, it reflects the importance of public life during the Roman era. It has an elliptical shape that (apart from the southern section) was hewn out of the rock in the 3rd or 4th century AD. Below the *cavea* you can see the access corridors, or *vomitorium*, and the tunnel through which wild beasts came into the arena. The *podium*, or royal box, can still be seen in the centre of the cavea.

Panoramic road AB1

One way of visiting the rest of the archaeological zone is to drive along the panoramic road beginning with viale Rizzo, AB1, which twists up around the Greek theatre. The belvedere overlooks the whole area.

A little farther along on the right, on the corner of via Teracati, is a monument known as the **Tomb of Archimedes**, A2. This is not, as was believed for centuries, the burial place of the famous Syracusan, but it is a simple Roman *columbarium* (niche for sepulchral urns) from the 1st century AD. Continue along via Romagnoli, which runs beside the Latomiae of Santa Venera, now a garden, and the Grotticelli necropolis containing Greek, Roman and Byzantine tombs. Then take viale Augusto on the left and turn into viale Teocrito, A2, where we recommend you leave your car. This central district is rapidly being built up.

The unfinished Sanctuary of the Madonnina delle Lacrime stands in the middle of a park enshrining a venerated statue of the Virgin that is believed to have miraculous powers.

Catacombs of San Giovanni (St. John)* A2

Guided visits only. March 15-Nov 15 at 10am, 11am, noon, 4pm, 5pm, 6pm. Nov 16-March 14 at 10am, 11am, noon. Closed Wed.

Across the avenue from Madonnina delle Lacrime, via San Giovanni leads to the former church of the same name. Originally Byzantine, it was gradually destroyed by invaders and earthquakes and all that remains is the façade and portico of columns with capitals.

You will be shown into the church, now overgrown, and then down a small staircase to the 1st-century crypt of San Marziano (St. Marcianus).

Venus Landolina

This white-marble work depicts the goddess leaving the sea, where she has been bathing, her left hand grasping to her thighs a garment, which falls behind and beside her feet like a shell. Her right arm, which has been broken off above the elbow, was held across her body in a gesture of modesty: the protuberances in the marble, designed to hold the arm in place, are still there, one just below the breasts, the other on the left arm. Beside her feet rises a dolphin, the goddess's own symbol, which serves here also to symbolize the sea. As well as the right arm the head of the statue is missing: a fact that Maupassant held to be of the utmost signifiance, for it seemed to illustrate his belief that in the final analysis woman is a purely animal creature, without rational or spiritual faculties: a figure of pure passion.

In the whole statue nothing is more inspired than the line of the garment Aphrodite holds across her body. It is a commotion of light and shadow which sets off the white smoothness of the flesh, a crumpled stormcloud that menaces the figure's orderly lines, a stretch of undulating country separating sea and sky. It is the barest of coverings, this narrow drapery, and the half-modesty of the retaining gesture is calculated to accentuate its inadequacy, just as the right arm, which in the original was stretched across the body, extended below the breasts without hiding them. The line of that arm repeated in a higher octave the same note achieved by the drapery, while the diagonal line of the left hand obviates too stiff and angular an attitude.

The figure, composed of sea foam, rises from the waves: the whole body is smooth, but the legs have a specially polished surface to suggest the glistening of water. Indeed, at moments the goddess seems to be standing in the sea, such is the equivocal quality of the lower part of her drapery, which forms now a grotto, now a stretch of waves. It is this affinity with the sea that is the essential feature of the work, an extraordinary achievement gained entirely by suggestion, for only the dolphin is there to set the scene. The marble has a melting quality, as if it really were the snow its colour says it is; the flowing, liquid lines of the drapery are drawn up through the fingers of the hand into the body itself, which assumes the undulating lines of a breeze-swept sea. The fingers serve another purpose, also, for their alternation of light and shade dovetails with the drapery, so that the hand, arm and body appear to continue in a calmer form the line of water which beneath the drapery appears turbulent and swept by tides.

Vincent Cronin
The Golden Honeycomb
Rupert Hart-Davis, 1954

The Venus Landolina in Syracuse.

This was one of Sicily's first churches. St Paul is believed to have preached here on his way to Rome. Note the traces of frescoes and the pilasters topped by capital bearing symbols of the Evangelists.

The catacombs of San Giovanni (St John) consist of a vast underground necropolis that has not yet been entirely explored, so stick to the lit route. The catacombs were first and foremost a Christian cemetery recognized by the pagan authorities. Because Roman law guaranteed their safety, Christians could take refuge there during persecutions. They consist of a network of galleries containing thousands of tombs, some of which lead off to circular chapels housing the sepulcres of martyrs. The most interesting of these is the Rotonda d'Adelfia from which the beautiful sarcophagus, now in the adjoining museum, was taken.

Museo Archeologico Nazionale: Paolo Orsi** A3

Open Tues-Sun 9am-2pm; closed Mon.

The National Archaelogical Museum was specially designed for its collections and has recently opened after many years of work Its displays follow the development of art in Sicily from prehistoric times through the Greek and Roman eras and up to the Palaeo-Christian. The works are classified according to their place of origin. The most remarkable include: **bronze finds*** from Adrano (8th century BC); a Paros marble funerary *statue of a kouros*** dating from the end of the 6th century BC that was found in the necropolis at Megara Hyblaea (the name of the deceased is inscribed on the right thigh: 'Sombrotidas, a doctor, son of Mandrokles'); a collection of **vases*** from Camarina and Gela; and part of a **marble cornice*** with a winged Gorgon from the Temple of Athena in Syracuse.

The museum's major piece is the headless *Venus Anadyomene* (meaning 'rising from the water'), also known as Venus Landolina, named after the archeologist who discovered it in 1804. The museum has not yet decided on a permanent place to exhibit it. The statue is a Roman copy of Hellenistic-style statues, probably the creation of a Syracusan workshop. It depicts Venus emerging from the water, modestly covering herself with a robe held in her left hand (see box).

Latomia dei Cappuccini and Santa Lucia*

Return to viale Teocrita, turn left following it until you reach via von Platen, A3, on the left. On the road to the left is the entrance to Villa Landolina, a small Protestant cemetery and garden. The Catacombs of Vignia Cassia (closed to the public) are a little farther on to the right. At the end of via von Platen, via Bassa Acradina and via Politi lead to the Church of the Capuchins, A4. The entrance to the Latomia dei Cappuccini is a short distance from here. According to Thucydides, 7000 prisoners of the Athenian army were held here in 413 BC.

Return to via Bassa Acradina and turn left at via Torino, then right at via Bignami, which leads to piazza Santa Lucia, B3. Here you will see the 12th-century Church of Santa Lucia, which has been recently restored. According to tradition, it was built over the site where Santa Lucia, the virgin of Syracuse and patron saint of Italy, was martyred. The church was altered in the 17th century but has retained its doorway, the base of the campanile and the three apses, all of which date from the Middle Ages; the portico was added in the 18th century. The interior once contained the *Burial of Santa Lucia* by Caravaggio, that is now in the Palazzo Bellomo (see p. 166).

San Sepolcro, the octagonal chapel by Giovanni Vermexio on the square, contains Santa Lucia's shroud. Although it was originally intended for the body of the saint, the Arabs took the body to Constantinople, and later to Venice where it lies today. In the crypt (closed) there is a statue of Santa Lucia believed to be the work of a Florentine artist.

By following the railway line right at the end of the square you will come back to corso Gelone, where the itinerary began, near Foro Siracusana.

ENVIRONS OF SYRACUSE

Castello Eurialo★★

Open Tues-Sun 9am-dusk.

Leave Syracuse on viale Teracati and after crossing the Catania road (N114) continue along viale Epipoli. Then take the country road to Belvedere, A1. After about 5 mi/8 km north-west of Syracuse take the road to the right, which leads to the Castle of Euryalus.

The fortress is the largest military construction in the Greek world, and covers an area of 161,460 sq ft/15,000 sq m. The fascinating ruins throw light on the strategic problems of the day. Dionysius the Elder had intended to extend the fortifications of the city to the plateau of Epipolae and to enclose the town by a wall that, according to Strabo, was 20 mi/32 km long. Building lasted five years but was never finished. More than 60,000 men, aided by women and boys, helped construct the building under the orders of the tyrant, who directed operations himself. The site includes three ditches and (on the western wall where the catapults stood) five towers, each originally 49 ft/15 m high. A wall to the east that joins the Epipolae ramparts by means of two towers encloses three cisterns that supplied the garrison with drinking water. The outer walls were between 7 to 10 ft/2 to 3 m wide. A large number of tunnels were hewn into the rock to form an underground city; the complicated network of its tunnels ensured that the inhabitants had a quick means of escape.

Fonte Ciane

You can either take the boat from Porto Grande, E4, Foro Italico, or Molo Zanagora (a round trip takes about four hours) or come by road (5 mi/8 km). If you choose to drive, leave Syracuse on viale Ermocrate or viale Paolo Orsi, C1, toward Floridia, then turn left at via Necropoli del Fusco toward Canicattini Bagni.

We suggest that you go on this country outing toward the end of the afternoon. The Ciane (Greek for 'blue') is a little river that flows from a spring in the Anapos Valley down to Syracuse harbour. It is a charming stretch of water lined with papyrus hedges. The two humpback bridges along the way mean you can cross from one bank to another. According to mythology, the nymph Cyane was turned into a spring by Hades because she opposed his abduction of Persephone.

SYRACUSE TO CATANIA: IONIAN SICILY

Invasions, volcanoes and natural calamities have all left their mark on this part of the country. But like the phoenix, Ionian Sicily always rises from its ashes.

Catania is 37 mi/59 km north of Syracuse on the N114.

MEGARA HYBLAEA

12 mi/20 km north of Syracuse.
Leave Syracuse on corso Gelone, A2, toward Catania. After 12 mi/20 km a road to the right leads 0.6 mi/1 km to the site of Megara Hyblaea, the ruins of one of the earliest Greek colonies in Sicily. It was founded by Megarians who set sail for Sicily with the Chalcidians, who settled at Naxos. Today the site is being excavated by French archaeologists in Rome; so far an archaic city and a Hellenistic town have been discovered.

In the 6th century, about two hundred years after the arrival of the Megarians, powerful ramparts were built around the city, and the first ruins you see (on the right) are of the wall, which was unearthed in 1888. Beside it is a group of sarcophagi. Continue driving along the track and cross the bridge to the Hellenistic fortress, where the walls are more than 984 ft/300 m long. At the end of the walls there are the ruins of a large gateway, the entrance to the ancient town. Of the town itself, only the foundations of the main monuments remain. Nonetheless, a large amount of pottery has been found as well as an outstanding **kouros** of Paros marble (dating from the middle of the 6th century BC), one of the major exhibits in the Syracuse museum, and a headless **statue** of a woman suckling twins, also in the museum. Megara Hyblaea has a small, informative antiquities collection.

AUGUSTA

19.8 mi/32 km north of Syracuse.
Return to the N114 from Megara Hyblaea. After 1.2 mi/2 km, a road leads right for 7 mi/11 km to the port of Augusta.

This is an industrial town (containing a thermoelectric centre, oil refineries, cement works and chemical factories) with a population of 40,000. It is built on an islet, linked to the mainland by two bridges. Although the town itself, with its ordered layout, offers nothing of great interest to the tourist, it does have two harbours, Megarese to the west and Xifonio to the east, which lend it both commercial and military importance.

You enter the town through Porta di Terra, which dates from 1681. Leaving the castle of Frederick II, now a prison, on the left, you reach via Principe Umberto, where you can see the 17th-century Church of the Anime Sante, Palazzo Municipale (1699) and the Chiesa Matrice (1693-1769).

Telephone area code: 0931.

▲ **Villa dei Cesari,** in Monte Táuro, 1.8 mi/3 km from Augusta, ☎ 983 311. 24 rooms. Comfortable hotel with private beach.

LL Trattoria Donna Ina, in Faro Santa Croce, 3.7 mi/6 km from Augusta. *Closed Mon.*

Direct Augusta-Catania route: the N 114 passes via Agnone Bagni (holiday village) and Lido di Plaia, both with beaches.

LENTINI

14 mi/23 km north-west of Syracuse.
Return to the N 114 from Augusta and at the intersection take the road left to Lentini.

Ancient Leontinoi was founded by Chalcidians from Naxos in 729 BC and once rivaled Syracuse. Today the town is a commercial and agricultural centre on the northern slopes of the Iblei Mountains, specializing in the export of citrus fruit.

The **Chiesa Madre** (also known as Sant'Alfio) contains a 3rd-century Christian hypogeum in the right-hand aisle, and in the left-hand one, a 9th-century Byzantine icon. The **Museo Archeologico** *(open Tues-Sun 9am-2pm; closed Mon)* contains local finds.

The **Archaeological Site*** of the ancient city on Metapiccola Hill can be reached by car from nearby Carlentini. Excavations have revealed ramparts that were apparently rebuilt four times between the 7th and 5th centuries BC. You can also see a vast Hellenistic necropolis, the foundations of a 6th-century temple and the ruins of a Swabian castle. Finally, in the grotta del Crocifisso in the San Mauro Valley there are several Byzantine frescoes of interest.

Militello in Val di Catania is 16 mi/26 km west of Lentini, via Scordia. This little town, with its population of 10,000 is beautifully positioned, facing Mount Etna and the Catania plain. The new Museo della San Nicola near the Chiesa Madre has an interesting collection of religious works of art.

Lentini-Catania direct route: 18.6 mi/30 km.

CATANIA:
UNDER THE VOLCANO

The fate of **Catania**★★ has always been linked to the caprices of Etna. As the saying goes, 'every time the volcano sneezes, Catania trembles'.

Catania is Sicily's second largest city, with a population of over 400,000. Known as 'the Milan of the South', Catania has a large appetite for modernism. It is the economic and financial centre of the island and also its noisiest, most frenzied town; buildings go up faster, traffic jams are bigger, car horns are louder, the people are more hurried and overpopulation is more out of control than anywhere else in Sicily! The *scippi* — those wayward boys who strip you of your possessions with such disconcerting skill — positively abound in Catania. But things aren't all bad — Catania is also the town with the finest shops and the most elegantly dressed people.

A SERIES OF TRAGEDIES

The former Sikel stronghold was colonized by the Greeks (729 BC), the Romans (263 BC), the Byzantines (AD 535) and the Arabs (AD 900), who called it Balad-el-Fil ('town of the elephant'). The Normans took over in 1071 and under Aragonese rule, Catania became the capital of the island.

The history of Catania reads like an endless succession of disasters. The earliest known destruction of the town was in 476 BC when Hieron, a Syracusan tyrant, exiled its inhabitants. They returned 15 years later, but when their new reconstructed town began to thrive again, another jealous tyrant, Dionysius, sacked it furiously in 403 BC. In AD 121, Etna erupted and leveled the city. On February 4, 1169, a terrible earthquake killed about 15,000 people. Catania rose from its ashes once again only to be beaten down by the pirate Barbarossa's son, who avenged himself on the inhabitants of Catania for having taken sides with the Normans. The Angevins ransacked Catania during the rebellion of the Sicilian Vespers, and after that the town was ravaged by two plagues, one in 1423 and the other in 1576. On March 11, 1669, when Etna erupted once more, the earth split open over an area of about 9.3 mi/15 km in the Nicolosi district

The barren slopes of Mount Etna, still an active volcano.

(where the Rossi Mountains stand today), and a river of lava flowed into the city, covering the port and spreading into the sea for about 1.2 mi/2 km. The eruption continued until May of that year; because of the extent of the catastrophe, Charles II of Spain exempted the town from paying taxes for ten years. On January 11, 1693, while 12,000 people were attending a service in the Duomo, another earthquake demolished the town, killing two-thirds of the population. There was another damaging tremor in 1818 and, in 1928, a nearby village was buried under lava. The most recent eruptions were in 1971 and 1985.

▬ PRACTICAL INFORMATION

Map coordinates refer to the map pp. 180-181.
Telephone area code: 095.

Access

Boat: Many shipping lines have a stopover in Catania. There are regular services to Reggio di Calabria, Malta, North Africa and Naples. For information contact: **Agenzia Tirrenia**, piazza Grenoble 26, ☎ 316 394.

Car: Catania is 47 mi/75 km south of Messina, 31 mi/59 km north of Syracuse, 124 mi/199 km east of Palermo, 45 mi/73 km east of Enna and 25 mi/40 km south of Taormina.

Plane: Catania receives flights from Palermo and the Italian continent. Fontanarossa, 4.3 mi/7 km south of the town, is Sicily's most modern airport, and many charters from northern Europe arrive here. It has a tourist information office (☎ 341 900), shops, a self-service restaurant, a bar and a parking lot.

There are buses to the centre of town, to Taormina, Ragusa and, on certain days in summer, to Milazzo.

Train: Catania is a stop on the Messina-Syracuse line and there is also access to Caltanissetta, Palermo and Caltagirone. Information: **Stazione Centrale**, C5, ☎ 531 625.

Accommodation

▲▲▲ **Central Palace**, via Etnea 218, C3 c, ☎ 325 344. 99 rooms. Rather antiquated but right in the centre of town, with a swimming pool and restaurant.

▲▲▲ **Excelsior**, piazza Giovanni Verga 39, B4 a, ☎ 325 733. 167 rooms. One of Catania's better hotels, with a restaurant and private garage.

▲▲▲ **Jolly Trinacria**, piazza Trento 13, B3 b, ☎ 316 933. 159 rooms. Located just north of the city centre, with private parking.

▲▲ **Moderno**, via Alessi 9, A3, ☎ 325 309. 47 rooms. Simple but comfortable hotel.

▲▲ **Villa Dina**, via Caronda 129, A3, ☎ 447 103. 22 rooms. Recently renovated, with a garden.

In Ognina-Cannizzaro:

▲▲▲ **Baia Verde**, via Musco 8, lungomare, ☎ 491 522. 127 rooms. Garden, swimming pool and private beach. Good view.

▲▲▲ **Sheraton Hotel**, via Messina 45, ☎ 271 557. 168 rooms. Swimming pool and private beach. Good view.

▲▲ **Motel Agip**, via Messina 626, on the N114 at km sign n° 93, ☎ 712 2300. 56 rooms. Standard comfort of the Agip chain of hotels; recently renovated.

▲▲ **Motel Plaja**, in La Plaja, viale Kennedy 42, ☎ 340 871. 45 rooms. On a private beach with a garden, restaurant and bar.

▲▲ **Nettuno,** via di Lauria 121, ☎ 493 533. 80 rooms. Pleasant location, with a swimming pool and restaurant.

On the Palermo road

▲▲ **Gelso Bianco,** 5.5 mi/9 km out of town, ☎ 345 657. 90 rooms. Garden and tennis courts.

Campgrounds

Jonio, via Acque Casse, ☎ 491 139. In Ognina, 0.6 mi/1 km north of the centre of town. *Open all year.* Bungalows for rent.

Villagio Turistico Europeo, lungomare Kennedy 91, ☎ 591 026. 1.8 mi/3 km south of the centre of town. *Open June 1-Sept 30.* Bungalows for rent.

Villagio Turistico Internazionale, lungomare Kennedy 47, ☎ 345 440. 1.8 mi/3 km south of the centre of town. *Open May 1-Sept 30.* Bungalows for rent.

Festivals and entertainment

During the **Festa di Sant'Agata** (Feb 3-5) there's a superb procession of people carrying *candelore,* large candles of gilded wood, and *vara,* relics of St Agatha.

Catania's parks include the **Botanical gardens,** via Etnea 397, AB2 *(open 8am-2pm)* and the **Bellini gardens.**

During summer, jazz and classical music concerts are held in the **Bellini theatre,** ☎ 312 020.

The wine and grape show is in September.

Food

LLL Costa Azzura, via De Cristofaro, ☎ 494 920. *Closed Mon and throughout Aug.* Panoramic view, terraces overlooking the ocean. Good food. Frequented by business people.

LLL Giardino d'Inverno, via Asilo Sant'Agata 34, B5, ☎ 532 853. A new restaurant with an exceptional decor, which alone is worth the visit. Nouvelle cuisine.

LLL La Siciliana, viale Marco Polo 52, circonvalazione N., ☎ 370 003. *Closed Sun evening and Mon.* A beautifully decorated former villa with a summer garden. Regional wines and dishes. Extremely well-run establishment.

LL Il Commercio, via Riso 8, AB4 s, ☎ 447 289. *Closed Sat.* Simple trattoria, good food.

LL Da Rinaldo, via Simili 59, B5 x, ☎ 533 212. *Closed Tues.*

LL Dom Pietro, viale Vittorio Veneto. Picturesque *trattoria* run by a former puppeteer. Collection of old *pupi* on the walls. Good food.

LL Don Saro, via Libertà 129, ☎ 317 184. Family *trattoria.* Ordinary decor but excellent traditional cooking. Among other dishes, the pasta with garlic and parsley is delicious.

LL Selene, via Mollica 73, beside the Baia Verde Hotel in Ognina, ☎ 494 444. *Closed Tues.* Large dining room with porthole windows overlooking the sea. Mainly fish dishes. Good service. Best to reserve, especially in the evening.

LL Stella Antica Friggitoria Catanese, via Ventimiglia 66, ☎ 325 429. *Closed Mon. Trattoria* recommended — you can eat well here for a very reasonable price.

Cafés and ice cream

There is a good selection of small bars and pastry shops, mainly along via Etnea. We recommend **Savia** — opposite the Bellini gardens, on the corner of via Umberto I, for its ice cream (the best in Catania), and **Mantegna,** a little farther up, for its unforgettable sorbets.

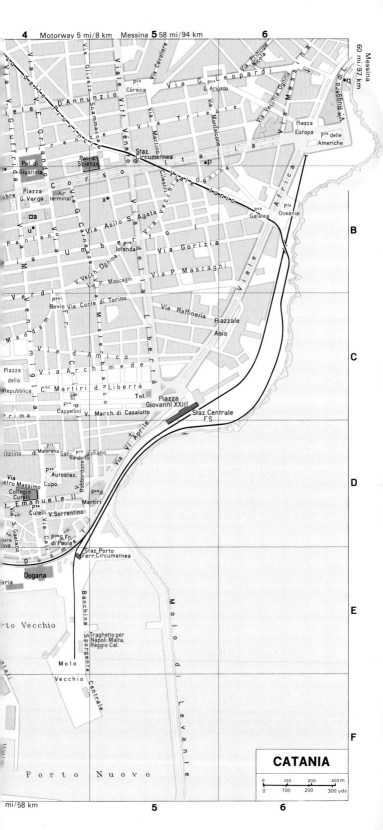

Messina 60 mi/L... km

Via Ruggero di L...

Via della Libertà
Via d'Annunzio
Pro Prov.le
Via Cavaliere
Via Cantiere
Via G. Leopardi
Via Principe Nicola

Corsica
P²a L. Ariosto

Via Oliveto Scammacca
Viale Vitt. Véneto
Via Martino
Via Trieste
Via Montalcone
Via Vecchia Ognina
Via Messina

Piazza Europa
P.le delle Americhe

Via Giuffrida
Via Orlando
V³a della

Staz. Circumetnea
●p
Via Africa

Pal. di Scienze
Corso
Viale Ognina
P.le Oceania
P²a Galatea

Pal. di Giustizia
x●

Piazza G. Verga
Air terminal

□a

Via C. Colombo
Via Asilo S. Agata
Via Vecchia Ognina

u●

Panian
Umberto
P²a Jolanda
Via Gorizia

V. Vecch Ognina
Via P. Mascagni
Via P. Mascagni

Via P. Mascagni

Verdi
P²a Bovio Via Conte di Torino
Via Raffineria
Piazzale Asia

Via Martino
Libertà

Mad...
Via d'Amico

Via Archimede

Piazza della Repubblica
C.50 Martiri d. Libertà
Tel.

P²a Cappellini
V. March. di Casalotto
Piazza Giovanni XXIII
Staz. Centrale F.S.

prima

Viale VI Aprile

ntonino
P²a di Maiorana San- P²a giuliano Gandolfo

Via
tro Massimo Lupo
P²a Autostaz.

Collegio Cutelli
Emanuele II
P²a d. Martiri

V. Via Cutelli V. Sorrentino

S. Gaetano
uca
ova
P²² S. Fr. di Paola
Staz. Porto
Ferr. Circumetnea

Dogana

Banchina Sporgente Centrale

to Vecchio

Traghetto per Napoli, Malta, Reggio Cal.

Molo di Levante

Molo Vecchio

eria

B

C

D

E

F

CATANIA

| 0 | 100 | 200 | 300 m |
| 0 | 100 | 200 | 300 yds |

P o r t o   N u o v o

Markets

A *pescheria* (fish market) is set up every morning around Porta Uzeda, D3, near the Duomo.

There is another market (for clothes, knick knacks, fruit and vegetables) between via Pacini, piazza Stesicoro and piazza Carlo Alberto.

Useful addresses

Air France, corso Martiri della Libertà 158, C5, ☎ 532 741.

Airport, Fontanarossa is 4.3 mi/7 km south of the town centre, ☎ 340 937.

Alitalia, corso Sicilia 113, C4, ☎ 327 555.

American Express, La Duca Viaggi, via Etnea 65 *(open Mon-Fri 9 am-1pm, 4:30-7:30pm; Sat 9 am-12:30pm).*

Bus station, piazza Bellini and Autostazione Etna, C2. For information contact: **SAIS,** via Teatro Massimo 41, ☎ 316 942, and **AST,** via La Rena 25, ☎ 348 083.

Car rental: Italy by Car Budget, airport, ☎ 349 888. Europcar, airport, ☎ 348 125. Holiday Car Rental, airport, ☎ 346 769. Avis, via La Rena 87, ☎ 347 116; via De Roberto, ☎ 374 095; airport, ☎ 340 500. Maggiore, via Gioieni 6, ☎ 338 306. Tirreno, piazza Vittorio Emanuele 32, ☎ 325 816.

CIT, via di Sangiuliano 208, D3, ☎ 327 555. *Closed Sat.*

Police, piazza San Nicolella 8, ☎ 317 763.

Post office, via Etnea 215, C3 *(open Mon-Sat 8am-8pm).*

Stazione Centrale, piazza Giovanni XXIII, C5 ☎ 531 625.

Stazione Porto Circumetnea, E5, ☎ 531 402.

Taxi ranks: Via Etnea, piazza Giovanni XXIII, piazza Trento and piazza del Duomo. Dispatched taxis, ☎ 330 966.

Telephones: Via San Euplio, near the Bellini gardens, B3 *(open daily 8am-10pm)* and in Stazione Centrale, C5.

Tourist information, AAPT, via Etnea 89, C3, ☎ 313 993. *Open Mon-Fri 9am-1pm, 4-7:30pm; Sat 9am-1pm.* There are other offices at the airport, in Stazione Centrale, in the harbour and on the highway to Messina.

▬ GETTING TO KNOW CATANIA

Map coordinates refer to the map pp. 180-181.

A single day is enough to give you a general idea of Catania. Below are two suggested itineraries that take in the main sights and can be followed on foot. You should try the first in the morning, because it includes the market, and the second in the afternoon. It is a good idea to split up the itineraries so that you can take full advantage of all the town has to offer. Because driving in town is so difficult you really must park your car in the centre the moment you find a parking place. Via Etnea is closed to traffic on Saturday afternoon, Sunday and on certain holidays.

▬ PIAZZA DEL DUOMO TO THE ROMAN THEATRE

The first walk begins in the city centre, piazza del Duomo, D3, a lively square surrounded by Baroque buildings dominated by the impressive mass of the cathedral. In the middle stands the **Elephant Fountain** sculpted by Giovanni Battista Vaccarini in 1736. An elephant, carved out of lava, trunk readied, seems to be watching over the town from its pedestal in the basin of the fountain. It has become Catania's main symbol, the emblem on the coat of arms.

Palazzo Senatorio, also known as the Municipio, stands across from the piazza on the other side of via Vittorio Emanuele. Work on it began in 1695 and was completed when the architect Giovanni Battista Vaccarini

ook over in 1741. You can see the difference in style between the rather
heavy, studded walls on the ground floor and the elegant windows,
doorway and central balcony. Opposite is the fine **Palazzo dei Chierici,** a
former seminary, built in a rather austere Baroque style. In 1937
Mussolini addressed a crowd from its balcony. Just beside the palace is
Porta Uzeda, which overlooks a railway viaduct and the harbour.

Duomo (Cathedral) D3

The cathedral was built during the 11th and 12th centuries, under the
Normans, and later rebuilt several times. After the 1693 earthquake, for
example, Vaccarini undertook the reconstruction work, which lasted six
years. The Baroque façade is sumptuous.

The majestic interior is completed by a dome, a high transept and three
apses. The **tomb of Vincenzo Bellini** is beside the second pillar on the
right after the entrance. The first notes of a tune from his opera *La
Sonnambula* have been carved on his funerary urn and the heroines of his
operas sculpted on the bronze bas-relief.

In the right-hand transept a marble portal by Giovanni Battista Mazzola
(1545) with scenes from the life of the Virgin leads into the **Cappella
della Madonna.** The original Norman architecture has been preserved
and contains the sarcophagi of the royal family of Aragon.

In the apse to the right of the choir is the **Cappella di Sant'Agata** (Chapel
of St Agatha)*, patron saint of the city. You look through a beautiful
wrought-iron grille to see the collection of Baroque works of art. The
grille, altar and marble altarpiece are by Antonio Freri and date from the
15th century.

The choir contains pictures illustrating the life of Saint Agatha and finely
sculpted stalls by Scipione di Guido (1558). In the left-hand transept is
another marble portal, identical to the one leading into the Cappella della
Madonna (Chapel of the Madonna). The two columns and capitals here
date from the original church. From an architectural point of view, this
part of the Duomo is by far the most interesting, giving an idea of what
the former basilica was like before Vaccarini's embellishments. Finally, in
the **Sacristy,** there is a large painting of the volcanic eruption that
occurred in 1669.

Palazzo Biscari** D4

On leaving the Duomo, turn at via Vittorio Emanuele to see another work
by Vaccarini, the Church of **Sant'Agata,** crowned by a vast dome and
adorned with its fine curvilinear front. Continue along the street for a few
yards to n° 159 and go into the courtyard of the bishop's palace to see
the Duomo's three tremendous lava apses and transept, remains of the
original building. The two towers, which once flanked the former basilica,
now correspond to the two side chapels of the Madonna and the Crucifix.

Continuing along the street you reach piazza Placido, D4, and the church
of San Placido (1769). At n° 56 there is an extremely elegant circular
courtyard* designed by Vaccarini for the Collegio Cutelli. Return to the
church of San Placido and take via Porticello, which leads to one of
Catania's most beautiful palaces, **Palazzo Biscari,** by Antonino Amato.
During his visit to Sicily, Goethe fell into ecstasy over its rich museum
collections belonging to the prince of Biscari, Ignazio Paternò Castello.
Walk around the palace to appreciate the architecture fully, and notice
the Baroque ornamentation around the windows — frolicking *putti*
(cherubs), grotesque faces and monsters. The palace was partly built
over the former 16th-century Spanish fortification.

La Pescheria** D3

As you walk along via Dusmet you will be guided by the shouts of
fishmongers and the rising odours to one of the most interesting markets
in Sicily. You definitely shouldn't miss La Pescheria (but watch your
handbag, as this is one of the *scippi's* favourite haunts).

Return to piazza del Duomo through Porta Uzeda, DE3, a gateway that
dates from 1696.

Castello Ursino* E3

On your way back toward the Duomo you pass a beautiful fountain adorned with a statue of Amenamos, the ancient river god of Catania, sculpted by Tito Angelini (1867). Take via Garibaldi from here to **piazza Mazzini**, a square surrounded by a peristyle of 32 columns, all from a former Roman basilica. Via Garibaldi is a long street and one of the most lively in Catania. It ends with a triumphal arch, E1, erected in 1768 for the wedding of Ferdinand III of Sicily and Maria-Carolina of Austria.

Via Auteri leads from piazza Mazzini to Castello Ursino, an impressive military building constructed under Frederick II between 1239 and 1250. Many of Catania's important historical events took place within its walls. In 1282 Peter of Aragon set up headquarters there to organize resistance against the Angevins; viceroys later used it as a palatial residence; in 1669, when the flow of lava from Etna's eruption of that year reached the sea, it was completely surrounded by a black volcanic mass. Today, the remaining walls form a solid square with a round tower 98 ft/30 m tall in each corner. The castle houses collections of the **Museo Civico** *(open Mon-Sat 9am-1pm, Sun and holidays 9am-noon).*

You can walk back from the castle towards via Vittorio Emanuele along via Castello Ursino (lined with shops selling coffins).

Bellini's House D3

Open daily 9am-1pm; admission free.

Cross via Vittorio Emanuele onto piazza San Francesco, D3. The Church of San Francesco (see p. 187) is on the right. An imposing monument of Cardinal Dusmet stands in the middle of the square, and to the left, at n° 3, you will find the house where Bellini was born. Inside, in the **Museo Belliniano,** you can see momentoes of the composer's life, including 19th-century prints of Catania, a piano, portraits, original scores, manuscripts and autographs. There is also a large music library (open to students only).

Teatro Romano* D2-3

Open Tues-Sun 9am-sunset; closed Mon.

The entrance to the theatre is on via Vittorio Emanuele, n° 266. The lava edifice you see today was built by the Romans over an

---

Bellini, father of bel canto

Vincenzo Bellini, Catania's most famous son, was born into a modest family on November 3, 1801. His father taught the organ and harpsichord, and Bellini began composing at the age of seven. At 18 he went to study in Naples. When he was 25 his first work, *Bianca e Fernando,* was performed at the San Carlo theatre in Naples and won the enthusiasm of Donizetti. His following works now form part of the standard repertoire of international opera; notably *La Sonnambula,* first performed on March 6, 1831, in Milan, where it was a triumphant success. On December 26 of that year, however, the opening of *Norma* with singers Giuditta Pasta and Giulia Grisi, was a failure. Bellini moved to France and settled in Puteaux, where he composed his third masterpiece, *I Puritani.* The first performance at the Théâtre des Italiens on January 25, 1835, with Giulia Grisi, was such a brilliant success that Queen Maria-Amelia, daughter of Ferdinand I, King of Two Sicilies, asked that the work be dedicated to her.

The fair-haired young composer was charming, exceptionally elegant and much sought after by Parisian ladies, although we don't know of any attachment. While his heroines never stopped singing their passion, he remained steadfastly single. He died suddenly at the age of 34, eight months after the opening of *I Puritani,* leaving nine major works, three of which are considered masterpieces of early 19th-century Italian opera. In 1876 his remains were returned with great pomp and ceremony to his native town, where he was buried in the Duomo.

earlier, 5th-century BC site. The diameter of the semicircular theatre is 318 ft/97 m, that of the orchestra is 95 ft/29 m. The rows of seats could hold 7000 spectators and were divided into nine sections cut by two circular corridors. This is the theatre where Alcibiades is believed to have harangued the inhabitants of Catania to side with Athens (415 BC). The **Odeon** is beside the theatre and dates from the same period. Used for philosophic discourse, concerts and rehearsals, it was part of an ancient acropolis (no longer extant) and could hold 1300 spectators. You have a better view of it from via Teatro Greco, which runs up behind the theatre. From here turn left at via Rotonda and walk to via Vittorio Emanuele, where you will see the 18th-century Church of the Trinita on the corner. Continue along the street to piazza del Duomo.

PIAZZA DEL DUOMO TO GIARDINO BELLINI

Via Etnea* AD3

Set out from piazza del Duomo, D3, on via Etnea, the city's main thoroughfare and the favourite haunt of Catanians. It is lined with fine buildings, luxurious shops and many cafés. Traffic is limited to buses and taxis; no private cars are allowed.

Via Etnea was the first of the four main streets to be rebuilt after the earthquake of 1693. It crosses **piazza dell'Universita** where you can see a harmonious series of fine buildings that benefited from Vaccarini's architectural genius. The palace of San Giuliano (1745), now occupied by Credito Italiano, stands on the right, and on the left is the university designed by Antonino Battaglia at the beginning of the 18th century. The sober, elegant interior has an arcaded **courtyard*** by Vaccarini. Beyond the square on the left, between two 18th-century palaces, stands the **Collegiata** (1768) with an unusual concave façade by Stefano Ittar. Inside you can see frescoes by Giuseppe Sciuti.

Teatro Bellini D4

Continuing along via Etnea you reach Quattro Canti, the intersection where via Antonino di San Giuliano leads left to the Church of San Nicolò, D2, and right to Teatro Bellini. The town's fine tribute to the composer stands on a small square that you reach from a street on the right. It was inaugurated on May 31, 1890, with a performance of *Norma*. The façade is neo-classical and is fittingly adorned with busts of musicians as well as fauns, lyres and eagles. The musical season begins in January and generally lasts until the end of May. Maria Callas and Luciano Pavarotti have performed here, as has Benjamino Gigli, who considered it the most beautiful concert hall in the world.

Piazza Stesicoro, the Roman amphitheatre C3

Return to via Etnea and follow it past the Prefettura and the Church of San Michele until you reach piazza Stesicoro, with its monument to Bellini. To the right is corso Sicilia, a wide avenue lined with modern buildings (banks, shops, travel agencies) and to the left, the remains of a Roman amphitheatre. The ruins give only a faint idea of enormity of the theatre, which could hold up to 16,000 people. It measured no less than 410 ft/125 m by 344 ft/105 m in diameter, and its arena was 233 ft/71 m by 167 ft/51 m.

Beyond the square and the Church of the Capuchins is the Church of the Santo Carcere, C3, so named because it was built over the site of a Roman prison where St Agatha was incarcerated. Its fine 13th-century doorway was taken from the former Duomo. From here via Cappucini leads to the church of **San Domenico**. Inside, on the first altar on the left, is one of the most beautiful Madonnas by Antonello Gagini. There is also a *Virgin with Rosary* (1531) above the second altar on the right.

Giardino Bellini* BC2

Keep to the left side of the Church of San Domenico and walk to the

upper entrance of Villa Bellini. This is a vast peaceful garden, lush with
beautiful trees and flowers. Cross through the garden to viale Regina
Margherita, and go left to the Church of **Santa Maria del Gesù**, B2. It
was built during the 15th and 16th centuries, and altered in the 18th. As
you enter on the left there's a finely sculpted doorway by Gagini (part of
the original building), who also carved the Virgin by the second altar on
the left. The crucifix above the main altar is by Fra Úmile da Petralía.

Church of San Nicolò D2

Walk back along viale Regina Margherita and then turn right into via Santa
Euplio, which leads to the Roman amphitheatre, C3. Continue along via
Corcifieri, D3, and then turn right at via Gesuiti. This ends at piazza
Dante, opposite the unfinished Church of San Nicolò, D2.

The largest church in Sicily, San Nicolò was part of a Benedictine convent
measuring more than 1,076,400 sq ft/100,000 sq m. Building began in
1558, but the terrible eruption of Etna in 1669 put a stop to the work.
The monks called upon a Roman architect to restore the church when the
1693 earthquake thwarted construction once again. Finally, the interior
was completed, but not the façade. The six columns you see today were
intended as a support for a pediment, as in a Greek temple. The
impressive interior is white and bare, measuring 344 ft/105 m long with
a width of 157 ft/48 m at the transept.

All that remains of the organ behind the altar, which the young Bellini may
well have practiced on, is the richly-worked case, dating from 1765. Even
the 2916 organ pipes had to be dismantled for restoration. The finely
carved cupboards in the sacristy once held the convent's religious
ornaments, and 11 superbly decorated candles carried through the town
in processions during the feasts of St Agatha are stored in the church.
Ask the sacristan if you would like to climb the cupola (203 ft/60 m high,
about 200 steps) for a panoramic **view*** of the city.

Benedictine convent** D2

The former Benedictine convent with its sumptuous façade adjoins the
church, hidden from prying eyes by high walls. After the 1693 eruption, it
was rebuilt by Antonino Amato, the architect of the Biscari palace
mentioned above. There are rows of magnificent **windows**** and
balconies set between white pilasters adorned with diamond-shaped
studs — each frame sculpted with inventiveness. The decorative images
include alluring siren-like caryatids, graciously frolicking cherubs and coats
of arms. This 'palace-convent' is at present being restored to its
former splendour.

Inside, wide corridors lead to two courtyards: the first has a faux-Gothic
cloister, and the second, which is far more beautiful, a graceful arcade
and windows.

Via Crocifieri** D3

Via Gesuiti leads off from the middle of piazza Dante to via Crocifieri, one
of the oldest streets in Catania.

Turn right onto this quiet street, which slopes down a hillside lined
with churches. An exceptional example of 18th-century religious urban
architecture, via Crocifieri offers a succinct view of the development of
the Baroque style. During the 18th century, poverty was widespread, and
there was no social welfare, so religious groups played an essential role in
society by aiding and educating the destitute. Convent churches were
built on the street, often proving their wealth with elaborate façades,
whereas the far more sober convent or monastery was always relegated
to a secondary position behind. This accounts for the number of
remarkable churches on via Crocifieri.

San Giuliano Church**, one of the finest examples of the local Baroque
style, is the first church on the left. It was built in the shape of a Greek
cross by Vaccarini between 1738 and 1760 and has not been altered
since. Its curvilinear façade is adorned with outstanding wrought-iron

work and girandole cornice decoration. The well-proportioned interior is crowned with a cupola and bears a painted 15th-century cross above the main altar.

Church of the Gesuiti, on the right, was by Father Angelo Italia di Licata, who designed the vigorous façade with twin columns — a style that heralded classicism. The sober building beside the church is a former Jesuit college which now houses the Fine Arts school. You can go in to see its beautiful inner **courtyard**** with its extremely elegant portico and loggia and a black-and-white stone carpet of inlaid paving.

San Benedetto Church*** is entered from the side; unfortunately it is often closed. The rich façade is by Alonso di Benedetto and the doorway (1704-13) by Vaccarini. The nave was raised above street level to avoid the danger of flowing lava, and Vaccarini gave the white entrance hall a tiered staircase to lead up to it. Its magnificent balustrade sets off eight statues of angels. The **painted ceiling** is exceptional, and the floor has kept its original paving of different-coloured marble that matches the colours of the **paintings*** on the vaulting. The two tribunes in the nuns' choir are made of gilded wood and have fine wrought-iron railings.

Once outside, continue along the street and walk beneath an arch, said to have been built overnight to connect two parts of a former monastery.

San Francesco Church is on the left when you reach piazza San Francesco, D3, described in the first itinerary (see p. 184). Its impressive façade is by Angelo Italia.

To return to piazza del Duomo, turn left at via Vittorio Emanuele.

These two walks will have taken you to Catania's main monuments, but there's still a lot more to see. Apart from over 25 churches, the town has collections of vulcanology, geology and minerology in the **Palazzo delle Scienze,** AB4, corso Italia 55 (contact the university to visit the collections). There are also a great many fountains, of which the most famous is the Abduction of Proserpine (1904) opposite the station.

ETNA, THE FIRE UNDER THE ASH

Etna is one of the most active volcanoes on earth and the largest in Europe. It is Sicily's main attraction, changing colour by the hour according to the light.

The vast Catania plain was formerly covered by a gulf that gradually disappeared as a series of underwater eruptions brought Etna into view. The volcano covers an area of 606 sq mi/1570 sq km and has a perimeter of 103 mi/165 km. Its height, which varies according to its state of eruption, was 10,902 ft/3323 m in 1980. Etna can be divided into three zones: the lower slopes are under cultivation, those just above are wooded and the uppermost are desert. In the cultivated zone there are vineyards and fruit trees, including orange, lemon and tangerine trees that can grow at an altitude of up to 3937 ft/1200 m; you can even find pear and cherry trees located at attitudes up to 4921 ft/1500 m. The wooded area is covered in chestnuts, beeches and birch trees. The desert zone begins at 6561 ft/2000 m and is an extraordinary landscape consisting of immense lava fields and secondary craters, surrounded by scoria flows. It isn't completely barren, however, because some herbaceous plants, such as juniper, grow up to 9842 ft/3000 m.

Remarkably beautiful, Etna's black lava desert slopes alternate dramatically with fertile stretches of flowering fruit trees. An even more striking contrast is created by the crater, snow covered for seven months of the year, which stands out like a white crown against the azure sky.

Well before the arrival of the Greeks in Sicily, the Sikels in the Etna region honoured their god Adranos as 'master of the turbulent depths of the earth'. The Greeks were in turn struck by Etna's volcanic violence and determined that giants, Typhon and Enceladus, lived on the mountain. Greek mythology often alludes to the volcano; it is here that the Cyclopes aided Vulcan who had his forge in the crater.

There have been no less than 135 fatal eruptions since Antiquity. A number were recorded during the Middle Ages, including that of 1381, which completely destroyed Catania. Borelli, a physician, described the tragic eruption in 1669 that caused the formation of the Rossi Mountains. A cleft opened from the crater right down to Nicolosi and out poured a river of lava that spread over a kilometre into the sea, devastating everything in its path and killing 20,000 people. The 1693 eruption took 60,000 lives. During the 18th century there were 16 eruptions, and during the 19th and 20th centuries volcanic activity has shown no signs of slowing down. On May 27, 1911, lava almost reached the Alcántara river. During the night of June 27, 1917, a unique phenomena was recorded: a fountain of lava about 2624 ft/800 m high shot up from the crater and, in just a few minutes, threw out more than 106 million cubic ft/3 million cubic m of lava. In May 1923, a cleft appeared in the mountain 6562-8202 ft/2000-2500 m long and spread over a distance of 1.8 mi/3 km. On November 2, 1928, during the most deadly eruption of the century, two cascades of fire shot up from a deep fracture in the mountain and destroyed the town of Máscali. The longest eruption was recorded in 1950-51, when three explosive cones formed in the middle crater. The highest of these reached 10,912 ft/3326 m, the present height of the volcano. The amount of lava produced during the eruption was an estimated 28,252 million cubic ft/800 million cubic m. The 1971 eruption destroyed the second cablecar station and the vulcanological observatory; that of 1983 destroyed the Sapienza refuge and that of 1986 the new cablecar installation. There is an observatory that monitors the volcano's activity, and from time to time tourist visits are cancelled if conditions are not considered safe.

Access

Catania and Taormina are good departure points for a visit to the volcano. You can go around it on foot or by car or, better still, take the routes that crisscross its slopes to the summit (map opposite).

There is a difference between an ascent up the mountain, which can be done by car up to the departure point of the former cableway, and the actual ascent of the summit, which you begin in a tracked (caterpillar) vehicle and continue on foot. The first part of the trip can be accomplished by anyone (provided warm clothes are worn) but the second requires certain precautions.

Useful addresses

SITAS Funivia dell'Etnea, agency and office for mountain guides, in Nicolosi, piazza Vittorio Emanuele 45, ☎ 914 209 and (facilities) 914 141.

Tourist information, Largo Pasiello 5, in Catania, ☎ 312 124. **Italian Alpine Club** (CAI), in Catania, via Vecchia Ognina 169, ☎ 387 674. **Pro Loco** in Linguaglossa, piazza Annunziata, ☎ 643 094. **Pro Loco** in Nicolosi, piazza Vittorio Emanuele, ☎ 914 201.

Train tour of Etna (four hours)

This is a 70.8-mi/114-km trip around Etna by train that begins at Giarre-Riposto and takes about four hours. Reservations for the tour can be made at Catania train station or with a travel agent. You can reach Giarre-Riposto station from Catania directly by train (35 minutes) or by bus.

The **Ferrovia Circumetnea** route passes through Linguaglossa, Randazzo, Maletto, Bronte, Adrano and Paternò. You have a good view of Etna for almost the entire journey and you pass through varied countryside; areas under cultivation or natural vegetation zones alternate with desolate lava landscapes.

Climbing Etna

The classic excursion up the mountain will be described in the way it is organized by travel agents in Catania. Because the buses leave early in the morning you can do the trip in one day. You should make sure you have warm clothing and good walking shoes.

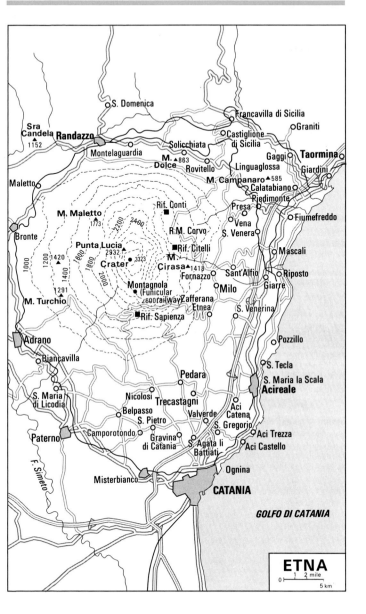

If you have a car, you can drive from Zafferana Etnea to Linguaglossa on Etna's eastern slopes, described on p. 194.

The drive from Catania via Nicolosi to the departure point of the former cable car is 21 mi/34 km.

Leave Catania on via Etnea, pass piazza Gioeni and turn left for Barriera del Bosco where you turn left again, passing between two obelisks. In **Gravina di Catania** (5 mi/8 km) you will see two craters dating from the 1381 eruption. **Mascalucia** (6 mi/10 km) is a town of 3000 inhabitants renowned for its Del Bosco wine and its carpets, woven by local women. After 6.8 mi/11 km you come to the **Convent of Santa Maria delle Grazie** on the left. **Massannunziata** (8 mi/13 km), at a height of 1794 ft/547 m, stands in a formerly active volcanic area.

Nicolosi (10 mi/16 km north-west of Catania)

This large market town, 2290 ft/698 m above sea level with a population of 4500, is known as the Gateway to Etna. Before the many roads were built across the slopes, Nicolosi was the departure point for climbs to the crater.

Nicolosi to the cable car

The **Strada dell'Etna** runs below the Monti Rossi Mountains and then between the San Leo Mountains (3940 ft/1201 m) to the left and the Albano Mountains (4071 ft/1241 m) to the right. It twists between lava flows, runs alongside Bosco della Fernandina and passes near the cone of Monte Manfrè (4790 ft/1460 m).

After 20 mi/32.4 km a road on the left leads to **Serra la Nave**, 5626 ft/1715 m above sea level, where there are ski slopes and pine forests.

Strada dell'Etna then climbs to **Casa Cantoniera** (6174 ft/1882 m) and on to the first station of the former cable car. Here you will find a vast parking lot and a selection of restaurants, among them **La Cantoniera, Corsaro, Esagonal** and **Monti Silvestri.**

Excursion from Nicolosi

Take time out for the walk in the Rossi Mountains, which should take just over an hour and a half, there and back. You will see one of Etna's largest secondary cones (with a perimeter of 1.8 mi/3 km). It is, in fact, the one that erupted and devastated Catania in 1669.

Telephone area code: 095.

Accommodation (in Nicolosi)

▲▲▲ **Biancaneve,** via Etnea 163, ☎ 911176. 69 rooms. Swimming pool and tennis courts.

▲▲ **Gemellaro,** via Etnea 160, ☎ 911373. 44 rooms.

Useful addresses

Excursions up Etna: SITAS Funivia dell'Etnea, piazza Vittorio Emanuele, ☎ 911158.

Tourist information, piazza Vittorio Emanuele, ☎ 914201.

Ascent of the summit

This is one of the oldest excursions in the world, renowned even in Antiquity when the emperor Hadrian climbed to the summit of Etna to see the sun rising in all the colours of the rainbow. Today, as a safety measure, visitors are no longer allowed to climb to the edge of the central crater.

Recent eruptions have destroyed the meteorological observatory at 9593 ft/2924 m, the *funivia* (cableway), the refuge and the new automatic cable car — one of the most modern in Europe. It could carry 1200 people per hour to 8556 ft/2608 m, reaching that altitude in only 15 minutes. A normal trip is described here in the hopes that the cable car will soon be brought back into service.

Special all-terrain vehicles (buses for 20 passengers) leave from the old *funivia* and drive up to 9514 ft/2900 m in an hour and a half. Expect to pay L25,000 for an adult and L14,000 for a child. You arrive at a refuge where you can have drinks and snacks. From this point, guides can accompany you to an opening in the earth, which may, depending on its mood, spew forth sulphurous vapours.

It is possible to visit underground corridors at 8202 ft/2500 m formed in the lava by the 1985 eruption. This information is given only as a guideline because the volcano, being active, can change its features quickly.

This excursion poses no problems and can be done by anyone, from April to October. However, certain precautions should be taken whatever the season. Strong winds, usually from the west, blow around the summit, and the temperature can fall to below 32°F/0°C even on summer nights. Come well-prepared with warm clothing, good walking shoes if you do not have climbing boots (these can be rented), and glasses to protect yourself not only from the sun but also from volcanic ash. Bear in mind that there's a temperature drop of 68°F/20°C between Catania and the summit. Furthermore, snow begins to fall in November and continues until spring. Finally, if you want to walk to the summit rather than take the minibus you must be accompanied by a guide.

Night excursions by jeep can be organized (you leave at 3am and return at 7:30am), which gives you the chance to watch the sunrise. Leaving from **Piccolo Rifugio,** you are driven up to 9842 ft/3000 m, about 656 ft/200 m below the crater. On the way up you pass the Torre del Filósofo refuge (under reconstruction). There is a small Roman monument nearby, probably erected in honour of Emperor Hadrian's climb. You then pass the site of the vulcanological observatory, which was destroyed along with the second cablecar station during the eruption of 1971. As you near the vast crater you see smoke emanations: chloride of sulphur and sodium sulphate gases. There are three cones inside and bubbling at the bottom is the incandescent lava. Once the sun is up, the panoramic view is spectacular: on a clear day you can see the whole of Sicily and as far as Malta. On the return journey you will be able to see the extraordinary lunar landscape of the **Valle del Bove.**

Excursions around Etna

Count on a minimum of half a day to drive the 87 mi/140 km around Etna. You will have extremely varied views of the volcano and its unusual contrasting landscapes enhanced by the 200 or more subsidiary craters that riddle its slopes. It's amazing to find so many villages on such an inhospitable mountain, although you'll understand why they're there when you go through a market and see farmers weighing their plump sun-drenched tomatoes, aubergines and heavy bunches of grapes. It takes barely 20 years for volcanic ash, like lava, to develop into rich, fertile soil.

Catania to Linguaglossa

Take the highway from Catania to Fiumefreddo as opposed to the coast road, described on p. 196, which is often very crowded. The N120 twists up the mountain from **Fiumefreddo,** offering beautiful views of the coast. It goes through **Piedimonte Etneo** (1142 ft/348 m), the departure point for excursions into the Arsi Mountains (2887 ft/880 m), and after another 13 mi/21 km reaches Linguaglossa.

Linguaglossa

This is a centre for the timber industry (6000 inhabitants) and is a good base for walks or for climbing the craters from the northern slopes (which can be done from June to October). There is also a ski resort with a National Ski School.
Telephone area code: 095.

Accommodation (in Linguaglossa)
▲▲ **Happy Day,** via Mareneve 3, ☎ 643484. 14 rooms.
▲ **Centrale,** piazza Municipio 4, ☎ 643548. 8 rooms.

Excursions
We strongly recommend that you take the Mareneve road to Linguaglossa pine forest (10.5 mi/17 km) and to the Chalet delle Ginestre at 4675 ft/1425 m (where there's a restaurant). A road from the chalet leads on for 4.3 mi/7 km to the Pouchoz refuge at 5905 ft/1800 m (Italian Ski School and bar). If you choose this route you can continue directly on to Randazzo without having to return to Linguaglossa.

Useful address

Tourist information, Pro Loco, piazza Annunziata, ☎ 643094. *Open Mon-Sat 9am-12:30pm, 4:30-7:30pm.*

Randazzo (12.4 mi/20 km west of Linguaglossa on the N120)
Randazzo (12,000 inhabitants) is located 9.3 mi/15 km from the central crater on the northern slopes of Etna, 2474 ft/754 m above sea level. Although the town has not been damaged by volcanic eruptions for centuries, much of its former character was lost during the bombardments of the last war. You need about an hour to see its three churches, which survived the 1943 bombings. Each served as a cathedral for alternate periods of three years in Randazzo's history.

On entering Randazzo along via Regina Margherita, on the right you come to via Umberto I which crosses the whole town and leads to the Church of **Santa Maria***. Built between 1217 and 1239 in the Norman style, the church was disfigured in the 19th century by a partial reconstruction of the façade and campanile. You should walk around it to see the powerful lava apses and the 15th-century doorways on the sides. Inside, the aisles are separated by monolithic lava columns with capitals. Note the marble baptismal fonts from the Gagini school, the beautiful 17th-century Crucifixion from the Messina school in the third chapel on the right and on the left, above the side door, a 12th-century fresco of the Virgin. The Sacristy contains fine carved walnut cupboards dating from the 17th and 18th centuries.

Via Duca degli Abruzzi leads from the square to San Nicolò, a 13th-century church that was altered in the 16th and 17th centuries. The ruined campanile is 18th century. Inside the church you can see the 14th-century baptistry, some bas-reliefs and a statue of San Nicolò by the Gagini school. Outside, in front of the square, there is a statue known as Randazzo Vecchia (1757). In the same street at nº 57, immediately on your right, is the Gothic-Renaissance façade of Palazzo Finocchiaro (1509). By continuing along the street you join up with via Umberto I and so reach **San Martino,** a 13th- or 14th-century church that has retained a lovely crenelated 13th-century **campanile*** built of lava and white limestone. Inside on the right there are octagonal baptismal fonts of red marble resting on eight carved columns (1447). The last chapel on the right houses a magnificent statue of *The Virgin and Child by* Gagini. In the left apse you can see a large Gothic tabernacle of richly worked marble.

Food (in Randazzo)

LL Arturo, via Roma 8, ☎ 921565. *Closed Sat and Sept 15-30.*
LL La Trottola, via Basile 27, ☎ 921187. *Closed Tues.*

Randazzo to Nicosia (50.3 mi/81 km)
From Randazzo you can make an interesting foray inland by taking the N120, a mountain road, for 50.3 mi/81 km to Nicosia. After 8 mi/13 km you turn right for about 1 mi/1.6 km to the former Benedictine abbey of Santa Maria di Maniace, founded in 1174 and now a sumptuous private residence. Ask the guardian to show you around. The church has a wooden ceiling dating from Norman times.
Troina (30.4 mi/49 km)
This picturesque town at 3674 ft/1120 m has a Norman church, Chiesa Matrice, that was altered in the 18th century. The fine tower beside it, also Norman originally, was given additional arches and pointed windows in the 16th century.
Cerami (38 mi/61 km)
This town stands at 3182 ft/970 m and is dominated by the remains of a castle. The road twists down from here into the Serra di Falco. After 13 mi/21 km you reach **Nicosia,** see p. 230.

Randazzo to Adrano
On your way out of Randazzo leave the N120 on your right and take the N284 to the left. This crosses a wooded region and then leads up

through a beautiful volcanic landscape to an altitude of 3412 ft/1040m. You have a splendid descent from this point to **Maletto** (3116 ft/950 m), the highest place on Etna.

After about 3 mi/5 km a side road leads to Castello, the former 12th-century abbey of Santa Maria di Maniace. It was given to Admiral Nelson, who became Duke of Bronte, in 1799. The town of **Bronte,** about 3.7 mi/6 km away, is a farming centre best known for its pistachio nuts.

Adrano (64.6 mi/104 km)

With 34,000 inhabitants Adrano is an agricultural centre set on a lava terrace over the site of a sanctuary to the god Adranos. Local excavations have brought a number of ancient objects to light, including a small bronze statue of an ephebus making a libation, now in the Syracuse museum.

Once in via Roma beside the Vittoria gardens, you will see on the right the former monastery of **Santa Lucia***, founded in 1158 by Countess Adelesia, Count Roger's niece. Its monumental façade, restored in 1596, is interrupted by a church with two towers, each consisting of a square base and a cupola. The oval interior is covered in gold and sky-blue stuccowork. There are rococo organ cases and, in the choir, a skill-fully arranged velvet-and-silk hanging with gold embroidery. The decor is more suggestive of a ballroom than a convent chapel. The nuns attended service here in tribunes closed off by railings as delicately worked as lace.

A little farther along you come to a Norman castle on piazza Umberto I. It was built in the 11th century, during the reign of Roger I, and altered in the 14th. Protecting the massive building is a bastion with small corner towers. The castle houses the **Museo Archeologico** *(open Tues-Sun 9am-1:30pm, Sun 9am-12:30pm; closed Mon)*. To the left is the Chiesa Madre, a Norman church that was altered several times and is now hideously disfigured by an incomplete modern façade. Inside there is a painted wooden crucifix dating from the 15th century. Outside the church to the right via Buglio leads to the walls of the ancient Greek city (4th century BC).

South-west of the town (4.3 mi/7 km) there is an experimental solar station equipped with Eurelios mirrors. Financed by France, Germany and Italy, it produces one million watts a year.

Festivals (in Adrano)

Diavolata di Pasqua is held on Easter Sunday in piazza Umberto I. This is a holy performance of the 'Redemption of Humanity' in which the archangel Michael, symbolizing the sun, frees a chained angel represent-ing Humanity, while the figure of Death submits with a symbolic breaking of a bow.

During the **Volata dell'Angelo** ceremony, held on August 3, a child dis-guised as an angel enacts flying over the grave of the patron saint.

Useful address

Tourist information, via Spampinato 31, ☎ 681938.

Adrano to Enna (43.4 mi/70 km)

This itinerary includes Regalbuto, Agira and Leonforte on the N121 and a short detour to Centúripe. To reach the latter, after 6 mi/10 km on the N121, take a road left for 5 mi/8 km.

Centúripe

Once a small Sikel city, this town of 6800 inhabitants is perched on a hill 2395 ft/730 m high, between the Simeto and Dittaino river valleys, with a splendid panoramic view of Etna. The Municipio houses a small museum *(open mornings during office hours)* with a collection of local finds. Take via Umberto I and then viale Corradino to reach the ruins of a Roman mausoleum known as Castello Corradino, where views of the Catania plain and Etna are magnificent. Other sights of interest nearby include remains of Roman houses in vallone Difesa and contrada Panneria and a ruined thermal spa in vallone dei Bagni.

At Catenanuova, 8 mi/13 km from Centúripe, you can join the N192 and the Catania-Palermo highway.

Return to the N121 and continue to **Regalbuto** (14 mi/23 km), a market town 1722 ft/525 m above sea level. It is not far from Pozzillo (3 mi/5 km), an artificial lake on the Salso built to supply a power station.

Agira (23 mi/37 km)

This town has a population of 15,000 and is located on the slopes of a hill 2198 ft/670 m high, dominated by a medieval castle. Ancient Agyrion was a Sikel city colonized by the Greeks in 339 BC. It had the honour of being the birthplace of Diodorus Siculus, a historian who, in the 1st century BC, was the first to write a history of the world. In piazza Roma the Church of San Salvatore, with its 16th-century façade and part-Gothic campanile, contains an invaluable treasure of vestments and 12th-century parchments. The Church of Sant'Antonio in piazza Garibaldi contains a 16th-century statue of San Silvestro. In the treasury there is a painting on marble of the Adoration of the Magi. The Church of Santa Maria del Gesú nearby houses a painted crucifix by Fra Úmile da Petralía (1580-1639).

Leonforte (31 mi/50 km)

This small town was founded by Prince Branciforte at the beginning of the 17th century and is best known for its large fountain (Granfonte) with arches.

Enna (43.4 mi/70 km): see p. 130

Adrano to Catania

The N121 for Catania bypasses Biancavilla (a town founded in 1480 by Albanese families) and then traverses lush orange groves to **Santa Maria di Licodia**. The name of the place derives from a former Benedictine abbey, now the town hall. The Church of Santa Maria preserves a lava bell tower dating from the end of the Middle Ages.

Paternò (74.5 mi/120 km)

With a population of 45,000, this town is set above the Simeto valley at an altitude of 915 ft/279 m and is dominated by a Norman castle. Via Matrice leads up to it, passing the Chiesa Madre on the way. To the left of the Chiesa Madre there are two other ruined churches and their convents, and to the right is the castle with a wonderful view of Etna. Built by Roger the Norman in 1073, it was altered in the 16th century and restored in 1958. There is also a zoological park 3 mi/5 km away on the Catania-Palermo highway (☎ 918057).

After Paternò the road crosses the Etna railway line and a lava track dating from 1669. **Misterbianco** (82 mi/132 km), a town dominated by churches, has a population of 15,000 and spreads over two hills.

Accommodation (in Paterno)

▲ **Sicilia,** via Vittorio Emanuele 391, ☎ 841700. 24 rooms.

Catania (87 mi/140 km): see p. 177.

ETNA'S EASTERN SLOPES BY ROAD

There are excellent roads on Etna's eastern slopes. The following is a 27-mi/44-km itinerary from Catania to Linguaglossa, via Zafferana Etnea.

Leave Catania on via Etnea, pass piazza Gioeni and turn left for Barriera del Bosco, then right for Sant'Agata li Battiati. Go through San Giovanni la Punta and turn right toward Viagrande. A road leads left to **Trecastagni** (1922 ft/586 m), where the fine Renaissance Chiesa Madre is thought to be by Antonelli Gagini. **Viagrande** (1804 ft/550 m) stands at the crossroads of the road to Acireale and Nicolosi. The road then passes below the volcano's secondary cones before arriving at **Zafferana Etnea**

— a resort on the slopes of Etna and a starting point for excursions. The local park has lovely trees and a wide variety of camellias.

From Zafferana to Linguaglossa the road crosses the Bove Valley, where guides can take you to see the fantastic cliff walls of lava and tuff that sometimes reach a height of 3281 ft/1000 m.

Near **Milo** (17 mi/28 km) there are signs of lava from the 1950 eruption that stopped a mere 984 ft/300 m from the village. **Fornazzo** (18.6 mi/30 km) is a departure point for excursions. A road leads up to the left from here to the Citelli refuge and the ski slopes (5712 ft/1741 m) before continuing 18.6 mi/30 km farther to Linguaglossa. A shorter, more direct road (8.6 mi/14 km) leads down from Fornazzo to Linguaglossa (see p. 191).

Accommodation

▲▲ **Ares,** contrada Savoca, San Giovanni la Punta, ☎ 827 651. 44 rooms. Peaceful location.

▲▲ **Madonna degli Ulivi,** via Umberto 266, Viagrande, ☎ 616 177. 54 rooms. Swimming pool and garden.

▲▲ **Primavera dell'Etna,** strada Mareneve Sud, Zafferana Etnea, ☎ 708 2348. 66 rooms. A quiet hotel in a good location.

Food

LL **Al Mulino a Vento,** via Mulino 48, Trecastagni, ☎ 616 634.

LL **Nuovo Calatino,** via della Regione 62, San Giovanni la Punta, ☎ 822 055. *Closed Tues.* Good regional dishes.

LL **Al Parco,** via Libertà 3, Zafferana Etnea, ☎ 951.222. *Closed Tues and throughout Nov.* Recommended for its regional cooking.

Useful address

Tourist information, piazzo Municipio 1, San Giovanni, tel: 822 604.

CATANIA TO MESSINA: SICILY'S EASTERN SEASIDE RESORTS

You can take the N114 (Orientale Sicula) along the coast from Catania to Messina (60 mi/97 km) or the A18 highway, which is more direct and less crowded than the coast road and which affords even better views of the sea. The itinerary below describes the seaside resorts along the coast road, the N114.

━━ CATANIA TO TAORMINA

Leave Catania on the coast road via Ognina and Cannizaro.

Aci Castello (5.5 mi/9 km north of Catania)
This is a seaside resort dominated by a basalt rock which dramatically sticks out of the sea. A Norman castle perches on the top. Climb to the terrace and castle keep for a good view of the coast and the Isole de Ciclopi.

Accommodation

See Catania, p. 178.

Food

LL Villa delle Rose, via Nazionale 15. *Closed Mon and throughout Nov.* ☎ 271024. Good food served in a garden setting. *Pappardelle* is the speciality.

Aci Trezza (6.8 mi/11 km north of Catania)
This is a fishing centre and seaside resort (population 15,000) set opposite the Isole de Ciclopi. The town has several claims to fame: Visconti filmed *Terra Trema* here, one of the masterpieces of Italian neo-realist cinema; Aci Trezza is the backdrop for one of the best-known 19th-century Italian novels, *I Malavoglia,* by Giovanni Verga (1840-1922); and last but not least, the inventor of the sorbet, Francesco de'Coltelli, was born here.
Telephone area code: 095.

Accommodation

▲▲▲ **I Faraglioni,** lungomare dei Ciclopi 115, ☎ 276744. 82 rooms. On the beach, with a good restaurant.
▲▲▲ **Kristal,** via Provinciale 5, ☎ 276543. 14 rooms. On the beach.
▲▲ **I Malavoglia,** via Provinciale 1/a, ☎ 276711. 86 rooms. Swimming pool and tennis courts. A peaceful establishment.
▲▲ **Lachea,** via Dusmet 4, ☎ 276784. 24 rooms. Swimming pool.

Food

LL La Cambusa del Capitano, via Marina 63, ☎ 276 298. *Closed Wed.*

LL Holidays Club, via dei Malavoglia 10, ☎ 277 575. *Closed Mon.*

LL II Pirata, via Provinciale 180, in the harbour, ☎ 274 529. *Closed Fri.*

LL Trattoria da Federico, piazza Verga 115, ☎ 276 364. *Closed Mon.*

Useful address

Tourist information, via Provinciale 214.

Acireale (10.5 mi/17 km north of Catania)

Acireale is a health resort and thermal spa with a population of 48,000. When the town was almost entirely destroyed in the 1169 earthquake, the inhabitants left to settle in neighbouring villages, taking the name 'Aci' with them.

You enter town on via delle Terme. On the right are the baths, Terme di Santa Vénera, which are open all year and where the temperature of the waters is 71.6° F/22° C. Corso Vittorio Emanuele leads to piazza Vigo where you will see the sumptuous Baroque façade of the Church of **San Sebastiano***, preceded by a balustrade adorned with 10 statues by Marabitti. The interior was decorated with frescoes by Pietro Vasta in the 18th century.

Continue on to piazza del Duomo, the town centre. Around the square stand the **Palazzo Communale** (1659), with its elaborate doorway and wrought-iron balcony, the church of **Santi Pietro e Paolo** flanked by 18th-century towers, and the **Duomo.** This was built between 1597 and 1618, but the façade was altered and given a Gothic look in the 19th century. The church, however, has kept its beautiful Baroque marble portal and some frescoes inside dating from the 18th century. In the chapel of Santa Vénera, on the right of the transept, there is a silver statue (1651) of the patron saint of the city.

Take via Cavour opposite the Church of Santi Pietro e Paolo and then turn right into via Marchese di San Giuliano where, at n° 15, you will find the **Pinacoteca dell'Accademia Zelantea** *(open Mon-Fri 10am-1pm, 3-6pm, or 4-7pm in summer; closed Sat afternoon and Sun).* Among other works is a bust of Julius Caesar, known as the *Bust of Acireale**, and a painting attributed to Rubens.

Back on piazza del Duomo, take corso Umberto to Villa Belvedere, where you have views of the sea and Etna. About 1.5 mi/2.5 km from here you will find **Santa Maria la Scala,** a picturesque little fishing village and harbour where you can take a boat trip to see the Grotta delle Palombe. **Telephone area code: 095.**

Accommodation

▲▲▲ **Santa Tecla Palace,** via Balestrate, Santa Tecla, ☎ 604 933. Private beach, swimming pool, tennis courts, and garden. It has a renowned restaurant, **Barbarossa,** *open June 15-Sept 15.*

▲▲ **Aloha d'Oro,** viale de Gaspri 10, ☎ 604 344. 90 rooms. Park, swimming pool, and private beach. *Closed throughout Nov.* Good restaurant.

▲▲ **Maugeri,** piazza Garibaldi 27, ☎ 608 666. 40 rooms. Private beach in a lovely park.

▲▲ **Orizzonte Acireale,** via Colombo, ☎ 886 006. 128 rooms. Swimming pool and thermal facilities; on the beach.

▲▲ **Park Hotel,** N114, Capomulini, ☎ 877 511. 101 rooms. Beach, swimming pool, and garden. *Closed Nov-Mar.*

Campgrounds

Al Yag, via Altarellazzo, Pozillo, ☎ 871 666.

La Timpa, via Santa Maria la Scala 33, Santa Maria la Scala, ☎ 894 420.

Festivals and entertainment

The **Carnival** takes place in February with a masked ball and procession of floats. The **Opera dei Pupi,** piazza San Francesco 1, in the church, is renowned for its shows (held in Aug and Sept). Enquire at the tourist office for performance times. At Christmas a manger scene is displayed in a lava cave with life-size characters.

Food

Apart from the restaurant at the Aloha Hotel and the Barbarossa in the Santa Tecla Palace, which we recommend, there are also:

LL Bettola, La Grotta di Don Carmelo, in Santa Maria la Scala, Scalo Grande 46, ☎ 894 414. *Closed Tues.*

LL Panoramico, in Santa Maria Amalati, 2.4 mi/4 km north, via Jonio 12, ☎ 885 291. *Closed Fri.* Beautiful view, good regional dishes.

Useful address

Tourist information, corso Umberto 179, ☎ 604 521. *Open daily 8:30am-2pm, also in summer 5-7pm.*

Acireale to Naxos

Giarre (18.6 mi/30 km north of Catania)

This is a business centre, its main street lined with souvenir shops. Giarre-Riposto station is the departure point for the train trip around Etna. (See p. 188).

Máscali (21 mi/34 km north of Catania)

This small town was originally situated a little farther to the west but was destroyed in 1928 by a lava flow and rebuilt on the present site.

Fiumefreddo di Sicilia (24 mi/39 km north of Catania)

Here the N120 branches left toward Randazzo, for those who wish to drive around the mountain (see p. 191).

After 28.5 mi/46 km the mountainous N185 branches left from the N114 to the Alcántara gorges (p. 203). It continues to Francavilla di Sicilia, Novara di Sicilia and ends at the N113 on the northern coast near Castroreale Terme (p. 226). Meanwhile the N114 continues to the bay of Taormina near Capo Schisò, where the first Greeks landed to found the colony of Naxos.

▬ *GIARDINI NAXOS**

This is a rapidly expanding seaside resort (population 8500) stretching along a magnificent beach where the **view*** of Taormina is exceptional.

Ancient Naxos, the first Greek colony in Sicily, was founded by Chalcidians from Euboea and Ionia in 734 BC and soon became an important religious, commercial and political centre. Because it sided with Athens against Syracuse during the Great Expedition, it was destroyed in 403 BC by the tyrant Dionysius who gave the territory to the Sikels and moved the Naxian refugees to another town, Tauromenium, on the mountain. When the Greek geographer, Pausanias, took an interest in the region, the city had totally disappeared. But excavations have brought to light a temple to Aphrodite, Hellenistic tombs, city walls and street plans implying that settlers returned intermittently to Naxos.

Archaeological Park

Open Tues-Sun 9am-sunset.

As you enter the site you see the **city walls** (6th century BC) made of large, irregular blocks of lava that stretch for about 918 ft/280 m. You pass the West Gate, and after a right-angle bend, the wall continues parallel to the sea up to the Sea Gate. The charm of the place is due more to its marvelous setting amid luxuriant lemon groves than to the modest ruins.

Museo Archeologico
Open Tues-Sun 9am-2pm, holidays 9am-1pm.
Excavations have revealed vestiges of the Neolithic era and the Bronze Age and Iron Age. These are displayed in a small museum on the tip of Capo Schisò, where you have a splendid **view★** of the coast, Etna and Taormina.

Telephone area code: 0942.

Accommodation

▲▲▲ **Arathena Rocks,** via Calcide Eubea 55, ☎ 51 349. 37 rooms. Attractive building set in a small bay with a garden, swimming pool and tennis courts.

▲▲ **Assinos,** in Alcantara, via Nazionale 33, ☎ 53 837. 56 rooms. Garden, swimming pool, tennis courts and private beach.

▲▲ **Kalos,** via Calcide Eubea 29, ☎ 52 116. 27 rooms. *Closed Nov-March.* Peaceful hotel with garden.

▲▲ **Ramada Inn,** via Jannuzzo 41, ☎ 52 654. 305 rooms. Garden, swimming pool and tennis courts.

▲ **Sirenetta,** via Naxos 177, ☎ 53 637. 14 rooms. *Closed Dec and Jan.* Private beach.

The above is only a small selection of hotels; the resort has more than 30. Most of them require you to take half board, especially in the holiday season.

Food

LL **A Massaria,** via Arancio 6, ☎ 50 243. *Closed on Mon in the off-season.*

LL **La Cambusa,** in the harbour near the jetty, ☎ 51 437. *Closed on Tues in the off-season.* Good regional specialities.

LL **Rendez-vous,** via Lungomare, ☎ 51 405. Enormous dining room overlooking the beach.

LL **Sileno,** via Stracina, ☎ 52 708. *Closed Tues.* Garden.

There are more than 50 restaurants and *trattorie* in Giardini.

Useful addresses

Post office, via Erice 1 and via Naxos 151.

Taxis, ☎ 54 245.

Tourist information, via Tysandros 76, in the middle of the lungomare, ☎ 51 010. *Open Mon-Sat 9am-1pm, 4-7pm.*

TAORMINA★★

Map coordinates refer to the map pp. 200-201.
Set on a 700 ft-/213 m-high terrace in the Peloritani Mountains, overlooking the sea, with Mt Etna behind, this lovely medieval town is Sicily's centre of international tourism. It was popularized at the turn of the 20th century, when the leisure classes of Europe started to winter there. Since the 1920s, when D.H. Lawrence lived in a villa in Taormina, the town has attracted both the great and would-be great and has developed into a bustling year-round resort.

For centuries Tauromenium, as it was then called, was a quiet outpost of the Greek colony of Naxos. After Dionysius of Syracuse destroyed Naxos, he founded the town of Taormina and the refugees of Naxos were taken there. The town prospered and the Romans gave it the privilege of a *'civitas foedecata'* until it was transformed into a strategic military colony by Octavian Augustus. Much later, in 902, the Saracens destroyed the

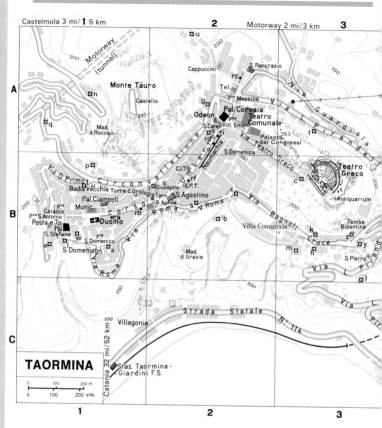

TAORMINA

city and then rebuilt it. Most of the monuments that survive today bear the stamp of the Arab-Byzantine-Norman style you see throughout Italy.

The itinerary below takes in the whole town with all the main monuments, passing through the places with the best views of the coast and Etna. You should park your car at the top of via Luigi Pirandello, or better still, leave it in the parking lot in Mazzarò, A4, and go up to Taormina by cable-car. You need at least a day to see the main sights and several days to savour all of Taormina's charm.

Palazzo Corvaia* A2

Our starting point is Porta Messina, where the main street, corso Umberto I, begins and runs the whole length of town. Standing to the right is Palazzo Corvaia, seat of the Sicilian parliament in 1410. It's a beautiful crenelated edifice dating from the beginning of the 15th century. The austere façade has four pairs of elegant twin windows above which runs a decorative cornice of limestone and lava. On the side there is a triple window and a Catalan-Gothic portal. In the courtyard you will see a pretty outside staircase with a bas-relief depicting the birth of Eve and the Fall from Eden. Inside, on the first floor, temporary exhibitions are held in the great hall.

The Church of **Santa Catarina** nearby is interesting for its three altars set between cabled columns. The nave has a wooden roof. On the right side you can see parts of the ancient Roman odeon upon which the church was built. In 1893 further ruins of the odeon were found outside, behind the church. The front of the *scena* was once part of an earlier Greek temple of the Doric order.

4 Messina 31 mi/50 km

MAZZARÓ

Isola Bella
33

4

Piazza Vittorio Emanuele spreads out in front of the church and opens into via del Teatro Greco, which leads to the Greek theatre.

Greek theatre*** B3

A *Open daily 9am to a quarter of an hour before sunset.*

The theatre is without doubt one of the finest existing monuments of Antiquity as much for its grandiose setting as for the remains of the building. It stands on a splendid site facing the sea on a hill 702 ft/214 m high.

First built in the Hellenistic period under Hieron (3rd century BC), it was then enlarged by the Romans in the 2nd
B century AD. It consists of a vast semicircle with a diameter of 357 ft/109 m divided into nine sections embedded into a natural hollow in the hillside. The *scena* has been remarkably well preserved with a two-tiered outer wall where five granite columns, four Corinthian capitals and part of the marble entablature have been reconstructed. Note also the statue niches and the side doorways for the actors. Because the wall has crumbled in the mid-
C dle you now have a beautiful panoramic view, especially from the top of the *cavea,* of the town, Etna, the Castiglione mountains, Monte Venere, Castel Mola and Capo Schisò at the far end of the bay. Above the rows of seats there is a small **museum** *(open 9am-1pm)* housing several interesting works, including a fine **oval sarcophagus** made of Paros marble. There are also statues of two male torsos, attributed to the school of Praxiteles, and the carved head of a woman, found in the theatre orchestra.

Corso Umberto I* B1-2

Return to piazza Vittorio Emanuele and turn left at corso Umberto I, a lively street lined with shops and interesting house fronts. The house at nᵒ 42 has an arch and a rose window taken from the former church, Santa Maria del Piliere (16th century), built by the governor of the Order of Malta. When you reach nᵒ 102 go down the alley on your left for a short way, walk under an arch and you come to the **Naumachia,** a vast Roman edifice, possibly used as a cistern for the baths during the Empire. All that remains is the wall — 400 ft/122 m long — in which large statue niches alternate with smaller rectangular ones. Return to the corso, which soon opens onto piazza IX Aprile, a terrace overlooking the sea, from which you have a fine view. To the right is the Church of San Giuseppe (late 16th century), and to the left is the former Church of Sant'Agostino (1448), restored in about 1700 with a lovely Gothic door-way, a small rose window and a graceful campanile.

The street runs under the arch of the clock tower, Torre dell'Orologio (not open to the public), and enters the medieval part of the city, which contains several vestiges from that time. Especially interesting are the façades of nᵒs 147, 154, 172,174, 176 and 190.

At nᵒ 185 there's a former chapel with the date 1533 inscribed on the lintel. Standing back from the street above a flight of steps at nᵒ 209 is Palazzo Ciampoli, built in 1412, as is indicated on the doorway. It is a

Catalan-Gothic building with five windows on the first floor of the façade and on the right side an arched portal, decorated with two medallions depicting the heads of Roman emperors.

Duomo (Cathedral)* B1

A little farther along past Palazzo del Municipio (1704) and its Baroque windows, you come to piazza del Duomo, with a charming statue that dates from 1635.

The Duomo was built in the 13th century, altered in the 15th and 16th centuries and then restored in 1636. It has a massive, austere façade, relieved by two small pointed windows that flank the doorway, which is adorned with a series of medallions. There are portals on the sides of the church: the one on the left is marble and dates from the 15th century, and the one on the right is 16th-century Gothic. The interior has a wooden roof and consists of three aisles separated by pointed arches which curve out from monolithic columns.

There are four lovely Renaissance arches at the top of the main apse. In the first chapel on the right you can see a painting of the Visitation by Antonio Giuffrè (mid-15th century), and in the second, a remarkable polyptych by Antonello de Saliba (1504) of the Madonna and Child, four saints and a pietà. In the right-hand apse there is a 15th-century alabaster statue of the Virgin, and in the left-hand apse is the chapel of the Holy Sacrament with an 18th-century marble altar. The second altar in the aisle on the left has an elegant statue of St Agatha by Montinini (16th century).

Mazullo foundation* B1

Corso Umberto I ends at Porta Catania, crowned by a small construction bearing the city's coat of arms and the date, 1400. Just before the gateway vico Spuches leads to the left for a few yards to Palazzo del Duca di Santa Stefano, an elegant example of 14th- to 15th-century Sicilian architecture. It looks like a tower with an outside staircase and two floors of twin windows, above which runs a cornice of limestone and lava inlays. The palace holds temporary exhibitions *(open 9am-1pm, 3:30-7:30pm)*.

Public gardens* B2

Beyond Porta Catania you come to piazza Sant'Antonio, where you will find the post office and the Church of Sant'Antonio with its Gothic doorway of white limestone. There is a good view of the bay from the terrace on the right side of the church. From here a road descends to Taormina's train station.

Return to piazza del Duomo and walk down to via Roma past the former monastery of San Domenico, now a luxury hotel (open to guests only). The adjoining church was destroyed during bombardments by the Americans and British in 1943, and all that remains is the Baroque campanile. Follow via Roma (fine views) around the monastery to the public gardens. From the terrace you have a wonderful **view*** of Etna and the coast, all the way from Giardini to Acireale.

At the beginning of the century the gardens belonged to an eccentric Englishwoman who designed the strange 'chicken coop' and 'Chinese pagoda' follies you can see here — images straight out of Walt Disney.

A network of picturesque alleyways leads back to piazza Vittorio Emanuele.

Environs of Taormina

Castello, Castel Mola and Monte Venere

This is a 10 mi/16 km drive round trip, and there is an 8am-8pm bus service from Taormina.

Setting out from Porta Messina, follow the Circonvallazione, which runs along the upper side of town past Badia Vecchia. A large battlemented tower, this is the ruin of an abbey built toward the end of the 14th century, with attractive pointed windows and carved lava.

Turn left off via Dioniso, which leads down to piazza Sant'Antonio, and continue along the winding Circonvallazione. After about 1.2 mi/2 km, leave your car and follow the path to the right up to the sanctuary of Madonna della Rocca *(only open on holidays)*. For a superb view take the steps on the left up to the Castello, a medieval edifice at the top of Monte Táuro (1305 ft/398 m).

Return to the fork in the road and head right (3.1 mi/5 km) for Castel Mola, a picturesque village at a height of 1804 ft/550 m, dominated by the ruins of a castle from which you have a magnificent panoramic **view***. You can climb on up to Monte Venere (2900 ft/884 m) in about two hours or admire the view from the terrace of the San Giorgio cafe, which has an extraordinary collection of autographs. There are also two well-positioned restaurants, with terraces, where you can lunch in very pleasant surroundings.

Alcántara Gorge (18.6 mi/30 km round trip)

Drive down to Giardini and just as you leave the village turn right onto the N185 for Castroreale. Leave your car at Contrada Larderia (10.5 mi/17 km) where there is a parking lot and a restaurant. Come equipped with swimsuit and plastic shoes (the shoes can also be hired at the entrance). You don't have to worry about the climb down because there's an elevator (admission charge).

Map coordinates refer to the map pp. 200-201.

Telephone area code: 0942.

Access

Cable car: It is a two-minute ride from Lido Mazzaró, A4 ad, to via Luigi Pirandello on the edge of town, A3. Frequent departures.

Car: Taormina is 33 mi/53 km north of Catania, 31.6 mi/51 km south of Messina, 69 mi/112 km north of Syracuse and 83 mi/134 km north-east of Enna.

Train: Taormina is on the Messina-Catania line. A bus service works in conjunction with the trains linking the station at Giardini with Taormina.

Accommodation

Taormina has at least 100 hotels and boarding houses. The following is a selection.

▲▲▲▲ **Bristol Park,** via Bagnoli Croce 92, B3 k, ☎ 23006. 54 rooms. Very good establishment in a magnificent location. Swimming pool and private beach.

▲▲▲▲ **Excelsior Palace,** via Toselli 8, B1 e, ☎ 23975. 89 rooms. *Closed Feb 15-March 1.* Park and swimming pool. Neo-Gothic style hotel in a splendid location.

▲▲▲▲ **Jolly Diodoro,** via Bagnoli Croce 75, B3 m, ☎ 23312. 103 rooms. Remarkable setting overlooking the sea. Lovely garden and swimming pool. Recommended.

▲▲▲▲ **San Domenico Palace,** piazza San Domenico 5, B1 a, ☎ 23701. 101 rooms. One of the most famous luxury hotels in the world. A 15th-century Dominican monastery with cloisters and garden in an exceptional position. Antique furniture in all the rooms. Swimming pool. Priced accordingly. **Les Bougainvillées** is the renowned restaurant.

▲▲▲ **Capo Taormina,** via Nazionale, Capo Taormina, C4 d, ☎ 24000. 208 rooms. *Closed Nov 1-April 15.* Large round construction overlooking the sea opposite the Faraglioni (rock islands). Swimming pool, private beach and garden. Good restaurant with a panoramic view.

▲▲▲ **Méditerranée,** via Circonvallazione 61, B1 p, ☎ 23901. 50 rooms. *Closed Nov-Mar.* Lovely garden, swimming pool.

Taormina's Greek theatre, one of the most beautiful in the world. ▶

▲▲▲ **Monte Tauro,** via Madonna delle Gracie 3, B2 b, ☎ 24 402. 67 rooms. Extraordinary architecture, with the hotel seemingly suspended in mid-air. Splendid view. Panoramic elevator. Swimming pool.

▲▲▲ **Vello d'Oro,** via Fazello 2, B2 i, ☎ 23 788. 59 rooms. *Closed Nov-Feb.* Fine view and private beach.

▲▲▲ **Villa Fiorita,** via Pirandello 39, A3 f, ☎ 24 122. 24 rooms. View, garden and swimming pool. Recommended.

▲▲▲ **Villa Paradiso,** via Roma 2, B2 x, ☎ 23 922. 33 rooms. View and private beach.

▲▲▲ **Villa Sirina,** contrada Sirina, ☎ 51 776. Lovely garden, pool, modern rooms and good restaurant.

▲▲ **La Campanella,** via Circonvallazione 3, A2 g, ☎ 23 381. 12 rooms. Garden.

▲▲ **Continental,** via Dionisio 1, B1 t, ☎ 23 805. 43 rooms. Garden and private beach.

▲▲ **Corona,** via Roma 7, B2, ☎ 23 022. 33 rooms. *Closed Nov-Feb 15.*

▲▲ **Sole Castello,** rotabile Castelmola 83, A1 n, ☎ 28 036. 57 rooms. Swimming pool and private beach.

▲▲ **Villa Kristina,** rotabile Castelmola 23, A1 q, ☎ 28 366. 32 rooms. *Closed Nov-Jan.* Swimming pool.

▲▲▲ **Villa Riis,** via Rizzo 13, B1 l, ☎ 24 874. 30 rooms. *Closed Nov-Feb.* Garden, swimming pool and private beach. Very peaceful.

▲▲ **Villa Schuler,** piazza Bastione 16, B2 s, ☎ 23 481. 27 rooms. *Closed Dec-Feb except over Christmas.* Private beach and lovely garden.

Campground
San Leo, on the cape, ☎ 24 658. *Open all year.*

Festivals

The **Carnival** takes place in Feb-Mar; the **Festival of Sicilian Costumes and Carts** is at the end of May; the **Film Festival** is held in July in the Greek theatre, and the **Grape Festival** is in Sept. **Opera dei Pupi** performances are held every Friday at 5:30pm in the San Nicoló cinema-theatre.

Processions
On **Palm Sunday** and **Good Friday** there is a beautiful procession through the town. In June there's the **Corpus Domini** and **Sant'Antonio** processions and another, **San Pancrazio,** July 9. On **Christmas Eve** there are peat fires and a procession.

Food

There are so many restaurants in Taormina it is impossible to list them all. The selection below of the best is simply an indication of the enormous choice.

LLLL Granduca, corso Umberto I 170, B1 rb, ☎ 24 420. Rightly deserves its reputation as the best in town. Excellent food in an exceptional 15th-century residence.

LLL Giova Rosy Senior, corso Umberto I 38, A2 ri, ☎ 24 411. *Closed Mon.* Excellent food served on an immense covered terrace overlooking the old theatre. Good fish and seafood.

LLL Luraleo, via Bagnoli Croce 31, B2, ☎ 24 279. *Closed Jan 10-Feb 15 and on Wed in the off-season.* Rustic setting, a pleasant terrace opening onto the street. Good food for a very reasonable price.

LLL Trattoria Rosticepi, piazza San Pancrazio 10, A2, ☎ 24 149. *Closed Wed.* Authentic Sicilian cooking. Good antipasti and cheese.

LL La Botte, via Giardinazzo. *Trattoria*-pizzeria, serving Sicilian dishes. Pleasant dining room and small garden.

LL La Buca da Nino, corso Umberto I 140, B2 rf, ☎ 24 314. *Closed Mon.* Lovely garden. Both international food and traditional local dishes.

LL La Giara, vicolo Floresta, B2, ☎ 23 360. New decor and new management introduced in 1989.

LL La Griglia, corso Umberto I 54, A2 rd, ☎ 23 980. *Closed Tues.* Good value for money. Attractive dining room on terrace. Recommended.

LL Trattoria Poco Pago, via Patricio 12, ☎ 24 165. *Closed throughout Nov and on Wed in the off-season.* Small inside garden. Good, reasonably priced food.

Cafés and pastries

Arco Rosso, beside Gambero Rosso, via Naumachia, B2, Sicilian wines and draught beer. *Closed Wed.*

Caffè Wunderbar, piazza IX Aprile, B2. In the historic centre of town beside the clock tower. A pleasant, comfortable place with a good view from the terrace.

Granduca, corso Umberto I 170, B1 rb. An elegant setting for tea and an excellent choice of cakes. *Closed Mon.*

Pasticceria Etna E. Tamako, corso Umberto I 112 and 141.

Pasticceria Chemi, corso Umberto I 102. Their specialities include Sicilian cakes and marzipan.

Useful addresses

Bus station, via Luigi Pirandello, B3.

CIT, corso Umberto I 101, B2, ☎ 23 301. *Closed Sat except in summer.*

English books and newspapers, corso Umberto I 37.

Gas coupons, via Largo La Farina 8.

Hospital, contrada Sirina, ☎ 53 068 and 53 722.

Markets, Every Wednesday morning in Taormina and every Saturday, except the first of the month, in via Vittorio Emanuele in Giardini-Naxos.

Post office, piazza Sant'Antonio at the end of corso Umberto I, B1 *(open Mon-Fri 8am-6pm).*

Public telephones, at Avis, via San Pancrazio 6 and at Santa Maretta, piazza Santa Caterina 13 *(open 8am-1pm; 3-8pm; holidays 9am-1pm).*

Stazione Centrale, in Giardini, C1, ☎ 23 751.

Tourist information, AAST, Palazzo Corvaia, A2, ☎ 23 243. *Open Mon-Fri 8am-2pm, 2:30-7pm; Sat 8am-noon.*

▬ TAORMINA TO MESSINA

Mazzarò* (2.4 mi/4 km north of Taormina)
Beyond the branch off to Taormina the road runs into Mazzarò, a seaside resort comprised of a series of beaches and creeks lined with hotels. The advantage of Mazzarò, especially in summer when it is almost impossible to drive around the whole area, is that it has a fast cablecar up to Taormina.

You can make a lot of boat excursions from Mazzarò, to Isola Bella for instance, where an oceanographic museum is being planned, or to Capo Sant'Andrea, where there is a wonderful cave.

Telephone area code: 0942.

Accommodation

▲▲▲▲ **Mazzarò Sea Palace,** via Nazionale 147, A4 aa, ☎ 24 004. 81 rooms. *Closed Nov-March.* Attractive architecture blending in with the surroundings. The rooms have flower-covered balconies looking out to sea. Swimming pool.

▲▲▲ **Villa Sant'Andrea,** A4 ab, ☎ 23 125. 48 rooms. Recommended. Beautiful garden and private beach. Excellent restaurant, the **Oliviero.**

▲▲ **Ipanema Hotel,** via Nazionale 242, A4, ☎ 24 720. 50 rooms. 164 ft/50 m from the cablecar. Swimming pool and solarium on the terrace. A good hotel for its category Very reasonable prices and good restaurant.

▲▲ **Lido Méditerranée,** via Nazionale, Lido Spisone, ☎ 24 422. 72 rooms. Garden. *Closed Nov-March.* Restaurant Caravella Club, just beside the hotel. Attractive terrace and private beach. Good food in a refined setting.

Food

LL **Il Barcaiolo,** on Lido Mazzarò beach. Tables set out attractively beneath a climbing vine overlooking moored fishing boats. Simple, very reasonable food.

LL **Il Delfino da Angelo,** on the N114, B4 rg. Terrace overlooking the sea. Good food. Sometimes rather casual service.

LL **Il Pescatore,** on the N114, B4 re, ☎ 23 460. *Closed Mon.* A real institution. The restaurant clings to a rock that juts out over the water. Magnificent view. Excellent food, especially the fish dishes. Recommended.

Capo Sant'Alessio, 37 mi/60 km north of Catania, is a sheer rock hanging above the vast bay. There are two high points on the promontory, one crowned by a Saracen castle that was rebuilt in the 19th century and the other crowned by a Spanish fortress.

Forza d'Agrò (8.6 mi/14 km)

A road leads up left for 2.4 mi/4 km to Forza d'Agrò, a small medieval centre 1407 ft/429 m above sea level dominated by the ruins of a 16th-century castle. On the left as you enter the village you will see the Church of San Francesco, which contains a statue of St Catherine of Alexandria (1558). Via del Municipio leads right to the Church of the Triade. The façade, rebuilt in 1576, is flanked by a fine campanile with an eight-sided pyramidal roof. Inside there is a 15th-century painting of *Three Angels Visiting Abraham* and a carved gilt gonfalon (16th century) shaped like a Gothic shrine. The Chiesa Matrice has a Baroque façade and houses a 14th-century painted cross and a 1559 statue of Santa Catarina.

An excursion to Casalvecchio Sículo to see the **Santi Pietro e Paolo*** Church is not to be missed if you are interested in Roman architecture. Return to the N114 and, after crossing Sant'Alessio Sículo, take the well-signposted country road to the left for 4.3 mi/7 km. After the bridge drive down to the Forzo d'Agrò river and you will see the church on the opposite bank. The crossing is difficult unless the river bed is dry. The church is a beautiful Norman construction, resembling a slender fortress. The external polychrome decoration bears the stamp of Muslim art, and the domes show a Byzantine influence. Two partly damaged towers flank the narthex. Ask the guardian if you would like to see the inside. The interior is surprisingly sober with its three aisles separated by columns and arches. The three apses rise from a rectangular base.

The N114 continues through rather uninteresting surroundings, but when you reach Itála Marina a road leads left for 1.5 mi/2.5 km to **Itála,** where you can see San Pietro, another Basilian church, built by Count Roger in 1093 to celebrate his victory over the Saracens. It's a basilica with three aisles and three apses which has been disfigured by clumsy restoration.

The outside decoration of multicoloured interlocking arches is not unlike that of Santi Pietro e Paolo.

MESSINA*: GATEWAY TO SICILY

Map coordinates refer to the map p. 211.

The town stretches along the shore in a crescent shape at the foot of the Peloritani mountains. It has always taken advantage of its exceptional position as guardian of the Straits between Sicily and the Calabrian coast. Now the third most important industrial city (after Palermo and Catania), it has a busy port and a population of 263,000.

Like the rest of this cataclysmic zone along the road from Catania, Messina has had its share of disasters: plagues, cholera epidemics, earthquakes and tidal waves. It was also badly bombed during the war.

The Graeco-Siculian town was founded by Chalcidian trader-pirates from Cumae in the 8th century BC and called Zancle (from the Sikel word *zanklon,* meaning 'sickle') after the shape of its peninsula. It was renamed Messana by the tyrant Anaxilas, who was born in Messenia in Greece and who captured the Sicilian port in 493 BC. Himlico, a Carthaginian, sacked the town in 397 BC; Syracuse later rebuilt it. Then it was occupied by the Marmertines (sons of Mars) — a group of mercenaries who controlled much of Sicily until they were conquered by Hieron II — from which point Messina became a Roman ally. In AD 843 it was captured by the Saracens and then in 1061 fell into Norman hands.

In 1190 and 1191, the English king Richard the Lionhearted attacked the town and then rebuilt the Castle of Matefriffon. Charles of Anjou tried to take the town in 1272 but was successfully resisted. By the end of the 15th century, Messina was a prosperous port, famous for its monastery.

In the 17th century, the town fell to the Spanish, who decimated the local population. This marked the beginning of a long series of diasters: in 1743, the plague wiped out 40,000 people; in 1783, a terrible earthquake flattened the entire city; in 1848, the Bourbons quelled a Sicilian independence rebellion with massive bombardments from the sea. A cholera epidemic broke out in 1854, and it was followed by another serious earthquake in 1894; then in December 1908, the strongest earthquake experienced in the region struck in the early morning hours and left 84,000 people dead. The city took protective measures against future quakes by constructing wide avenues and low buildings, aided by international organizations. Allied bombs killed 4500 more people during World War II. One result of this list of devastations is that Messina is the most modern of all Sicilian cities. Its location on an unindustrialized coast at the foot of the Peloritano Mountains adds to its appeal.

Two or three hours are enough to see the town; you will need more time if you visit the Museo Regionale.

Setting out from piazza Cairoli, D2, the town centre, take via Garibaldi, a long street that runs parallel to the port. You pass the Baroque Church of Santa Caterina Valverde and then on the right via Santa Maria di Alemanna, which leads to the ruins of a Gothic church destroyed during an earthquake.

Further along via Garibaldi on the left stands the Church of **Annunziata dei Catalani***, C2, a particularly fine 12th-century Norman construction. In the 13th century it was badly damaged by an earthquake. The façade and three portals date from this period while the transept, the charming cupola and the apse, all with beautiful blind arcading, are original 12th century.

Opposite the central porch there is a statue by a Tuscan sculptor dating from 1572. It portrays Don Juan of Austria, victor of the Battle of Lepanto, who returned to Messina with his fleet. Via Lepanto leads behind the statue to piazza del Duomo adorned with its beautiful **Orion Fountain*** (1574) by Montorsoli.

Duomo (Cathedral)* C2

Begun by Roger II toward the end of the 11th century, the church is one of the oldest in Sicily, but it was reconstructed after it was almost completely destroyed by the earthquake of 1908. It had already been damaged by fire in the 13th century and by earthquakes in the 17th and 18th centuries. Rebuilding began in 1919 but the church was badly damaged again in 1943. Restoration has since been carried out as much in keeping with the original plan as possible — it is still a basilica with three aisles, three apses and a tall transept. Of the façade, the lower part is the oldest, and the three wonderful portals date from the 15th and 16th centuries. The side doors are also noteworthy; one dates from the Renaissance and the other is a pointed 15th-century entrance with decorative mosaic strips.

The campanile was erected after the 1908 disaster and contains the largest astronomical clock (open daily 9am-1pm) in the world, built in 1933 by Ungerer, a company in Strasbourg. The tower is 213 ft/65 m tall; on it are a number of dials showing hours, days, months, planets and religious feasts. There are also mechanical figures, the most spectacular of which illustrate a local legend where the Virgin Mary gives an angel a letter for the people of the town. The clock strikes and activates the figures every hour, although the most interesting performance occurs at noon when the figures move for a quarter of an hour to musical accompaniment.

The interior of the Duomo consists of three aisles with monolithic columns and a painted wooden ceiling. The 12 side altars in the aisles and the statues of the Apostles are copies; only that of St John the Baptist (first altar on the right) by Antonello Gagini is original (1525). You should also see the **tomb of Tabiatis*** by the Siennese sculptor Goro di Gregorio (1333). The 14th-century mosaics in the apses have been largely restored. Near the side exit on the left there is a relief of St Jerome (15th century). The Duomo houses a rich treasury, currently being reorganized.

At the end of the cathedral square take corso Cavour to the right. This leads through piazza Antonello and runs alongside the Mazzini gardens where there is a municipal aquarium (open Tues, Thurs, Sat and Sun 9am-1:30pm). Continue along the corso to piazza Unità d'Italia, B2-3, with its **Neptune Fountain*** by Montorsoli (1557). You have a good view from here of the harbour and San Salvatore, the Spanish fort.

Museo Regionale* A3 (off the map)

Open daily 9am-2pm, holidays 9am-1pm. In summer also open Tues, Thurs and Sat 3-6pm or 4-7pm.

Via della Libertà leads from piazza Unità d'Italia along the shore past the buildings used for the Messina Trade Fair (held in August). After about 1.2 mi/2 km you come to the entrance to the museum at n° 461 on the left.

The archaeological department is still being reorganized, but exhibitions of medieval and modern art give you a good idea of the town's artistic heritage. Of note among the works displayed at present are: *Madonna degli Storpi** (1333) by Goro di Gregorio, the Siennese sculptor (mentioned above) who made the tomb of Tabiatis in the Duomo; *Polyptych of St Gregory*** by Antonello da Messina (1473); *Circumcision** by Girolamo Alibrandi (1519) and two paintings by Caravaggio, *Adoration of the Shepherds** and *Raising of Lazarus**, which he painted during his stay in Messina in 1608-9. There are also interesting collections of minor works, such as the nine gilt paintings dating from the beginning of the 19th century that illustrate the legend of the Sacra Lettera.

A tour above the town and the cemetery

We suggest that you finish your visit to Messina with a drive along the boulevards that twist up the hillside affording lovely views of the town and

the Straits. Set out from piazza Cairoli on via Cannizaro and when you get to the end turn right into viale Principe Umberto, BC1-2, which leads to piazza XX Settembre and the botanical gardens, C1. Continue past the Santuario di Montalto (a short way off to the right) and the Church of Christo Re (on the left). You then take viale Regina Margherita, which ends at via Palermo. By turning right at this street you soon reach via Garibaldi and the centre of town.

Don't miss the **cemetery,** F1, on any account. One of the loveliest in the whole of Italy, it resembles a park and covers the hillside with a variety of luxuriant vegetation. You have enchanting views across the Straits to Calabria. There's nothing gloomy about this visit, in fact some of the funerary monuments are quite exquisite.

Environs of Messina

Leave Messina on viale della Libertà and go past the museum. The N113 follows an ancient Roman road and runs beside the shores of Lake Ganzirri. A 1.2 mi/2 km detour leads to Torre di Faro and Capo Peloro, the point nearest to the Italian peninsula, dominated by the enormous pylon that receives Sicily's electricity supply from the mainland. The road leads on to **Lido di Mortelle,** Messina's most popular seaside resort and then to **Spartà** (15 mi/24 km), where you have a panoramic view of the Aeolian Islands. When you reach Divieto (21.7 mi/35 km) leave the Palermo road opposite and take the N113 back toward Messina. This winds across the Monti Peloritani through pine and eucalyptus forests. From **Scala** (31 mi/50 km), a path leads (20 minutes) to the 12th-century ruins of the Benedictine monastery of **Santa Maria delle Valle.**

Map coordinates refer to the map p. 211.

Telephone area code: **090.**

Access

Boat: There are ferries for Villa San Giovanni and Reggio di Calabria: **Ferrovie dello Strat,** ☎ 773 811; **Caronte,** ☎ 44 982; **Tourist Ferry Boat,** ☎ 41 415 (lines also to Malta and Tunisia). There are *aliscafi* (hydrofoils) several times a day to Reggio di Calabria, once a day in summer to the Aeolian Islands and several times a week in summer for Naples: **SNAV,** ☎ 364 044.

Car: Messina is 60 mi/97 km north of Catania, 119 mi/192 km north-east of Enna, 161 mi/260 km east of Palermo, 97 mi/156 km north of Syracuse and 31 mi/51 km north of Taormina.

Train: All Italian trains from the mainland arrive at the station in Messina. They cross the Straits by ferry in about 30 minutes.

Accommodation

▲▲▲ **Jolly Hotel dello Stretto,** via Garibaldi 126, C2 a, ☎ 43 401. 99 rooms. Comfortable hotel with restaurant and bar.

▲▲▲ **Riviera Grand Hotel,** viale della Libertà 516, A3 off the map, ☎ 57 101. 144 rooms. Located to the north of the centre.

▲▲ **Paradis,** via Pompea 441, A3 off the map, ☎ 650 682. 92 rooms. Private parking, restaurant and bar.

▲▲ **Royal Palace,** via Cannizzaro 224, E3 c, ☎ 21 161. 83 rooms. No restaurant.

Campground

Il Peloritano, in Rodia, contrada Tarantonio, ☎ 848 021. *Open May-Oct.*

Festivals

Giganti parade, Aug 13 and 14; **Varette procession** on Good Friday; **Vascelluzzo procession** on Corpus Christi (the Thurs after the festival of the Trinity); and **Vara procession** on Aug 15. There's a big trade fair in August and various exhibitions (especially in winter).

Food

LLL Agostino, via Maddalena 70, DE2 m, ☎ 718 396. *Closed Mon and throughout Aug.* Intimate decor. Very good cooking.

LLL Alberto, via Ghibellina 95, D2 s, ☎ 710 711. *Closed Sun and Aug 5-Sep 5.* One of the best known in Sicily.

LLL Pippo Nunnari, via Bassi 157, E2 r, ☎ 293 1568. *Closed Thurs and July 1-15.* Luxurious setting and regional specialities.

LL Antonio, via Maddalena 156, E2 u, ☎ 293 9853. *Closed Sat.* Regional cuisine.

LL Donna Giovanna, via Risorgimento 16, D2 v, ☎ 718 503. *Closed Sun.* Traditional *trattoria* with regional dishes.

LL Il Galeone da Pietro, viale della Libertà 516, ☎ 57 101. Attractive terrace with a panoramic view.

LL Trattoria da Piero, via Ghibellina 121, D2 n, ☎ 718 365. *Closed Sun and throughout Aug.* Good food.

Useful addresses

Bus companies: AST, via Alemanna, D2, ☎ 293 7548 and **SAIS,** piazza della Repubblica, D1, ☎ 771 914.

Hydrofoils *(aliscafi):* **SNAV,** via Cortina del Porto, ☎ 43 095 and **Tirrenia Navigazione,** via Garibaldi 146, ☎ 43 095.

Post office, piazza Antonello, C2.

Stazione Centrale, D3, ☎ 775 234.

Tourist information, APT, piazza della Repubblica, D3, ☎ 777 0731. *Open Mon-Sat 9am-7pm.* **AAPT,** 45 piazza Cairoli, D2, ☎ 293 3541.

MESSINA TO PALERMO: TYRRHENIAN SICILY

The itinerary from Messina to Palermo is 161.5 mi/260 km long on the N113, a direct highway that is only partially open. You can also take the coast road, the N113 dir., from Messina, which takes you right to the tip of the island and adds another 9.3 mi/15 km to your trip. This little road is lined with daisies, geraniums and oleanders. It occasionally leaves the shore to climb promontories with views of the whole coast, the most beautiful in Sicily.

Leave Messina on via Palermo and take the N113.

MILAZZO (28.5 mi/46 km west of Messina)

Ancient Mylai, now Milazzo (31,000 inhabitants), is located at the base of a narrow strip of land that juts 3.7 mi/6 km out into the sea. The old town is on a hill and the newer quarters line the shore. Milazzo has one of the largest oil refineries in Italy, and its busy port is the nearest departure point for the Aeolian Islands.

You enter town on via XX Luglio, which runs alongside the port and then splits. If you go right, you follow via Marina Garibaldi along the shore — a pleasant tree-lined drive. It leads on for quite a long way to a little fishing harbour with boats moored on the beach. If you take the left branch you go up via Umberto I to the top of the town into the old quarter, still partly surrounded by walls. To the left, opposite a small church, via Duomo leads to the 16th-century Duomo Vecchio. At the top of the hill there is a 13th-century castle that retains a fine Gothic doorway and 15th-century towers.

We recommend you go to **Capo Milazzo lighthouse** where you have a magnificent **view*** of the Aeolian Islands, the coast and Etna. A panoramic road takes you right around the cape.

Telephone area code: 090.

Accommodation

▲▲▲ **Eolian Inn Park Hotel**, via Cappuccini, ☎ 928 1633. 250 rooms. *Closed Oct 16-Mar 15*. Modern hotel facing the sea. Spacious, prettily decorated rooms with balconies, but far from the centre. Garden, swimming pool and tennis courts. Recommended.

▲▲▲ **Residenzial**, piazza Nastasi, a few minutes from the port, ☎ 928 3548. *Closed Nov-Mar*. Convenient location.

▲▲ **Flora**, via Tenente la Rosa 1, on the corner of via Umberto I, in the centre, ☎ 928 1882. 23 rooms. Simple and reasonable.

One of the lovely beaches near Milazzo, on Sicily's north coast.

▲▲ **Silvanetta Palace Hotel,** via Acquaviole 1, 1.2 mi/2 km from Milazzo on the Messina road, ☎ 928 1633. 130 rooms. Modern with garden and swimming pool.

▲ **Mignon Riviera,** via Tono 68, outside the centre in Litoraneo d Ponente, ☎ 928 3150. 10 rooms. *Closed Oct 15-Mar 15* Inexpensive, simple hotel.

Campgrounds

Riva Smeralda, in Capo Milazzo, ☎ 928 2980.

Sayonara, in Gronda on the Ponente beach, ☎ 928 3647.

Tourist village La Tonnara, contrada Tono, ☎ 928 8144.

Villagio Cirucco, in Capo Milazzo, ☎ 928 4845.

Festivals

Way of the Cross, costumed performance, on the Sat of Holy Week feast day of **St Francis of Paul** on the second Sun after Easter; feast da of **St Anthony of Padua** on the evening of June 12 and feast day c **San Stefano,** the patron saint of the town, on the first Sun in September

Food

LL Al Gambero, via Rizzo 4, in the port, ☎ 928 6041. *Closed Mon* Fish dishes and a reasonably priced set menu.

LL Diana, piazza della Repubblica, ☎ 928 1322. *Closed Tues.* Good food.

LL La Bussola, via Cortina del Porto, in the port, ☎ 928 2955 *Closed Tues.* Tables set out on a terrace.

LL Il Covo del Pirata, via Marina Garibaldi, ☎ 928 4437. *Closed Wed.* Excellent food; mainly fish. The best address in town.

Useful addresses

Hydrofoils (aliscafi) **and ferries** for the islands: **COVEMAR,** ☎ 928 1213 **LEM Travel,** ☎ 928 2073; **NGI,** ☎ 928 3415; **Siremar,** ☎ 928 3242 **SNAV,** ☎ 928 4509.

Travel agent, Placido Musicò, via Cavour 1, ☎ 928 2073. *Oper 8am-1pm, 3-7:30pm.*

Tourist information, Pro Loco, piazza Caio Duilio. *Open Mon-Sa 9am-12:30pm, 4-8pm.*

▅▅ AEOLIAN ISLANDS

The Lípari or Aeolian Islands form an archipelago of seven volcanic islands, two of them active (Vulcano and Strómboli). The largest of the seven are Vulcano, Lípari and Salina, with Filicudi and Alicudi west c Lípari, and Panarea and Strómboli to the north-east. There are also seven uninhabited islets in this unusual little archipelago. All the islands belong to the Messina province and are between 19 to 50 mi/30 to 80 km from the coast. Their 35,000 inhabitants are spread over a surface area c 45 sq mi/117 sq km.

The climate is similar to that of Sicily although much windier. Legend has it that the god of winds, Aeolus, still rules the region, controlling the winds with magic, allowing them to escape from animal hide bags in his cave whenever the fancy takes him. Naturally, with high winds, the sea around the islands is choppy — probably the most violent water of the entire Mediterranean. Wind erosion and volcanic eruption have formed rugged, foreboding coastlines of inimitable beauty. Inland, dry zones alternate with soft, green hills covered with sweet-smelling herb bushes that give way to slopes of white pumice or black volcanic rock. The vineyards on most of the islands produce excellent Malvasia wine, and capers and olives are grown in abundance. But because of the lack o water, most fruits have to be imported. The main resource is of course fish, which abound in the warm, clear water.

Lípari was first inhabited in 3000 BC by a people from the Near East, after which the islanders appear to have discovered obsidian, which they mined and sold on a large scale. Examples of that volcanic glass — used for making tools — have been discovered as far from Lípari as France and Spain. But for reasons unknown, the flourishing obsidian trade suddenly disappeared around 2350 BC. The period that follows is referred to as the Aeolian Medieval Period, and it is during this time that the islands gained importance as ports on the trade route connecting the Tyrrhenian and Aegean seas. New settlements were formed on Salina, Filicundi, Panarea, Ginostra and Strómboli, and all flourished as commercial centres.

Bronze Age peoples apparently attacked the settlements sometime in the 13th century BC, and they were resettled by an Appenian tribe called the Ausonians, who produced bull's head vessels typical of that time. According to Diodorus Siculus, the ancient Sicilian historian, this was the period in which Líparo, son of King Auson of southern Italy, founded a colony on one of the islands, which he named after himself. By Siculas's account, Líparo also had a friend with him — Aeolus — who married one of the island girls and stayed there as king, entertaining Odysseus, Homer's famous character, when he landed on the island after sailing through the Strait of Messina.

Somewhat more historically certain is the notion that Greek colonists from Rhodes and Cnidos landed on Lípari on their way home from a failed attempt at colonizing the west coast of Sicily, in 580 BC. Attracted by the rich volcanic soil of the island, and welcomed by the 500 Líparasi, they decided to stay.

The new colonists built a fleet to combat marauding Phoenician and Etruscan pirates. According to another legend, the Líparisi received an oracle from Apollo to fight the Etruscan pirates with as few ships as possible. Thus when the Etruscan captain saw only five ships defending the island, he sent only five of his own to attack; the natives, who knew their dangerous waters much better, vanquished the ships. The Etruscan captain sent five more ships and, to his dismay, the islanders met them with five more of their own, and so on until finally the Etruscans retreated. Celebrating their victory, the Líparisi built a treasury at Delphi and erected a statue of Apollo for every ship they had beaten.

The Líparisi, who had allied themselves with Syracuse, also managed to repulse attacks from the Athenian mariners in 427 BC. But perhaps more impressive than their skill as seamen, the Líparisi instituted a system of self-government in which all members of the community owned land, ships, houses and goods in common. The island people divided themselves into 'people of the earth' — who farmed not only their own island but others as well, and even parts of the mainland — and 'people of the sea' — fishermen, pirates, and sailors who defended the island. All the bounty was shared, with yearly tributes religiously sent off to Delphi.

During the Punic Wars most of Sicily, including Lípari, sided with Carthage, and in 251 BC the Roman force of 60 ships put an end to the Líparisi's luck, destroying the island and leaving almost no survivors. From that point on, the history of the Aeolian Islands falls more or less in line with the history of Sicily.

AD 836 saw the arrival of the Saracens, who were in turn driven out by the Normans, who built a Benedictine monastery in Lípari where Count Roger created a diocese. In 1340 Robert I, King of Naples, seized the town. Two centuries later it was looted by the pirate Khair er-Dîn Barberossa, commander of a fleet of 114 ships, and the inhabitants were deported as slaves. Charles V of Spain then rebuilt Lípari and repopulated the islands, which were annexed by the kingdom of Sicily in 1610.

The recent history of the islands has been a hard one. Until about 20 years ago, the inhabitants struggled to maintain a basic survival level, fishing, tending vines and mining pumice. During the past 20 years, a great number of people have migrated, either to the mainland or to Australia, leaving the resources to be divided by fewer people.

Tourism is still growing in the region and contributes a large amount of income to the local economy. The Aeolian Islands are by far the most popular of the islands off Sicily's coast — with good reason. Rich in ancient history, with a variety of natural wonders, the sheer beauty of this intimate archipelago is positively other-worldly.

On average, one day on each island is enough to form a general impression and to see the main sights. If you are planning to visit the islands at the end of your stay in Sicily, it is a good idea to schedule in an extra day, in case the boats are delayed. If you are traveling in summer you should reserve your hotels ahead of time. A half-board minimum is required by most. Rates vary according to the season, so it is best to inquire beforehand.

Lípari

Lípari is the largest island in the archipelago (145 sq mi/37.6 sq km) and has the most inhabitants (9000). The focus of regional activity in Antiquity, it was once a centre for the obsidian trade and is now the world's most important producer of pumice stone. Geologically, it is the most complex of the islands, and although there has been no known major volcanic eruption here, there is evidence of post-volcanic activity: smoke and gas emanations, sulphur and hot springs. The highest points on the island are Monte Chirica (1978 ft/603 m), Monte Sant'Angelo (1945 ft/593 m) and Monte Guardia (1210 ft/369 m).

The capital of the island — also of the archipelago — is a lively little town, **Lípari**, on the east coast, dominated by a natural promontory known as 'il Castello'. This is located between two ports, **Marina Lunga** to the north, used for large boats and ferries and **Marina Corta** to the south for hydrofoils.

Lípari

Il Castello* is a vast, steep lava rock that was inhabited in prehistoric times. You can climb up to it from Marina Lunga by the stairway that begins at piano della Civita and ends at piazza Municipio. Follow the ancient Greek walls to the Gothic doorway that until the 18th century was used to close off the ancient upper town or citadel.

The buildings on the left are occupied by part of the museum. On the right are three churches: Santa Caterina in front and Addolorata and Immacolata in back. The archaeological zone spreads out before them.

The **Duomo** (cathedral) stands on the summit of the hill. Originally Norman, it was rebuilt in the 13th century and then altered inside in 1654. The façade dates from 1861. The Baroque interior is adorned with frescoes and paintings which, in the nave, illustrate scenes from the Old Testament. A rich altar to the left of the choir holds an unusual silver statue of San Bartolomeo, patron saint of the island. There are 18th-century cupboards in the Sacristy.

A wide staircase facing the cathedral leads down into the town. Beside it is the former 17th-century episcopal palace, now part of the museum.

The **Museo Eoliano**** (open Mon-Sat 9am-2pm, Sun and holidays 9am-1pm; admission free) is located in several buildings around the cathedral. Begin with the rooms in Palazzo Vescovile (17th century) to the right of the cathedral. As the museum was being enlarged in 1990 the contents of each room are not listed and may change, but the main works are mentioned.

In the first part of the museum (rooms I to X) there are mainly finds from the four phases of the Aeolian Neolithic era (from the 4th to the 2nd millennium BC), the Bronze Age and the Ausonian civilization (1250 to 800 BC) as well as objects from Milazzo.

In the second part (rooms XI to XXVI) you can see necropolises from the middle of the Bronze Age, such as the one discovered in May, 1952 at

Sottocastello, which has been faithfully reconstructed. There are also some important collections of local **pottery*** and **miniature masks**** made of terra cotta. During the second half of the 4th century BC there was a flourishing school of renowned potters on Lípari. The artists drew their inspiration from the theatre of the day to produce masks of comic and tragic characters.

The collection of **kraters**** (Greek jars) is no less fascinating. One of them illustrates an episode of the Odyssey. Another representing Dionysius watching actors and a nude acrobat is attributed to the painter Assteas. Room XXVI's underwater archaeological discoveries complete the displays in this part of the museum. The oldest piece here is a fragment of a stirrup from the Mycenaean period (16th to 15th century BC). All the amphorae (two-handled vessels) come from cargoes of sunken ships.

An extremely well-organized building opposite Palazzo Vescovile houses art from the smaller islands as well as an interesting section on vulcanology.

The archaeological site spreads out in front of the cathedral and includes a prehistoric village with oval huts from the first Bronze Age.

The **Archaeological Park** *(closed Sun)* in a garden at the end of the street is far more interesting. It contains different types of tombs found at what is called the 'site of Diana' (6th to 2nd century BC) at the foot of the acropolis. The **view*** from the ramparts over Marina Corta harbour and the Purgatorio peninsula makes this one of the loveliest places on Lípari.

Around the island

The following two excursions can easily be done on foot, by scooter or by bus. There's a good road all the way around the island (24.8 mi/40 km).

Canneto* (3.1 mi/5 km from Lípari)

The tourist office can give you a timetable for the buses that leave from opposite the Esso station on corso Vittorio Emanuele. If you go by car take the road through Monte Rosa tunnel on the outward journey.

Canneto (1000 inhabitants) is a pumice mining centre. Eruptions on Monte Pelato formed pumice and also caused obsidian flows. The Forgia Vecchia flow is more than 1640 ft/500 m wide and 0.6 mi/1 km long. Allow 30 minutes to walk there from Canneto.

The obsidian deposits on Lípari are the only ones known in Europe. Obsidian is lava that solidified rapidly before crystalization occurred. In the past it was used to fashion tools and knives for human sacrifices; today it is made into luxury articles. It looks like glass when highly polished and has a glossy, black anthracite colour.

Obsidian is no longer valued as it was in Antiquity; the island has nevertheless made up for the loss with the exploitation of pumice stone. Not far along the road out of Canneto (toward Acquacalda) you can see the huge, white mountain from which the pumice is taken. The deposits are spread over 3.2 sq mi/8.4 sq km, covering about a quarter of the island's surface area. Pumice stone is porous volcanic rock formed when acid magma solidifies rapidly. Lípari's pumice, considered to be the best in the world, is so light it floats on water. On the beach below the road the water is 'so saturated with white dust that it looks like a good, strong pastis' (A. t'Serstevens).

The road leads on to Acquacalda (6.8 mi/11 km), another pumice centre, and then continues around the island.

Piano Conte and Quattropani (6.2 mi/10 km)

There is a bus service to both places. The road from Lípari leads to belvedere dei Quattrocchi where you have a wonderful view of Vulcano. It continues onto the plateau in the middle of the island to the white houses of Piano Conte. If you are looking for a restaurant, try **La Ginestra**.

From Piano Conte the road leads north to the village of Quattropani, set attractively among vineyards. You can return to Lípari via Acquacalda and Canneto on the road described above.

Telephone area code: 090.

Access

Since hydrofoils were introduced, transport between Sicily (see 'Useful addresses' for Milazzo p. 216) and the Aeolian Islands, and between the islands themselves, has been excellent. Because the frequency of crossings varies according to the season, you should ask one of the various maritime companies for a timetable. These companies have representatives in the harbours of each island.

Accommodation

▲▲▲ **Carasco,** in Porto delle Genti, ☎ 981 1605. 89 rooms. Modern hotel overlooking the sea. Garden and swimming pool.

▲▲ **Augustus,** via Ausonia 16, ☎ 981 1232. 28 rooms. Very charming hotel run by the owner. Small patio with a pleasant café. Magnificent palm tree.

▲▲ **Gattopardo Park Hotel,** via Diana, ☎ 981 1035. 53 rooms. Cottages situated in a beautiful garden. Pleasant dining room and comfortable sitting room. Reception and service unfortunately casual.

▲▲ **Giardino sul Mare,** via Maddalena 65, ☎ 981 1004. 30 rooms. *Closed Nov 1-Mar 20.* Swimming pool, garden and lovely sea view. Recommended.

▲▲ **Rocce Azzurre,** via Maddalena 69, in Porto delle Genti, ☎ 981 1582. 33 rooms, each with balcony overlooking the sea.

▲▲ **Villa Meligunis,** via Marte, ☎ 981 2426. 40 rooms. A former 17th-century residence in the centre; sometimes noisy.

▲ **La Filadelfia,** via Mancuso 2, ☎ 981 2795. 22 rooms. *Open all year.*

▲ **Hotel Poseidon,** via Ausonia 7, ☎ 981 2876. 11 rooms. Simple, pleasant, and charming. *Open all year.*

▲ **Oriente,** via Marconi 35, ☎ 981 1493. 25 rooms. *Open from Easter to Oct.* Simple, very pleasant new hotel with a garden. Efficient, friendly service.

▲ **Villa Diana,** in Diana Tufo, ☎ 981 1403. 13 rooms. In a lovely park. Outside the city centre.

There are a lot of other places to stay, including apartments to rent, among them the Mendolita establishments run by the **Filippino** restaurant, ☎ 981 1002 and 981 2152. The **Augustus, Oriente** and **Filadelfia** hotels are run on a half-board basis in conjunction with the **Filippino** and **E Pulera** restaurants, where their guests can go for meals.

Campground

Baia Unci, via Garibaldi in Canneto ☎ 981 1909. *Open April-Sept.*

Holiday Club

Lípari, 1.8 mi/3 km south of town at Punta di Capistello, ☎ 981 2331. 25 bamboo huts in a magnificent setting. Minimum stay of 3 days. Specialized in short sailing cruises ideal for visiting the islands.

Food

LL Al Pirata, in the harbour opposite the hydrofoil wharf. Attractive terrace on the seafront.

LL E Pulera, stradale Nuovo, beside the Oriente Hotel, ☎ 981 1158. *Open May-Oct.* A branch of the Filippino restaurant. Garden setting and folk music orchestra. Local specialities served on ceramic tables.

LL Filippino, piazza Municipio, ☎ 981 1002. *Closed Nov 15-Dec 10 and on Mon in the off-season.* Has been run by the Bernardi family since 1910. Over the years its large flowery terrace has gradually invaded the square. You can always be sure of having a good meal here.

L Trattoria d'Oro, via Umberto I 28. Almost on the corner of corso Vittorio Emanuele. Simple decor. Authentic Sicilian cooking at modest prices. The set menu is a good value.

Cafés

La Vela, in the harbour. Very pleasant cafe with parasol-shaded terrace. Excellent cappuccino and good daily specials. Recommended.

Useful addresses

Car rental, ☎ 981 2352 (also scooters, bicycles and boats): **Foti,** top end of Marina Longa beach.

Travel agents: Meligunte, corso Vittorio Emanuele 123, ☎ 981 1870, for all kinds of excursions, rentals and reservations. Exchange office *open on holidays*. **Menaldatours,** corso Vittorio Emanuele 235, ☎ 981 3131, for all tickets and reservations. Exchange office *open daily 9am-1pm, 5-8:30pm.*

Tourist information, AAST, corso Vittorio Emanuele 253, ☎ 981 1580. *Open Mon-Sat 8am-2pm, 4-7:30pm.*

Vulcano

The island has often changed its name over the centuries and, according to legend, is the dwelling place of Aeolus, the god of winds. It has a population of less than 500 and a surface area of 8 sq mi/21 sq km. Geologically interesting, the island consists of different volcanic formations all knitted together. The largest of these, Vulcano Vecchio, takes up the entire south-east part of the island. The craters of mounts Aria (1637 ft/499 m) and Saraceno (1578 ft/481 m) have been extinct since prehistoric days; only Fossa di Vulcano (1266 ft/386 m), also known as Gran Cratere, is still active.

Because of Vulcano's proximity to Milazzo, it has become a popular spot for vacation homes. This means that its scenic landscape is giving way to development.

Porto di Levante

Arriving by boat at Porto di Levante, on the left you will see Gran Cratere, dominated by Monte Aria, and on the right a strange rock of sulphur crystals. Across from Porto di Levante, on the other side of a narrow neck of land, is Porto di Ponente. The isthmus between them was formed by a lava flow from Vulcanello (a volcanic cone now on the northern tip of the island) and served to link the two volcanic masses together to create a single island.

A path leads to Porto di Levante beach after passing a natural pool where people 'take the waters' for their renowned therapeutic properties — mainly to ease the pain of osteo-arthritis and rheumatism. You will see patients covered in mud sitting on stones among emanations of carbonic anhydride that rise up from the earth. Before entering the pool, choose a place where the water will not scald you; it can come up out of the ground at a temperature of almost 212°F/100°C. After bathing you can rinse yourself off in the sea. Here too, on the shore, you will see bubbling caused by underwater *fumaroles* (holes emitting volcanic gases).

You can cross the isthmus on foot in about 15 minutes to **Porto di Ponente,** where the black sand contrasts dramatically with the yellow sulphur colour you see on most of the island. From here, boats leave on excursions to **grotta del Cavallo.** While the cave itself is not particularly interesting, the trip is well worth your while because the coast is fantastic. A boat trip around the whole island takes about four hours — don't forget to discuss the price beforehand.

Fossa di Vulcano **

A climb up Fossa di Vulcano, or Gran Cratere (1266 ft/386 m), takes barely more than an hour from Porto di Levante. The best time to do this is late afternoon.

The vast, regular crater with its diameter of about 1640 ft/500 m has multicoloured sides where sulphur yellow predominates. It is usually possible to walk down to the bottom without difficulty.

The last eruption took place at the end of the last century when large quantities of volcanic bombs known as 'bread crusts' were thrown sky high.

Vulcanello *

If you feel uneasy about the ascent of Fossa di Vulcano, you can climb the extinct Vulcanello (406 ft/124 m) in only 30 minutes. This small volcano rose out of the sea in about 183 BC and its lava flows formed the isthmus of black sand linking it to Vulcano, as mentioned above. You have a beautiful **view*** of Lípari and Vulcano from the summit.

Telephone area code: 090.

Access

Vulcano is easy to reach from Lípari; there are frequent boat departures from Marina Corta.

Accommodation

▲▲ **Archipelago,** in Vulcanello, ☎ 985 2002. 80 rooms. Swimming pool, garden. *Open May-Oct.*

▲▲ **Conti,** in Porto di Ponente, ☎ 985 2012. 61 rooms in cottages. Pleasant setting and friendly atmosphere. Recommended.

▲▲ **Eolian Hotel,** in Porto di Ponente, ☎ 985 2152. 98 rooms. Lovely garden. Peaceful. *Open May-Oct.*

▲▲ **Garden Vulcano,** in Porto di Ponente, ☎ 985 2069. 30 rooms. Unusual decoration. *Open April-Oct.*

▲▲ **Les Sables Noirs,** in Porto di Ponente, ☎ 985 2014. 27 rooms. Garden and private beach.

Campground

Sicilia, in Porto di Levante, ☎ 985 2164. *Open June-Sept.* Facilities for 240.

Useful address

Tourist information, AAST in Porto di Ponente, ☎ 985 2028. *Open June-Sept, Mon-Sat 8am-2pm.*

Salina

Salina was called Didyme (twin) in ancient times because of its two volcanic cones. It is the second most populated island, is the most fertile and has the highest peak, as Monte Fossa delle Felci (3156 ft/962 m) is a little higher than Strómboli. The rich soil produces an excellent grape, yielding red and white wines renowned for their bouquet and high alcohol content.

Tourism is not as developed here as on Lípari, but many regular visitors return every year to enjoy this charming island with its green hillsides and little pebble beaches. Excavations begun in 1955 have brought to light a Bronze Age village and traces of a settlement dating from the 6th and 5th centuries BC.

Unlike the other islands where the inhabitants live mostly in one town, Salina's population is centred in four: Santa Marina, Lingua, Malfa and Rinella. **Santa Marina,** on the east coast, is the port for boats and hydrofoils, and the point of departure for the ascent of Monte Fossa delle Felci (extinct) with its crater of andesitic rock. From the summit you can see the whole archipelago.

A coast road from Santa Marina leads south for 1.5 mi/2.5 km to the little village of **Lingua** set among vineyards and olive groves. You can still see the old salt marsh that gave the island its present name. Another excursion, this time in the opposite direction, north of Santa Maria, takes you 3.7 mi/6 km to **Malfa**. From here the road twists along the shore and

then turns inland through the Giovi Valley, where you can see the sanctuary of the Madonna del Terzito. It then crosses Leni, a market town set 656 ft/200 m up on Monte Fossa delle Felci, and descends toward **Rinella**, a little fishing village considered a harpooning paradise.
Telephone area code: 090.

Accommodation

▲▲ **Ariana**, via Rotabile 11, 1.8 mi/3 km from Leni (between Leni and Rinelli), ☎ 980 9075. 15 rooms. *Open Easter-Oct.* Private beach.

▲▲ **Punta Scario**, in Malfa, ☎ 984 4139. 17 rooms. *Open May-Oct.* Garden. Very peaceful.

▲ **Mamma Santina**, via Sanità 26, Santa Maria, ☎ 984 3054. 11 rooms. Simple boarding house with good view.

Campground

Tre Pini in Rinella, ☎ 984 2155. *Open June-Sept.*

Food

LL Portobello, in Santa Marina with a fine view of the harbour.
LL Marinara, in Lingua.

Filicudi

The ancients called the island Phoenicoessa, probably inspired by the ferns *(felci)* that covered it. It looks like a cone in the middle of the sea, about 12.4 mi/20 km from Salina; the water reaches a depth of 3280 ft/1000 m in places. There are three extinct volcanoes on the island: Fossa delle Felci (2536 ft/773 m), Montagnola (1092 ft/333 m) and Torione (922 ft/281 m). The island has a surface area of 3.6 sq mi/9.5 sq km, and the 200 inhabitants live in the hamlets of **Filicudi Porto**, **Pecorini** and **Valdichiesa**. The first two are on the coast while Valdichiesa, with its Church of San Stefano, is nestled inland against a background of greenery.

Of the many walks one can take on the island, the most interesting is to **Capo Graziano**, which reaches a height of 570 ft/174 m and is connected to the island by a narrow strip of land. Excavations have revealed the ruins of a prehistoric site dating from the Bronze Age.

Another memorable excursion to make is a boat tour around the island to see the dramatic coastline of sheer rock drop to the sea. During the trip you can also visit a few extraordinary caves (enquire at the port for details) of which **Bue Marino**, an hour's boat ride from the island, is the most famous. Its name derives from the seals that are said to have lived here. You enter Bue Marino through a pointed archway, then move into a deep cavity, at the back of which you can see a little beach. There are also some impressive rock obelisks off Filicudi (that of La Canna is 233 ft/71 m tall). When the sun sets, the contours of the rocks soften and the landscape becomes surreal.
Telephone area code: 090.

Accommodation

▲▲ **Phenicusa**, via Porto, ☎ 980 9955. 36 rooms. *Only open in summer; a minimum stay of a week is required.* Private beach.

Alicudi

Alicudi, once known as Ericusa from the Greek *erike* meaning 'heather', is a wild conical island. It is the most westerly of the Aeolian Islands, with a surface area of 2 sq mi/5.2 sq km and about 20 inhabitants who live on the eastern slopes. Timpone delle Montagnola, at 2171 ft/662 m, is the highest point on the island. You arrive at **Palomba** in the south-east. A path leads from here to **Piano del Fucile,** where tombs were discovered containing a collection of beautiful vases and clay artifacts.

Accommodation

▲▲ **Ericusa,** viale Regina Elena 5, ☎ 981 2370. 12 rooms. The only hotel on the island with a restaurant.

Panarea

The smallest island in the archipelago (1.2 sq mi/3.24 sq km; 270 inhabitants) is located 9.3 mi/15 km north of Lipari. The eastern slopes of the highest point on the island, Punta del Corvo, 1381 ft/421 m, are under cultivation, while the rugged western slopes form a sheer drop to the sea.

On Panarea's inhabited eastern shore the three successive centres of **Iditella, San Pietro** and **Drauto** form a kind of elongated village. Boats arrive on San Pietro quay, the starting point for the two following walks.

The first and most interesting, to **Punta Milazzese,** takes about an hour there and back. Follow the coastline south along a path to Caletta dei Zimmari and at the end of the beach you will see a promontory, on top of which, in the 14th century BC, there was a village known as Milazzese. This is also the name given to the art form that prevailed in the Aeolian Islands during the middle Bronze Age. Below, on the opposite side of the headland from Caletta dei Zimmari, is the pebble beach of **Calajunco bay.**

The second walk from San Pietro quay takes you north to **Calcara,** where there was probably a volcano in prehistoric times. Today there is evidence of volcanic activity: fumaroles and little geysers of hot water that bubble up from the sea. There is a mud pool here like the one in Vulcano, and a hot spring (122°F/50°C) near San Pietro quay, used by the local inhabitants for its medicinal properties.

Boat trips have been recommended around the other islands and Panarea is no exception. An outing by boat is particularly attractive here because of the many islets to visit. The most impressive is **Basiluzzo,** formed from vitrified lava, which rises out of the water 1.8 mi/3 km north-east of Panarea. It spreads over an area of about 7.4 acres/3 hec and is mainly used for growing capers. You can see the ruins of Roman buildings and traces of mosaic paving.

Telephone area code: **090.**

Accommodation

▲▲ **Cincotta,** via San Pietro, ☎ 983001. 19 rooms. Park and swimming pool.

▲▲ **Lisca Bianca,** via Lani 1, ☎ 983004. 25 rooms. Quiet, with restaurant.

▲▲ **La Piazza,** loc. San Pietro, ☎ 983003. 25 rooms. Swimming pool.

▲▲ **Raya,** in Costa Galetta, ☎ 983013. 10 rooms. Recommended.

▲▲ **La Residence,** loc. San Pietro, ☎ 983029. 9 rooms.

▲ **Tesoriero,** via Comunale Lani 7, in San Pietro, ☎ 983098. 11 rooms. Pleasant park-like setting.

All the above are closed during the off-season.

Strómboli

From the sea, this island (4.8 sq mi/12.6 sq km; 380 inhabitants) looks like a smoking volcanic cone. Strómboli takes its name from the Greek *strombos,* meaning 'round', and is the most famous of the Aeolian Islands because of its active volcano. Its summit, Serra Váncora, is often dramatically wrapped in clouds and rises 3038 ft/926 m above sea level, but because the cone continues underwater for another 3608 ft/1100 m, the total height can be estimated at more than 6561 ft/2000 m.

Most of the inhabitants live on the north-east side of the island in three villages, **Piscita, San Bartolomeo** and **San Vincenzo,** all bordering the beach of **Ficogrande.** Hydrofoils stop at the Scaro Scari jetty in Piscita.

Low white houses with flat roofs and exterior staircases rise in terraces over the green eastern slopes of Strómboli. Black, however, is the predominant colour on the island, prettily setting off the attractive houses and brightly coloured boats. Once on shore, you have a strong impression of being near a large stove — there is always a lingering smell of coal in the air. It is enjoyable to walk along the narrow paths between the hamlets.

Live volcanic activity takes place in a crater 656 ft/200 m below the summit on the western side of the island and is partly obstructed by two crests of heaped lava known as Filo del Fuoco and Filo di Baraona. Inside the crater there are constant eruptions which, every 15 minutes or so, throw out incandescent scoria accompanied by explosions. These eruptions pose no danger to the inhabitants because the volcanic matter is channeled down Sciara del Fuoco (*scaria* is Arab for road), a corridor 765 yds/700 m long and about 0.6 mi/1 km wide leading to the sea.

The volcano was once thought to produce explosions alone, known as 'Strombolian activity', but lava flows have also been recorded. The only major eruption so far this century took place on September 11, 1930, and lasted 11 hours, during which a black cloud rose 8202 ft/2500 m above the crater.

Ascent of the volcano*

This can be done by anyone in good health with a little walking endurance. Count on three hours to go up and two to come down. Because of the heat, the best time to do the climb is in the early morning or evening with a guide. The Club Alpino Italiano (☎ 986 093) organizes daily excursions from April to October for groups of ten people (minimum) that leave in late afternoon and return before midnight. Come equipped with warm clothes, sturdy walking shoes or tennis shoes, a snack, water and a flashlight with spare batteries. Despite what the locals say, it is also quite possible to do the climb alone, as long as you are fit. It is also fun to take a sleeping bag and spend the night at the top in the reed and lava shelters.

Sciara del Fuoco

There are organized excursions to the foot of Sciara del Fuoco, where you can watch the explosions from the sea. The boat trip there takes about 25 minutes. When the blocks of volcanic matter fly out from the crater and land on the Sciara they burst into a spray of sparks like continuous fireworks. About ten times yearly, when the activity gets more intense, the fiery pieces roll down the slope and shoot into the sea, producing columns of steam as they hit the water.

Ginostra, an hour's boat ride away on the south coast facing Panarea, is a little hamlet with about 20 inhabitants and a port so small it can handle only one boat at a time.

A boat trip right around the island is also recommended. All along the wild coastline you'll find small creeks and black sandy beaches where you can swim. Over the last few years Strómboli has become increasingly popular for deep-sea diving as well.

To finish your visit you could take a 20-minute boat trip out to **Strómbolicchio,** a striking rock that rises out of the sea a mile from the island. From afar it looks like a medieval castle. Its steep sides (141 ft/43 m at the highest point) drop straight to the sea. A rock-hewn stairway of more than 200 steps leads up to a terrace where the view is splendid.

Telephone area code: 090.

Accommodation

▲▲ **La Sciara,** via Soldato Cinotta, ☎ 986004. 62 rooms. Small villas with antique furniture, in a garden setting. Tennis courts, swimming pool and private beach.

▲▲ **La Sirenetta Park Hotel,** via Marina 33, in Ficogrande, ☎ 986025 and 986082. 43 rooms. A modern, extremely well-run hotel complex. Attractive Aeolian architecture. Well-appointed spacious rooms. Patio, solarium, bar, shops, swimming pool and private beach. Recommended for its comfort and efficient friendly reception.

▲ **Villagio Strómboli,** via Regina Elena 38, ☎ 986018. 30 rooms. Modest, reasonably-priced hotel.

Food

Of the many restaurants open in the holiday season **Alla Brace, Puntazzo, Barbablu, Il Gabbiano, La Nassa** and **Il Canneto** are recommended. There are also several *trattorie.*

Useful address

Tourist information, in Ficogrande. *Open in the holiday season.*

▬▬ *MILAZZO TO MONTI NÉBRODI*

Return to the N113

Barcellona Pozzo di Gotto (28 mi/45 km west of Messina)
This farming centre (population 38,000) is set in the middle of fertile countryside. From here you can make a 5.5 mi/9 km excursion to Castroreale.

Castroreale

This little town stands 1292 ft/394 m above sea level at the foot of the Peloritani mountains and has some very fine churches. The **Chiesa Matrice,** now restored, is flanked by a 15th-century crenelated campanile and contains several statues, including one of St Catherine by Antonello Gagini. The **Santa Marina** church houses a 1570 triptych from the Flemish school. In the **Sant'Agata** you can see an Annunciation by Antonello Gagini and a crucifix, believed to have miraculous powers, that is carried in a procession through the town on August 25. The Church of **Santa Maria di Gesù,** near the cemetery, contains the sarcophagus of Geronimo Rosso by Antonello Gagini.

Castroreale Terme (31.6 mi/51 km west of Messina)

This is a thermal spa and seaside resort in the middle of Golfo di Patti bay. Its sulpho-sodic, alkaline-ferruginous waters are used in the treatment of rhumatism and liver and respiratory disorders. The season lasts from May to October.
Telephone area code: 090.

Accommodation

▲▲▲ **Grand Hotel Terme,** viale delle Terme, ☎ 9781078. 65 rooms. Best hotel in the town, with tennis and thermal spa facilities.

▲▲ **Belvedere,** via Nazionale 132, ☎ 9781338. 24 rooms.

▲▲ **Gabbiano,** via Marchesana, ☎ 9781385. 26 rooms. *Closed Oct-May.* Pleasant location.

San Biagio (33.5 mi/54 km west of Messina)

A mountainous country road, the N185, leads left to Taormina through Francavilla di Sicilia.
On leaving San Biagio, you come to the ruins of a 1st-century AD **Roman**

The volcano on the Aeolian Island of Strómboli is still very much active.

villa on the left-hand side of the road. It is a Hellenistic building with several rooms arranged around a peristyle; the *tablinum,* or reception room, retains fine marble paving and the *frigidarium,* or cooling room, contains a large mosaic depicting a fishing scene.

Tíndari★ (42 mi/68 km west of Messina)

Tíndari, located near the cape of the same name, is the site of the ancient town of Tyndaris, founded in 396 BC by Dionysius I of Syracuse. The town remained faithful to the Romans during the Punic Wars and became successful under the Empire but was eventually destroyed by the Saracens.

The road leading to the ruins (0.7 mi/1.2 km) runs beside Greek walls which date from the 3rd century BC and ends on a vast esplanade (with a parking lot) 918 ft/280 m above the sea. You will see a large **sanctuary** — a huge painted-concrete edifice, convered in tiles. This was built onto the original 16th-century church, which retains a portal. The monument is considered an important place of pilgrimage because it houses an icon known as the Black Madonna, venerated since the 16th century and believed to have come from the Near East.

The splendid **view★★** from the belvedere nearby takes in the Golfo di Patti and the Aeolian Islands beyond. Below you can see a lagoon where sea currents have created unusual sand formations.

Archaeological zone★

Open daily 9am to an hour before sunset; free admission.
As you enter the site, walk past the little museum, which is best visited at the end of your tour. On the left is the 3rd- or 2nd-century BC **Greek theatre★** that was altered by the Romans. Its *cavea* faces the sea and is divided into 11 sections with 28 rows of seats. Parts of the original Greek *scena* remain.

Returning along the Decumanus, or main street, that once linked the theatre to the forum, you reach the impressive **Gymnasium★**, a kind of basilica built in imperial times. Of its three original floors only the bottom one remains. It was restored during this century and now looks like a vast vaulted hall with nine arches. It was designed so that it could be shut at both ends for meetings with the ancient forum spread out before it.

Beside the Decumanus, in front of the basilica, is a thermal edifice with a portico on either side of its entrance. The mosaics here represent a bull and the Dioscuri — symbols of the town of Tyndaris — as well as Trinacria, symbol of the island. The baths consist of a number of rooms in some of which you can see the remains of ancient mosaics.

As you walk down toward the sea, you pass insulae (Roman houses) and tabernae (shops), some fairly well preserved. The museum contains archaeological finds and a partial reconstruction of the theatre *scena.*

Patti (47 mi/76 km west of Messina)

Beyond the Tíndari junction the road descends inland between the sea and the mountains toward Patti, a little terraced town on a hill. The N113 then passes under the highway and runs beside the fine beach at Marina di Patti on the shores of the gulf.

The town of Patti has a population of 13,000 and looks out over Marina di Patti beach below. In the **Duomo** there is a painted Madonna by de Saliba (16th century) and the Renaissance sarcophagus of Adelasia, the wife of the Norman king, Roger I. East of Marina di Patti, under a highway viaduct, you can see a grand **Roman villa★** *(open daily 9am to sunset)* with several rooms, a fine peristyle and polychrome mosaic floors.
Telephone area code: 0941.

Accommodation

▲▲ **Park Philip Hotel,** on the lungomare, ☎ 361 322. 45 rooms. *Open all year.* Swimming pool across the street.
▲▲ **La Playa,** outside the town centre, overlooking the sea,

☎ 361 319 and 361 326. 70 rooms. Swimming pool and beach. Very pleasant.

Campground

Simenzaru Beach, contrada Galice, ☎ 37 110.

Tourist information, piazza Sciacca, ☎ 21 327.

Gioiosa Marea (52.8 mi/85 km west of Messina).
This small town (7,000 inhabitants) lies beyond Capo Calavà and its magnificent beach. The narrow beach here, crossed by a railway line, is mediocre by comparison. A two-hour walk takes you up to the abandoned village of Gioiosa Guarda, 2608 ft/795 m above sea level, where there's a splendid view of the Aeolian Islands, a mere 12.4 mi/20 km away.

Telephone area code: 0941.

▲▲ **Capo Skino Park Hotel,** in Capo Skino, ☎ 301 167. 98 rooms. Park, tennis courts and swimming pool.

Campground

Cicero, in San Giorgio, contrada Cicero. Facilities for 420.

Tourist information, via Umberto 197, ☎ 301 211.

Patti to Sant'Agata di Militello

The N113 continues to **Brolo,** which has a beach and a panoramic view. The town is dominated by a large square tower.

After 64.6 mi/104 km from Messina there's a junction with the N116, which leads left to **Randazzo** (41 mi/66 km; p. 192) and right to **Capo d'Orlando,** a seaside resort above which rise the ruins of a 14th-century castle. The town offers little of interest but has a wide choice of hotels.

The N113 leads west keeping close to the coast.

Sant'Agata di Militello (75 mi/121 km west of Messina) is a seaside resort (13,000 inhabitants) with a fine beach.

Telephone area code: 0941.

▲▲ **Parimar,** via Medici 1, on the Messina road, ☎ 701 888. 48 rooms.

▲▲ **Roma Palace,** via Nazionale, the Palermo road, ☎ 703 516. 48 rooms.

MONTI NÉBRODI

This chain of mountains is not unlike the Apennines with its wooded hills and lakes. Because of the relatively cool temperature that reigns over the area, summer is the best time for a visit. The Nébrodi date from the Tertiary period and reach an average height of 4265 ft/1300 m. Monte Soro, 6059 ft/1847 m, is the highest point. The 43 mi/70 km-long chain forms a richly vegetated mass covered in beech, ilex, oak and elm trees. The largest woods are those of Caronia, Troína, Grappida and Foresta Vecchia.

The itineraries below begin at the coast and then take little mountain roads into a part of Sicily where you can go on long walks and where the natural surroundings and the customs and traditions of country folk are still respected.

Villages in Monti Nébrodi

Setting out from Capo d'Orlando, the N116 twists through olive groves up into picturesque villages — such as Naso, Castell'Umberto, Castell'Umberto Vecchio and Ucria — and on to Floresta at an altitude of 4183 ft/1275 m. You cross beautiful countryside from here to Randazzo (p. 192) — a distance of 12 mi/20 km.

A winding road leads from La Rocca to **Frazzano** (8 mi/13 km), famous for its Norman church of San Filippo Fregala perched on a wild hilltop outside the village. There's a network of little roads to Floresta on the N116 (see above) passing through Longi and Tortorici on the way.

The first of two itineraries from Sant'Agata di Militello is to **Alcara li Fusi** (9 mi/15 km), the starting point for interesting walks. The second route is along the N289, which traverses the centre of the Nébrodi mountains. After 8 mi/13 km you reach the isolated village of **San Fratello**, dominated by a large rock, where the inhabitants still speak a Gallo-Italic dialect. Traditions are kept very much alive here, such as the mysterious Festa dei Giudei celebrated on Maundy Thursday and Good Friday. The N289 then climbs through lovely cork tree forests to **Fossa di Lupo** (3966 ft/1209 m), **Portella Fémmina Morta** (5000 ft/1524 m) and on to **Portella della Miraglia** (4803 ft/1464 m), one of the most interesting places in the mountains where you can see both the Ionian and the Tyrrhenian slopes. The road continues to **Cesarò** (3773 ft/1150 m; population 5000). On the left you can see Etna and a little farther away, Monte Soro with Biviere, a small artificial lake, at its foot.

From San Stéfano di Camastra you can take the N117 to Nicosía, one of Sicily's most unusual inland towns. After 11 mi/18 km you reach **Mistretta,** a large market town 3116 ft/950 m above sea level, dominated by a feudal castle. The feast of the Madonna takes place in September when *giganti*, giant warrior figures, accompany the statue of the Virgin in procession. The Chiesa Madre is worth a visit in spite of all the alterations it has undergone over the centuries, but Mistretta is especially important as a departure point for excursions into the mountains. In two hours you can climb Monte Castelli (5118 ft/1560 m), in three hours, Monte Sambughetti (5249 ft/1600 m) and in four hours, the Pumeri Pass (5249 ft/1600 m).

The road continues up to Portella di Contrato and then to Portella San Martino (3444 ft/1050 m) before descending to Nicosía.

Nicosia

This ancient city was particularly prosperous in the Middle Ages as the halfway point between Palermo and Messina before the coast road was built. It's a picturesque town spread over four hills, with 15,600 inhabitants. A dialect still spoken here originates from the Lombard and Piedmontese colonists who settled in the area under the Normans.

The 14th-century **Cathedral of San Nicola** in the centre of town has a magnificent pointed doorway bearing the emblems of the Princes of Aragon. Flanking the façade is a fine 13th-century **campanile***. In the Baroque interior of the cathedral, to the right of the entrance, you can see the funerary monument by Marabitti (1753). There is also a marble pulpit by Antonello Gagini (1566) and a painted wooden crucifix by Fra Umile da Petralia in a chapel to the right of the choir.

Behind the church, off piazza San Leone, via Francesco Salomone leads up to the **San Vincenzo Church,** decorated with frescos by Gugliemo Borremans (1777). On turning left from here you come to the **Santa Maria Maggiore Church,** which was founded in the 13th century and rebuilt in the 18th. It contains a large marble polyptych by Gagini (1512) at the back of the choir and the so-called throne of Charles V on the side, supposedly used by the emperor during his visit in 1535.

Sperlinga is 6 mi/10 km from Nicosia along the N120 heading toward **Gangi**. It is dominated by the ruins of a castle where the French took refuge after the revolt of the Sicilian Vespers in 1282. There is also a

wonderful **view*** of the entire region from the castle. Gangi is only
9 mi/15 km away (see Monti Madoníe p. 237).
Telephone area code: 0935.

Accommodation

▲▲ **Pineta**, in San Paolo, ☎ 647 012. 48 rooms. Lovely setting.

Food

LL **La Cirata**, on the N117, ☎ 647 095. *Closed Mon.* Well worth a
visit for its good food and hospitality. Recommended.
LL **La Pagoda**, 2.4 mi/4 km from Nicosia on the Troína road.
Closed Fri.
LL **La Vigneta**, 3.1 mi/5 km from Nicosia on the Mistretta road.
Closed Tues.

SAN STÉFANO DI CAMASTRA TO CEFALÙ

San Stéfano di Camastra (93.8 mi/151 km west of Messina) is a village
of 5000 inhabitants rising in tiers up a hill. It has a Ceramics Museum, a
school of ceramics, numerous workshops, and shops selling pottery. The
Chiesa Matrice has a fine Renaissance portal and 17th-century statues
inside.

After San Stéfano di Camastra, the N113 winds through wild verdant
countryside towards Cefalù. After 100 mi/161 km (from Messina) at the
little seaside resort of Castel di Tusa, a branch left leads to Tusa
(6 mi/9.5 km) leaving the ruins of ancient **Halaesa** on your right. This
city was founded in 403 BC and flourished under the Romans. The
foundations of a **Hellenistic temple** remain, along with some ancient walls
*(open Tues-Sun 9am-2pm in winter, 9am to an hour before sundown in
summer; closed Mon).*

The Palermo road continues toward Cefalù's limestone crag, leaving
Caldura beach on the right.

CEFALÙ**

Map coordinates refer to the map p. 233.

Cefalù is an unforgettable stop on a tour of the island. It is famed as a
seaside resort thanks to its fine-sand beach, the best on the coast, and
also as an important cultural centre because of its cathedral, one of the
most magnificent monuments of the Norman period in Sicily. The old
town has managed to keep its character and the 15,000 inhabitants
make their living mainly from tourism, so much so that the sleepy little
port seems to exist solely for the pleasure of photographers.

The Sikels settled Cephaloedium in the 9th century BC. The name of the
town comes from *cephalus* (head) — a reference to the large, craggy
rock resembling a human head that overlooks the town. Cefalù is first
mentioned by Diodorus Siculus whose account purports that Greeks from
Himera found refuge here after their town was destroyed by the
Carthaginians. Cefalù surrendered to the Romans in 254 BC and then, on
the fall of the Roman Empire, the inhabitants settled on the rock. In 857
the town was taken by the Arabs, who in turn were ousted by the
Normans in 1063. The Normans rebuilt the town on the shore, using
what little remained of the original houses — the Arabs having burned
their homes when the Normans invaded.

The city flourished under Norman rule. In 1152 the geographer Isrisi
wrote that Cefalù was 'a fortress just like a town, with markets, baths and
even mills inside the town, above a spring of water that gushes from the
rock, sweet and cool for the inhabitants to drink. It has a fine port where
boats come from everywhere.' In this idyllic spot in 1131, Roger II started
construction on one of the most beautiful religious monuments on the
island — the cathedral — in thanks for having landed safely on the island

after a violent storm at sea. Later on, the town was ruled by bishops whose power extended not only over the garrison but also over the port and the sea trade. In 1430 town magistrates took over, promising that Cefalù would remain in the hands of the state. Today, Cefalù is a popular tourist town, due in part to the 'magic village' — one of the first and best known of the Club Med villages.

Count on a minimum of half a day for a quick visit, although Cefalù is worth more time if you can manage it.

The road from Messina leads into piazza San Francesco, C2, where you turn left, then right onto via Matteotti, which passes the Villa Communale and the post office to end at piazza Garibaldi, B2. On the right you will see the base of a campanile and the 18th-century limestone church of Santa Maria della Catena preceded by a porch of Ionic pilasters. Remains of the old walls can be seen behind the church.

Corso Ruggero*, B2, the main street, is a narrow lively thoroughfare lined with shops. On the left, at n° 75, is a house known as Osterio Magno, the former residence of King Roger. Today all that remains is a fine triple window*. The communal theatre is a little farther along on the right, followed by the **Purgatorio Church,** whose name derives from the fact that the church once adjoined the oratory of the Brotherhood of the Dead, whose members had the painful task of helping those condemned to death onto the scaffold. On their own deaths, they merited the dubious privilege of being embalmed in the catacombs of the sanctuary. First the bodies had 'the fat trimmed off' by boiling lime and then were dressed in their most sumptuous vestments before being hung for display in macabre catacomb niches.

Duomo (Cathedral)*** A2

The corso opens onto piazza del Duomo, the former scene of public executions. It is a vast sloping terrace with palm trees, at the back of which rises the Norman cathedral and behind it the great rock.

There are a number of palaces around the square. Palazzo Maria is noteworthy with its Gothic-Catalan doorway, as is Palazzo Piraino, which is adorned with 16th-century balconies.

The cathedral will of course draw your attention more than anything else on the square. This magnificent edifice — a basilica in the shape of a Latin cross — took almost a century to complete.

During recent restoration, a mosaic from the Palaeo-Christian period was discovered together with part of a Roman street, proving that the basilica was built over an earlier edifice.

Façade**

The original façade, like that of Monreale, was very different from the one we see today. The façade designed by Giovanni Panettera in 1240 was originally covered in mosaics illustrating the king 'in his relations with the church'. The portico, originally intended to protect frescoes which have since disappeared, was added in 1471 by Ambrogio da Como. It blends in well with the rest of the building thanks to the three elegant arches that shelter the richly decorated central doorway.

The façade is flanked by two tall towers, each with three sets of windows. These two campanili, surmounted by minarets with sloping, coloured roofs, dominate the entire town.

Before going inside, walk around the right side of the cathedral through a little door into a garden where you will see the powerful **apses*** behind. The Norman style is unmistakable, but it is also likely that Muslim and Lombard artists took part in the building. The unfinished apses of different levels are decorated by a frieze of interlacing arches with slender supporting columns while the raised transept is massive and grandiose. Apparently, King Roger intended to make the church his family pantheon and brought in two porphyry sarcophagi for his queen and for himself in 1145. They were transferred to Palermo by Frederick II in 1215.

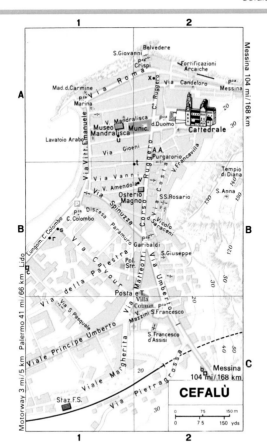

Interior★★★

Open daily 7:30am-noon, 3:30-7:30pm.

You enter through a side door on the right. The nave is separated from the aisles by 12 columns taken from antique monuments. They have Roman and Byzantine capitals supporting stilted Gothic arches. A grandiose Gothic **arch**★ resting on huge columns with capitals decorated by an artist from the Pouilles region in Italy (1140-50), marks the entrance into the transept. This latter has intersecting ribbed vaulting on the right side. The left column of the arch bears a 15th-century fresco of an enthroned woman covered in jewels and wearing a tiara of heavy pearls. The style of the picture is Byzantine, and it could be the portrait of the Greek queen, Irena. She holds a casket containing the remains of her husband and son.

The ceiling of the nave was burned in 1888 but it still bears traces of paintings completed in 1263 during the reign of King Manfred. A Renaissance work on the main pillar in the left part of the transept depicts an enthroned Virgin and Child surrounded by angels. The fine painted wood **crucifix**★ is attributed to da Pessaro (1468). Note also the two 18th-century organ cases between the nave and the transept.

The 12th-century **font**★ in the right-hand aisle is decorated with four leopards, symbols of the Altavilla family. A door in the left-hand aisle leads into the former Augustinian convent, the order to which King Roger II entrusted his church. All that remains of the convent (which was destroyed by a fire in the 14th century) is the magnificent **cloister** with twin columns. The Franco-Catalan, Roman-Lombard capitals are among

Christ Pantocrater of Cefalù

Of the three comparable figures in Sicily, this is probably the earliest and certainly the most Near Eastern in appearance. Only the round line of the halo prevents the face, with its curling beard, from appearing unduly long. If the lines of the face suggest asceticism, this is confirmed by the attenuated fingers. The eyes, on account of their large size and their dominant position in the cathedral, are all-seeing: nothing in the church is hidden from them: they symbolize light to which the text refers. They are inscrutable and severe, yet not without compassion and love, illustrating the inscription that overarches the figures, where Christ is described on the one hand as redeemer, on the other as judge.

For there is no questioning the fact that these mosaics are among the supreme examples of Christian art. In scale as in conception, in line as in colour, which, thanks to the excellence of the materials employed, remains undimmed, the Pantocrator at Cefalù is unsurpassed by any other representation of Christ. Moreover, since this figure was created in the tradition preserved from apostolic times by the mosaic-working hermits of Mt Athos, it may be taken as an authentic portrait of the Saviour. Like the inscriptions, written partly in Greek, partly in Latin, the mosaics are the fruit of the fusion between Eastern and Western Christendom, resultant upon that curious historical process whereby the Normans surged down from Hauteville to act as the fertilizing insect between two cultural flowers. The humanism and compassion of the West are in this figure linked to Near Eastern majesty, austerity and unlimited power.

Vincent Cronin
The Golden Honeycomb
(Rupert Hart-Davis, 1954)

the finest Sicilian sculptures of the day. The cloister was originally embellished with a corner fountain like the one at Monreale but this unfortunately no longer exists. Since 1952 there has been a competition for a restoration plan, but none has yet been chosen and the stones lie scattered around, waiting for the authorities' decision.

Mosaics***

Although the cathedral is Roman, some of its features are Near Eastern, such as the raised choir covered in mosaics. It is more or less certain that King Roger intended the entire interior to be decorated with mosaics, but by 1148 only those in the apse were finished and six years later the king died. There is an immense, solemn figure of *Christ Pantocrator****** set against a golden background, with Christ lifting his right hand in blessing and holding an open Bible in his left. The Latin text surrounding the portrait lends it meaning: 'Made man, administrator of man, redeemer of man created by me, as God incarnate I judge the bodies and hearts of men'. The Bible text reads: 'I am the light of the world, he who follows me will not walk in darkness but will have the light of life.'

Immediately beneath the figure of Christ is the Virgin Mary surrounded by archangels. St Peter and St Paul are on either side of a window on the level below, with the Apostles Matthew and Mark on one side, Luke and John on the other. Saints and prophets are arranged at the sides in rows according to a precise theological hierarchy. A medallion on the left contains the bust of Melchisedec, and one on the right contains that of Abraham. The vault above has fine intersecting ribs and is decorated to represent a golden firmament with angels and cherubs.

Old town** AB1-2

Cefalù's cathedral is not its only attraction; to see more of the town take a walk through the old quarters, which are laid out in a fishbone pattern on either side of corso Ruggero.

Rocca district, B2, to the right of the corso, consists of picturesque alleys like via Costa, where you can see the Bellipani courtyard and, at n° 8, a 16th-century doorway. Via Francavilla and Lo Duca are also worth a stroll, as is via Caracciolo, which rises (in steps) toward the Church of San Domenico.

The left-hand side of the corso, AB1, has kept its authenticity and consists of nine parallel alleys stretching down to the sea. There's a great charm in this part of town, where washing is strung between houses belonging to ages past. At the end of via XXV Novembre, A1, you can see a medieval public bath house, the Lavatoio Arabo. Continue along via Vittorio Emanuele to the **marina***, A1, a little harbour with a view of the beach. In the foreground there are fishermen's houses and coloured boats lying on the shore of a creek.

Museo Mandralisca** A1
Open daily 9am-12:30pm, 3:30-7pm.

This wonderful little museum, at via Mandralisca 1, houses the collections of Baron Mandralisca, the first deputy of Cefalù in the newly created Italian parliament of 1861. He also promoted excavations and was a great art lover who spent much of his time searching for rare objects.

The most interesting exhibits include **coin collections***; a **krater****, with an illustration of a fishmonger cutting up tuna fish on one side and on the other a picture of two young lovers (4th-century BC); Veneto-Cretan icons; inlaid cabinets; works from Spanish, Flemish, Neapolitan and Venetian schools of painting; and a 17th-century Christ crowned with thorns.

The finest work of all is the *Portrait of an Unknown Man****, a masterpiece of 15th-century Italian painting by Antonella da Messina. Mandralisca is believed to have found it behind a cupboard door belonging to a pharmacist in Lípari. The pharmacist's maid was so infuriated with the man's mocking look that she damaged the painting by scratching it. The expressive face is that of a 'deceitful man, a man who is used to all life's little failings, a man who is sure of himself, who always knows how to deal with a situation, who gives careful advice' (P. Saja).

Via Vittorio Emanuele opens into lungomare Giardina which runs beside the **beach*** all the way to Santa Lucia, affording good views of the town and the cathedral situated against the famous head-shaped rock.

Environs of Cefalù

Cefalù rock

The ascent up the enormous limestone crag behind the town is an easy excursion that can be done in an hour. Simply set out from corso Ruggero and take Vicolo dei Saraceni, B2, to the top (882 ft/269 m). Apart from the splendid panoramic **view** you can see the ruins of various ancient constructions.

You can also go around the rock by car or on foot (2.4 mi/4 km of good road) After piazza Duomo, turn right and take the road overlooking the sea, which runs past the foot of the lighthouse and leads to a little harbour and Caldura village — an area covered with restaurants and hotels. Presidiania beach nearby is where the goddess Diana is said to have come to bathe.

Gibilmanna

A panoramic road from Cefalù leads up 9.3 mi/15 km to the sanctuary of Gibilmanna on the slopes of Pizzo Sant'Angelo, 2624 ft/800 m above sea level. It is a popular centre of pilgrimage (festival on Sept 8). The church dates from the 17th and 18th centuries and contains a Madonna by the Gagini school and a statue of Sant'Elena by Fazio Gagini. There is also a fine altar which is thought to have been built from a drawing by Paolo Amato.

From here a country road leads up to the Istituto Nazionale di Geofisica (3297 ft/1005 m).

Cefalù is an excellent departure point for a tour of the Monti Madonie (see p. 237). The direct coastal route from Cefalù to Palermo is on p. 240.

Map coordinates refer to the map p. 233.
Telephone area code: 0921.

Access

Car: Cefalù is 92 mi/148 km north of Agrigento, 120 mi/194 km west of Catania and 46 mi/74 km east of Palermo.
Train: Cefalù is on the Messina-Palermo line.

Accommodation

Hotels in town

▲▲ **Astro**, via Nino Martoglio 8, ☎ 21 639. 30 rooms.

▲▲ **Riva del Sole**, lungomare Colombo, B1 c, ☎ 21 230. 28 rooms. Very well situated. Also has an annex with 5 rooms.

▲▲ **Tourist**, viale Lungomare, B1, off the map, ☎ 21 750. 46 rooms. Garden and swimming pool. Good service.

In Caldura (1.2 mi/2 km east of Cefalù toward Messina)

Kalura, ☎ 21 354. 76 rooms. Beach, garden, swimming pool and tennis courts.

▲▲ **Le Calette**, ☎ 24 144. 50 rooms. Swimming pool, garden and beach.

▲ **Al Pescatore**, villagio Pessatori, ☎ 21 572. 14 rooms.

▲ **La Siesta d'Oro**, beside the road, ☎ 21 761. 27 rooms.

▲ **Pink Hotel**, ☎ 22 275. 35 rooms. Swimming pool and garden.

In Santa Lucia (1.8 mi/3 km west of Cefalù toward Palermo)

▲▲ **San Lucia Sabbie d'Oro**, ☎ 21 565. 213 rooms. Large tourist complex with two hotels, private beach, swimming pool.

In Mazzaforno (2.4 mi/4 km west of Cefalù toward Palermo)

▲▲ **Baia del Capitano** contrado Mazzaforno, ☎ 20 005. 34 rooms. Set in a vast olive grove with swimming pool, small private beach 437 yds/400 m away.

In San Nicola (3 mi/5 km west of Cefalù toward Palermo)

▲▲ **Costa Verde**, ☎ 20 209. 373 rooms. Garden, swimming pool, tennis courts and beach.

In Capo Plaia (3.7 mi/6 km west of Cefalù, towards Palermo)

▲▲ **Carlton Riviera** contrado Capo Plaia, ☎ 20 200. 144 rooms. Attractive club-hotel on the seafront. Private beach, swimming pool, tennis courts, organized activities, and excellent food. Contact the hotel beforehand for booking information.

Campgrounds

Costa Ponente, in Ogliastrillo, 1.8 mi/3 km west of Cefalù, ☎ 20 085.

Plaia degli Uccelli, in San Ambrogio, 3 mi/5 km from Cefalù, ☎ 999 068.

San Filippo, in Ogliastrillo, 1.8 mi/3 km west of Cefalù, ☎ 20 184.

Tourist resort

Hotel Villagio Valtur, in Finale di Pollina, 8 mi/13 km from Cefalù. *Open Apr-Oct.*

Festivals and entertainment

Folklore performances and sailing competitions in the summer.
Feast of San Savatore, patron saint of the town, on August 4, 5 and 6. The cathedral and the old bath house are lit up in the evening. Not to be missed.

Food

LL Al Bastione, via Cortile Pepe, A2 x. Simple *trattoria* where you are served outside on the little square. Tourist menu.

LL La Brace, via XXV Novembre 10, A1 u, ☎ 23 570. *Open only in the evening. Closed Mon and throughout Dec and Jan.* Best restaurant in Cefalù and throughout the whole region; Palermitans don't hesitate to come here for dinner. Relatively short menu, excellent daily specials. Always reserve in the holiday season.

LL Da Nino Alla Brace, Lungomare, B1, ☎ 22 582. Stands out from the other restaurants along the lungomare for the quality of its cuisine, fish specialities, the efficient service and warm welcome. The menu is in French. Recommended.

LL Kentia, via Nicola Botto 15, AB1-2 t, ☎ 23 801. *Closed Thurs.* Renowned for its food and decor. Small indoor garden.

LL Osteria del Duomo, via Seminario 5, A2, on the corner of piazza del Duomo, ☎ 21 838. Authentic local cuisine served in a pleasant little dining room or out on an attractive terrace at the foot of the cathedral (illuminated at night). *Closed Mon.* Try the *caponata* and *penne* (small pasta cooked Palermitan style).

LL Osterio Magno, via Amendola, B2 v. *Closed Tues.* Traditional restaurant with rather plain decor. Good food.

Useful addresses

Hydrofoils *(Aliscafi),* services for Lípari and Vulcano three times a week in summer. Departure in the morning, return in the evening.

Car rental: Barranco, via Umberto I13, ☎ 21 525.

English newspapers, on sale opposite the post office and at Muffoletto, corso Ruggero 98.

Hospital, via Aldo Moro, ☎ 21 121.

Post office: via Vazzana (off map C1).

Taxis: piazza Duomo, ☎ 21 178; piazza Garibaldi, ☎ 22 158 and piazza Stazione, ☎ 22 554.

Telephones, Roma Palazzo EGV Center, A1.

Train station, piazza Stazione, C1.

Tourist information, AAST, corso Ruggero 77, ☎ 21 050. Efficient, well-documented office. *Open Mon-Fri 8am-2pm, 4:30-7:30pm; Sat 8am-2pm.*

MONTI MADONÍE: CEFALÙ TO CAMPOFELICE DI ROCCELLA

The itinerary suggested below takes you inland into a relatively unknown part of Sicily, one that is usually forgotten on a classic tour of the island. Yet it is in these remote villages, untouched by modern development, that you will find the heart of the real Sicily. You pass through large dormitory towns where the houses huddle timidly around the Chiesa Madre's campanile. The fields spread out around them in beautiful strips of changing colour. This part of Sicily is home to a people who, throughout the ages, have been forced to live on the defensive, to protect themselves from the influence of foreign invaders.

You will need a day to drive the 119 mi/192 km inland from Cefalù and back to Campofelice di Roccella on the coast, halfway between Cefalù and Términi Imerese.

The Madoníe region, called Maronius by Pliny, covers an area of 563 sq mi/1460 sq km. Like the Peloritani and Nébrodi mountains, the Madoníe form part of Messina province's upland mass and include the highest points on the island after Etna, with the peaks of Carbonara (6492 ft/1979 m), Antenna (6486 ft/1977 m) and Palermo (6414 ft/1955 m). The chain's luxuriant vegetation includes forest of oak, maple, fir and beech. Although its eagles and vultures have disappeared you can still come across wolves and wildcats.

Monti Madoníe

Isnello

After traversing olive groves and pine woods the road reaches the sanctuary of Gibilmanna (see p. 235) with good views of the Sant'Angelo slopes (3546 ft/1081 m). It then descends to Isnello, 1935 ft/590 m above sea level, in the Castelbuono river valley. The town is dominated by the ruins of a Byzantine castle and has a number of old churches which contain interesting paintings and sculptures. Among these are the 15th-century Chiesa Madre, the Church of San Michele and the Baroque Church of the Annunziata. You can also visit the Abisso del Vento caves that reach depths of 656 ft/200 m.

Isnello is a good base for mountain excursions to the Monte Cervi and Ostello della Gioventù refuges or to rifugio Orestano (31 rooms), 3608 ft/1100 m above sea level in Piano degli Zucchi (10 mi/16 km), ☎ 62 159. Good food.

Telephone area code: 0921.

Accommodation

▲▲ **Baia del Faggio**, loc. Acque del Faggio, ☎ 62 194. 24 rooms. Garden.

▲▲ **La Montanina**, loc. Piano Zucchi, ☎ 62 030. 42 rooms.

▲▲ **Villa del Parco**, loc. Piano Zucchi, ☎ 62 080. 9 rooms.

Festivals

Sagra delle Fave in June and **Sagra del Tuma** in July.

Castelbuono

This small town at the foot of Pizzo della Carbonara (6486 ft/1977 m) is the main centre of the Monti Madoníe with a population of 10,000. A castle dating from the beginning of the 14th century dominates the town. The first monument you see is the Church of Santa Maria d'Itria, just in front of the Renaissance fountain that was taken from the castle. The bas-reliefs illustrate scenes from the cult of Venus.

The **Matrice Vecchia*** is preceded by a 15th-century Gothic-Catalan portal and a 16th-century portico. The columns inside are painted with the figures of saints. The most interesting work is the large **polyptych*** (1510) by Antonello de Saliba. The Chiesa Nuova houses a 16th-century riptych and a painted cross from the same period. You can see various 16th-century sculptures and a Madonna by Antonello Gagini in the Church of San Francesco. Via Sant'Anna leads up to the chapel of castello dei Ventimiglia, a Baroque edifice with stucco decoration by Giuseppe and Giacomo Serpotta (1683) set against a golden background (ring for the guardian).

Among the displays in the **Museo Civico** is a fine herbarium of Madoníe mountain flora. A panoramic road leads 6 mi/10 km to the Crispi refuge at a height of 4593 ft/1400 m.

Geraci Sículo (33 mi/53 km south-east of Cefalù)

This ancient Arab citadel is now a market town with 3000 habitants. Its houses blend in with the rock background, and the pinnacles of the Chiesa Matrice campanili are covered in tiles decorated with Arab patterns. The whole region is known for the production of excellent cheese.

When you reach Bivio Geraci, leave the N286 and take the N120 for 5.5 mi/9 km to Gangi.

Gangi* (45 mi/73 km south-east of Cefalù)

The village of Gangi (population 8000) stands on Monte Marone (3444 ft/1050 m), which once served the Sikels as an observation point. The houses huddle close together, forming a regular solid mound; even the Chiesa Madre tower, an elegant late-Gothic **campanile***, does not rise above the other roofs (although this is partly explained by the fact that it was never finished). Inside the church you can see Giuseppe Salerno's *Last Judgement*, considered his masterpiece. Salerno was born in Gangi, as was Gasparo Vazzaro, another Renaissance painter whose works can be seen in churches all over Sicily.

Inside the crypt known as Fossa di Parrini (which cannot be visited), there are rows of the mummified bodies of priests who died between 1729 and 1880. The skeletons make a macabre spectacle, dressed in their vestments and hanging in niches like marionettes. The catacombs were much larger originally, but the room containing the bodies of the inhabitants of Gangi was walled up, probably at the beginning of the century, and only the space for the clergy was saved.

Other interesting historical buildings include the Catena Church, the Church of San Cataldo, the 14th-century Ventimiglia castle, the Bongiorno palace with its 18th-century frescoes and the 16th-century Monastery of the Annunziata.

Telephone area code: 0921.

Accommodation

▲▲ **Miramonti**, via Nazionale 13, ☎ 44424. 15 rooms.

Festivals

Sagra della Spiga in Aug; **Festa delle Palme** the week before Easter and **A Cravaccata** in Feb-Mar.

Useful address

Tourist information, Municipio, ☎ 44076.

Sperlinga (see p. 230) is 9.3 mi/15 km to the east.

Return to Bivio Geraci to continue the itinerary on the N286. The road leads around the mountains to their southern slopes and the town of Petralía Soprana.

Petralía Soprana (54 mi/88 km south of Cefalù)

The second highest town in Sicily, with an altitude of 3763 ft/1147 m, Petralía Soprana was once an Arab military centre and has kept its medieval character. The late Gothic Chiesa Madre has a fine doorway and an elegant 17th-century portico on the right side. Apart from some Renaissance pieces, the most important work inside is a 17th-century wooden crucifix by Fra Úmile da Petralía. Other churches in the town

include San Salvatore, with a circular design, probably buil
over a mosque; the 18th-century Santa Maria di Loreto Church with a
harmonious, convex façade, an elegantly winding staircase and a
splendid panoramic **view***; and the 18th-century collegio di Maria
Church, where the influence of the architect Borromini is apparent. Strol
through the streets of the town to see a fascinating series of doorways
and balconies.

Petralía Sottana (56 mi/91 km south of Cefalù)

A younger town than Petralía Soprana, Petralía Sottana is located on a
spur at an altitude of 3280 ft/1000 m. The village (4000 inhabitants) is
built around a Norman castle dating from 1046 and is surrounded by
churches. The church has an unfinished 18th-century façade and a late
Gothic portal on the right-hand side. Its grandiose interior contains
Baroque and Renaissance works, among them a triptych by an unknown
artist, probably dating from the 15th century. Behind the 15th-century
façade of the Trinita or Badia is a veritable treasure — a marble **altar-
piece****, probably by Domenico Gagini, that is one of the largest in Sicily
and that illustrates 23 scenes from the life of Christ. Inside the San
Francesco Church, adorned with a 16th-century doorway, you will see
exquisite frescoes and a carved wooden **pulpit****.

Festivals

Ballo della Cordella in Aug and **Sagra delle Castagne** in Sept-Oct.

Useful address

Tourist information, Pro Loco, via Carapezza.

Polizzi Generosa (67 mi/108 km south of Cefalù)

Another charming Norman village at the foot of a ruined castle, Polizzi
Generosa became famous after the visit of Charles V in 1535 when the
generous monarch thanked the Minorites (Franciscan friars) for their
warm welcome with a gift of the canopy above his throne, now on view in
the Chiesa Madre. This church also contains several sculptures by the
Gagini school and a wonderful Flemish **triptych****. Note the design of the
tomb of Notarbartolo illustrating a dog lying at its master's feet. The
Church of the Gesuiti is a fine octagonal edifice crowned by a dome,
beside which stands the Collegio, dating from 1761.

There are also several palazzi (palaces) — Carpinello, Gagliardo — in
the village and some interesting Spanish doorways. Hazelnuts are widely
grown in the region and are made into renowned pastries.

If you are looking for somewhere to eat, Polizzi Generosa has a good
selection of pleasant *trattorie*.

Polizzi Generosa to Campofelice di Roccella

The road twists around Monte San Salvatore to the Battaglia plain
(5406 ft/1 648 m), a winter resort. You then descend to the Zucchi plain
(3608 ft/1100 m above sea level) near the Orestano refuge (see p. 238)
and continue down the slope toward the Tyrrhenian sea to the foot of
Monte Cucullo (4675 ft/1425 m). You pass the village of **Collesano**
(96 mi/155 km) looking out over the valley of the Roccella River. Its
Chiesa Matrice with a Gothic-Catalan side door houses a carved painted
cross dating from 1555.

After a farther 23 mi/37 km downhill you arrive at **Campofelice di
Roccella,** which stands at the foot of a castle built over a small Arab fort.
Here you can join the coast road from Cefalù to Palermo.

▬ CEFALÙ TO PALERMO

The 46 mi/74 km itinerary described below includes places along the
N113. You also have an alternative route, the A19, which takes you to
the capital in less than an hour.

Himera (127 mi/205 km south-west of Cefalù)

After Cefalù, the N113 traverses the Làscari crossroads, followed by the Campofelice crossroads, the Palermo-Catania highway and the Imera Settentrionale road. Immediately after this last road, you will see the ruins of ancient Himera on the right, on the opposite side of the railway line *(open daily 9am-1 hour before sunset).*

Himera was founded in 678 BC by Zancle (Messina). In 480 BC it witnessed the historic defeat of the Carthaginians by Gelon of Syracuse. But 70 years later, Hannibal avenged himself on the Greeks by destroying ancient Imera. The city was never rebuilt and all that remains today is the base of a Doric temple built by the Syracusans in 480 BC to commemorate their victory over the Carthaginians.

The temple had 14 massive columns on the sides; some enormous pieces remain. The 56 lionhead waterspouts that adorned the cornice are now on view in the archaeological museum in Palermo (see p. 71).

Excavations on the hill have revealed traces of the ancient town and several objects are now displayed in a small local museum (ring for the custodian).

Continuing along the road toward Palermo you cross the Torto River and drive up through olive plantations before reaching Términi Imerese.

Términi Imerese (138 mi/222 km west of Cefalù)

Términi Imerese (26,000 inhabitants) is a thermal spa and seaside resort spread over a hillside. It is also an industrial centre with a busy port. The town is divided into an upper and a lower region.

You enter the town through Porta Messina and arrive at piazza Crispi, where you are advised to leave your car because of the daunting network of one-way streets. Corso Umberto Margherita leads off the square and ends at via Roma. Take the stairs from here up to piazza del Duomo in the upper town, where you will find most of the interesting buildings.

You can also reach the square by an alternative route: start at the foot of the via Roma stairs and take via Erculea to the right. This leads to the baths, praised by Pindar, where Hercules supposedly came to bathe after his fight against Eryx. The waters rise at a temperature of 107°F/42°C and are used to relieve rheumatism. Beyond the baths, on the left, you come to via Serpentina, which twists up to belvedere Principe Umberto, the site of the ancient forum. The view from here is magnificent. Via Belvedere leads to piazza del Duomo.

The 17th-century **Duomo** has a modern façade that dates from 1912 adorned with 16th-century statues by Marino. Inside, in the second chapel on the right, you will find a Madonna by Milano (1487), and in the fourth chapel is a marble medallion by Marabitti. There is a crucifix by Ruzzolone (1484) in the third chapel on the left that is used in processions. Two streets, via del Museo and Mazzini, lead off the square opposite the Duomo. The first goes to the Museo Civico, presently being reorganized, and the second runs past two churches, Church of the Monte on the right, which contains two 16th-century tombs and the **Santa Maria della Misericordia Church** on the left, which has a triptych* by da Pesara (1453). Via Garibaldi, to the right of via Mazzina, runs beside the Biblioteca Liciniana and the public gardens (Villa Palmieri), where you can see parts of a Roman *curia* (senate building) and the remains of an amphitheatre. Via Garibaldi ends at the old Porta Palermo.

Cáccamo

We recommend you make a short (6.2 mi/10 km) excursion from Términi Imerese south to Cáccamo, a picturesque village perched on a spur dominating the whole San Leonardo Valley (leave the town on via Amedeo). As you approach the village you will see a splendid 12th-century **castle**, one of the largest and best preserved in Sicily, which was built during the days of the Carthaginians. It has been restored and enlarged several times and looks like a medieval fortress with turrets and crenelations. From its towers you have a good view of the fertile countryside below. You can go inside and see the *salone della congiura* where rebellious barons plotted against William the Bad in 1160. Corso Umberto and via Cartagine lead to the Norman Duomo (San Giorgio), which was rebuilt in 1477 and altered in 1614. Inside there are statues by Francesco Laurana in the transept and gold and silver-plate treasures in the sacristy.

Other churches in the village include San Domenico, dating from 1487, which contains a statue of the *Madonna* by Antonello Gagini; San Marco with a 14th-century doorway; and the churches of the Annunziata and Santa Maria degli Angeli, both adorned with Baroque façades.

Términi Imerese to Palermo

The N113 crosses the San Leonardo River near an old Roman bridge rebuilt in 1625. It is a beautiful work of art, 141 ft/43 m long, with a wide central arch flanked by two smaller ones.

The road continues to **Trabía** (140 mi/226 km), where the fine Vetrana beach spreads out below a castle. You then cross the town of **Altavilla Mílicia** (146 mi/236 km).

Large hotel complexes stretch along the coast to **San Flavia** (150 mi/242 km), where a road right leads to the ancient city of **Solunto** and to **Capo Zafferano** (p. 85). The N113 passes near **Bagheira** (p. 85) and crosses **Ficarazzi** and **Ficarazzelli** to arrive in Palermo (p. 47) on the seaward edge of the Conca d'Oro.

USEFUL VOCABULARY

Common words and phrases

Yes	*Si*
No	*Non*
Mr.	*Signore*
Mrs.	*Signora*
Good morning	*Buongiorno*
Good evening	*Buona sera*
Good night	*Buona notte*
Good-bye	*Arrivederci*
Excuse me	*Scusi*
Please	*Per favore*
Thank you	*Grazie*
You're welcome	*Prego*
Why?	*Perchè?*
Far	*Lontano*
Near	*Vicino*
Again	*Ancora*
Can you tell me?	*Puo dirmi?*
Do you have...?	*Ha...?*
I don't understand	*Non capisco*
Speak slowly	*Parli lentamente*
A lot	*Molto*
A little	*Poco*
Too much	*Troppo*
Enough	*Abbastanza*
All, everything	*Tutto*
Nothing	*Niente*
How much?	*Quanto costa?*
It's too expensive	*E'troppo caro*

Numbers

One	*Uno*
Two	*Due*
Three	*Tre*
Four	*Quattro*
Five	*Cinque*
Six	*Sei*
Seven	*Sette*
Eight	*Otto*
Nine	*Nove*
Ten	*Dieci*
Eleven	*Undici*
Twelve	*Dodici*
Thirteen	*Tredici*
Fourteen	*Quattordici*
Fifteen	*Quindici*
Sixteen	*Sedici*
Seventeen	*Diciassette*
Eighteen	*Diciotto*
Nineteen	*Diciannove*
Twenty	*Venti*
Twenty-one	*Ventuno*
Twenty-two	*Ventidue*
Thirty	*Trenta*
Forty	*Quaranta*
Fifty	*Cinquanta*
Sixty	*Sessanta*
Seventy	*Settanta*
Eighty	*Ottanta*
Ninety	*Novanta*

One hundred	Cento
Two hundred	Duecento
One thousand	Mille
Two thousand	Duemila
Three thousand	Tremila
One million	Un milone
One billion	Un milliardo

Time

Monday	Lunedi
Tuesday	Martedi
Wednesday	Mercoledi
Thursday	Giovedi
Friday	Venerdi
Saturday	Sabato
Sunday	Domenica
Spring	Primavera
Summer	Estate
Autumn	Autunno
Winter	Inverno
Today	Oggi
Yesterday	Ieri
Day before yesterday	Ieri l'altro
Tomorrow	Domani
Day after tomorrow	Dopo domani
The morning	Il Matino
In the afternoon	Nel pomeriggio
The evening	La sera

At the station or airport

To arrive	Arrivare
To change	Cambiare
Closed	Fermata
To leave	Partire
Left luggage	Deposito
Luggage	Bagagli
Platform	Binario
Porter	Facchino
Sleeping berth/Couchette	Cuccetta
Station	Stazione
Suitcase	Valigia
A ticket for	Un biglietto per...
Ticket inspector	Controllore
Timetable	Orario
What time does... arrive?	A che hora arriva?
What time does... leave?	A che hora parte?

By car

Attention, take care	Attenzione
Automobile	Macchina
Carwash	Lavaggio
Danger	Pericolo
Entrance	Ingresso
Exit	Uscita
Forbidden	Vietato
Fuel	Benzina
Greasing	Lubrificazione
No parking	Divieto di sosta
Oil	Olio
Parking	Parcheggio
Roadworks in progress	Lavori in corso

Slippery road	*Fondo sdrucciolevole*
Tyre (tire)	*Pneumatico*
Tyre (tire) pressure	*Gonfiaggio*
Toll	*Pedaggio*

In town

Alley	*Vicolo*
Avenue	*Viale*
Cemetery	*Campo santo, Cimitero*
Church	*Chiesa*
Cloister	*Chiostro*
Courtyard	*Cortile*
Garden	*Giardino, orto*
Main square	*Piazzale*
Market	*Mercato*
Museum	*Museo*
Palace	*Palazzo*
Promenade	*Passeggiata*
Ruins	*Rovine*
Square	*Piazza, largo*
Stairway	*Scala*
Street	*Via*
To the right	*A destra*
To the left	*A sinistra*
Way, Promenade	*Corso*

At the hotel

Inn	*Locanda*
Hotel	*Albergo*
Family boarding house	*Una pensione familiare*
I want a room...	*Vorrei una camera*
With one bed, with two beds	*A un letto, a due letto*
Double bed	*Letto matrimonale*
Bedroom with bath	*Camara con bagno*
On the street	*Sulla strada*
On the courtyard	*Sul cortile*
What is the price, service and tax included?	*Qual'e il prezzo, servizio e tasse comprese?*
Everything understood?	*Tutto compreso?*
English breakfast	*Colazione all'inglese*
What time is lunch served?	*A che ora il pranzo?*
And dinner?	*E la cena?*
Wake me at... o'clock	*Mi svegli alle ore...*
The bill, please	*Il conto, per favore*

Menu Guide

Italian may be an easy language but interpreting a menu in a restaurant *(ristorante)* can pose problems. To help you find your way, here is a selection of the vocabulary you are most likely to come across:

Antipasto misto	*Assorted hors d'œuvres*
acciughe	anchovies
asparagi	asparagus
barbabetiole	beets
carciofi	artichokes
cetrioli	cucumbers
cetriolini	gherkins
cotechino	small spicy sausage
funghi	mushrooms
insalata	salad
oliveripiene	stuffed olives

pate	pâté
prosciutto — crudo	ham — raw
— cotto	— cooked
— affumicato	— smoked
ravanelli	radishes
sedano	celery
uova	eggs

Frutti di mare / Seafood, shellfish

calamari	squid
cozze	mussels
gamberi	prawns
gamberetti	shrimps
granchio	crab
insalata di mare	seafood salad
ostriche	oysters
ricci	sea urchins
scampi	large prawns
vongole	clams

Pesce / Fish

anguilla	eel
aragosta	crayfish/lobster
branzino	bass
fritto misto	assortment of small fried fish
marluzzo	whiting
mugine	mullet
nasello	hake
pesce spada	swordfish
polpo	octopus
razza	skate
rombo	turbot
salmon	salmon
seppia	cuttlefish
sogliola	sole
spigola	sea bass
tonno	tuna
triglia	red mullet
trota	trout

Carne, pollame, cacciagione / Meat, poultry, game

abbacchio	roast lamb
agnello al forno	lamb cooked in the oven
anatra	duck
beccacce	woodcock, snipe
bistecca	steak
brasato di manzo	braised beef
cervello	brains
coniglio	rabbit
costata	steak
costoletta	chops
cotoletta alla Milanese	breaded veal cutlet
fagiano	pheasant
fegato	liver
filetto	fillet
gallina faroana	guinea fowl
lepre	hare
maiale	pork
oca	goose
osso buco	shin of veal

pernice	partridge
piccione	pigeon
pollo	chicken
porchetta	suckling pig
quaglia	quail
rognoni	kidneys
salsicce	sausages
tacchino	turkey
trippa	tripe
vitello	veal

Verdura mista

Assorted vegetables

cavolfiore	cauliflower
fagioli	beans
fagiolini	French beans
fave	broad (fava) beans
finocchio	fennel
granturco	sweet corn
lattuga	lettuce
lenticchie	lentils
patate	potatoes
peperoni	bell peppers (red or green)
piselli	peas
pomodori	tomatoes
porri	leeks
radici	radishes
riso	rice
sedano	celery
spinachi	spinach
zucchini	courgettes (zucchini)

Zuppa

Soup

brodetto	broth with eggs
brodo di carne	meat broth
brodo vegetale	clear broth with vegetables
minestra di spinaci	spinach soup
minestrone	vegetable soup

Uove

Eggs

alla coque	boiled
bazotte	soft boiled
sode	hard boiled
affogate	poached
fritte	fried
strapazzate	scrambled
fritatta	omelette

Frutta, dolci

Fruit and desserts

albicocchi	apricots
anguria	watermelon
arance	oranges
ciliegie	cherries
datteri	dates
fichi	figs
fragole	strawberries
lampone	raspberries
limone	lemon

mandorle	almonds
mele	apples
more	blackberries
noci	walnuts
nocciole	hazelnuts
pere	pears
pesche	peaches
pompelmo	grapefruit
prugne	plums
uva	grapes
formaggi	cheese
gelato	ice cream
granita	sorbet
dolce	pastries
torta	cake, tart
zuppa inglese	trifle

At the end of the meal

coffee	*un caffé*
coffee with milk	*un caffé macchiato/un capuccino*
espresso	*un espresso*
How much?	*Quanto costa?*
The bill, please	*Il conto, per favore*
Is everything included?	*Tutto e incluso?*

Table essentials

a plate	*un piatto*
a glass	*un bicchiere*
a cup	*una tazza*
a bottle	*una bottiglia*
a knife	*un coltello*
a fork	*una forchetta*
a spoon	*un cucchiaio*
a table napkin	*un tovagliolo*
bread	*del pane*
butter	*del burro*
mustard	*della mostarda*
oil	*dell'olio*
pepper	*del pepe*
salt	*del sale*
sugar	*dello zucchero*
water	*dell'acqua*

▬▬ GLOSSARY

Acropolis: Citadel of an ancient Greek city.
Agora: Public square or market place in an ancient Greek city.
Amphora: Two-handled ancient jar for oil and other liquids.
Andesitic rock: Volcanic rock with plagioclase and some ferromagnesian mineral.
Antiquarium: Museum of antique finds.
Apse: Domed semicircular or polygonal recess in a church, especially at the end of the choir.
Architrave: Lowest division of the entablature, resting immediately on the upper section of a capital.
Atlantes: Male figures serving as columns in a building.
Basileus: Greek word for 'king'
Bouleuterion: Council chamber in an ancient city.

Campanile: Bell tower, especially a tall one detached from the church, often divided into several levels.
Capital: Top part of a column.
Caryatid: Female figure used as a column.
Cavea: The seating section, in rows, of a theatre or amphitheatre.
Crenel: A notch in a parapet. From crenellations or battlements.
Drum: a) Upright part of a cupola. b) Cylindrical block of stone used to form a column shaft.
Entablature: The part of a classical building above the capital comprising the architrave, frieze and cornice.
Ephebus (ephebos): Young male citizen (aged 18-20) in ancient Greece.
Ex-voto: Votive offering expressing gratitude to a saint, often in the form of a decorated tablet or small painting.
Fluting: Design of longitudinal grooves often on a column or pillar.
Forum: Open space in a town serving as a market or meeting place.
Frieze: a) Often ornamented part of the entablature between the architrave and cornice. b) Ornamental band on a wall.
Fumarole: Vent in a volcanic area from which spurts smoke and gases.
Hypogeum: Undergound chamber often used for Christian tombs.
Incunabula: Early printed books, especially before 1501.
Kouros: Statue of nude male youth of the Archaic period.
Krater: Ancient conical bowl with rounded base.
Loggia: Covered gallery or balcony.
Majolica: Glazed or enameled earthenware.
Metope: Panel between triglyphs on the frieze of a temple.
Naos: Inner cell of a temple.
Narthex: Vestibule inside a Christian basilica.
Odeon: Roofed concert hall usually in the shape of a Greek theatre.
Pediment: Triangular part above the portico of a classical building.
Pendentive: A triangular segment of the lower part of a hemispherical dome, between two adjacent penetrating arches.
Peristyle: Court or garden surrounded by a columned portico.
Polyptych: Painting or tablet in more than three sections.
Praetor: Magistrate of ancient Rome of lower rank than a consul.
Pronaos: Porch or vestibule of a temple leading into the cella.
Propylaea: Entrance gates to a sacred enclosure.
Quadriga: Two-wheeled chariot drawn by four horses abreast.
Quaestor: Official of ancient Rome with financial and other duties.
Scena: Stage structure of an ancient theatre.
Scoria: Piece of cinder-like lava with steam holes.
Stylobate: Platform on which a columned temple is built.
Telamon: Supporting column in the shape of a male figure.
Tribune: Stall, throne, speaking platform or raised gallery in a church, also the apse in a Christian basilica containing the bishop's throne.
Triglyph: Tablet with vertical grooves on either side of a metope.
Triptych: Painting or carving in three joined sections.
Tuff: Porous rock composed of fine volcanic fragments and dust.
Volute: Stone decoration in the shape of a spiral scroll.

SUGGESTED READING

Allcroft, Arthur. *A History of Sicily* (Gordon Press, 1977).
Aziz, Ahmed. *A History of Islamic Sicily* (Edinburgh University Press, 1953).
Cronin, Vincent. *The Golden Honeycomb* (Dutton, 1954).
Dolci, Danilo. *Outlaws* (Orion Press, 1961).
Sicilian Lives (Pantheon, 1982).

Durrell, Lawrence. *Sicilian Carousel* (Viking Press, 1977).

Finley, M.L. *A History of Sicily: Ancient Sicily to the Arab Conquest* (Viking Press, 1968).

Guido, Margaret. *Sicily: An Archaeological Guide* (Faber, 1977).

Norwich, John Julius. *The Kingdom in the Sun* (Harper & Row, 1970).

Runciman, Steven. *The Sicilan Vespers* (Cambridge University Press, 1982).

Sciascia, Leonardo. *The Day of the Owl and Equal Danger* (Godine, 1983).

● *Sicilian Uncles* (Carcanet, 1986).

● *The Wine Dark Sea* (Carcanet, 1985).

Verga, Giovanni. *Short Sicilian Novels* (Hippocrene Books, 1985).

▬ INDEX OF ARCHITECTS, PAINTERS AND SCULPTORS

INDEX